HERE'S

BOB KNIGHT

"I want that kid to go away and say,
well, I learned more in basketball
than in any class I took at Indiana."

"Sometimes I regret it
when the chair's halfway across the floor."

"Part of getting a kid
not to make mistakes
is getting him to a point
where he doesn't want to make mistakes...
because he doesn't want to hear me."

"I will scream and yell at you
all the time.
But I'll make you
as good as you can be."

BOB KNIGHT
HIS OWN MAN

JOAN MELLEN

AVON BOOKS ◆ NEW YORK

Grateful acknowledgment is made for those photographs that appear courtesy of the Indiana University Athletic Department.

Grateful acknowledgment is made for those photographs that appear courtesy of the author.

AVON BOOKS
A division of
The Hearst Corporation
105 Madison Avenue
New York, New York 10016

First Avon Books Printing: November 1989

FOR RALPH SCHOENMAN
with gratitude

Acknowledgments

When Don Fine approached me with the idea for this book, I had to consult Bob Knight. Practices at Indiana University are closed to the press. And such a book would be meaningless without his voice. Having heard him tell an Indiana audience, "Nobody else is going to write a book while I'm here unless it's me." I had my doubts about whether he would go along with the idea.

"I have no problem with that" was his reply to my inquiry about doing a book. And so I began.

Not only did Knight make no attempt to influence this book, but he never even asked me for the name of the publisher. There were no rules, no agreements, oral or written, and no stipulations about what might or might not be said, regarding language or anything else.

Bob Knight is so often open and uncalculating, even garrulous, that I think some of his friends were concerned that his privacy would be violated. But he never expressed a word of caution. In retrospect it seems clear that he had decided that was the way it would be, a decision that was implemented from the moment he agreed to open the doors of Assembly Hall to me, despite his friend Father James Higgins' warning, "If you ever trust another writer, you'll go to hell for sure."

"True to you, fair to him," Tom Callahan of *Time* advised. I hope I have been both.

This book exists by virtue of Bob Knight's great quixotic generosity, but I would now also like to acknowledge some of the other people who were kind enough to grant me their time and their thoughts.

Tough-minded and bemused, Bob Hammel, sports editor of the Bloomington *Herald-Telephone*, helped whenever I asked. Any errors about basketball are my own. Many of the errors from which I was saved are owing to Bob Hammel's gentle persuasion as he set me straight all along the way, right down to Hartford.

I am indebted to the athletic department of Indiana University, most particularly to athletic director Ralph Floyd, for many courtesies and to Sports Information Director Kit Klingelhoffer, who accomplished the impossible for a book writer, given the NCAA's determination that only newspaper and magazine people are worthy of tournament credentials. I would also like to thank Eric Ruden, and Academic Advisor Elizabeth (Buzz) Kurpius for her abiding assistance.

I saw from the first the camaraderie that prevails in the basketball program at Indiana. Coaches Ron Felling, Joby Wright and Dan Dakich taught me a lot, as did Julio Salazar. Bob Knight's secretaries, Mary Ann Davis, B.J. McElroy and Kyle Parmenter were always warm helpful and cooperative.

To the Indiana players who suffered my presence in their locker room and who talked with me, I am also very grateful.

The Indiana managers assisted me in a host of ways, but I would like to single out Greg Burton and Stephen Trust for being especially considerate and ready with help even when I wasn't aware that I needed it.

For their willingness to recall old times, I thank these graduates of the Indiana University basketball program: Tom Abernethy, Steve Ahlfeld, Quinn Buckner, Jim Crews, Steve Downing, Phil Isenbarger, Steve Green, Ted Kitchel, Landon Turner, Jim Wisman and Mike Woodson.

I am especially grateful to Coach Mike Krzyzewski for his graciousness to me in Raleigh-Durham.

And there are many others whom I would like to thank: Ira Berkow, Brad Bomba, Rita Bomba, Dr. Donald Boop, Pauline Boop, Tom Callahan, Brad Duggan, Gary Eiber, David Ferrell, Tim Garl, David Israel, Father James P. Higgins, Tim Knight, Jeff Marx, Bob Murrey, Robert Quay Norris, Dick Otte, Billy Reed, Satch Sanders, Mark Stephens, Mya Shone, Fred Taylor, Joe Vecchione.

In Bloomington Nancy Salmon, Harry and Maryrose Pratter and Eleanor Byrnes became friends. I thank them for everything. But, most, for the extraordinary interest he took in this project I thank Distinguished Professor Emeritus of History Robert F. Byrnes, my alter ego in Bloomington.

Coach Jay Norman at Temple was a solace and a support, as was my pal Bill Van Wert, who taught Larry Bird freshmen English for a few days at Indiana University. I would also like to thank for their good insights those basketball fans-to-be Michael Pakenham, Natalie Robins and Francine Toll.

More than thanks, my deepest appreciation to my agent Jane Gelfman and to Mrs. Judith Burnley of London, England, who, never having seen a game of "roundball", knew the right questions to ask. For her advice about titles I thank Dorothea Straus. I would also like to thank my editor, Susan Schwartz, for her consideration, for her good taste, and for the interest she took in this project.

The dedication reveals the source of my nurture during this unlikely enterprise.

Contents

PART I

PART II

PART III

But that is the way people are. They want talent, which is in itself something out of the ordinary. But when it comes to the other oddities that are always associated with it, and perhaps are essential to it, they will have none of them and refuse them all understanding.

THOMAS MANN,
Confessions of Felix Krull, Confidence Man

Part
One

CHAPTER ONE

A Man without a Mask

"I want him to go away and say, well, I learned more in basketball than in any class I took at Indiana. Basketball was by far the most educational experience that I had when I was at Indiana. And if that kid says, well, Chemistry 401 was my best, then I want to find out what the hell that guy is teaching in Chemistry 401 because I ought to be teaching it in basketball."

"The General," ABC's Dick Vitale calls Indiana Coach Bob Knight, the basketball genius who has won three NCAA championships, the NIT, eight Big Ten championships, the Olympic and the Pan American gold. Yet for most writers covering college basketball his name at once evokes an obligatory reference to: a chair, an LSU fan, a Puerto Rican policeman and, of all unlikely people, the Russians.

Few know him beyond formal press conferences; few have observed Knight's Indiana team at practice.

To paraphrase a scene in which he confronts his team later in this book: Who is he? What is he? Where is he? And does Bob Knight the coach or the man bear any resemblance to the stereotypic profane bully, his mouth open in a shout, his arms up in the air ready to descend upon a student we meet so often on the sports pages?

In fact, his flamboyant public image notwithstanding, Bob Knight is a teacher first, a purveyor of subjects not covered in any known college curriculum. To the chosen few young men who come to him, he imparts deceptively simple and yet invaluable lessons of hard work, self-sacrifice, self-reliance and effectiveness.

Through basketball, a "kid's game," he'll call it, he reveals to his players not only what their particular talents are but how to respect themselves sufficiently to develop them. And he demands what few teachers do: that they ask of themselves nothing less than what he asks of them. He requires that they take themselves seriously, settle for nothing less than excellence, and that through competition they discover the secret of how to live well, how to survive.

Through an unending struggle for perfection in basketball, Knight offers a model for how his players might best conduct the rest of their lives. Winning becomes nothing less than taking yourself seriously enough to demand excellence. Basketball is the activity through which these truths are taught at Assembly Hall, the games themselves the proving ground. The rest of life awaits their application.

The photographs convey a man with his mouth open in disbelief, his eyes flashing in anger, his arms raised to the heavens in exasperation. That is not the man you will encounter in these pages. Nor once you meet him will it be difficult to forget that shrill icon, that caricature, however endlessly perpetuated.

That image vanishes because there's a viable alternative— the man as he is rather than as he's been presented in the media.

This Bob Knight is a man of profound moral significance who has changed for the better the lives of the young men under his charge. If such a description seems uncharacteristic, it's because he will not trouble to help strangers understand. It may be that the deception amuses him, this enormous disparity between appearance and reality. And the misunderstanding grows because he is a man who will neither demand his due, defend himself nor clarify misconceptions.

Instead he defines his existence on his own terms, and, as

always, his teaching, his work, unfolds behind closed doors. No doubt you expect in the pages that follow to read a lot of profanity, but you will not. It's not that Knight is never salty, although he's less so than you might imagine. In the environment of sports, even college sports, he would be robbing himself of an effective tool to attract the attention of young male students. But profanity actually occupies a small proportion of his speech. Listen to him in these pages in a variety of situations, at work and at home, at dinner and in the locker room, and because I am there so frequently I realize that he can't be adjusting his language to the presence of a woman, a writer.

There are occasions when, if only for the fun of it, he'll string together a chain of expletives of the most dramatic variety. But such occasions are rare. In trying circumstances, coaching a team playing abysmally, losing a first round game at the NCAA tournament, he is not profane. To present him as spewing forth obscenities at every turn would be simple bad faith.

But there's something else that needs to be said. Most coaches use profanity. They do it in the confines of the locker room while in public they may appear mild, unemotional and controlled. A visitor at practice forces an adjustment, not only of the coach's language, but of his entire personality.

With Knight, there are no such disguises, no masks. He's the same everywhere. Once he amazed a houseguest, Clippers' assistant Don Casey, by suddenly walking into a room stark naked. That's Knight, never cloaking an action in pretense, a man without a mask.

Knight *is* a man obsessed. What drives him is a need, almost indeed a compulsion, that his students grow strong, competent and sure of themselves. He's adamant that in the destructive element of the basketball game, which will become, as Joseph Conrad had it, the deep sea of life itself, they discover how to keep themselves afloat.

He looks at his twelve players sitting before the open lockers, identified with little plaques by the names of those who have been there before them, and he asks that they compete. Primarily, they must compete against their own recalcitrance, against the resistance of all students to change, to grow, to think in ways other than they have thought before. Then they must compete against his disenchantment with them as they carelessly fail to do what they can do best, as they fail to be all they can. Never does he demand feats that a player lacks the ability to achieve. Always he is unrelenting in his insistence that what they can do, they do well, consistently and with increasing flair.

As a teacher he brings to his students his historical imagination as he recaptures for them the exploits of his former players. At speaking engagements, at a restaurant over dinner, but mostly to his team, all those who played for him inevitably reappear. Together they form a visionary company, to be recalled at will. There is a promise he makes to those enduring his constant criticism, which even accompanying praise does not wholly mediate: they know they will one day join that roster, many of whose members turn up at Indiana games, keepers of the flame. Having passed through this crucible of effort, they are now friends of the coach.

Often Bob Knight seems a happy man whose days are full. As he enlarges their lives, so does he reach out to the community, those in distress, illness, old age, recipients of catastrophe, whose lives might be brightened by Indiana basketball—a telephone call from him, a letter, an appearance at a hospital or nursing home These visits, unheralded and unreported, form an inextricable part of the texture of his days, rich in the presence of people and events, made doubly pleasurable for him by the presence of his two sons, Tim and Patrick, and by his wife. There is something sacred to him not only about family, but about one's personal history, and he is reflected in these pages by the friends of his own youth, by co-workers of his father, and students of his mother some seventy years ago.

With a prodigious memory, alert to all he has done and where he has been, he recounts for players, friends, assistants and strangers the truth he has learned. He insists by the vitality of his enthusiasm that life is worthwhile, which is why his friends are not only gratified by his invitations, but cannot stay away.

He lives by what he teaches. He takes his own life seriously, even surprising the outsider by the unselfconscious pleasure he takes in the achievements of his teams: the Pan American medal, the Olympic gold, Big Ten championships tenaciously extracted, the three NCAA national championships in 1976, 1981 and 1987. He remembers these victories through those who achieved them, his team leaders whose names he has raised to Indiana legend. And so after the 1987 championship he would spend a season talking not only about Steve Alford, but about Daryl Thomas and Todd Meier too, all three having become the bulwarks of that team.

There is nothing of precision, concentration, effectiveness or hard work demanded by that apocryphal chemistry professor that he will not wrest from his own students. He made that remark at the NCAAs in New Orleans in April of 1987. When he is reminded of it, he half-smiles as he says, matter-of-factly, simply and indubitably, "But I know they don't learn more in chemistry than they learn here. I know that."

CHAPTER TWO

A Voice from the Heart of the Country

"I'm not difficult to deal with like these people think I am. But, you see, they won't take the time to find out. They're afraid to find out."

One hot sunny June afternoon in 1986 in a telephone conversation of no particular significance, a friend asked, "Aren't you watching the NBA finals?" I wasn't. Not only didn't I know which teams were playing, but I hadn't seen a basketball game in years. Idly I turned on the television. And it couldn't have taken three minutes for me to discover a game I hadn't known existed.

You could see it immediately, the player of startling concentration who at once saw the entire floor and everyone on it, knew what they would do, where they would move, what they were thinking before they themselves knew, a player who used this sense seamlessly and unselfishly to create opportunities for his teammates to participate, a player whose own scoring was woven into the texture of how the other members of his team performed. It was that fusion of thought and action that makes basketball a paradigm for the fulfilled life. It was the unselfish team game much vaunted but little seen.

I was no reader of the sports pages and so I had no idea

who that player was. The morning newspapers, however, emblazoned his name over half a dozen stories. He was from Indiana. One of the articles referred to a short sojourn at Indiana University. There was a very intelligent coach there, but somehow it didn't work out. I might have seen that coach's name in print somewhere although I couldn't remember in what connection.

I put the pieces together. By some twist of fate, the brilliant coach, practitioner of the team game, had lost the unselfish, creative player who exemplified that game better than anyone who had ever played it.

So when late that summer I saw an advertisement for a book about that coach, I ordered it to find out how that unlucky accident had happened, how the coach who stood for team play had lost the player who best understood how it leads to greatness in basketball.

I read the book. There was no real explanation of why Larry Bird left Indiana University. The book itself seemed to be unedited transcriptions of a coach endlessly, furiously criticizing mediocre players. As if aware of its own banality, it would race forward to new displays of temper, only to subside into long descriptions of basketball games, victories and defeats merging toward no particular end.

Nonetheless, I saw through those pages a teacher facing the same struggles with students I faced at Temple University, so I decided to review the book. Unlike most teachers these days (and I hoped, like me), he would not give up on a single one of his students. He battled with them all, believing they all could learn not because he was waiting for their thanks, but because he cared. These students weren't mastering Sir Philip Sidney, but "help side defense," and while it may be natural to Larry Bird, it was not easy for them. They faltered. Sometimes they even cried, as my own students will on occasion when they receive a grade lower than B. But he never gave up on them and he wouldn't allow them to give up on themselves, even if it meant shaking them to bring them to their senses.

He also had a larger vision, this teacher. He was helping them to grow up, encouraging them in manners where before they had none. He had also rescued a former player from the depression that was an outcome of a devastating accident. I thought I had seen an extraordinary teacher buried in those pages.

One day in January the secretary of the Temple English Department, Catherine Hence, called to say she thought I ought to know about a telephone message taken by one of her assistants. Bob Knight? Was that important? He had left no forwarding number, but he wasn't difficult to find.

"I just wanted to tell you I really liked what you wrote." There were no introductions, greetings, prefatory awkwardnesses. Nobody's name need be spoken. (Yet when he speaks to his players, when he's teaching, in a given sentence he's likely to speak someone's name not once, but twice. So he assigns responsibility, as in, "There you are, Keith, ten feet away from anybody, not creating problems for anybody, you're just there, Keith, where you want to take it," or, "Dean, look at him walk right over you, Dean.") His voice was as lucid and clear as a cold mountain stream, his pronunciation defiantly middle western, precise, definite, loud, uninhibited, unambiguous, a skeleton key to his character.

"You're a professor of literature?" he chuckled.

There was some more talk. But what I remember most was the energy of his silence: his silence was palpable, more aggressive than other people's words. It made you examine your own words as you spoke them; it never left you in doubt that there was a presence on the other end who would hold you accountable for whatever you said.

At that moment it seemed inconceivable not to suggest that I would like to come to Indiana to write a story about him.

Time passed.

The first time I saw him on television was at the tail end of a game. Suddenly, as he shouted "Ricky!", his voice thundered across the court with such force and velocity that you thought all must be lost, now and forever. So I was incredulous to discover that his team was winning by more than ten points with less than half a minute to play. He was yelling instructions although the game was in fact over. At the time, this seemed utterly inexplicable.

There was no straight line to Bloomington. Delays followed. In one telephone coversation, as the 1987 season drew to a close, I told him I hoped he would win. This was greeted by the overwhelming silence. I thought then that I had jeopardized my chances, exposed my ignorance, because winning might not be what he was about at all.

I read everything I could find out about him, and the stack of clippings grew. Scarcely a day went by that he was not quoted, mentioned, attacked. There seemed to be three Bob Knights of my potential acquaintance, the affable, friendly, quick-witted man on the telephone, the dedicated teacher I perceived through the book—and this other strident, belligerent person of the newspapers, a person I discovered had just been censored by the Indiana University faculty for physically and verbally abusing his students.

One editor to whom I spoke revealed the certainty with which those who didn't know him concluded what he was.

"I don't like him," the man said. Then, oblivious of the contradiction, he asked:

"What's he like?"

"He was courteous, rather kindly," I began.

"Ah, he's faking," came back the answer. The case was obviously closed.

At last a date was set. It was October 15, the first day of basketball practice. I expected an extensive lecture, spelling out all the rules, for personal behavior no less than for basketball from the coach whom I had read was supposedly an admirer of General Patton and ran his practices like boot camp in the marine corps.

"We just start practicing," he said simply.

The details of my arrival, however, were not left to chance. It would be met, he told me, by someone six foot five inches tall, with sharp features.

"You carry a carnation and have the New York *Times* under your arm," he said in that definite way of his, "and he'll have the *Wall Street Journal* and carry a red rose."

CHAPTER THREE

Valparaiso, Indiana, Population: 23,000

"Most of us go on to other things."

At first meeting he seems a foot taller than the six foot five he is, and his aura can be measured on the Richter scale. Get too close and you experience the sense of danger that comes when you put your hand too close to a fire. You feel as if you're nowhere you've ever been before. Later a professor friend of his, a man old enough to be his father, will confide, "He makes me feel like a boy." "It's very hard to become something if you don't already look the part," Bob Knight will say. In many ways he resembles the stereotype: he's large and commanding, authoritative and definite and physically powerful. You believe that if he had to impose his will by force, he could do it. A tall gray-haired man in the vigor of early middle age with eyes that turn instantaneously from green to gray to hazel—hardly unique and yet there's something about him that defies whatever your expectations might have been. There's also an incipient air of impatience, or even derision, which already insists that there's no time for trivialities.

Look again and it's a pleasant-seeming man in an old blue sweater and a plaid shirt that sticks out in back and wrinkled gray corduroy pants. He has appeared without being announced and now leans against the door with a half-smile on his face. He's long and lean with only a gentle paunch, nothing like the belly-bulging firebrand you've read about. It's obvious that there's too little personal vanity here for him to be considered handsome. When he speaks, it's to tell me I don't have to get dressed up for the speech he's giving in Northern Indiana. He walks with his shoulders thrust slightly forward so that effortlessly he covers great distances, in this case the ramp leading down from his office to the lobby of Assembly Hall. In the basketball office an air of cheerful energy and good humor pervades among secretaries and assistants, and a sign reads, "Everyone Who Visits Here/Brings Happiness/Some By Coming In/Others By Going Out."

The voice is as I've heard it, the accent evoking the sounds of frontier a century and a half ago. Before we leave, he disappears into the coaches' locker room to change into the costume by which he is known: the red sweater, the blue pants, the black loafers.

On the late afternoon flight in the tiny Indiana University jet to Valparaiso, a steel town more in the sphere of Purdue than Indiana University, he sleeps. He is obviously exhausted, having been "roasted" in Atlantic City the night before, an event hosted by Howard Cosell. ("I told Don King he had to get a haircut or he couldn't play on my team.")

The plane is met by Gary Dunne, an FBI agent friend whom Knight immediately ribs: "You guys did a great job on the Kennedy assassination. It rivals the Normandy invasion." "Getting needled is part of being here," he'll say. No one escapes. The needling both expresses and wards off intimacy: it's an affectionate way he has of distancing himself from people, rather like a magnetic screen that comes up and down at will. It's part of the world of sports, of course, men ribbing each other. It evokes feelings only to pull back from them; it admits sentiment while at the same time rejecting it. And it forms a barrier between the man and himself, just as sports provide an outlet for emotions and actions our lives may be too pallid to admit. (The needling is also fun for Knight, who will admit to frequent boredom. "That's an absolute needle I give to every FBI guy I've ever met. I stick 'em with that. Have you sons of bitches ever decided to release the facts on the Kennedy assassination? They're sensitive about that; I enjoy it.")

Dunne counters: He'll hang Knight's picture in his office next to Reagan's.

"Not too close," Knight murmurs.

We are bound for the Valparaiso high school gym, which, like so many Indiana high school gyms, seats more people (6,600) than many university arenas. A young reporter from the local newspaper, dressed in white shirt, suit and tie, squeezes into the car. Knight tries to find out what he's supposed to speak about. The reporter has questions of his own.

"What would you like to have written about you?" Knight sinks back into his seat and says, quietly, "Nothing."

And then come the seemingly endless questions: How would he write his job description, how does he see his relationship with his players, what specific characteristics does he look for in recruits? Fatigued, he answers almost in slow motion, and he replies to every one, but when it comes to this: "Of all the teams you've had at Indiana University, could you name an all-time starting five?"

"Yes, I could, but you'll never hear them."

The reporter laughs. Young as he is, he has been schooled to place his need to get the story before considerations of his subject's comfort. Finally he raises the subject of Isiah Thomas. Eliciting no reply whatsoever, undaunted, he wants to know, "Are you as fine a fisherman as I've read you are?" The subject revives: "Damn near as good as anybody!" And, finally, "What are you gonna do when you quit coaching?"

Knight cannot resist this one.

"Become a writer."

He began this ribbing of the press, not with an attack on a writer who wronged him, but as one of those needles bestowed upon one of his closest friends, the sports editor of the Bloomington *Herald-Telephone,* Bob Hammel. How convenient, some might smirk. How sycophantic, others might scoff. And yet behind Hammel's affable exterior and his easy laugh, he is a tough-minded, unsentimental man of principle, more rigid and unbending of purpose than his seemingly less sensitive, more rough-hewn friend. What they have in common is not only the belief that college athletics can be played successfully and honestly at the same time, but also that neither is what he seems.

The incident occurred at a suburban Kiwanis Club dinner in November of 1973 at a Bloomington motel since torn down. Hammel had been at practice and now wanted to go home. Knight invited him to the dinner: "You're going to miss some really good stuff," an appropriate needle for a writer.

Hammel declined. Then, half way home, he turned back and went to the dinner, heading for a seat in the back, hoping he would not be noticed.

During the question period, one of the inevitables turned up. "You're rated third in the pre-season . . ."

"Well," Knight said, "polls come from sportswriters. All of us learn to write in the second grade. Most of us go on to other things."

There was only one writer in the room. Heads swiveled around; everyone looked. The writer, who blushes easily, blushed.

"What exactly is this thing tonight?" Knight asks again.

"It's a ladies' sorority. Haven't you been up here?" Dunne asks him, as if Valparaiso, Indiana, were the capital of the Western world.

"These people up here are basketball fans. Any given home game you get three or four thousand people; they just like their basketball," says the reporter. "Twenty-five hundred tickets have been sold."

"Who else is on this thing with me? Do they have Michael Jackson also?"

"Only you."

He enters the gym and the president of Kappa, Kappa, Kappa, Iota Chapter, a "not-for-profit organization for women whose goal is to further charity, culture and education," is waiting to greet him. He puts his arm around her shoulders and asks what she wants him to talk about. "Inspire us and motivate us," she says. The printed program defines his talk: "Motivation"—Bob Knight.

Inside, the Valparaiso high school band plays. The crowd awaits him, the old, the middle aged and the young, men, women and children. A sign above the podium is emblazoned with the dates of the Indiana championship seasons.

The twenty-two hundred give him a standing ovation as he walks down the aisle with a sheepish smile on his face, ducking his head. All that's missing is "Hail to the Chief." He likes being "Coach Bob Knight," there's no mistaking that. But standing ovations have not made him pompous or preten-

tious; his notoriety has not led him down paths of narcissism
or self-aggrandizement. When I ask him how he feels to be so
glorified, he replied, "What pleases me is that it's a recognition of what basketball in Indiana means to those people, the
players, the way they conduct themselves. They're probably
telling kids, Indiana's basketball players are graduating,
they're going to class, that pleases me. What they're saying is
that Indiana University basketball stands for something they
like." Somehow, I believe him.

II

"Don't you worry about old fat-ass catching you."

He needs no introduction in Valparaiso, and the Tri Kappa is
too nervous to say much anyway. "He's gonna cut me off,"
she says quickly, "so with that, Coach Bob Knight!"

"Reagan should have had you present Bork," he begins.
"He might have had less trouble." He's a practiced speaker
with a sense of timing not unlike Bob Hope's. "I'm a little bit
concerned that you say this affair here tonight will take in
more money than your cookbook did. What you ought to do is
find better cooks to give recipes."

His subject is Indiana basketball, what happens that the
audience might not see on television. He speaks from memory
with energy, forcefulness and good humor.

Early on, he asks the audience for a five-second period of
complete silence "from the time I say start, 'start!'" only to
conclude, "That gives the news media here in attendance
something that can be quoted with absolute accuracy."

He invokes the stereotype forged by the press to poke fun
at himself. "There have been a lot of distorted images projected of what goes between players and coaches at Indiana
University," he says. With play in progress, he asks the audience to picture him asking Steve Alford, "Steve, would you
mind coming over here a second?" And he questions his star
player, "Would you guys have any objection if I took a time-
out here?"

In this parody of Indiana basketball, Alford first confers
with Daryl Thomas and only then returns with his answer:

"That would be fine." The team is down 24 to 10; coach tells them: should they continue at the present pace, they will "get beat 211 to 63."

Knight now politely suggests to Alford that for two or three minutes they run the offense that "we set up for this game and play the defense that we have set up for today's game." Alford looks around; Todd Meier says, "Well, coach, would you mind letting us alone for just a moment to talk this over?"

"Sure."

The coach retreats to the scorer's table, where, "fortunately," he mocks himself, "they did not put any telephones. That's the most expensive phone call ever made," he adds, referring to the NCAA's ten thousand dollar fine at the 1987 tournament for his bringing his hand down on the phone during the LSU regional final.

By a close majority, Alford and his teammates vote to use Knight's offense for three minutes.

"I couldn't have asked for anything more from you."

His point, of course, is the reverse. Coaching does not permit a democracy. Like any teacher, the coach leads by virtue of his superior knowledge, wisdom, guidance and leadership. Coach and players, teacher and students, are separate and unequal.

One of the constants of Knight's approach to Indiana basketball has also become apparent. The anecdote has starred Alford, Thomas and Meier, all last year's seniors and now remembered as their team's leaders. As he recounts their exploits, and their foibles, they become Indiana players once more, participants in a living history, sharing a continuity with each other and with those at Indiana now. All have come through the experience of playing for him stronger and better able to survive in the world they have since entered.

The members of this endlessly present visionary company are remembered not for their weaknesses, which can no longer be amended, but for the seemingly impossible feats they accomplished. The invocation of their names even takes on a religious, a spiritual quality.

It all comes down to recruiting, Knight goes on, describing Randy Wittman's living room, the Wittman who now in the autumn of 1987 still plays for the Atlanta Hawks, and will later be traded to Sacramento. But then he was a senior at Ben

Davis High School in Indianapolis. "He's one of the all time great players that I've coached," Knight adds.

He tells the audience not of an NBA star, but of Wittman as a ninth grader at Knight's basketball camp. The formidable, frightening coach, a giant of a man, beckons the boy to his side. "He didn't know what he had done, but he was sure he was in trouble for something."

"Is your name Wittman?"

"Yes, sir."

"Wittman, would you like to come to Indiana when you get out of high school?" The voice is gruff, forbidding. No one would enjoy this interrogation.

"Yes, sir."

"All right. Keep playing and we'll try and see that that happens."

The scene flashes forward to Wittman as a senior in high school with the same coach now ensconced in his living room, reminding him of that day in basketball camp.

"Are you still coming to Indiana?"

"Yes, sir."

"And that," says Knight deadpan, "is the intricacy of recruiting at Indiana. You get the kid when he's a ninth grader, make sure he's afraid to say no to you, and then make sure he stays that way when he's a senior."

He now evokes one of his favorite characters, the mother of one of his top players, who wanted her son to come to Indiana because "she thought I was the next best thing to a convent." Many of the mothers of Knight's former players remain friendly with him; they all receive gifts at Christmas, and tickets whenever they wish, as if they too will forever share in the living history of Indiana basketball. They are not, however, exempt from his needling.

Knight portrays this woman as a mother who wants to keep her son alongside her, innocent of sex, innocent of adulthood as long as she can. "This player and his wife are now about to have a baby," Knight reveals, "and his mother's not sure how that came about." He's providing background to a story about a rebellion of players who want to live off campus, which Knight had permitted up to 1980 only for seniors.

He considers their arguments and agrees. All the parents are notified; none, of course, is more incensed than this player's, with whom Knight makes a deal.

"Have I ever done anything else wrong as far as your son's development as a person is concerned in your eyes?"

Reluctantly, the mother admits he has not, and agrees to a month's trial period. Her son moves off campus. In a month she receives a telephone call from Coach Knight.

"Hi, this is your old friend, Coach Knight."

"I hate to admit it," the woman says immediately, "but you were right. It's much better for him living off campus."

The coach appreciates her having given him that month, adding, "I'll tell you something. You'd absolutely adore the girl he's living with."

The dead silence is interrupted only by the player's father coming on the line: "What the hell did you just tell her?"

"I can't believe you haven't told her about the girl your son is living with. You and I took her to lunch last week." And Knight hangs up the telephone. Slightly ribald, invoking the parental authority the members of this audience would retain over their children, the story strikes at the heart of their concerns, and it brings down the house.

Knight tells another story illustrating how coaches get players to do things. It stars his 1976 championship team and its captain Quinn Buckner, that hero who inevitably comes to the fore in these events perpetually made legend, the player who walked out onto the practice floor his first day as a freshman and became the team's leader.

Indiana is down a point to Alabama in this story, with two minutes to play in the first game of the 1976 regionals. A fourteen-point lead has been reduced to one. The coach orders Buckner to take the ball out of bounds, and Wilkerson and Abernethy to screen for May, while Benson breaks across the baseline toward the ball. No one in this Valparaiso audience will have trouble with these names, members of that undefeated team.

A time-out is taken.

"I went over everything I wanted and when they told me they understood everything that I wanted, I grabbed Benson by the shirt, I wrapped his shirt up in my fist, and I said, 'Benny, they're going to come down the floor and they're going to get the ball in to their center. Benny, if he gets the ball and scores, I'm going to chase your ass up the turnpike to Bloomington."

While Benson is left hanging in the wind, Knight digresses to a game against Texas A&M. In the huddle, Knight has his team chant, "One, two, three, four," the four passes they must make before they shoot the ball.

"May has been playing really well. But he takes a fifteen-foot shot on two passes and misses. We get the rebound and it comes back out to Buckner at the top of the key. I'm playing better on the bench than Buckner has in the game for these ten minutes.

"Buckner's just been chewed from end to end at this time-out and this is what made Buckner great. May is his best friend in all the world. Right in front of me, he puts the ball under his arm, May's down in the corner, and in a voice that everybody in Market Square Arena can hear, Buckner says, 'Goddamn it, make four passes!'"

But however gratifying Knight finds Buckner's assimilation of his teaching, as soon as he hears this comment, he jumps up from the bench and yells over to Buckner, "Yeah, you just better make damn sure you've got somebody counting for you too!" If you listen between the lines, you will hear a teacher whose students are never off the hook.

Knight returns to the story of Benson, Buckner and Alabama, with Buckner taking Benson by the arm, while Benson leans down and nods his head. Back on the bench, isolated from the action, the coach wonders what Buckner has come up with. What has he changed? What will happen?

"Remember, I said I wanted Buckner taking the ball out of bounds. Abernethy takes it out of bounds. So I have a suspicion that things aren't going to work the way I want them to here. I had Benson breaking across the baseline. They put Wilkerson on the baseline. I had Wilkerson and Ab [Abernethy] screening for May. Somehow Buckner's got them screening for him.

"The pass comes in. A kid named T.R. Dunn deflects the pass and it goes to May, the guy I want to shoot. I look up and say, 'There is a just God up there.' May has the ball, he turns, he shoots it, and it goes in." (He can't resist this.) "A play we work on a lot. We draw the defensive man into a position where he can't quite get the pass and just deflect it into the hands of our good shooters and we go on to win the game!"

Knight then takes his Valparaiso audience to the locker room after the game, where Buckner is sitting calmly taking off his shoes.

"Quinn, what'd you tell Benson after that time-out?"

Buckner continues to remove his shoes as if he doesn't hear.

"Quinn, what the hell did you tell Benny?"

Buckner still does not look up. But coach knows that Benson at least will not ignore him. Benson, who now plays for the Cleveland Cavaliers, was always afraid of him.

"Kent, what did Buckner tell you?"

Suddenly a grin lights up Benson's face.

"Coach, he just came right up to me and grabbed me by the arm, and he said, 'Benny, don't you worry about old fat-ass catching you if Douglas scores, 'cause I'll have you before he ever gets off the bench!'"

III

"Don't let me intimidate you."

"You girls don't have to introduce anybody else?" So he begins the question period. "I don't want any dumb questions. We play the Russians on the fourteenth of November, and from that night on, following the game, I'll get all the dumb questions I care to hear until sometime in March."

After this prescient demand, he goes on to mock himself: "So ask me whatever you want, don't let me intimidate you."

Then he orchestrates, it's the habit of command. "What I would like you to do, if you would, is simply stand, and don't face me, but let everybody hear your question. Speak loudly and clearly."

A speaker asks how much playing time Jay Edwards and Lyndon Jones will receive; both were high school stars winning three state championships at a school called Marion. "This guy's a Marion alumnus," Knight informs the audience. "I don't give a damn where you went to high school. That doesn't mean anything to me."

Knight's bluntness might cause discomfort, but the man has indeed asked a dumb question: playing time, of course, is something earned. Even the coach who is treated here as a cross between Paul Bunyan and Davy Crockett cannot know how Jay and Lyndon will develop.

At his peril, the man remains standing. "You ask some question and then you sit right back down," Knight orders.

Of course they want to know about this season's team. Keith Smart is compared to Mike Woodson, who was "the epitome of a real scorer. He constantly looked to drive it, to shoot it, any way he could get it in. That's what I want Smart to think about."

Optimistically, Knight draws a line from Woodson to Smart, as if greater ability would be infused in Smart by virtue of his connection with the visionary company—all team players.

Someone asks about Daryl Thomas and is told he had "trouble finding the classroom and we took what steps we thought we had to take to show him the direction. To a degree he found it, but not to as great a degree as I would have liked, however." In fact, Knight was disappointed that Daryl Thomas did not graduate.

Here in Indiana, north or south, Larry Bird is always on someone's mind, no matter that it's nearly fifteen years ago that Knight recruited him.

The big classes were "just something that he was totally unprepared for," Knight says. And he adds, "I made a couple of mistakes, how I roomed him . . ."

Bird's pride indeed suffered at Indiana. He arrived with a few shirts and a few pairs of pants, so that the clothes of his roommate, Jim Wisman, seemed formidable. Wisman, from Quincy, Illinois, didn't have much, but he had more. Bird took bowling as a physical education elective and one day came back upset that he had to buy special bowling shoes. "I thought I was on a full ride," he said indignantly. The truth was, of course, that he couldn't afford the shoes.

Bird hated the big classes and began almost at once to say, "I'm getting out of here. I can't stand it. There's 260 people in there. How can I learn anything?" Worse, in a scrimmage he was one of the last chosen by his teammates, although he knew he was better than more than a few, including roommate Wisman.

It rankled. And so one night three weeks after he arrived, and long before basketball season began, he waited until Jimmy Wisman was asleep and went out onto the *highway with his bag, hitch-hiking back home to French Lick.*

Bird the Celtic, his frontier wit transplanted to Boston, laughs and says, "It was the closet. I was afraid of Jimmy's clothes." And the elegance that permitted him to disallow Isiah Thomas's remark about how if he were black, he wouldn't be special ("If the statement doesn't bother me, it shouldn't bother anybody.") notwithstanding, there is no reason to doubt his present assessment: "If I knew then what I know now, I've have run right back. Coach Knight and me wouldn't have had no trouble."

In an aside, Bird added that he got Isiah Thomas off the hook! "Bird probably shouldn't have gotten him off the hook," Bob Knight reflects. "It would have taught him a little lesson."

Knight reveals that he appreciates best those players who recognized that his dominating ways are directed toward helping them grow strong. Michael Jordan, he tells them, is "the best player who ever played the game, I can't imagine anybody being any better than Michael Jordan physically." The word "physically" is not idly added—the most intelligent player, he'll tell his team was (of course) Bill Russell.

"My experience with Jordan was simply this," he confides. During practice for the 1984 Olympics, "When Jordan wasn't playing well, I walked up to him and I grabbed him by the arm, and I just squeezed his arm. I'd say, 'You're too damn good to play like this.' And Jordan looked me in the eye and said, 'You're right,' and he'd play better."

Has he ever hit a player? No. Has he ever touched a player? There is no self-consciousness about that. The Jordan story has a parallel in Knight's coaching of Michael Brooks during the Pan American games of 1979. He was a player who made many mistakes. One day that summer after one of their morning workouts Knight ripped him "from pillar to post." Brooks then walked over and took his free throws, only to return to say, "I'm twenty-one years old and no one has ever talked to me like that in my life and I just wanted to thank you." Eight years later Knight remembers: "I love the kid. I just love the kid be-

cause of the significance of what we were saying to him, he grasped. He understood it."

As for other coaches, his favorite joke on his colleagues involves the original voting on the three-point shot. In the spring of 1982, believing he had the only two kids in the league who could shoot the shot, Knight deliberately voted against it. His strategy was that this would ensure the other coaches voting the reverse.

Outvoted nine to one, with the three-point shot in place, he wins the Big Ten championship. Meanwhile, prior to the season, he had told reporters that there were *three* players in the league who could shoot the three-pointer and he had two of them. Who was the third? He wasn't telling. "I watched us play eighteen games with every kid who thought he could shoot the ball trying to prove to me he was the third guy. It was the best defense we played in fifteen years!" Practical joker meets basketball coach; the man who is a genius at the "kids' game" entertains himself.

"There were more bad shots taken against us that year than any year I've been coaching," he insists. "Out of a gesture of magnaminous appreciation of the friendship of my fellow coaches, at the meeting that spring following the 1983 season, I said, 'I want to apologize to you guys because you were right about the three-point shot. It's a hell of a rule.' And they voted it out nine to one!" By now he has his Valparaiso audience shrieking in delight, for they well know he was never an advocate of this innovation.

("The friendship of my fellow coaches": he knows they recruit against him, describing to prospective recruits how difficult it is to play for him. This season, Digger Phelps, a man Knight considers a good friend, called Eric Anderson, a senior at St. Francis de Sales high school in Chicago with a 3.65 scholastic average, and a future McDonald's All-American, a boy recruited heavily by Notre Dame and Purdue as well as by Indiana. Although Anderson had already made an oral commitment to Indiana, Phelps called to talk him into changing his mind and choosing Notre Dame.

Far from retaliating, after Indiana's defeat of Notre Dame, Knight sat in the locker room explaining to Phelps

*how David Rivers had been too easy to guard, and that if
he came off the screen in either of two ways, rather than
always in the same way, it would make a difference. And it
did; it has.*

*Notwithstanding Phelps' call, justice did prevail. Eric
Anderson honored his commitment to come to Indiana.)*

There are more jokes. He tells his oft-repeated story of
how he came to throw the chair: a grandmotherly woman
called to him from the other side of the court, "If you're going
to stand up the whole game, throw me your chair!" Someone
wants to know whether the baskets should be raised to bring
the game "back to the little guy."

He offers a ready answer: "I say, the hell with the little
guy," says Knight with gusto. "Let him play golf. Let him
play second base. This isn't a game for little guys!"

His voice grows hoarse. At times he seems to draw into
himself, abstracting himself from the situation. He is thinking, perhaps, of tomorrow, the first offical day of practice.
But he summons the energy to make his most important point.

Part father, part teacher, part role model, Bob Knight defines Indiana basketball in terms of what happens to kids. His
life's work is helping kids grow up strong. If this audience
listens to him, it is because it accepts the sincerity of his
mission, and the sincerity of his complete disdain for the business big-time college sports has become.

He begins by replying to a question about drug testing.
He's for it. There's applause. He tells the Tri Kappa host-
esses, "There ·isn't a bigger community project, girls, than
helping your school system to get funds to drug test athletes.

"Let me speak to you kids for a second," he says. "Parents
are beyond help at this point." He invokes Len Bias, the Boston Celtic recruit dead of cocaine poisoning. I "felt no em-
pathy whatsoever for Len Bias, none."

He expects them to be shocked at his callous lack of feeling for the young man cut down in his prime. But there is a
larger message for young people here. Len Bias, Knight tells
the kids, had "the world by the tail," and he lost everything.

"Each of us is free to make up our minds as to what's best
for us as individuals," he argues. "The worst thing that any
one of you kids can ever say is, 'I did it because the other kids
did it.'"

The "absolute best word in the English language for you kids ever to learn is the word 'no.' 'No' is the best word you can ever learn. No, I won't. No, I can't. No, I don't. No, I'm not." This is Knight at his best, using his success as a winning basketball coach to reach young people, as their parents and their teachers may fail to do.

He pauses. "And if that doesn't work, you call me, and I'll give you a couple of stronger words you can use." Never is the applause greater than it is now. "You are a hell of a lot more important to you than anybody else is, and you have to learn to take care of you because you can change it to 'yes' if you should, but it is damn difficult to change 'yes' to 'no.'"

There's something more he has to say to these kids, and it involves his whole philosophy of teaching. It's about discipline, the mode of the caring teacher. He knows full well that kids do not always appreciate the hard demanding teacher.

"I'll tell you kids something," he begins. "Find someone who'll kick you in the ass once in a while, because that's the person who really cares about you. When that person delivers that kick, don't think about it. Think about the many pats on the head, or the pats on the fanny you've got from the same person. You all have a tendency as kids to focus in on a particular moment when you're probably getting just what the hell you deserve. Think about the times when you've been praised by that guy or that lady who doesn't worry about kicking you in the ass."

He proposes a game. Let them think of the most demanding teacher they've ever had and then the best teacher. "And I'm willing to bet that over ninety percent of you have the most demanding teacher and the best teacher as one and the same person."

He wishes for them: "demanding teachers who are parents, who are coaches, demanding teachers who are classroom teachers and demanding teachers who are friends."

He comes to the end of his sermon.

"Demand a little bit from each other," he says, "but most of all demand something from yourselves, you kids." And the gymnasium is so silent you could hear a pin drop.

A final question comes from a child who wants to know who will write the next book about him.

"Nobody else is going to write a book while I'm here unless it's me. When I write one, you make damn sure your Mom and Dad buy it for you."

The evening closes with his invocation of the line from "America, the Beautiful." "God shed his grace on thee." He says he never wants to hear the phrase "Born-again American." And so he stands there before them as a man proud of what he has built, or who he is and of his country.

Exhausted as he is, he is not yet free to go. The lottery must be called, with Coach Knight standing patiently on the stage picking numbers out of a giant wastepaper basket. Some of the winners will get basketballs which he will then sign; one will get a photograph of Keith Smart making his winning shot, "the shot" which will so haunt him in the season to come.

The audience is now free to ascend the stage for autographs. There are as many in middle age, men and women, grandmothers, and teenagers as there are kids; autograph hunting is not a sport for the young here, and only a few even bother with the excuse that they're doing it for their children.

(A Bloomington feminist requests that Bob Knight sign a sweatshirt for her thirty-year-old son-in-law. Could he use an indelible laundry marker so that it will not wash off? Could he insert a cardboard inside so that the signature will not bleed through to the other side? Coach Knight obliges. And the gift is received with due solemnity: "Bob Knight touched my sweatshirt.")

He poses for pictures with someone's wife on his knee, or holding a baby. He signs photographs, caps, programs, Bob Hammel's book about the 1987 championship season, *Beyond the Brink with Indiana,* or paper napkins. Always he asks the name of the person for whom he's signing.

On the sidelines a gray-haired man is annoyed that he has to wait for Knight to sign the basketball he won in the raffle: "Why didn't he do it before all the kids lined up?" he whines.

Knight is about to depart at last, when another reporter wants an interview, and so he stands before the glass doors leading out of the gym for another fifteen minutes. But a beige suede jacket covers the red sweater.

At last he can depart. In the car, he turns on the Giants-

Cardinals playoff game. By the fact that the Giants have eight hits and a certain batter is up, he figures out what inning it must be. About the evening, he wants to know: "How many people came? How much did they raise?" Fifteen thousand dollars, he's told.

The pilots are nowhere in sight on the deserted airstrip. "You may have to drive us back to Bloomington," he threatens Dunne, a three-hour journey by car.

But the pilots materialize out of the darkness, and the twin-engine eight-seater lifts off smoothly into the night.

Clutching a box of flies (they knew he was an obsessive fisherman) and one of the cookbooks of the Tri Kappa sorority, he sleeps. When he awakens, it's to rib the pilot. "Hey, Wally," he calls, "is that Indianapolis?"

"Yes, it's Indianapolis."

"I thought it was Kokomo."

Back in Bloomington, he heads for a midnight dinner at a fast-food place called "The Big Wheel." On the floor of his car is John McPhee's *A Sense of Where You Are,* which he has been reading. Bradley for President? The Democrats? "The last time they didn't have anyone, he became president."

With a final thought he sums up the evening, and simultaneously his chronic warfare with all those he deems the enemies of promise. By way of Benjamin Franklin, he offers the following look at a disillusioning world he believes neither he nor anyone else can hope substantially to alter for the better. "If the rascals understood the advantages of virtue, they'd be virtuous for the sheer rascality of it."

IV

"Never gamble and don't hang out with queers."

It can't be news that a deep cultural conservatism still pervades the heartland of America. Bob Knight's Indiana base is founded not on the cultured immigrants from Germany who brought symphony orchestras and the fine arts to Indianapolis and the North.

Rather, his characteristic supporter traces his ancestry to the pre-Civil War southern migration. These were people from the Carolinas, who settled in Southern Indiana and had little to do with their civilized neighbors; they were a group so fierce that Union recruiters making the mistake of heading south of Indianapolis simply didn't come back. When the great aunt of the leading Hoosier novelist married a bookseller from Louisville, they refused to sell in their shop the novels of her nephew Kurt Vonnegut on the grounds of "taste." Of the raw conservatism of this side of the heartland, Vonnegut muses: "I thought the whole world would be as mean as that and it wasn't." As for why some Hoosiers were so mean—"It was because they lost the Civil War!"

The world in which Bob Knight is treated as folk hero and legend remains uneasy with change. It is rooted in the belief that before duty and moral obligation, personal inclination, and impulse toward happiness, must at critical moments give way. Intellectuals and professionals, distinguished professors and doctors no less than ordinary folk live traditional lives. They go to church on Sundays and raise large families.

Young people marry and settle close to home; for the quintessential Knight basketball player, Illinois to Indiana has been a frequent migration. Living still in Milwaukee (having been a Milwaukee Bucks draft pick), Quinn Buckner, Illinois-born, talks today of moving to Indianapolis. If Keith Smart and Dean Garrett represented departures from that norm, Eric Anderson is a return to the type of young man who has provided the muscle and bone of the Indiana program, from Jim Crews and Jim Wisman to Randy Wittman to Ted Kitchel and Tom Abernethy to Mike Woodson and Buckner himself. At Indiana all these people flourished under the coach, whom they still say reminds them of their fathers and their grandfathers and their teachers.

You have only to cross one state line from the heartland to Ohio, where Bob Knight was born in 1940. With its agriculture and iron foundries, Orrville remains the prototypic small town, population eight thousand. If there is uniqueness to Orrville, it is that it was a railroad town to which blacks were brought to handle the creosote used for making the railroad ties at Koppers because it was thought to be too toxic for whites.

Here the same values of conformism, moral uprightness and patriotism dwell. Knight, who attended church Sunday as a child, was raised in the same values as his constituency. So it should not be surprising that as he finished speaking in Valparaiso, as he will in hundreds of places large and small throughout Indiana in any given year, he intones in that loud, clear and defiant voice of his, "America, America, God shed his grace on thee." He is welcomed as one of them by people whose faith in America has been unshaken either by Vietnam or by the struggle for civil rights. "God truly did shed his grace on us," Knight says, "and I hope we appreciate just what we have."

And yet he is no longer quite one of them. Were he merely an advocate of received truths, he would not be the folk hero that he is, one whose aura draws people like a magnet. For he is also a rebel, a man who would dare speak his mind and stand up for what he believes despite the consequences. A provincial in his origins, and so at once recognizable to them, he is no less an immensely sophisticated man who has seen the world and suffered its ways. Yet he prefers being among people like those with whom he grew up, sharing the simple pleasures of rural America. And for those many who chafe under the rigid structure of small-town life, through his activism he offers vicarious transcendence.

For the acceptance of conformity breeds its opposite: the appetite for rebellion, for outrage, for defiance of the repressiveness that settles over life led in the predictable lanes. In his fierce individualism, Knight fulfills for his wide heartland constituency what they will not do for themselves: he cultivates an independent spirit and implements it through actions that embrace the risks even as they accept the consequences.

Vicariously through him the Hoosiers, who have raised Bob Knight to the status of folk hero, exorcise the repressiveness. Their quasi rebellion is achieved with neither guilt nor bad faith because while he speaks his mind, at the same time Knight stands for the very principles they hold dear: justice and self-determination, honesty and competence, and hard work, the "work ethic" they call it. That he will defy acceptable norms of behavior in pursuit of these principles, that aggressively, flamboyantly and outrageously he is willing to defy hypocrisy, greed and corruption, wins him to their hearts.

There is a line in Rudyard Kipling's "If," displayed in Knight's office, which invokes "the will" to hold on, and which expresses what he loved best about his father, "the strongest-willed man I ever met." One of thirteen children born in the Arkansas hills and growing up in Oklahoma, Carroll ("Pat") Knight, a freight agent for the Wheeling-Lake Erie Railroad, was a man of few words. Stoicism was his credo, his definition of what it meant to be a man. He would walk four miles every day, to work, back home for lunch and back to work and home again at night. One day he slipped on the ice on the porch, went to work (writing with his left hand this day) and visited the doctor to set his broken right wrist only when the workday ended.

Simple needs, simple desires, sufficed. Pat Knight never earned more than eight thousand dollars a year, his son remembers. He owned a total of three automobiles in his life, including one which survived ten years with only eleven thousand miles on it. He would not be a slave to money, to material things, and so paid off the twenty-year mortgage on the first house he ever owned in four and one half years.

He was a man who never told his son he was proud of him, who never once spoke to his son about feelings. His advice to his son was "never gamble and don't hang out with queers." He did once tell Fred Taylor, the basketball coach who had recruited his offspring, that he was "awful glad" Bob had gone to Ohio State since that meant he could come to all the games. (Their father believes that "Pat" Knight's grandsons, Tim and Pat, would not have managed very well with so stern a father as their grandfather was. He makes this point matter of factly, not as criticism, if perhaps implying that in needing praise, approval, affirmation they are softer than the generations which preceded them.) Out hunting one day, Pat Knight suffered a heart attack—a cardiogram confirmed the fact— one which did not prevent him from returning to work, where his wife and family friends descended upon him in a quixotic effort to bring him home.

But if Pat Knight could fend off this crew, he was no match for his strong-willed son, who immediately dismissed his mother and the neighbors. Then he proceeded, in no uncertain terms, to "blister" his father. In response, Pat Knight put on his hat, left the railway freight office, and got into the car— on the passenger side. As his son drove him to the hospital, he did not utter a word. He never worked again after that. He was sixty-four years old.

His wife, Hazel, was a schoolteacher, an old-fashioned schoolmarm who one day in the third grade paddled a pupil named Danny Markley hard with a ruler because he walked on grass where he shouldn't be walking. Once, her son remembers, she paddled him too, but he places his emphasis on that singular: once.

A month before she died, on New Year's Eve of 1987, a family friend remarked to Hazel that she hoped Bob would beat Kentucky. "I hope he behaves," returned Hazel Knight, then in her mid-eighties. She adored her only child, often letting him win at cards. She was so fiercely proud of this son that she once upbraided a friend for being too busy to take her child to a game. She would have taken her son herself.

Hazel Knight never learned to drive, but was dependent on her mother, Sarah Henthorne, who moved in with the Knights before Bob was born.

It was Grandma who taught Bob Knight to make his bed every morning, and it's Grandma's words Knight more often quotes today, as in, "Never tell a lie, then you don't have to remember what you said." It was she who took him to visit colleges, and baked strawberry shortcake for Fred Taylor out recruiting.

She died in her favorite chair. Having driven downtown that day, she had placed her hat and bag and gloves neatly on her bed. Always she was elegant; her hair was set in what they called "marcelled waves," and she would wear a matching suit and hat and gloves, always the most appropriate attire. It was she, this exemplary woman, everyone agreed, who provided the most physical affection to the boy, and whom Orrville people remember hugging his Grandma.

He was not popular with his peers, the child whose mother could not envision him with a broken heart. But beloved as he was by his parents, he was not showered with worldly goods. Through high school he wore khaki pants in which you put metal stretchers to form the crease.

He was different, gifted. He liked adults better than children. His mother was tough on him when she had him in her second-grade class, for much was expected of this unusual child. He was a fun-loving boy, who liked practical jokes. Willful, rambunctious, at sixteen he watched his neighbor Pauline Boop working in her garden only to grab the garden hose and drench her. Caught at one of his pranks, he would grin sheepishly and blush.

If he was a good student, who could have been a better one had he tried, he also played sports—all sports, for in the world in which he grew up a boy would not do otherwise. It was a culture which at its best acknowledged no separation between mind and body, student and athlete. But sports fascinated him, and were his preference. The lessons he learned from all the coaches of his childhood are as real and alive for him today as they were on the day they were spoken.

So he will remember playing baseball in junior high only for the coach to admonish him for not leading off first base far enough.

"I was never very quick, so the lead I took was very short. This coach said to me, 'Bob, I want to tell you something. You can't steal second by keeping one foot on first.'" Sports becomes a paradigm for all of life, not only a metaphor for excellence, but also a training ground for learning how to cope, to mature, to excel.

As a youth, he must already have been articulate because his Grandma and his dad told him they wanted him to become a lawyer. His dad had said he couldn't understand why you had to go to college to become a coach. Bob Knight wasn't stuck for an answer to that one: "I couldn't understand why anyone as honest as my dad would ever want to admit that he had a son who was a lawyer."

There are light years between the speaker of that remark and the playing fields of Orrville. For in those words you meet the man of the world transplanted back to the heartland, the person who understands Kipling's definition of what it means to be a man, as one who "can bear to hear the truth you've spoken/twisted by knaves to make a trap for fools . . ."

To his constituency, Bob Knight brings news from elsewhere, a knowledge of the wider world in all its infamy. Through his basketball program he has shown them how the principles by which they have all been raised might yet defeat iniquity. That he bears the laurels, the national championships, garnered without cheating, testifies to the rightness and the longevity of these beliefs; that he aggressively and forcefully argues for these principles relieves the pressure of his constituency's thwarted desire to act at times more forcefully themselves. If they, mired in conformity, have eschewed risk-taking, he has not.

You listen to him and you see the warfare between the boy from Orrville, raised to do "what was right," and the man whose credo is to do what's right, but only as he defines it.

In many ways, he is not a rebel. Too extreme a defiance meets a resurgence of the pull of Orrville. What was written in childhood cannot be erased, not by all the slogans from Patton to Vince Lombardi. The adult feels a loss of self-respect in violating the childhood norms. Too great a departure from what you have always known brings depression, or, perhaps, loneliness, a recklessness that allows you to cast all caution to the winds . . . to throw a chair, to refuse to leave a game after the third technical foul has been called, to use a phrase like "rape is inevitable," susceptible to misinterpretation and then, naively, to challenge a media celebrity not to use it.

You might think of him as Huckleberry Finn, who got stopped before he could light out for the territory. Before he could do anything about it, he got enrolled in high school, where he played sports. Very bright and increasingly savvy, he found himself coaching at West Point.

He's accepted his fate in civilization, but he remains that independent-minded, ornery boy. Every once in a while he goes too far in his orneriness. He may seem wild, even reckless, anything to protect himself from the taint of civilization, which has long since taken over small-town America. Boyish intransigence becomes his familiar weapon. No wonder that he enlists it in frequent patterns. It's all he has to protect himself from those cold nights out there on that precarious platform that he is destined never to escape half-way between the frontier and progress.

CHAPTER FOUR

The Litany

"No one ever knows when I'm happy or sad. I cry inside."

"Let's just go through the whole litany," Bob Knight said, offering what he had granted no reporter before me. He would even talk about Puerto Rico, a subject which for years he had refused to discuss. I was to assemble a list of every incident of his untoward behavior I could come up with, everything bad that had been written about him, with no restrictions. He would respond to each item.

"Talk to a lot of other people," he ordered. He planned no apologia for his own foibles, but an attempt at discovering what actually happened. It was another of those opportunities which "might be interesting."

They think they know him. He's the one who "scuffled with,"[1] "punched,"[2] "slapped,"[3] "hit,"[4] "slugged,"[5] and "as-

---

1. *USA Today,* November 23, 1987
2. New York *Daily News,* November 24, 1987.
3. Washington *Post,* November 25, 1987.
4. Philadelphia *Daily News,* November 24, 1987.
5. Santa Barbara *News-Press,* June 30, 1987.

saulted"[6] a policeman during the 1979 Pan American games in
Puerto Rico. Then, at the 1981 Final Four, after some uncomplimentary remarks were tossed his way, he "stuffed" a taunt-
ing LSU fan into a garbage can.

Four years later, in the process of losing to a hated rival,
another Indiana team, he violently jeopardized life and limb
of the players by throwing a chair onto the basketball court.
And two years after that—if you believe what you read—incensed at losing to the Soviet National team, rabid right-
winger that he is, he defiantly led his team right off the court
and by so doing ended the game. He alone of coaches quarrels
with officials; he alone is profane; in sum, his behavior is
worse than that of any basketball coach in America.

No wonder then that his players defect in droves, as the
popular wisdom has it. In other programs the students never
leave, only in his. And he abuses them. Wasn't it reported
how he grabbed Steve Eyl by the jersey during a 1988 loss to
Michigan, shoving him several feet down the bench? Sure,
he's a legend out there on the edge of the frontier, in the heart
of the country that's not even a swell place to visit. In Southern Indiana all they care about is basketball, so they like him
because he'll do anything to win a basketball game.

This litany, with variations, is invariably chanted whenever
Bob Knight's name is mentioned in print—which is often.
Sometimes the frenzied effort to pour forth the litany results in
an error. The Puerto Rican policeman may be dumped in the
garbage can.[7] Knight, and not the NCAA, suspends Steve
Alford for posing for a sorority calendar.[8] When Buddy Martin, a columnist for the Denver *Post*, is questioned about that
statement, he replies that he read it in John Feinstein's *A Season on the Brink*. In fact, Feinstein accurately reports that the
NCAA did the suspending. After the Russian incident, NBC
is reported by several newspapers to be "reconsidering"
whether they want to hire Knight as a commentator at the
1988 Olympic games.[9] In fact, Knight had already been offered the job and turned it down. The NBC producer was

6. *Sporting News*, December 14, 1987.

7. New York *Times*, November 25, 1987.

8. Denver *Post*, April 1, 1987.

9. New York *Daily News*, November 25, 1987. New York *Times*, December
1, 1987.

concealing his failure to garner Knight by suggesting that now they might not want him anyway!

Are hostile sportswriters motivated by malice? What accounts for so many deliberate attempts to smear Knight, lie about him at every turn? Certainly it seems that people are willing to go into print without checking the facts. One might even conclude that he was being treated as a resident scapegoat, a stock Satan destined forever to enliven the sports pages with his antics.

It's also true that having been burned too often, and over the years watching this litany proliferate and multiply, with the attendant inaccuracies, he is no longer accessible to most writers. When then neophyte sportswriter Ira Berkow traveled to Bloomington in 1981 to cover the story of Isiah Thomas's decision to turn pro after his sophomore year, Knight's distrust of the media was already in place. Berkow did not get in to see Bob Knight.

"What I am is really honest with them, and they don't like that," Knight says. Is he then alone among coaches in distrusting sportswriters? "What did you mean by *that?*" Temple coach John Chaney's friend Tony Penne demanded one day a few years ago. "Don't you run a three-guard offense?"

"That's what I tell *them!*" Chaney replied. And when a year later reporters began calling the Temple dorms at four A.M. in search of "the freshman," Mark Macon, Chaney refused them access to Macon for the rest of the season.

Less diplomatic than Chaney or former Marquette coach and now NBC commentator Al McGuire, Knight, with vestiges of the mischievous boy who turned the hose on his neighbor Pauline Boop, taunts his adversaries. "Like after the Olympic Gold Medal game. I pick out about three guys in the press, and I just did it intentionally. I said, 'Hey, why don't you guys come back here with me.' That just infuriates the others."

Knight is also happy to be proven wrong about a sportswriter's willingness to treat him fairly. Years ago Larry Merchant, then of the New York *Post*, just (to use Knight's term) "blistered" him. Knight tells what happened next:

"Then he became a TV guy. There was a crew from NBC to talk to me after we won the championship in 1976 relative to a show for 1977. I go downstairs and it's Larry Merchant! I just say to myself, 'I can't believe I'm doing this.' But I went ahead and did it. He says something and I say, 'Larry, have you ever seen us play this year?' He says, 'No.' 'Have you ever been to one of our practices?' 'No.' 'Then I don't know how you could make a comment like that.'

"I know this will be edited out of it. But it wasn't. I called him later and I told him, 'That was really good that you would leave that in.'

"'Well,' he said, 'I was wrong.'"

Merchant at once became one of the writers with easy access to Bob Knight.

Nor was this an isolated occurrence. An "undisciplined disciplinarian . . . a coach who orders haircuts while throwing furniture," write Tom Callahan in *Time* magazine.[10]

But two years later, writing about the 1987 tournament, Callahan referred to the litany by invoking Puerto Rico. He wrote: "The officer's story collapses when he swears that Knight called him a 'nigger.' Any other vile expression would be eminently believable. But a legion of young black men can testify that Knight does not think in those terms."[11]

It isn't that Callahan's article was an all-out rave. He also wrote that had Knight played more at Ohio State, "basketball might be a little seemlier today." Judging from Feinstein's book, Callahan adds, "He may be the most profane coach in history." And he concludes that Knight "doesn't have the restraint born of good taste. It's the way he defines himself a man."

Yet Knight was gratified by that column. A month later he ran into Callahan at the Kentucky Derby.

"Hey, Callahan, what the hell's wrong with you? What's with the article in *Time* magazine on the NCAAs? That's the best thing I've ever seen anybody write about Puerto Rico and about the only accurate thing. You're a lot friendlier to me lately."

"Maybe one or the other of us has grown up."

"I think you have more growing up to do than I do," says the coach.

Then he adds, "Why don't you come to Bloomington?"

Callahan has not been "converted." But Knight so appreciates even the single note of fairness that at once he opens the doors to the Indiana basketball program.

* * *

10. *Time*, March 18, 1985.
11. *Time*, April 13, 1987.

For good or ill, sports remains one of the few arenas of experience where there remains leaders, and hence followers, heroes and villains. There are those whom many agree are sportsmanlike people: Larry Bird and Earvin Johnson, for example. And there are unsportsmanlike people, drug users, people who violate the law, coaches who cheat and solicit students to cheat, or who look the other way while others are bribing students on their behalf.

Yet although most writers grudgingly grant that Knight runs what they call a "clean" program, he has overwhelmingly been pilloried in the press, while writers only occasionally report on the endemic cheating in college basketball. Only the Lexington *Herald-Leader* has distinguished itself through its vigilance on this issue.

It may be that, insecure about being relegated to the "toy department" of their newspapers, many sportswriters become uneasy with the notion of the leader who takes command. Admiring a hero who rules by dictatorial methods seems to exclude them from the ranks of intellectuals; it seems unworldly. Yet sports each day brings its heroes, those who excel above others. Sportswriters may compensate for this contradiction by postulating a demonology, villains whom they can criticize, whose very existence reveals that they as writers care more about the real questions than they do about the day's scores.

Paradoxically, they choose their villains not on moral criteria, but on more superficial grounds. Knight's aggressive style offends them. He has attacked them for not knowing the game as well as he does; he has refused many of them access; and they have used their pens to retaliate. Were this not true, surely there would not be so many inaccuracies in the reporting about him. The desire to attack him sometimes outweighs their commitment to accurate reporting. Occasionally a newspaper will retract, as the New York *Times* did after readers were told that Knight threw the Puerto Rican policeman into the garbage can. More often errors are allowed to stand.

The truth about the press's treatment of Knight becomes apparent when we compare how the events in Puerto Rico were reported—and continue to be reported—with what actually happened.

II

"You do whatever you think you should do."

When he arrived in San Juan with his well-drilled players, Knight agreed to a scrimmage with the Puerto Rican team as a courtesy. Bill Wall, representing amateur athletics for the United States, suggested it. Knight complied, although he rarely practices with a team he will later play in competition.

Afterward, Knight conducted a clinic sponsored by Converse, during which he remarked, "I'm not here to pimp for Converse." He meant, obviously, that he was not there to sell anyone anything. At once the local press labeled him a "racist," suggesting the mood of Puerto Rico—and all of Latin America—that summer.

While the Puerto Rican movement for independence had been waning, there was enormous anti-American sentiment that summer. It was fueled by the brutalities of Somoza's last two months in power, which many saw as fostered and made possible by the North Americans. Anti-American feeling ran high, especially after the June insurrection in Masaya; even General Torrijos of Panama, to whom Jimmy Carter had signed over the Panama Canal, was engaging in strong anti-American rhetoric. There were large demonstrations throughout the Latin American continent on behalf of the resurgent Sandinistas, who would defeat Somoza at last five days after Bob Knight's departure from San Juan.

Because he was highly visible, outspoken and perceived as an American patriot, Bob Knight was a likely candidate on whom Puerto Rican sympathizers with the Latin American revolution could vent their political outrage. It began from the opening ceremonies when American flags were burned, and would last until the conclusion of the championship game.

Accompanying Knight as his assistants were Fred Taylor, who came out of retirement to be "delegation manager," and Mike Krzyzewski, currently the coach at Duke, once Knight's player at West Point and his assistant at Indiana, and at that time the head coach at Army.

In his first game, against the Virgin Islands, with the

United States thirty-five points ahead, Knight protested a bla-
tantly bad call. He had thought to himself: the players were
letting the officiating affect their play (they had been assessed
thirty first-half fouls!). Why not draw a technical to illustrate
to the students how futile worrying about calls would be on
their part?

When the officials seemed to change their minds about
what the call was (they had first called a charging foul),
Knight found himself asking for an explanation in English to a
Spanish-speaking referee near the Virgin Islands' bench. He
had passed the center line that serves in international play as a
limit. For this, he was assessed a second technical, which
meant expulsion. Hardly exemplary, the officiating was so
sloppy that in the confusion the Virgin Islands team never shot
a single free throw for his transgressions.

After the game, Knight conducted a press conference out
in the rainy parking lot, where he joked about how the cool
night air was superior to the steamy arena. The incident did
not seem unusual, until the International Amateur Basketball
Federation demanded that Knight appear before them the next
morning.

There he was told that the technical foul and the expulsion
amounted to strikes against him; a third transgression would
mean a sanction against him or his team. In retrospect, it
seems obvious that those in charge of the games on behalf of
international basketball were already reacting to the prevailing
mood of anti-Americanism in San Juan that July. While the
Latin coaches would put on fiery displays of temper on the
sidelines, abusing officials and receiving their share of technicals, it was Knight who was warned about expulsion from the
tournament; it was the Americans who were told that their
behavior had to be "exemplary."

In the press Knight at once became "temperamental" and
"controversial," although in the first week of Pan Am play
Knight was not the only coach ejected from games—two
others were, also.

The next "incident" came in a game against Brazil. With
the United States out to a fifteen-point lead, a pass came to
high school star and Indiana freshman-to-be Isiah Thomas.
Thomas put out one hand and the ball went off his hand out of
bounds—a turnover. Although he had not yet played for Indiana, he had been at Bloomington with the rest of the team

since May, about thirty-five days of practice. He should have known better. Knight yelled at him, as all the players would be yelled at during those games, Kevin McHale no less than eighteen-year-old Isiah.

Shortly after the turnover, Isiah got the ball on a fast break and raced down the open floor for a dunk. He missed the dunk. Meanwhile, coming right behind him had been Mike Woodson and Michael Brooks, two of the best offensive players in the tournament. Isiah should have dished it off to either of them—or laid it up. The failed dunk did not endear Isiah to the coach, no matter that the United States was leading by fourteen points at the time.

Before the half, Isiah was still in the game, but Brazil had gone ahead 38–36. The United States tied the game with less than a minute to play. Then, just before the buzzer, Brazil got the ball. One of their players was about to throw up a desperation shot from twenty-five feet out. There were two seconds left on the clock. Michael Brooks had his hands up, making the shot even more difficult when, suddenly, just as the shooter was cocked to fire, Isiah came up behind him and slapped him from behind, giving him a two-shot foul. While the Brazilian player made the two foul shots, Isiah was called over to the side and given the most bristling lecture of his life. To drive the point home, Knight benched him for the rest of the game.

The Americans won the game 82–78, but not easily. The Brazilian coach rose from his seat seventeen times to scream at the officials. But the press wrote only about Knight's "vicious treatment of a high school student." What Knight had seen was a high school player with bad habits, one about to join his Indiana team and whose instruction couldn't begin too soon. He wanted to make it clear he would not tolerate such play. "He got on me because I was wrong," Isiah said afterward. "And that's the way you learn. And that's why he's the coach."

"I didn't yell at him that much, did I? What do you think?" Knight asked a friend later.

"Well," he was told. "I'd put it in the top five."

(In fact, even now, with Isiah Thomas, one of the most successful professional basketball players in the country,

*Knight occasionally feels the impulse to coach him, to
make him better. "We used to play Isiah Thomas in the
post," he'll say, "because he was far better in the post
than the guy guarding him was defensively. Invariably. I'd
play him in the post with the Pistons a little bit just to keep
him from throwing the ball away." When Isiah dribbles too
much, Knight itches to correct him.).*

By Sunday July 8, the games were half over. Having
squeaked by Panama, the American team remained unbeaten
going into the championship round.

Five minutes before their allotted time at ten in the morning, the American team bus pulled up for practice at Espiritu
Santo High School gym. A policeman stationed at the door
named Jose Silva told them, "You can't come into the gym
until ten!"

"That's fine," said Mike Krzyzewski, "just let us know." It
was clear at once that the policeman was bent on asserting his
authority. The players were kept on the bus until just before
ten.

At ten, practice began, interrupted a short time later by
the Canadian women's team chattering as they left the gym.
Although the American team was preparing for its game
with Canada, no one complained. Knight was putting them
through a customary combination of practice and walk-
through.

Between 10:45 and 10:50, the Brazilian women's team entered the gym at the far end from where the Americans were
now seated on the floor. The players had their notebooks
open, and were taking notes from Knight on their match-ups
and other details of the game plan. The noise of the Brazilian
women talking and laughing became loud and the team could
barely hear what Knight was saying. It was clear that the
Brazilian women's team had not been required to wait outside, as the US team had been.

"You are either going to have to get them to be quiet or get
them the hell out of here," Knight called over to the coach of
the Brazilian women's team.

The laughing and talking only increased in intensity.

Krzyzewski went over to the scene of the disturbance. In
his calm and controlled manner, he said: "Could you please
keep quiet?"

"Hey, man, this is my gym. When you're in Puerto Rico, you do as I say," said Jose Silva in English. "They can come in. They've got a right to be in here. They stay here because I say they stay here."

"You wouldn't allow us in. Now you're allowing them in," Krzyzewski said indignantly.

"What the hell's going on down there?" Knight wanted to know. And now he got up and walked to mid-court, where Silva and Krzyzewski were standing. The American players were sitting against a stage on the baseline forty feet away.

"Who gave you the right to tell these people to leave the gym?" Silva demanded of Knight, shaking his finger in Knight's face. "You don't run this gym. I'm in control. What I say goes." To assert his authority, he stepped closer to his much-taller adversary, who weighed at least sixty pounds more than he did. Three, then four times, Silva shook his finger in Knight's face in a series of stabbing motions. The shaking finger stretched closer, shook again, closer, closer—until Silva poked Knight hard directly in the right eye.

Stunned, Knight ducked his head and raised his left hand, as if to protect himself, to push the policeman's hand aside. Unintentionally, he placed his open hand on Silva's right cheek and gave him a slight shove. It wasn't a smack, let alone a punch, a slug, a hit or an assault. The heel of Knight's hand rested briefly on the fleshy part of Silva's cheek at his chin.

It was a small gesture, a reflex of self-defense, but Silva interpreted it as a blow to his authority, to his very manhood. In rage, he grabbed Knight's arm.

Knight jerked his arm away. "Get your hands off me," he said, and as Krzyzewski stepped between them, Silva, by now out of control, shouted, "You're under arrest!" Again he tried to grab Knight's arm and again Knight jerked his arm away.

"You hit me! This isn't the United States. This is Puerto Rico. You hit a policeman! You're under arrest!" Silva shouted.

"I didn't hit you," said Knight quietly.

Obviously taking advantage of the moment of quiet reason, of his adversary's calm, Silva ordered Knight to the parking lot outside the gym, where he removed his hat and took a nightstick from an unmarked car. Then he touched Knight's nose twice with the nightstick.

"Goddamn you, brother, this is what I'd like to use on you. You want me to use this on you, don't you?"

"You do whatever you think you should do," Knight said.

Raising the club, Silva taunted Knight again, "You just want me to hit you, don't you?"

"You do whatever you think you should do," Knight repeated.

What Silva did was handcuff Knight and put him in the squad car. Then Silva took out a notebook and began speaking to a few Puerto Ricans at the gym entrance. Knight took the opportunity to ask the driver where they were headed and the driver obliged with the address. "Get moving on this," Knight told Krzyzewski as he gave him the address. "Something bad is going to happen."

Silva returned in time to push Fred Taylor away as Taylor tried to get into the car with them. And off they sped to a jail in Hato Rey.

Team captain Mike Woodson said, "Maybe someone better follow the squad car. No one knows what they'll do." Mike Krzyzewski and Fred Taylor did just that, while the players returned to the village in their bus.

That afternoon the charges were dropped. But in the evening Knight was arrested again. Puerto Rico had brought no charges, but Silva had appeared to bring a civil charge against Knight for "aggravated assault," claiming there was a hematoma—a bruise—on his cheek. Two days later he insisted that Knight had hit him on the jaw after he reprimanded Knight for calling the Brazilian women's team "dirty whores" because they made too much noise. He had asked Knight his name to report him to the Pan American games organizing committee, and as he was writing down the name, Knight hauled off and slugged him. (Under oath on August 22 Silva would testify that when he grabbed Knight by the elbow to arrest him, Knight said, "Take your dirty hands off me, nigger.") Now Silva said he had a broken jaw and had to take a leave of absence from his job. He denied that he had ever touched Knight.

That Knight's entire team, in addition to Krzyzewski and Taylor, were witnesses and heard exactly what he said didn't deter Silva from concocting this story. The entire team would later deny that Knight had used racial epithets. It is unlikely that the eight black players would have kept silent.

Knight counterchanged, the evidence of his reddened eye obvious and documented by Dr. Tony Daly, head of the Pan American medical group, as a corneal abrasion. But the judge dismissed Knight's complaint, while allowing Silva's to stand (and, even then, Silva's charge only involved a misdemeanor). Meanwhile a trial was set for Friday morning, July 13, with the championship game—which would turn out to be the United States against Puerto Rico—to take place that same night.

During those tension-filled days, Angel David Gonzalez, president of the San Juan Policemen's Benevolent Association, met with the press on Silva's behalf. "We feel there is a reality in this case," he confided, "and that is that there has been a violation of the law. There is a dignity of the policeman's uniform." It was not only Silva as an individual who had come to accuse Knight.

"I've given him all the resources of our organization," Gonzalez revealed. Should the district attorney not charge Knight, he already had plans for the legal division of the Policemen's Benevolent Association to submit the case on behalf of its members in their own right as private citizens.

And his plan, he admitted, was not to have Knight jailed, but to "get the man fired for moral turpitude." Relieved of the misapprehension that Knight was the permanent national coach, Gonzalez corrected himself. He would get Knight fired "here. He will not coach any of *these* games."

It was Wednesday and Silva's wife told anyone who would listen that she had to give her husband food "he doesn't have to chew very much." A doctor had filed a paper that Silva had suffered a "hematoma." Angel L. Tapia, president of the Puerto Rico Bar Association, told reporters that Silva had applied for state insurance benefits.

"It's almost like we're in the middle of a dime-store novel," Fred Taylor said. Meanwhile the Americans proceeded through the games but were unable to practice. Knight worked out plans for the game with Argentina in the police parking lot.

It would appear that Knight's behavior was indeed rather exemplary, that in fact, nothing happened! Why then are we wordlessly treated to Puerto Rico and the litany, and the endless resurrection of the story of Knight slugging the Puerto Rican policeman?

One reason certainly is that the US Olympic Committee would not allow Knight to talk to the press for two days after the incident. The only information available came from Silva and his allies. The American officials were so anxious to avoid charges of "ugly Americanism" that they eschewed not only common sense, but integrity in the process.

Whether or not Silva was influenced by a radical pro-Independence group bent on creating confusion and fanning anti-American sentiment, it seems obvious that the American officials played right into their hands by refusing to allow Knight to tell his story. And fan the flames the local press did.

The atmosphere was now about to turn even uglier. On Tuesday, during a game with the Cubans, with scarcely three minutes left and the Americans out in front, a Cuban guard named Thomas Herrera, twenty-eight years old, walked up to Kyle Macy and, entirely without provocation, hit him in the jaw with a sneak punch. The ball was on the other side of the court; the incident had nothing whatever to do with play.

Herrera then walked over to the Cuban bench and sat down, as if anticipating his punishment. Ultimately he was thrown out of the game, although given his action he could have been charged with criminal assault.

Groggy, Macy had dropped to his knees. He managed to play for another minute and then left the game. He sat on the bench holding an ice pack. In fact, his jaw had been fractured.

A starting guard, Macy had to fly home for medical treatment the next day. No one raised the cry of "Ugly Cubans," nor should they have denigrated the entire country for the unsportsmanlike behavior of one player. But the incident suggests that once more, the Americans were being treated as fair game.

By now the Americans were unified against adversity. At a team meeting after the incident with Silva, Knight told his players to vote on whether to leave or to stay for the remainder of the games. It was clear that the opponent in the final would be Puerto Rico. Knight suggested that maybe they should all just go home. They didn't have to stay; he wasn't going to make them stay.

After the first count, half the players voted to leave and

half to remain. But Kevin McHale and Michael Brooks argued that they had worked so hard during training, as well as having played in a tournament in Italy, that they wanted the gold medal. Mike Woodson, Knight's own Indiana player, agreed. A few others changed their votes then.

As for Silva's suit, there were those who still couldn't bring themselves to take it seriously, like Fred Taylor, who asked Knight every day what color shirt he would be wearing, red, white or blue.

"What the hell difference does it make what color shirt I wear?" Knight finally demanded.

"I just want to wear a different color from you. I don't want anyone remotely to connect us."

Taylor was obviously defusing tension because there were threats. On Wednesday, Knight moved the team to a downtown hotel, using the money he had raised at the practice games. The team had been placed on a high floor in a building without air conditioning.

At this hotel on the night before the final game, two men came up to Michael Woodson and threatened: "We have guns. If the game is close, we're going to shoot down onto the floor."

This remark was sufficient to frighten college students, if not the wry Taylor, who told Knight, "If they throw a grenade, don't expect me to use my body to cover you."

In terms of politics and power, public opinion and the press, the Americans had become the underdogs.

On the morning of Friday, July 13, the judge granted a continuance, postponing the trial. Knight's own Puerto Rican attorney chimed in with, "It's the responsibility of all of us to be prepared for tonight's game—which Puerto Rico is going to win!"

The San Juan *Star* in the morning's paper called Knight "an international embarrassment to his country," his actions "inconsiderate, rude and not a little uncivilized." It called Knight's contention that the case against him was built on lies and anti-Americanism "an act either of abysmal ignorance or acute paranoia." Yet Knight's contention was true.

The championship game against Puerto Rico was billed as the greatest sporting event in the island's history.

Thirteen thousand people crammed into the ninety-six-hundred-seat Roberto Clemente Coliseum. For hours before game time, people were jammed in everywhere, right up to the out-of-bounds lines on the court. Hard liquor was sold. Leading his team out onto the floor, the captain of the Puerto Ricans unfurled a gigantic Puerto Rican flag, which the crowd greeted by waving thousands of little flags of their own.

It seemed, however, that the Americans would have no trouble. They jumped to a 12-point lead and by the half were ahead 54–39. Then, in the second half, Puerto Rico began to catch up and after two free throws, with 9:35 left, the lead had melted to 73–70. At this point Knight called a time-out.

In the huddle, Knight grabbed Mike Woodson by the front of his jersey, startling him. He had played for Knight for three years and he had never been grabbed like that.

"What the hell's going on?" Knight yelled, seemingly in a rage against Woodson. "Get those guys together!"

Furious himself, but also stung, Woodson began to holler at his teammates. The hysteria of the crowd faded from his mind. All he cared about was never, not ever again being grabbed by Knight like that. The players returned to the floor, a team possessed.

Fear of Knight had released them from fear of the violent hostile crowd. Cleverly, Knight had chosen as his scapegoat his own player, Woodson, on whose reactions he could rely. It was a stroke of genius. The American players reached back into themselves, instantly transcending everything that had come before—the vicious press, the Cuban who had fractured Kyle Macy's jaw, and now the hostile drunken crowd. Knight was simply being Knight, the man of action for whom passivity is anathema.

Racing back onto the floor, eighteen-year-old Isiah Thomas took an out-of bounds pass on the fly. He bolted to the basket, got the basket, drew a free throw and sank it. It was the biggest single play of the game. Isiah then hit Michael Brooks for a three-point play and Woodson came up with the third three-point play in a row.

In four minutes Isiah Thomas had three baskets, two assists and a blocked shot, and the lead had jumped back up to 82–72. Later, Woodson would express his pride in baby Isiah, who had a 21-point, 5-steal, 4-assist game. "Isiah played his ass off," Woodson declared.

Refusing to permit his own jeopardy to interfere with his

responsibility, Knight led the Americans to victory, as they say in sports, "going away." The final score was 113–94. (Their average age twenty, the Americans had won nine games, each by an average of 21.2 points against older, more physically mature opponents.)

Remembering the threats, the players were worried as they lifted an elated Knight into the air, an easy target for a sniper. Again Knight was booed, lustily and long. He responded by raising a triumphal fist, which became an index finger, which, he explained later, stood for being number one.

After the medals were presented, Knight was accompanied back to his car by the policemen who had been assigned to protect him. He opened the trunk and to their delight presented them with all the T-shirts, pins and medals he had left. At the same time the superintendent of police in Puerto Rico apologized, expressing his regret for what had happened.

With some of the players still shaken by the crowd's hostility, the team raced out to their bus as soon as they could. Mike Woodson rememberes the crowd erupting, and the police using their clubs on the unruly. The team returned by bus to spend their last night not at the hotel, but back in the village with the other athletes.

"Do you want to know my appraisal?" Indianapolis lawyer Clarence Doninger, representing Knight, said. "We better get the hell out of here! Silva now has as many witnesses as you and it's a Puerto Rican judge."

The next morning, Bastille Day, Knight flew back to America. On August 22 he was tried in absentia, having forfeited his constitutional rights by "escaping."

At the "trial" Silva again told the story of how Knight had slugged him as he wrote on his pad. There were no witnesses for Knight, except the policeman at the Hato Rey station, who, of course, had not witnessed the event. Knight was convicted of charges of "aggravated assault," and was sentenced to nine months in prison and a fine of one thousand dollars, although the maximum penalty for a misdemeanor—which this was—is six months and five hundred dollars!

On the morning of the conviction, F. Don Miller, executive director of the United States Olympic Committee, immediately characterized the conviction as "blatant, outrageous, and unwarranted." Two weeks later Charles Neinas, chairman of the American Basketball Association, USA games committee, personally supported Knight's decision not to return to Puerto Rico.

From this reconstruction of events, Knight emerges as hero, the leader who rallies his team under adversity to defeat not only another team, but the forces of iniquity and injustice. Yet even those writers who admit that the events happened as the American team insists believe Knight's cause was injured by his comments at the heady moment of victory. John Papanek in *Sports Illustrated* points to Knight's remark: "Their basketball is a hell of a lot easier to beat than their court system. The only thing they know how to do is grow bananas . . . I didn't have any friends in Puerto Rico when I came here, so I don't have any fewer when I leave."[12]

Given what Knight had been put through, let alone how the incident has been distorted for a decade since, Knight's remarks seem, if undiplomatic, incommensurate with the injustice he had suffered.

The press coverage, both during the events and later, distressed Mike Krzyzewski: "Finally, when we did have a press conference a few days later, and we told our version," Krzyzewski was shocked to discover, "it was we who were the ones who were lying. I graduated from West Point. I was coaching at West Point. The one thing I don't do is lie. I don't lie. I'm not going to lie for Coach Knight. We're very close friends, but I would never lie for him. I've never lied for anybody. When we had the press conference, I thought truth and justice would come out and they [the press] would rally around us. Forget it . . ."

In September, Knight wrote a letter to Puerto Rican Governor Carlos Romero-Barcelo in an attempt to clarify events, which were continuing to be distorted in the press. Knight refers to comments he made "with a humorous intent . . . as well as some things said in the heat of the moment after the game that I should not have said." In this apology he makes reference as well to "several statements of an inflammatory nature attributed to me that I just simply did not make." The remarks he did make were meant for those involved in the incident.

In this letter, Knight speaks of his experience in Puerto Rico as a positive one and declares that he never had any

12. July 23, 1979.

intention to offend "a warm and friendly people." And he offers "most sincere apologies" if anything "I have done or said has been interpreted as being offensive to the people of Puerto Rico." That Romero-Barcelo did not have the matter dropped then and there, and allow Knight to pay the fine, may only be attributed to his own political agenda.

It did not matter where the facts lay, however. For most of the American press committed to the fable that had already seen its way into print, retraction or clarification might have seemed a blight on their original reporting, a doubt cast on their tough-mindedness, on their very manhood. By the time the Olympic Committee allowed Knight to speak to the press, the "facts" had been writ in stone. The slugging of the Puerto Rican policeman, no matter that it had never happened, had entered the litany, that series of tales about Bob Knight that seem destined for immortality.

III

"I think I anticipate the consequences and then I let my sense of saying exactly what I think run away with my ability to anticipate . . . at that point I think that the son of a bitch is wrong, that's unfair, that's unjust, that's not the way it should be and goddamn it, I'm going to tell him."

"Sometimes I regret it when the chair's half-way across the floor."

Rarely do the chanters of the litany forget either "the chair" or the "stuffing" of the Louisiana State University fan into the garbage can.

"No excuse," Knight says of the occasion when, protesting a foul early in a game against Purdue, he picked up the orange plastic chair on which he had been sitting and sent it across the court.

Most of the litanies make it sound as if he threw the chair at someone or in the direction of someone, neither of which is true. Or that he threw it so violently that you couldn't be certain where it would land, or whom it would hit, also untrue. He picked up the chair at its bottom and sent it spinning.

It skittered across the court. There was no one in its path, either along the way or at its ultimate destination. It was certainly not a sportsmanlike thing to do, but hardly was it the wild act portrayed endlessly thereafter.

Jim Crews, a Knight assistant coach at the time, argues that Knight's throwing the chair was a form of communication to his team, a calculated act. The floor was empty as the Purdue player was about to take his free throw. Knight turned around and stood facing his chair, his back to the court. He said nothing. Then, slowly, he lifted the chair and with a flick of the wrist sent it lightly across the court. His intention, as Crews interpreted it, was to bring his team together, even at his own expense. The score was 11–6, with fifteen minutes remaining in the first half, so he couldn't have been very angry at the officials yet. But he might have been communicating his disgust with a team whose play, as the season would reveal, was unworthy of the effort their coaches had been making.

Mention of the chair is usually followed by the incident in which Knight supposedly "stuffed" a supporter of the LSU basketball team into a garbage can. "Bouncing the Bayou Bengal loyalist into a trashcan," Bill Conlin writes in the Philadelphia *Daily News*.[13] Reporting on the 1987 NCAA tournament for *Sports Illustrated*, Curry Kirkpatrick reminds us that the LSU "loyalists" "hadn't forgotten the 1981 Final Four, when the Indiana coach slammed the LSU fan into a trash can."

For Knight, the Final Four has served as a reunion for old friends (particularly the fourteen of his former assistants who at the start of the 1987 season were head coaches elsewhere). On the particular Saturday afternoon in question, Indiana had defeated LSU to advance to the finals. A group was on its way through the bar to the special area of the restaurant set aside for them. In the group were Knight, Mike Krzyzewski, Ed Gottlieb, who had been the manager of Knight's Ohio State basketball team, and Ralph Floyd, Indiana's athletic director.

For two days LSU fans, staying at the same hotel where the Indiana players were staying, chanted their favorite slogan. Or they would walk through the lobby and yell in the

13. November 24, 1987.

students' faces: "Tiger bait! Tiger bait!" When the Indiana players went for their team walk after the pre-game meal, there was an LSU contingent calling after them, "Tiger bait!" Tiger bait!" Knight said nothing, did nothing—other than defeat LSU that afternoon.

Witnesses are unanimous about what happened, so it might be best to hear Knight's version. The scene is the bar beside which stood an empty trash can with a plastic liner used to hold ice, but at this time empty. As Knight attempted to pass, an LSU supporter had a few words for the Indiana coach:

> *"The fan is standing. He's got on a purple T-shirt with all sorts of buttons and emblems and bullshit. With a drink in each hand, he conversationally says, 'Nice game, Coach.'*
>
> *" 'Yep, yep, we weren't tiger bait after all, were we?'*
>
> *"Just as conversationally and I just kept right on going. And the guy screams, 'You're an asshole, Knight, you're an asshole!'*
>
> *"And with that I went back to the guy, and I said, 'You know, you people can walk around here just sticking it to our kids for two days with all this "here comes tiger bait," and then we beat your ass and it seems that you can't handle that. What's wrong with you people?'*
>
> *" 'Well, you're still an asshole.'*
>
> *"I just took the guy by the shoulders and with the heels of my hands I shoved him back up against the wall. He hit the wall and he just slid down. On the way down he hit an ashcan that spilled over on top of him."*

Knight grabbed the man by the shirt front, pushed him against the wall, and then abruptly let go so that the man slid and staggered sideways. On his way down, the empty garbage can fell on top of him. No damage having been done, Knight and his group proceeded to the restaurant, where dinner was already in progress. Happily seated at his table, Jim Crews heard the commotion, figured it was exactly what he had predicted, and went on eating his soup.

Knight did indeed grab the drunk and thrust him out of the way. "I'm an activist," he says.

In fact, most of the time when Knight is harassed in this manner, he does not retaliate. At a Michigan game three years ago, Indiana was one point ahead at the buzzer when Michigan put up a twenty-five foot (then) two-point shot and it went through. Knight sank back into his seat with his head down as the Michigan crowd exploded. Suddenly a fan walked right up to him and began to scream obscenities in his face. Knight looked up, then rose and walked away.

During the 1987 regional final in Cincinnati against, again, LSU, a spectator stuck his pom-pom in Knight's face each time he passed. At the Duke game and then at the LSU, Knight silently endured abuse from the stands. Whenever he passed the spot, the same thing happened. Finally, at halftime during the LSU-Indiana game, the fan got closer and took a swipe at Knight with the pom-pom stick. Indiana team doctor Brad Bomba, following Knight, grabbed the pom-pom and reported the fan to a policeman. Bomba didn't hear Knight say anything in reply to the obscenities that rained down on him from the stands. But Knight does remember:

"I haven't said a word. The eighth time that I go through there, I look up and say, 'Hey, why don't all you people take those pom-poms and just stick 'em up your ass!'"

At the press conference after the game, talking about whether the final basket would count, Knight said, "I watched the officials and as soon as those sons of bitches left the floor, boy, I was right with them." Later he was asked to explain to the NCAA tournament committee why he had "cursed the officials." His reply to this suggestion is in keeping with its absurdity: "Hey, you and I may choose different pronouns... in my language 'son of a bitch' is a pronoun!"

(It's one he'll use with no small amount of creativity. Teaching students to look for good shots, to pass the ball, he says, "Ricky, the son of a bitch won't go off. Have you ever all the time you've been here heard the son of a bitch go off?" The "son of a bitch" in question is, of course, the 45-second clock.)

Profanity often appears on the litany of sins, but in fact Knight uses it in its strongest manifestations rarely. Nor, probably, are there many coaches who choose never to address players in the language they themselves us. "I use 'choice words' when I'm talking to my players about drugs," Bob Wade, the Maryland coach said one day on national television.[14] Indeed profanity as a tool of persuasion is useful because, irreverent, it demands attention; its defiance of the norms of language evokes a similar emotion in those who hear it.

Another item that turns up in the litany involves Joe B. Hall, former Kentucky coach. The bare facts are these: Knight slapped Hall on the head during a heated exchange at courtside. A Kentucky assistant rose from the bench and demanded combat with Knight over this injustice.

What happened is somewhat different.

In a game against Kentucky, Indiana was way ahead, once by as much as thirty-four points. The incident occurred toward the end of the game. Indiana's substitutes, who had been in for some time, were now playing very badly, and the lead was shrinking. Steve Ahlfeld was then called for a foul.

"All right, Steve, that's all right," Knight called out.

"Way to go, Bobby," yelled a Kentucky assistant named Lynn Nance.

"Why don't you guys coach your end and I'll coach my end," Knight shouted and walked back to the Indiana bench.

At once Hall got up and walked over to the scorer's table and the two coaches met at center court. By now both were smiling.

"Let's get this game over with so you can get home and I can get home and we can get on to the next game," Knight said. And he reached over and hit Hall on the back of the head, as he will one of his players or a friend. Perhaps he hit him a little harder than he meant to because Hall was jolted a bit and his glasses moved, but both men remained smiling.

On the Kentucky bench Nance now popped up from his seat and called, "Do that to me, Bobby," and the press had its story.

The incident might have ended there had Hall told the reporters that Knight didn't mean anything, that Knight had been kind to him. Knight had recently praised Hall on national television for the fine job he was doing, having taken over from the legendary Adolph Rupp.

But instead, following Indiana's victory over Kentucky that

14. ABC-TV News, January 6, 1988.

day, Hall let the incident build so that it joined the litany, his motives for doing so unclear.

"If it was meant to be malicious," Knight says, "I would have blasted him into the seats."

But in the insular world of college basketball we find little evidence of the fellowship of coaches. LSU coach Dale Brown in a national magazine uses language fit for Idi Amin, Pinochet or Jaruzelski in a grotesque, unmotivated attack on Knight, to which Knight did not reply: ("What he *really* is," Brown declares, "is a despicable human being . . . who the hell appointed the self-righteous son-of-a-bitch judge anyway? Who is he, Barabbas?"[15]) Florida coach Norm Sloan charges Knight with misusing his influence to further his own recruiting during the tryouts for the 1987 World University Games. According to Sloan, Knight, without justification, arranged tryouts for Todd Jadlow and two potential recruits, George Ackles (who ultimately chose Nevada/Las Vegas) and John White. "Let me tell you," Sloan told whomever would listen, "there are a lot of different ways to cheat."[16] Meanwhile Sloan's own Florida player, Vernon Maxwell, failed the drug test during those tryouts.

In 1979, ironically, the press had chastised Knight for dismissing three students from the team for smoking marijuana during the team trip to Alaska for the Great Alaska Shootout. Counterculture sympathies among the press had Knight the "volatile adolescent" out of touch with contemporary youth, contemporary problems.

Out of fashion though it might be, Knight took the matter seriously. He questioned each student individually and discovered that there were eight students involved. Then he called each parent, told them what he had learned and received their support for what he planned to do. Cox, Roberson and Baker were dropped from the team; the other five were put on probation for the remainder of their stay at Indiana.

When David Israel, then of the Chicago *Daily News*, defended Knight, pointing out that most coaches were looking the other way on the drug issue, they became good friends, Israel's long hair and blue jeans notwithstanding.

For those who would perpetuate the litany still, it might be

15. *Sport*, February 1988.
16. *The Sporting News*, June 22, 1987.

instructive to remember how another coach handled his team infected with a drug problem. When Rollie Massimino of Villanova heard reports about Gary McLain's drug taking, and by no means were either the rumors or the facts confined to McLain alone, he chose not to pursue them. According to McLain, and he is supported in this by his high school coach Bill Donlon, Donlon warned Massimino during his very recruiting visit that McLain had already been caught with drugs.

Nonetheless McLain was recruited by Villanova. Later, when Massimino heard rumors of McLain's taking cocaine, he did nothing: "He had me in his office," McLain writes in *Sports Illustrated*,[17] "and he said 'I hear you're on cocaine or selling it. If I find out, you're gone.'" There was no urinalysis, only several more confrontations, concluding again with no consequences to McClain other than Massimino's saying, "If I hear it again . . ." Neither Massimino nor anyone at Villanova has disputed McLain's story, which *Sports Illustrated* courageously reported. With McLain, Massimino went on to win his national championship. Following his own 1979 problem with marijuana-smoking players, Knight went on to win only the NIT. He had to wait until 1981 for another national championship, but he did it without the marijuana smokers. Some may insist that Knight cares only about winning. In fact, in any conflict between winning and a principle that affects the moral development of his students, winning comes in a distant second.

If there is a common denominator in the litany where Knight would have been wiser to ignore a provocation, it is in his impulse always to teach someone a lesson. From anyone, strangers no less than players or assistant coaches, he will invariably demand acceptable behavior, whatever the circumstances.

One day Knight and then dean of the Indiana University Law School, Harry Pratter, were driving onto Kirkwood Avenue in Bloomington, traveling at about five miles an hour. At the same time a student on a bicycle was approaching the intersection. The student stopped; Knight slid through. He

17. "The Downfall of a Champion," by Gary McLain, as told to Jeffrey Marx, March 16, 1987.

was probably in the wrong, he admits, because he should have waited for the cyclist to cross.

Suddenly, however, without recognizing the driver of the car, the student began to scream obscenities.

At once Knight jerked the car, backed up, jumped out and confronted the rider.

"Coach, I had no idea it was you."

"What difference does it make? I'm not an asshole. The man riding with me is acting dean of the Law School. He's not an asshole. Maybe we were at fault, but you stopped and we proceeded on. What did it cost you, four seconds?"

When a photographer appeared on the scene and was about to take a picture, Knight just picked him up and set him into the hedges. (The next morning, however, Harry Pratter apologized to the photographer on Knight's behalf.)

"I wanted to teach the kid a lesson," Knight says. At such moments the cost in energy, time and misunderstanding matters not a whit.

A final example: one day before a game, Knight received a telephone call from a referee who was to officiate that night. All officials receive tickets to games, but this man complained about the seats he got and wanted more tickets. Such a request implied how the game would be called.

Knight's reaction was instantaneous. "I'm going to turn you into the head of officials for the Big Ten and tell him what you did!" That such a response might cost him the game at that moment of indignation obviously did not enter his head.

IV

"Nobody liked hassles less than I do. I'd just like to go through life without another hassle. But it will be unavoidable because I'll take certain stands on things and somebody will make some comment, and I'll say, 'That's an idiotic thing to say,' because it is idiotic to say."

The entire litany was revived at the opening of the 1987–88 season in the widely-reported "Russian incident." Unanimously, reporters wrote that in protest against the officiating

Knight took his team off the floor. Yet this is not what happened at all. After Knight had protested against leaving, referee Jim Burr had raced over to the scorer's table and written that the game was forfeited before anyone realized what was happening. Only then did Knight and his team leave.

This sequence of events might be contrasted with the December game in which Manhattan College coach Bob Della Bovi did indeed pull his team off the floor after he received his third technical. The referees had not signaled the game forfeited; Della Bovi, unlike Knight, simply removed his team. Yet the Della Bovi incident was reported and then duly forgotten with no one stopping to underline the significant difference between the two events. With Knight, normal standards of accurate reporting don't seem to operate.

Some background: the Russian incident was not the first time Bob Knight received three technical fouls. In 1974 at a CCA tournament, one of the consolations for those who are not invited to the NCAAs, Knight received two technical fouls (the limit then) only to remain in the stands and coach the game from there. Earlier in the tournament Tennessee coach Ray Mears and his assistant Stu Aberdeen had tossed off their coats and thrown clipboards onto the floor, yet had received no technical fouls. Now in the final game between Indiana and Southern California, an SC student palmed the ball.

Knight rose from his seat and shouted, "He carried the ball, he carried the ball!" He received a technical from the same referee, who had stood silently watching Mears throwing the clipboard. When Knight added, "You don't have any idea what the hell you're doing," he received technical number two and was supposed to leave. The game resumed with Knight in the stands offering advice to his assistants, a practice that has since been outlawed. The incident is significant only in that it had so profound an effect on Knight—it was his third season at Indiana—that he seriously considered resigning.

Knight's players rarely receive technicals. They are instructed that he'll take care of representing them should there be an unfair call. "I'll be your lawyer," he says. During that CCA tournament in 1974 Steve Green received a technical for raising his hand for a foul directly in front of the official's face and only then straight up. It was the first technical a

Knight player at Indiana had ever gotten and Green did it intentionally to express solidarity with his coach sitting up there in the stands.

"Keep your nose out of it!" Knight told Green after the game. The following year in that superb 1975 team's 92–90 loss to Kentucky in the regional final, Green got another technical. "Oh, no," he said to himself, "if I'm going to get a technical, at least let me say something." He hadn't said a single word.

After the game, the referee told Knight that Green had slapped his hand. In fact, when the referee had extended his hand to Green to help him up from the floor where he had landed, Green had waved him off, as it to say, "I don't need your help." There had been no slap, only simple disdain.

Although Indiana had played the Russians in exhibition games in the 1976, 1978, 1979, 1980, 1983 and 1987 seasons, this time Knight went on the record saying that in an Olympic year it was questionable whether the Americans should compete with the Russians and so help to train them for the summer games. Yet despite what some of his Indiana supporters believed—his supposed dislike of the Russians, his supposed right-wing politics and anti-communism—none of these beliefs had anything to do with what happened.

In fact, Knight would more accurately be labeled a democrat with a small "d," a midwestern populist restless with ideology, a proponent of hard work and the rights of the individual man. Loyalty and friendship seem to govern his political choices; he believes he has been labeled a Republican because of his long friendship with Otis Bowen, former Indiana governor and Secretary of Health and Human Services in the Reagan administration.

Knight supported liberal Senator Birch Bayh because Bayh called during the Puerto Rican events and offered to fly down to Puerto Rico to help. Knight refused the offer. "They'll just make a big issue out of your being here, it'll be worse," he said, a predictable response from him.

During the 1980 campaign, Bayh was singled out as a target by right-wing groups. Bayh's campaign workers telephoned Knight to request that he make a commercial.

"Will it put you in a bad position?" the Bayh campaign worker, hesitating, wondered.

"Hell, no," Knight said. And then he wrote the commercial himself:

> *"Hey, when it comes to politics, I vote for the guy that I think will do the best job. I've voted for Republicans and Democrats, and in this case I'm going to vote for a guy that I think has done a great job for Indiana and will continue to do so, Birch Bayh."*

Mail poured into then-IU President Ryan's office. Indignant, Knight held his ground: "As though I haven't a right. Because I work for the state of Indiana, that denies me the right to have a political leaning? Well, I just blistered their ass."

("It's instructive that Knight's language seldom goes beyond the anal stage," Frank DeFord wrote in his 1981 *Sports Illustrated* profile. Instructive to what end? At times the attacks on Knight are as subtle as this, slipped into a seemingly innocuous discussion of his profanity.)

Knight went on to note that no Democrat complained when he spoke on behalf of Governor Bowen, a Republican. To those who attacked him, he replied in a letter which said, in effect, "After the way I've supported Doc Bowen and now I do something positive for another guy whom I happen to like, that tells me if ever I have a party affiliation, which one it will be."

Oliver North was not a favorite with Knight for a simpler reason than Iran-contra politics: he lied. When people, schooled in misconceptions about Knight, came up and told him, "You must have loved Oliver North," he replied, "Hey, I'd have fired him in a second if it would have been me. I mean, he lied and he lied and he lied."

His politics? "I like people."

The game against the Russians was badly officiated. Jim Burr, who had worked the LSU game in the tumultuous 1987 regional, might still have been reacting to charges that he wasn't tough enough on Knight at the LSU game after Knight slammed his hand down on the telephone at the scorer's table. He may have felt it cost him an appearance at the Final Four: none of the referees in that game went on to work the championship games.

Early in the game, the Russians suddenly had six people on the floor with the ball in play. "Just give them the ball back," Knight told the official. "Forget it, let's go."

By this point the Russians had a twelve- or fourteen-point lead. Indiana cut it to eight. Then, with five minutes gone in the second half, six Russian players once again appeared on the floor. The matter was straightened out with no technical foul assessed to the Russians. A minute later as the Russians were shooting a free throw, one of their players stepped out of the lane and began to run to the other end of the floor, which should have meant Indiana's ball out of bounds. Referee Burr led the errant player back to the lane instead of calling an obvious foul lane violation.

Knight got up and walked down to mid-court. Up to this point the Russian coach had been out of the coaching box eight or ten times with the referees ignoring him or putting him back in the box, although, having played in America before, the Russian coach certainly knew the rules.

When Knight reached the scorer's table, Burr hit him with a technical foul.

Bill Wall, executive director of the Amateur Basketball Association/USA, was seated at the end of the Russian bench and Knight spoke to him.

"Bill, get these officials, the Russian coach and everyone together and tell the guy there isn't going to be any technical foul," Knight said.

"I can't do that. I can't interfere with the game," Wall said. "It's the official's game."

When Knight continued to complain, Burr hit him with his second technical. What could easily have been resolved soon became an international incident. Knight returned to his bench and play resumed. In a change of possessions, Burr was situated right in front of Knight for a few seconds, words were exchanged and Knight received the third technical.

Because of what he judged to be the bizarre way Burr had handled the game, frequently ignoring the rules, Knight refused to leave the floor. He did not take his team off the floor. Rather, Knight simply refused to go, as the rule demanded that he do. Burr went over to Wall to ask him to get Knight to leave the floor. But Wall again refused to intervene, although he might have demanded that play resume. Burr then ran over to the scorer's table and signed a forfeit. The game was over. It was then, the outcome of the game having been determined by Burr, that the Indiana team left the floor.

Weeks later, reporters, with the exception of Dick Vitale on ABC television, still had Knight removing his team from the floor as if it had been a matter of his choice, his decision. As in the case of Puerto Rico, the original error was perpetuated in the press: Knight petulantly had led his team off the court. "Grow up," wrote Harvey Araton in the New York *Daily News,* adding, "punch a cop in San Juan, if you must, throw a few chairs, but do get us into the Final Four." Even Andy Rooney of "Sixty Minutes" had his say via the Tribune Media Services: "Knight decided, on the spot, to take his team off the floor and forfeit the game."

There is a profound difference between a team leaving the floor after a forfeit and taking your team off the floor and by so doing forfeiting the game. Further, it might be argued that without rules sports is no longer sports. Knight was not depriving audiences of fifteen minutes of basketball (the time remaining) because the unruly play permitted had amounted to no game at all.

Acknowledging this fact, the Amateur Basketball Association apologized "for inconsistencies in the official's enforcement of the Russian coach's box, substitution and free throw lane rules," an apology which never made the newspapers. When several months later, however, Bill Wall suddenly sent a two-hundred-dollar contribution to the Oak Street Playground Fund in Orrville in memory of Knight's mother, Knight had the check returned. There is no substitute for doing the right thing at the moment when you must.

After the game, Knight apologized to the fans. "I just should have walked away from it," he said, no doubt true. He did not help to set the matter straight when he added, carelessly, "As far as taking the team off the floor, there are things I wish I could do over again. That is one of them." He *hadn't* taken his team off the court, as he later acknowledged.

The next day, Knight telephoned Indiana President Thomas Ehrlich, requesting that the University issue a reprimand. Ehrlich suggested to Knight that he, Ehrlich, send the text over to Knight's office for his perusal, but Knight declined.

* * *

Knight had acted on behalf of his principles, which include playing the game as it ought to be played. He failed, Bob Hammel believes, to live up to the fundamental demand he makes of his players, to anticipate. With his last outburst, he provided Burr with ammunition he was obviously seeking. "Knight would reply to the view that at such times he should cease and desist," Hammel speculates, "by saying 'You don't understand the number of times when I don't do that.'"

For Harry Pratter with his legal mind the Russian incident is the only serious sin in the litany because it breaks faith with the structure of the game by flaunting its rules: no matter the injustice, the coach must depart after receiving his third technical.

"Pseudointellectual," Knight pronounces this argument. "I would agree with Harry, but for a different reason. I truly mistreated seventeen thousand people and a television audience. I had no right to prevent them from watching the game."

All coaches, in one style or another, communicate with referees, and Knight's open approach might be preferred to John Wooden's. Silent to the crowd, Wooden would hiss at a referee whose call he wished to oppose, "You'll never work again and I can make it stick." With Knight, there are no threats, just very loud outrage.

Did he make a mistake in not departing after that third technical in the game with the Russians? Of course he did. And he'll tell you so, quoting Churchill in the bargain: "I believe this and I don't think people have much of a grasp of this as far as I'm concerned: 'Eating words has never given me indigestion.'"

V

"They don't care."

From the chair to the LSU fan to the "Russian incident," Knight's behavior is not always right, wise or appropriate. Yet these incidents have been blown out of all proportion. For when other coaches misbehave either the press is not overly bothered, praises the coach for his tenacity, or reports the incident once and then lets it die.

In March of 1987 Bob Dukiet, the coach of Marquette University, hit a referee across the arm with a rolled-up program. The referee turned around and gave Dukiet a technical foul. Then he put his whistle back into his mouth, ready to resume play. Enraged, Dukiet threw the rolled-up program at the official, knocking the whistle out of his mouth! For this he received a second technical and remained in the game. The Milwaukee press called it the turning point of the game, an inspiration for a team which, in fact, went on to win.

In a game against Oral Roberts, Bill Harrell, coach of Moorehead State, threw a chair *into the stands*. When someone called out, "You can't throw Oral Roberts' chairs into the stands!" he threw another.

The 1987–88 season produced the following examples of inappropriate behavior, none of which involved Bob Knight. On Saturday, January 23, 1988, Billy Tubbs raises his arms and snarls at an official, demanding a three-pointer instead of a mere two as Oklahoma leaves the floor at the half, nine points ahead of Pitt. On the same day, his face contorted in a wolflike grimace, his jacket long since thrown somewhere, Dale Brown, as Jim Nantz of CBS puts it, "loses his cool" and is slapped with two technicals. According to observers, each time Brown awards the referee an obscene gesture.

A few weeks later Villanova's Massimino accuses Pitt coach Paul Evans of calling him "a very serious and dirty name." At a game with Temple, Lasalle coach Speedy Morris berates and grabs a player by the jersey. More extreme behavior is not unknown either during this 1988 season. Michigan coach Bill Frieder slaps a television cameraman on the back of the head as the man tries to get a close-up of Frieder walking through the tunnel at half-time during a game in which Michigan is *leading* Iowa by 35 points. And Brown coach Mike Cingiser is arraigned on February 23 for striking a Fullerton State fan who had been heckling him during a December 30 game. Cingiser finally enters a plea of *nolo contendere* to disturbing the peace and is fined $100.

This is by no means to justify Knight's throwing the chair. Rather, it is to suggest that Knight's violation of decorum should be viewed within a context where emotions run high, and that a double standard is at work when he is involved.

Art Spander in *The Sporting News* writes of John Wooden, "If given the choice he would rather be remembered as a good person than a good coach. Wooden, of course, was both. Bobby Knight? Well, one out of two ain't bad."[18]

And yet in Wooden's basketball program, students were persistently bribed and corrupted by their benefactor Sam Gilbert (amusingly indicted for racketeering and money laundering in connection with a Florida marijuana smuggling ring—four days after his death!) and his predecessors. Happily the UCLA players drove among the palm trees in their new Toyotas, since, no doubt, upgraded. Wickedly Nevada Las Vegas coach Jerry Tarkanian once called Gilbert "the most important stone in Wooden's famous 'Pyramid of Success.'" As even the most jaded sportswriter will admit, there is no cheating in Knight's program.

Should the press focus more on this issue of the bribing of students? "They don't care," Knight says simply. "I don't think they have any interest in that."

"He's an isolationist," Mike Krzyzewski mourns, sorry that the man from whom he learned so much and who, he believes, has so much to offer, has absented himself from arenas of discussion within the sport. Because Bill Wall did not intervene to return a sense of fair play to the Russian game, Knight quietly resigned from the Olympic committee.

Meanwhile he builds his program—alone, scrupulously avoiding so much as a mention of the foibles, let alone the crimes, of any other coach—at least to this writer. "By your own soul learn to live," reads an unattributed plaque in his office. "And if men thwart you pay no heed/If men hate you have no care/Sing your song, dream your dream, Pray your prayer/By your own soul Learn to live." The warfare with the press provides an outlet for his not inconsiderable wit. In a 1981 commencement address he gave at Indiana, he told of how on the same day that the newspapers virtually ignored Lincoln's "Gettysburg Address." Edward Everett was soundly praised for his rhetoric. The press?—"An institution willing to praise undeserving people."

He's an easy target then, fair game. The exploits of the devil, real or ersatz, sell more newspapers than Adam, God,

18. December 14, 1987.

Christ and the angels put together. He's unfashionable, no matter that the atrocious plaid jackets have given way to red sweaters that do little to conceal extra pounds. It's also unfashionable for a teacher to be a stern disciplinarian and utterly to eschew democracy in the classroom.

Judging from appearances, there *is* something out of date in his style of masculinity, something anachronistic in an era of willed androgyny and the post-feminist view that men are no different from women. He's loud, strident and efficient, and the women I surmise he'd like best are those smart, competent, hard-talking women in the movies of Howard Hawks: Lauren Bacall in *To Have and Have Not* or Jean Arthur in *Only Angels Have Wings:* women who stand up to men, talk their language and won't wilt in a crisis, women who can roll up their sleeves and do the work of men. (A cassette of *Shane,* however, with its paean to the domesticated woman played by Jean Arthur, sits in his living-room bookshelves.)

Finally he doesn't explain himself, stoic that he is. He'll tell you how tough he is ("Yea, though I walk through the valley of the shadow of death, I will fear no evil, for I am the toughest son of a bitch in the valley"). He will readily defend others, but rarely himself. Judge him not by what you read, or by the persona viewed on television (the wire services have people at his games solely to photograph him at moments of anger), but perhaps by the fact that in the last five minutes of a game his students are less likely to make mistakes than those of other coaches. It's *their* grace under pressure that's at issue, not his.

He allows the press to misunderstand him and write that all he cares about is winning. In fact, his refusal to back down after a series of bad calls had nothing to do with the score, or whether the opponent is a Big Ten rival, or the Russians in the era of *Perestroika* and glasnost. If he grabs the shirt front of a drunk who vilifies him in a bar, it's *after* his team has advanced to the finals. You're your own man whether you win or lose.

Common sense decrees that you don't throw a chair to rouse a lethargic team. You don't grab someone who abuses you. And you resist those few more words to an official bent on your downfall, even if he thrusts his face right up to yours.

But for Knight, it would seem, the world is governed by rules other than the one that says that you cover yourself first, you don't get thrown out. In an era where the medium is the message, you don't put yourself in a position where you might be misunderstood. Meanwhile, to relieve the boredom that afflicts us all, but especially one whose commanding intellect might have led him to other pursuits, isn't it sometimes fun to play into the stereotype, to pretend to be what other people are so convinced you are—and so Knight quotes Bob Hope:

> "I play in a golf tournament that President Ford has every summer. In 1984 I couldn't play, and a guy that's a Hollywood personality that's on a whole lot of things, Wayne Rogers, is there as the MC. Among people that weren't able to be there that summer, he mentioned me.
>
> "And he said, 'As you all know, Bob's in Los Angeles trying to win the gold medal in basketball and keep us out of World War III.' And so everybody laughs at that.
>
> "Bob Hope comes on a little bit later. And he says, 'Wayne mentioned about Bob Knight being in Los Angeles and we all know that he's there doing everything he can to see that we win the gold medal in basketball. And those of us who really know him understand that he doesn't give a damn whether he get us into World War III or not to do it.'
>
> "Which I liked."

Part
Two

CHAPTER FIVE

The Art of Basketball

"It's like they're analyzing the participants in the Yalta conference, and I mean it just blows my mind. It's a simple goddamn thing. I just say, hey, kid, goddamn it, be the best player you can be."

It's Thursday, October 15, the first official day of practice. But other than a few remarks last night, addressed to last year's national champions ("The Bears beat the Giants before the strike; Detroit won more games than Minnesota; the same thing could happen to you!"), there is no lecture, no outlining of rules. "We just start practicing," Knight had said. Freshman players—and new assistant coaches both—are thrown headlong into the crucible with no guiding instructions. "We don't have any set working hours," Knight says. "We do what we have to do to get the job done."

(To his first full recruiting class at Indiana University in 1972, however, he said something else. "We're going to win the national championship," he told them. "That's everyone's goal. But we're going to do it with good people and do it the right way." He wasn't "Bob Knight" then,

73

*but some coach from West Point. Nonetheless, they be-
lieved him.)*

I am struck by the beauty of the room, the sparkling quality
of Assembly Hall, pristine in every detail, from the highly
polished floor to the seats. The colors red and white and blue
alternate so that you feel as if you are sitting inside an American flag. Overhead, swaying to the breeze of the ventilation
system, are the championship flags: 1940 and 1953 have been
joined by the three flags of the Knight era: 1976, 1981, and
1987, for he won his national championships with three completely different teams, different personnel. The 1975 undefeated regular season team is represented by a flag from the
NIT. Although he has won eight Big Ten championships,
there is only one Big Ten Championship flag, for 1983 for the
fans who never deserted that team. High above, flanking the
American flag, are those two hard-won triumphs, the Olympic
white and the Pan American blue.

The first person out on the floor with the players is assistant coach Ron Felling, lithe, limber and ready to go. But
there's also a new assistant this year, Taylor ("Tates") Locke,
who arrived yesterday at Indianapolis airport in hunting cap
and blue plaid shirt. He's a strong-featured man with light
eyes, gray-blond hair and a cleft in his chin. Twenty-five
years ago as head coach at West Point he honored his prede-
cessor's commitment to retain twenty-two-year-old Bob
Knight as his assistant. (He himself was only twenty-five.)
Today he remembers himself and Knight sitting with Joe Lap-
chick at a press conference in New York, two coaches in their
twenties listening and learning as the older coaches talked.

The intervening years have not been kind. There were recruiting violations at Clemson, where he coached. These included changing the grades of players, an assistant coach's
daughter taking a math test for a player, creating a phony
black fraternity to lure black players to a small Southern town,
and the usual cars and monthly spending allowances for
players from a slush fund. In 1982 Locke wrote a book called
Caught in the Net.[1] "Foolishly, I didn't listen to my con-
science," he wrote. Having read the manuscript, Bob Knight

---

1. Tates Locke and Bob Ibach, *Caught in the Net.* West Point, New York:
Leisure Press, 1982.

wanted to pay off whatever money had been put into the project and prevent publication of the book. There was no point in dwelling on what couldn't be changed.

Now the Bob Knight who hates and detests cheating of any kind has hired his old friend as an Indiana assistant.

A contradiction?

"He was good to me," Bob Knight says softly when Locke is out of earshot.

On this first day of practice at Indiana, Locke stands quietly on the sidelines, dressed in red shirt and white shorts. "I want to be with him," he has said. "I'll stay as long as he wants me to." In their telephone conversation as Knight invited him to come, Locke had brought up the past, but Knight had cut him off. Why should it be different for friends than for players? Knight's is a world of the clean slate, of starting over, of not giving up on people.

There are no reporters here today, none are permitted entry, but in the stands sit the professors: Drew Schwartz, the botanist; William Wiggins, of Black Studies; Harry Pratter; and Robert F. Byrnes, the distinguished professor of Soviet history who views Knight as the paradigm of the teacher.

As the players begin their drills, Knight is nowhere to be seen. But on the floor in his motorized wheelchair is Landon Turner, crippled for life in an automobile accident in the summer of 1981 and the recipient of the well-known Landon Turner trust fund created by his former coach.

(Not that Bob Knight will ever speak about this or any other of the acts of generosity with which he leavens his days. Once someone asked him for a ticket to a game, saying, "Well, I gave to Landon Turner's fund."

"If that's what it meant to you," Knight scathingly replied, "I'll give you your money back!")

Landon has been summoned to Assembly Hall today to be chewed out by his old coach for having quit his job at Indiana University in Indianapolis now that his lawsuit has been settled. He wants to become an agent representing athletes; his former coach is not so sure this is a good idea.

Last night at Valparaiso someone wanted to know what Landon was up to. One of the results of Knight's constant evocations of his former players is that they—and Landon

Turner in particular—remain of great concern to the fans of Indiana basketball long after their playing days are over.

"Landon and I are a little bit at odds right now," Knight confided to that audience of two thousand, "because he had a good job with the university that he gave up to pursue a couple of things, reminiscent of some of the shots he took while he was playing. I reminded him of that the other day, and he said, 'You think it's really that bad?' I said, 'Yeah, you'd better get down here on Thursday.'

"You should have talked to me first if you weren't pleased with the job," Knight tells him today.

"The job wasn't me," Landon says. "I didn't think I had to come to you." But Landon knows—Knight would have tried to set him up with something he did like, if only he had spoken to him first.

> *Indeed, Knight is always in search of opportunities to help people. "I try to let people know that I'm always here," he says, "and that if there are things that I can do to help you, I'll be glad to. Let me know. I'll do anything within reason that people I know ask me to. Just give me a break and ask me."*

It was Landon Turner, everyone agrees, who spearheaded the 1981 championship team, Landon who had started out that year in disfavor for not working hard enough.

During one of the 1979 Pan American practices, Knight sat down next to Landon Turner, who was watching from the stands.

"I talked with Buzz Kurpius [the director of Indiana's academic support program for athletes] the other day and she says you missed some classes."

"I haven't missed any classes."

"I know damned well you have because she showed me the figures. You know you could be the best player we have ever had; you could be better than Scott May was. You've got enormous talent. You simply haven't worked hard enough. If you do that, you'll make this a great team and you'll be a great players. You'll go on to an extraordinary professional career."

It was, thought Bobby Byrnes, sitting there in the stands eavesdropping, like father and son. But Turner somehow wasn't listening. He kept saying he was doing as well as he could and Knight kept getting angrier and angrier.

Finally Knight stood up.

"Why am I wasting my time with someone as dumb as you?" he roared, storming off, kicking a wastebasket on his way.

But soon Landon presented Knight with his significantly improved grades.

Yet again Knight berated him, because he hadn't done better before, and he could do still better than that. Unrelenting pushing, unrelenting pressure: ask Phil Isenbarger, former Indiana player, now an Indianapolis lawyer who is here today in the stands on October 15.

"Was Knight harder on anybody than on Kitchel?" (about whom, more later).

"Landon Turner," Isenbarger replies without hesitation.

Did Landon appreciate this much attention, this much caring? "When I was playing for him," Turner remembers, "sometimes I couldn't stand him and sometimes I enjoyed his coaching, but his personality stung with me. But I knew if he stopped hollering, that meant he just didn't care, that he had given up on me. But it's just the way he does it, he just cusses you out, he makes you feel like a little ant. You feel that you're a man and he makes you feel like a little kid."

Not that Turner was entirely browbeaten. One day after practice, Knight sat on his chair with the team gathered around him.

"You really worked hard today, you did a good job. Let's come back and work hard again tomorrow," he told them.

Then Landon Turner slapped Knight on the leg and said, "I think you did a good job today too, Coach." And with that he walked away quickly before even the rumble of a repercussion.

Now Turner reflects: "He wants perfectness, which is hard to get from humans."

The former players agree: there was no one Coach pushed more, loved more. In the hospital, after his accident, depressed, Landon Turner had given up—until Bob Knight laid down the law: "You're going to recover. I'm going to insist that you recover. Do you remember when you were having a bad time last year and you weren't playing at all? You finally got into the Northwestern game and you played badly. I took you out and I gave you one more chance and you played very well. You played well for the rest of the season and you really made that NCAA team. Without you, we wouldn't have won.

YOU'RE GOING TO GET UP AND RECOVER FROM
THIS!"

For a time after his accident that summer of 1981 Turner
sat in a chair, unresponsive. "I thought Coach was going to
pick him up out of that chair and throw him on the floor,"
Joby Wright, once an Indiana player, today down there on the
floor as a Knight assistant, remembers. "Landon had lost the
money, the career, his looks." Joby gestures. "He lost all that,
and Coach was so mad."

"What I got from him was love," Landon says.

At last, fifty minutes into this first day of practice in another post-championship season, Coach Knight, delayed by a
telephone call, appears in red warm-up jacket and blue pants,
his unvarying practice costume. He is speaking with two television people. One holds a steadicam. Beside the television
man, another reporter is holding up a tape recorder as Knight
gives an opening-day interview.

Knight thinks to himself, what the hell do the TV people
need this on tape for if they're getting it on film? It doesn't
make sense.

The interview lasts three or four minutes and then the man
with the tape recorder introduces himself as a reporter from AP.
Eric Ruden from the Sports Information Department of the
University is there as well, and Knight says, "Eric, what's this
guy doing here? I don't know him. I don't allow reporters in
practice. You know that. What the hell is he doing here?"

It is not a matter of the man's point of view; Knight does
not know what that is. But this is not how things are done.
The man leaves. Ruden explains. The reporter had told him,
"If the TV people can come in, I have a right to come in."

Has another potential mortal enemy in the press been
hatched? There are probably more observers at Knight's practices than at anyone else's, but practice is Knight's classroom,
something he takes very seriously, and he chooses his own
guests.

Knight spots Turner. Why isn't he helping with the practice? "I can get lots of guys to come around and sit on their
asses!" he yells. A moment later he stands beside the wheelchair, his arm around Turner, his irritation forgotten.

"What am I doing here?" Tates Locke asks Knight.

"Relax," Knight says, and he moves on.

He wanders from group to group. Nothing any one of his players does escapes him. He looks grim and they look grim. This is serious business because what they have to learn is hard: how never to abandon your effort, how to take pride in yourself, how to believe in your own value. He's an idealist, this man. He takes people nearly grown up and believes they can still learn character, if they choose to do so; there's still time. And he has figured out how to do it; if only they execute what he is teaching them in practice, they'll win against superior opponents.

They must concentrate every second, as he does, always moving from group to group. Under the generosity of his vigilance he never asks of a student what he can't give and is furious when one of them tries to do what he's not capable of. "These kids don't need a nice guy," he'll say. "They need somebody that's willing to say, I'll be the distraction, I'll be the pressure, I'll be what you have to play through." And so it begins.

"We've got a basket open and three guys here," he calls. He illustrates Todd Jadlow's run, slow and heavy. Some players have not spread out on the floor: "I could put a sheet over the three of you," he says in disgust. With Mark Robinson, the new junior college recruit from the same San Francisco program that brought him Dean Garrett, he is more patient: "One of the things you can't do is shoot it over someone six foot ten." Freshman Jay Edwards is taken aside by the arm for a talk. A moment later Knight is taking Jay's hand and twisting his head around: "Make sure you know what's behind you," he orders. Then Jay is awarded with a pat. Throughout, Edwards' expression does not change.

Knight is annoyed with his veterans for not having taught the freshmen the drills over the past month. He sure isn't "taking twenty minutes to do it." Jay indeed doesn't know the drills: four corners, three lanes.

"I was scared," he admits later. "After a week, I got adapted to it."

The issue of leadership has reared its head on this first day of practice: what Steve Alford did for Keith Smart, what Daryl Thomas did for Dean Garrett, what Quinn Buckner took on for his teammates from his first day of practice—as a freshman—who now will do these things for Lyndon Jones, who is even more frightened than Jay, and Jay himself and Mark Robinson?

Immediately Knight spots weaknesses, some old and some recently acquired. "I don't want any goddamned defense you developed over the summer," he tells Joe Hillman. Hillman, simultaneously animated and expressionless, doesn't miss a beat. Steve Eyl must use his advantage, defense, because, "unless there's been divine intervention over the summer, shooting isn't it."

"Good pass, Steve," Knight calls a moment later. "But be ready to take a shot."

Rangy Magnus Pelkowski, however talented an artist, needs to marshal all his forces when it comes to basketball: "Don't just stand. Make the play and get back into it. Don't let someone make the next play. If you don't want to play basketball, paint pictures!"

Knight increases his displeasure with those who will respond only to a firmer hand. Pelkowski is told he hasn't made a single play, "and on the basis of what I've seen tonight, you aren't going to."

Practice is made much more grueling than any game could be; stats are kept by the managers and films are made of each session, to be reviewed by coaches and players as a measure of how far they have come. Knight carries his famous index card, listing the drills he plans, and compares his card with Ron Felling's. Since Knight has arrived late, the players must repeat some of the drills while he leans against the basketball support watching.

At practice, there are no stars. You are only as valuable as the last play you have made—and how effectively you have gotten back on conversion. If there are students today who come in for the most criticism, they are Keith Smart, Dean Garrett, Joe Hillman and Steve Eyl, members of that (so long ago) championship team. "The shot," as reporters have called it, which won the 1987 NCAA championship game against Syracuse has never been praised by Knight; that, Keith Smart hopes, will come after graduation. What Knight does talk about is how Daryl Thomas, not in a bad position to take the shot himself, nevertheless passed the ball to Smart on the baseline.

Meanwhile, Garrett is told, "You aren't playing as well as

you did when you first came here. What do you think?" Garrett looks solemn. Then, quietly, sadly, he says, "No."

II

"We've got to set things up so that the kids can't screw it up. My feeling is that if we allow them to make the switch, we're not teaching. We're not setting up something that they can do well. Let's set it up so they can do it the best way possible. . . ."

On Friday, 402 high school and junior college coaches gather from around the country, and Taiwan, Japan, China, Yugoslavia and Egypt, for a clinic. From Friday night through Sunday noon, Knight will outline the principles by which he teaches basketball, the philosophy by which he understands it. There are no "good evenings," or "good mornings," no time wasted on the irrelevant.

On Friday night he goes over the schedule. "If you've got a question, the only way it won't be answered is if you don't ask it," he announces. And when they leave, the coaches will be told that practice is always open to any of them. They are even welcome to bring their teams.

The young coaches are treated as equals, as colleagues. Hes is anxious to share all that he has discovered about the game, all the rules of play upon which for over twenty-five years he has learned to depend. What binds him and the participants is this clinic is their common enterprise: teaching kids to play the game they all love so well. That Knight takes this clinic very seriously may be measured by his stated aspiration. He hopes that they will go away feeling "nothing you've ever done has been more beneficial to you as far as basketball is concerned."

He speaks without notes, occasionally using a clipboard projected onto a screen, through a wireless microphone—until it breaks down.

"I don't think I'm smart enough to operate this goddamned thing," he says, his voice booming out into the far corners of Assembly Hall without it. When the projector attached to the clipboard won't work, he has an answer for that too. "Where did you get this thing?" he calls out. "Puerto Rico?" The coaches, men, but with a sprinkling of women too, laugh. They've heard the litany, of course, but they're not victims of it. They're here for something else.

At the scorer's table, dressed in a red cap and a green high school jacket, Shawn Kemp sits with another potential recruit, a skinny high school junior named Patrick Knight. Kemp's visit is an official one, no small matter because he is the leading high school senior in the state of Indiana; as a junior he had averaged 25 points and 14.4 rebounds a game, shooting 58 percent from the field. There was a game where he scored 42 points with 21 rebounds. By his senior year at Concord he had scored 1,483 points.

Joby Wright, in charge of most of the recruiting, had been worried. Kemp "wasn't doing well in his books." Should he not receive a score of 700 on his combined English and Math SATs, or pass the ACT, he would be the first Indiana recruit to be ineligible to play as a freshman under the NCAA's Proposition 48. (The average score of black students in general on the SATs is 745.)

For most of the weekend, Kemp will be entertained by the players; now he seems as absorbed in the clinic as the coaches. The clinic itself is a project of Knight's older son, Tim, age twenty-three, who was working this season as his father's business manager. He resembles his father much more than his younger brother, his eyebrows darkly shadowing his eyes, his eyes themselves deep set, although he is shorter and stockier and less graceful than Patrick. Unlike their father, who speaks in standard American speech, Patrick and Tim surprise you with their Southern Indiana drawls.

Tim was the student of the family, attempting to please his father with his high grades. He was never an outstanding athlete, although he played baseball in high school, incurring his father's displeasure by not working harder at it.

> *Because of a bout with mononucleosis during his freshman year at Stanford, Tim did not graduate on time. In September of 1986, as his final semester began, his father made him an offer.*
>
> *"You're going to graduate at a bad time to get a job, Christmas. I have some stuff that you can do. You can work*

a few months for me. I'll pay you. Get that stuff done for me and then look for a job."

Knight had seriously doubted that his son would accept. There would be "no way. But I wanted him to know that I would like him to do that, that I thought enough of him."

A month later, Tim said, "I've been thinking and if you're serious, I'm going to come back."

Knight and Tim joke about their fantasy business firm, "Knight, Knight and Maybe." Patrick's interest at the moment residing exclusively in basketball, he is the "maybe."

"I enjoy it but it's not something I look to do for the rest of my life," Tim says. "I'd like it to be a start for me to go on my own in the next six to eight years, move away and run my business somewhere else."

At business he has always excelled, from the time he was twelve and ran the concession at his father's basketball camp. And he loves basketball too, having at the age of three sat on the West Point bench, being looked after by an assistant manager while his father coached the team.

Inevitably, the roles of father and son reverse. In part, Tim has accepted the job as a way of looking after his father. "The way I see it," Tim says, "there are a lot of people out there looking to take advantage of him. Who could be more loyal to you than your son?"

Knight explains the structure of his practices. He holds up a red notebook: these are kept by all the students in their lockers. They are taken on the road and emerge whenever coaches talk to the team. At the start of every practice, the team is taken off the floor to the locker room, where they are addressed by the coach about something important in practice, or a game, or a past game, or the season. Then they come back out and the practice starts. Always they begin with the four-corner passing drill, calling out each other's names, communicating.

The principle by which he teaches, Knight reveals, is to break everything down into parts, and then put it together as a whole. Basketball is broken down into its essence. He is teaching the game, not patterns, teaching people how to anticipate, concentrate and execute. And he attributes his methods to his mentors, Pete Newell, Clair Bee and Henry Iba, not so much because they are really responsible for what he is about to say, but because he sees himself as belonging to a living tradition, to which he is contributing. Most people who major in history in college, as Knight did, don't assume a historical approach to life as he does. But Knight approaches basketball and his participation in it as if it were living history.

The clinic becomes a clinic in teaching, its subject, basketball, at times almost irrelevant. A teacher, Knight explains, can never "assume."

"We have to teach what our kids can do and what they can't do," he says. "Kids will do first what's easy and what you will tolerate."

> "You leave it up to the kid. He comes down the floor and he makes the pass with two guys open. He's going to make the pass a lot of the time to the easier of the two to throw it to, although the other guy who's open is the much better shooter...."

The solution: rules. And there is a rule for practically everything: "When you catch the ball, unless you can drive to the bucket, you must face the basket for a count of two. As soon as you catch the ball, 1,001, 1,002. Just to see what the hell is going on." There are two things to do to set screens, seven things a passer can do. At once he eliminates three of the passer's options: "I don't want him to go behind to get the ball back; I don't like him to screen for the ball and I don't want him to stand where he is.'"

Four alternatives for the passer remain: inside cut, cut to the bucket, screen away, replace yourself. There are three things to do to distort the zone; there are three ways to use the dribble effectively against a zone (penetrate gaps, take the ball off the top, employ the freeze dribble). And with the dribble you must reverse the ball twice on each possession.

You can't distort a zone with passing. You don't go to the basket unless you have been screened. On defense, the further the ball is for your man, the further you should be from the man. On offense there are three things you must immediately learn to to: pass, cut and screen. The center can't go anywhere that he can't score from. But never do you teach patterns: "You teach kids how to play and what to look for."

There isn't anything that can happen on the basketball court that he can't predict, defend against, distort or maneuver beyond. He's there to lead, and he's comfortable with the habit of leadership. He's not permissive. In Knight's experience, students just don't learn on their own. They must be followers in his classroom, mastering these rules he has spent his lifetime developing. Yet leadership is something they must assume.

Thus he instructs these young coaches in their alternatives, particularly where they must not allow their players to make decisions. "I never let the players call out a switch," Knight says. "They're not smart enough to do that."

Where it is likely to produce mistakes, spontaneity is eliminated. If self-esteem and self-confidence are the goals, the players must not be put in situations where they are likely to fail. There will be frustration when they don't get it right and self-esteem when they do. But a student cannot gain confidence trying to do what he is physically incapable of accomplishing.

The players have come out to practice now, going through their drills, seemingly oblivious of the unusual gathering as Knight continues to address the coaches:

"I never trust the sons of bitches," he confides. "Don't trust them. You trust them and they're going to say to you, 'Well, I thought we should have switched.' Don't give them that option. Either they switch it every time on a high cut or they stay put every time on the low cut. That's as plain as it could be." The goal is to break basketball down into its individual elements so that his students can understand it, learn it, succeed at it.

"Keith Smart's a hell of a basketball player," Knight announces. He calls Smart forward and puts his arm around him.

"Do you think I have total trust in you?" Knight asks.

Smart, a quick-witted, modest young man with irrepressible high spirits, reveals the tail end of a barely suppressed smile. He shakes his head. No.

"The epitaph I want on my tombstone," Knight says, "is 'He didn't trust the sons of bitches.'"

In part, Knight's success is based on how well he perceives his players, who they are, and what they are likely to do. He is an astute student of their thinking. So his advice to the coaches is to get your players there on offense a second late —which may seem surprising until he explains:

"Never be on time because when they're on time they're always early. Kids are anxious. They cheat, they lean, they cut too soon. They think they're on time, but they're early.

Being there a split second late is far more important to the timing of what you're doing offensively than anything I'm aware of."

He emphasizes the distance, the separation, between himself and them—which is the appropriate distance between all teachers and students. On the first day of his coaching class he asks his eight students, male and female, "How many of you had a coach in high school that you didn't like?"

Every hand goes up; the students all smile to each other knowingly—for a moment.

"The first thing you people have to understand," Knight tells his student coaches in the classroom, "is we don't like all you little bastards either."

"So don't feel that they're going to think like you do," Knight tells the young coaches here today during this October Clinic weekend.

The cornerstone of Knight's teaching is making the students concentrate, the principle behind every practice. Only five minutes are spent on any aspect of play, then they go on to something else. "Four on four," he'll call, and they must immediately move into the next situation. "I really believe we can teach kids to be quicker by making them concentrate," he says.

Already on the weekend of October 15, problems that will plague Indiana during the coming season are apparent. Joe Hillman seems reluctant to take initiatives. By Saturday, Knight is complaining about the absence of communication among the players, the absence of leadership—which will be Indiana's greatest deficiency this season:

"Garrett's in white, and there was a red shirt up here with nobody guarding him, and that's the whole idea of communication. Hey, let's get somebody on him. Well, Garrett doesn't say a word. He just stands there. . . ."

One of the freshmen doesn't pick anybody up. And so coach screams at Ricky Calloway. "We've got no leadership here! Why didn't you tell him to get out there! You've got to see what's going on, Rick. Get everybody in position!" (And when, later in the season, Calloway fails in this challenge that he lead, having been a starting player on a championship team, he is benched.)

"Move, you have to come to the ball, Joe," Knight screams. "How many years have you played here?"

His curly black hair and blue eyes making him the handsomest member of the squad, Hillman is also the one who concentrates hardest. And when Knight speaks to him, he answers. This time, however, his answer is inaudible.

"This is the fourth year? Give me within six months of the date that I ever talked to you about soft lob passes in the middle of the zone. I never have? OK. I just wanted to check. I thought maybe I was losing my mind."

Suddenly, on this Saturday afternoon, in the middle of the practice floor, Knight descends on Tates Locke and engulfs him in a giant bear hug. Overcome with emotion, in tears, Locke tries to express his gratitude to Knight for having brought him to Indiana. Abruptly, Knight waves him off. In this world of men, where the expression of emotion is viewed as antithetical to the purity of it, Knight abruptly silences his friend.

By now the philosophy at the heart of Knight's teaching has become clear: "You win with people," he says, not with offense or defense. You find ways to use kids; you find a role for each individual based on his particular talents. You demand what he can do; you never allow him to attempt what he cannot, no matter how hard he tries.

Shooting is never "an equal opportunity situation." In high school, Knight confides, he was plagued by a coach who thought everybody should shoot the same amount of times: it was a terrible experience for him as a player far superior on offense than defense. Ability alone determines how a student will be used; some are scorers, some feeders, some primary screeners.

He turns to the tradition of Indiana basketball for his examples. As a freshman playing guard, Randy Wittman turned the ball over less than twice a game, and he didn't score. Later, as a senior, when Ted Kitchel was hurt, he did. Roles change. No point would be complete, however, without Quinn Buckner marching to center stage.

Knight recalls once more Alabama, the first game of the 1976 regionals. He set up a delay game, and he told his two guards, Buckner and Bobby Wilkerson, there were two things they were not to do: cross and provoke a three-second call.

"What do you want us *to do,* coach?" Buckner asked.

"Not one goddamn thing."

He didn't want them to go up and shoot free throws because they weren't good free-throw shooters. May and Abernethy would handle the basketball because they could make free throws. But, Knight says, he had never seen a kid leave a time-out as mad as Buckner was.

Roles in basketball, however, do change. And so Knight creates for the coaches an imaginary conversation with a potential recruit, a young man schooled in players being assigned, not only roles, but numbers to go with them.

"Coach, where would I play?"

"You'll play between the sidelines and the end zone."

"Would I be a one, a two, a three or a five?"

"You can be all of them, if you want. I don't care. What do you want to be?"

"Would I be a power forward or a small forward?"

"Well, you aren't real big, so you must be small. And you can't play unless you're a powerful son of a bitch, so you've got to be a small power forward. How's that?

"Hey, you come to Indiana and we'll teach you how to play the goddamn game. We'll play you anywhere. We'll play you in the post, we'll play you here, we'll play you there. You'll just learn to play and that's what basketball here is all about."

Students grow and develop new talents; and as they do, in basketball as in life, their roles correspondingly change.

As for the basis of offense, of course it's shot selection, along with everybody knowing who can shoot and who can't. After a week of practice, Knight confides, "I'll stop somebody on the red team and I'll say, 'Hey, Dean, who's the best shooter on your team?'

> *"And he better pick out the best shooter. If I say that to a kid who is the best shooter, he'd better say 'It's me.' And if I ask who the worst shooter is, he'd better look around and say 'It's me'—or he'd better pick one of the worst shooters. People talk about a kid's confidence. I don't give a damn about his confidence. I'm concerned about my confidence. When somebody goes up to shoot, I want to feel confident that the son of a bitch is going in."*

The coaches in the stands laugh, although Knight is exaggerating here. Trying to do what you can't reduces confidence; achieving what you can builds it. His entire basketball philosophy is founded on the principle of developing in each student a recognition of his abilities and then an insistence that he realize them, consistently, efficiently, and without respite. Not that this always happens:

"One day in practice Wittman gets the ball on the break. He starts down the floor, crosses mid-court and sees a red shirt coming in from the other side and makes the pass. The red shirt coming in from the other side was our center, Blab, who had a tough time catching the ball and a particularly tough time catching the ball on the run.

"Now we have a standard rule here that you only throw the ball to big guys if you expect them to dunk. Never throw it to them if they have to put it on the floor. As soon as he throws the ball, Wittman looks to see who it is, and he says, 'Oh, no.'

"The ball goes right through Blab's hands, out of bounds, and sails out to the wall.

"I came out on the floor, and I said, 'Goddamn it, Wittman, how many years have you been here? This is your fifth goddamn year here. How long have you watched Blab play? How well does he catch the ball?'

"Wittman sat there and he was so mad. He wanted to say something back to me in the worst way. But he knew he was wrong, so he couldn't. If they're right and they say something back, that doesn't bother me. But if they're wrong, they better not.

"Wittman seethes, as if to say, all right, all right, I know. For Christ's sake, leave me alone. But when I get them at that stage, I just keep at them. I had Wittman and Wittman is mad.

"We've never had a smarter player than Wittman. But ten minutes later, the same situation occurs. Wittman throws the ball again, but Blab, instead of trying to catch it, just runs right past, doesn't even make an effort to catch the ball.

"That, temporarily, takes me away from Wittman.

" 'Goddamn it, Uwe, the least you can do is try and catch it. I mean, knock it down, maybe you can deflect it and somebody else can come up with it. You can't help it that Wittman threw it to you, the dumb sob. But try to catch it, will you?'

"Uwe, a brilliant student from Germany, looked at basketball a little differently from the way we do.

" 'Coach,' he said, 'I want you to know if Wittman is so dumb he throw me the ball, I'm not so goddamn dumb I try to catch it!' "

Knight draws another example from his coaching days at West Point:

"A player named Schrage, who was my best defensive player ever, gets a rebound twelve feet from the bucket right in front of the free throw line. He goes up to shoot it. There isn't anybody within eight feet of him. He shoots it and misses it, which is predictable.

"We get the rebound, I call time, and I have him by the throat. I can remember my fingers slipping off his Adam's apple or I would have killed him. I had his shirt in my fist in the time-out and I said, 'I want to tell you something. Someday do you want to be a goddamn general?'

" 'Yes, sir.'

" 'You've got no chance of being a goddamn second lieutenant if you shoot that son of a bitch one more time. Do you understand that?'

" 'Yes, sir.'

"He isn't going to make it. He isn't going to make the son of a bitch the next one hundred shots he takes because he can't shoot." (Knight demonstrates.) "He shoots the ball like this, for Christ's sake, the worst goddamn looking shot I've ever seen. Well, I don't want him shooting, he can do enough other things. He was a hell of a player. But when it came to shooting, hell, no."

In practice, Knight explains, there are times when he will instruct that the only person who can shoot the ball is the scorer; he did this for Steve Alford, ordering the offense to get him open. On another day, he would say, "Steve, I don't want you to shoot today. Make everybody else score. You don't score today."

The lesson is literally "from each according to his ability." "We'll do the same thing with Smart this year," Knight plans. Knight envisions his post-Alford team with Keith Smart doing most of the scoring.

What Knight is proudest of in his teaching is that he praises the students inordinately for what they do right, but also never permits a mistake to pass unnoticed, no matter the score, or the situation. (Jim Crews says he has broken it down: joking, teaching and praising ninety percent, with ten percent devoted to yelling and criticizing.)

Suddenly Knight puts his arms around two players, as if to introduce them to the audience. "This is Hillman and Smart," he says. Hillman keeps a straight face; Smart has trouble:

> "Let me introduce you to Hillman and Smart. They're both fourth-year college students. They both played instrumental roles in our winning the national championship last year. They both played really well in the game against Nevada/Las Vegas and the game against Syracuse. We're going to have a little offensive change in about ten minutes where we're going to run triangle, post exchange and regular offense. Now with all you two have practiced and everything that you've done, as twenty-two-year-old young men, smart enough to leave Louisiana, smart enough to leave California, everything you've accomplished . . ."
>
> and then comes the punchline . . .
>
> "I hope I can trust you two not to mess up the next ten minutes . . . (pause) . . . you better not."

Out on the floor, Tates Locke begins to coach, using some rough language, rougher than what you would *expect* of Knight. Off the court during a break, Knight tells Bob Murrey, who has put together the clinic, that he hadn't said anything about his language to Locke in advance. but he'll straighten it out later. If an obscene word is used here, it is only by Coach Knight.

Meanwhile throughout the three days Knight's teaching is precise, self-explanatory, detailed and unrelenting. He takes extra time to help his fledgling freshmen:

> "Lyndon, don't dribble him back to his position. When you dribble down the floor, notice a skinny black kid, number 20 [Calloway] playing point. If you see a short white guy, number 44 [Hillman], you know it's not the point man. Get a point of recognition, his knee pad, what-

*ever you have to do to recognize him and then move him
further off the point."*

If you let the little things slide, Knight says, then the big
things will slide.

"The leadership out here is nonexistent," he yells. "How
can you let Edwards run a flare when he doesn't know what a
flare is." If they don't master the screens, Knight turns to
another new assistant coach, Dan Dakich, the sharp-featured
young man who met me at the airport, once also a Knight
player, "They're going to run the steps, and, Danny, you're
going to run with them."

(Later one of the coaches will ask Dakich, would he really
have made you run up and down the stairs? The answer comes
back: yes).

Freshman Jay Edwards is made to feel at home. "He stole
it from you, from you and from you," Knight points. "And his
last competition was a high school team. That's pretty good.
He must think you guys are awfully easy to play against."

Keith Smart, in particular, should know better:

"Keith, we need better penetration. I can stand here and
do this. I don't need you to do it. I don't need you to be on
the outside and pass the ball. I can do that. I think I can do
it better than you can do it the way I've seen you throw the
ball around for two days. What I can't do, Keith, is this."

Joe has the ball. Knight takes it back.

His voice grows louder.

"I can't penetrate like you can and pass like you can.
but I can sure as hell do that garbage."

He is not tolerant, nor does he believe he should be. "I
believe that kids are satisfied with what we tolerate," he says.
"If we're intolerant, then they're going to be hard to satisfy."
Intolerant people should coach a team, he insists. Nor does he
want his own children taught by tolerant people. Demanding
people are the efficient ones; they are the ones who get a job
done.

This lesson has little to do with basketball. Rather, it returns us to Knight's larger motive, turning out effective, competent human beings who will succeed at whatever they
choose to do. "I'm talking about turning out a kid that can

compete with other kids a little bit better than they can compete with him—because of his association with you or his association with me."

And so he believes in pushing people to their limit, an approach that, inexplicably, seems to bother so many sportswriters. But they are not teachers; they do not understand how difficult it is to change the behavior of students, and how great and unrelenting a physical and mental effort it demands of the teacher. Knight finds an example that would please those of his critics who would stereotype him as one who peppers his stories with military analogies. He recalls Colonel Blaik, the West Point football coach under whom Vince Lombardi was initiated into coaching:

"They've got Pete Dawkins on a two-by-four trying to get him up. He's got a torn muscle in his calf and they can't get Dawkins up. The colonel comes in and he gets behind Pete, and he says, 'Pete, get up! Get up, Pete! Damn it, Pete, get up, Pete!'

"Finally Dawkins turns and says, 'Goddamn it, Colonel, I can't.'

"You could have heard a pin drop. Everyone there was sure Dawkins would never play again, there would never be another play that Dawkins was involved in.

"But all Blaik did was turn and walk away. It didn't bother him because he knew he had pushed the kid to the limit."

It's clear that Knight loves to teach, to teach kids to recognize "what's going to happen." And he is no less fierce than he will be when there are not four hundred observers.

That Dean Garrett was picked "Big Ten Pre-Season Player of the Year" is sufficient cause alone for his coach to be hard on him: "Dean, where's the ball? You made no move to the ball. Come on, Dean, think, think, think. Come on, Dean, get the thing in play!"

"Garrett thinks he's a lot better shooter than I do," Knight confides, as if Garrett were not within earshot.

Those who know Indiana basketball only from the movie *Hoosiers* might be amused to hear the coach upon whom Gene Hackman's character is modeled demanding of his players what Hackman demanded of his. As the hero in *Hoosiers* instructs, so does the real-life model: four passes are crucial, especially with this team where there is no real shooter. Only with an Alford, a Woodson or a Wittman can one deviate from that rule: "Offensive play requires four passes on a half court," Knight instructs.

Another restriction he'll invariably insist upon is that they run the offense minus the dribble, which puts emphasis on cutting and screening. And he teaches the young coaches a game: four on four or five on five where, if the offense gets to eight passes, they score one point, and if they make a basket, a lay-up, they get two, while, if the defense gets a hand on the ball, it gets a point, and if the defense gets possession, no matter how, they score three.

"Dean, you've had the three worst practices since you came out of junior college," Knight tells him.

"That was really a good job of Hillman reading the screen," Knight calls. "He looked at the defensive man, not at the ball.

"If I look up again and see you walking back there, you're going back to San Francisco," this to Mark Robinson.

"Good move, Jeff, but come up with the ball. Good help. Come on, come on, who's got the ball? You're letting them take the ball where they want to take it." Smart hits the floor. Mark Robinson is taken aside for individual teaching.

Knight puts his arm around Lyndon Jones.

"Free throws," he calls, their rest period.

"Move, Mark, move," he yells. You have to move without the ball here or you won't play.

"The man isn't going to score," he calls. "I've never seen a man go through the bucket yet. It's the ball that's going in."

"Ricky, Ricky, see how far out of position you are. You're eight feet out of position."

Six on four. They must force the ball into the corner now. The corner man must take it as far as he can go. If the drive is stopped, he can throw it back out.

"Stance, Jay, stance. Move your feet. Don't play with your hands. Move your feet."

"Change!" Ron calls, and the five offensive men become defensive men.

"We're reacting slowly to making the change from offense to defense," Knight complains.

Pressure is kept up and everyone is playing hard. "Get back, get back!" Joby yells.

Knight asks Joby to demonstrate Jadlow's shot. Without hesitating, Joby moves into a perfect imitation. "I don't want that shot taken by you ever again unless you get your feet straight," Knight says.

Everything has been broken down into parts, what a coach can do in defensive play, what he can do in offensive play:

"First, let's take man to man. You're going to play man to man against my team. Here's what you can do and here's what I can do. You can decide who your players will guard. I don't have anything to do with that unless you're going to switch. And if you're switching, then I'll take your weakest defensive player and put him in a position where he has to switch to our best offensive player. We can easily do that in triangle or in post exchange . . . you decide who's going to guard our five players. But here's what I decide for you. I decide where they're going to play."

Against a half-court trap, he explains, he'll put his quickest player—Keith Smart—in the center of the court. Knight then discusses how he will use Smart. On offense, why not send your best scorer to set a screen twice to thwart the defensive player ready to shut him down on the first pass? Or—don't make two consecutive cuts in the same direction.

The day winds down. Knight shakes hands with Patrick Knight as he departs.

By Saturday evening, Knight has a splitting headache. Yet he remains into the early evening, signing autographs, posing for pictures, including one in which he holds a baby. Then he goes hunting. Grouse season started yesterday, but although he is out for two hours, he doesn't get a shot and returns home empty-handed.

III

"They get into those sessions with the pro players and pretty soon they start telling stories about me, and they become the focal point of attention. Because now it's, 'What was he like? What was it like playing for him?' Now they exaggerate. They forget the nine hundred and ninety-nine times I patted them on the ass, or patted them on the back, or said something good to them. Now it's 'Boy, I survived this, I survived Camp LeJune. I'm a

green beret now for what I survived.' And they don't mean that."

Him and them: Knight's relationship with his players also partakes of myth, forms a litany of its own. Harassed and mistreated, the newspapers would have it, his players leave in droves. In fact, Indiana falls midway among Big Ten schools in the number of players who leave to play elsewhere. Among basketball freshmen entering in 1974, by October of 1987 more players left Michigan State, Wisconsin, Ohio State, Purdue and Minnesota than they did Indiana.

That even this many players leave (36.7 percent at Indiana as of April 1988 as against a national transfer average of about 29 percent) may in part be attributed to the down side of the Hoosier obsession with basketball. As the Valparaiso aficionados revealed, towns like Marion, which sent Knight Lyndon Jones and Jay Edwards, expect their high school stars to start as college freshmen and to play many minutes. When some don't crack the lineup early in their freshman year, they are made to feel as if they're failures. And indeed at smaller schools, or at schools attracting less talent, they would be offered more playing time, as Indiana's Delray Brooks was at Providence and Marty Simmons was at Evansville, neither of whom would be drafted by the NBA at the close of their senior seasons.

"The people here are really great," Dave Minor said as he departed in the fall of 1987. "I wish I could have contributed a little more to the team." Sometimes, too, as we will see with one starter from the 1987 championship team, parents intervene, their only concern their own child's playing time. And it takes a strong child to withstand the demands of a parent's ego.

> *"Great game," Ed Vreeswyck told his son Michael after a Temple loss to Nevada/Los Vegas in the 1986 pre-season NIT in which Michael had scored twenty-two points.*
> *"What's that supposed to mean?" his son answered with cold disdain. "We lost, didn't we?" And the father, who tells this story on himself, learned something from his son and John Chaney.*

Shooters who are recalcitrant about learning to be strong defensive players encounter resistance at Indiana (where, as

Knight says and means it, the word team has no "I" in it). Steve Alford responded to Knight's insistence that he "defend someone," although it may not always have been easy. "He abused Steve Alford," Buddy Martin wrote in the Denver *Post*.

In fact, Knight forced Alford to be what Alford insisted he wanted to be—a creditable basketball player. "I love that man," Alford said at a press conference in the Market Square Arena in Indianapolis in the fall of 1987 as a rookie Dallas Maverick. When Delray Brooks played below the level of the rest of the team, rather than redshirting him, Knight encouraged him to transfer at once so that he would have two and a half more years to play.

Most of the defections came in one season. After the 1976 championship, everybody but Kent Benson had graduated, five of the top six players. In 1977 as the second best high school player in Ohio, Mike Miday announced he'd cut off all his hair to play for Knight. He started his second game, but not the third because he had already been missing class. He quit the following week with harsh words about his coach: "He dehumanized me."

That same season Bobby Bender, a sophomore, Billy Cunningham and Derek Holcomb left, disappointed in their playing time as Knight shuffled his lineup and began to rebuild. A football player named Trent Smock was allowed to come out for the team. When he complained that he didn't play in the first game, Knight called him in and said, "I don't need that. I think you're better off taking your time to do something else." A reluctant student, Mark Haymore, went to the University of Massachusetts because "Julius Erving played there." Later, he wrote to Knight, wishing he'd remained at Indiana, and Knight regretted it too: "We made a mistake in not keeping him."

Mike Giomi, the team's leading rebounder at a time when the team was struggling, was cut after having been warned about cutting classes. Ira Berkow has written sympathetically about Giomi's plight, contending that a student's development should be measured by means other than his attendance record. It's the more permissive approach to education, this view that students may choose how they are to learn, that the old-fashioned dictatorial approach, which includes a focus on discipline and attending class, has little place in education.

In fact, this permissive approach has few adherents in university education today. There is simply no student who doesn't profit from class attendance, from whatever level he begins, and athletes usually do not enter college with the best academic preparation or habits. (Only after Giomi left did Knight discover that he had left unpaid library fines, bills owing to merchants all over Bloomington.)

At the end of that 1977 season, Miday's roommate, Rick Valavicius, also departed. One night he was coming down the floor with the ball; Knight screamed at him from the bench so that it unnerved him. He accused Knight of being "arbitrary and violent" and went off to Auburn.

When at the end of that 1977 season Bob Hammel in the Bloomington *Herald-Telephone* printed Valavicius's statement, a rupture ensued with Bob Knight not speaking to Hammel for close to eight months. For Knight, coming as it did after a flood of defections, printing the words of still another disaffected student seemed superfluous and unnecessary. For Hammel, it was his responsibility to print what was happening in the Indiana basketball program, his biggest winter story. As two men of strong convictions, unyielding in their sense of what was right, neither would back down.

That summer, Hammel's son Rick worked at Knight's basketball camp. "It must be you," he told his father one night, "because he's pretty nice to me. You must be the one at fault."

In the autumn, Hammel greeted Knight's silence by writing pre-season columns about the players, not once mentioning Knight's name. Once the season began, Hammel believes, Knight responded to their feud by canceling all his post-game press conferences and having his comments distributed in mimeographed form so that he would not be accessible to Hammel. (Knight denies this action had anything to do with Hammel.)

And then one day there was a telephone call.

"Do you want war?"

Hammel laughed. His going to war with Knight seemed ridiculous.

"No, not really. Why?"

"Because if you want it, you can have it."

Such a telephone call could only mean that rapprochement had begun. But Hammel was not yet out of the woods. There was a banquet celebrating the Indiana Classic at which the four coaches sang "Jingle Bells" and Knight made a speech "ripping the devil out of me, in the nature of what a bad job I was doing," Hammel says. "It was savage." At the end of that speech President John Ryan went up and apologized to Hammel. "There's no problem," Hammel assured him. "This is OK."

Hammel knew that Knight had made his second overture. But Hammel would have to endure a chilly reception on a road trip before, at last, it was over. And meanwhile he continued to report, neither permitting Knight's intransigence toward him personally to affect his writing, nor ignoring any aspect of a story he happened to be reporting.

Hammel ponders it now: "Given the opportunity to take the clay and remodel it, I would probably change some things. I don't know that in my reshaping, I would come up with as effective a person as there is right now. In some mysterious way these rough aspects that I find removable add in some peculiar way to the effectiveness."

Now the two men meet in a shared ideal that Knight more than any other basketball coach has realized: you can win without cheating.

Knight's reputation of being rough on his players may date from that 1976 photograph in which he is shown pulling a player named Jim Wisman off the court by his jersey. Wisman looks perplexed. Looking at the photograph himself, he decides that he looks "goofy."

It happened during that extraordinary 1976 season when Indiana would go thirty-two and zero. In a game against Michigan, Wisman threw the ball away twice against the press. Knight couldn't get the game stopped fast enough.

"I called time-out and I saw a white shirt out of the corner of my eye," Knight remembers. "I reached out and grabbed the shirt. I had no idea whom I had. It ended up that I had Wisman, who had just thrown the ball away twice."

At first Wisman didn't realize who was grabbing him. "Oh, no!" was his sudden reaction, and he was embarrassed. But what made him mad was that right then and there Knight benched him. The wire services had a field day.

The next day, Sunday, in practice, Wisman again threw away the ball.

"Wisman, I'm going to tell you one thing," Knight said then. "You're either going to have to learn how to get the ball in against the press, or you'd better get a tearaway jersey to wear." The whole team laughed. In the championship game of the Final Four, against Michigan, Wisman came in off the bench and played well.

Knight, however, does not apologize for pressuring his players. "Hey," he says, "what is this kid going to do when somebody gives him something to do when he's out working and he screws it up like that? He's going to lose his job. He better learn to do things right now. That's one thing we teach our kids here in basketball. You have a chance to leave here and do things right later because you know that's what's expected of you."

In 1978, a senior now, Jim Wisman played his last game for Indiana. It was an NCAA tournament game against Villanova. Indiana was one point up. Villanova called time-out, with possession. "If they score, you race the ball down here and call time-out," Knight told Wisman. Villanova scored. Wisman raced the ball down, and called time. Indiana took the ball in bounds—and then they lost.

And all the way down the ramp to the lockers, Knight followed Wisman, saying, "Goddamn it, Jimmy next time . . ." He was still coaching, still teaching, so intent on improving Wisman's basketball that he forgot that Wisman would never play another college game.

Indeed, to some players, Knight's unrelenting teaching is difficult to accept. "When you get down on me," Patrick Knight has told him, "it's hard to remember you're my father." Because Knight is never one to "explain" his motives —not to players, let alone to the press—the mythology grows that, motivated by the need to win basketball games, he manipulates and tortures students.

Many players, in fact, do catch on. "Sometimes he yells at you for something he says you did wrong," Rick Calloway confides. "But you did it right, just to see how you're going to react. Are you going into a shell and not want to play tomorrow or are you going to come back and not worry about what he said and just keep on playing?"

It's October 16 and the players are eating dinner together after practice.

Shawn Kemp, whom they are entertaining, listens intently.

Are you planning to come here? he is asked.

"We hope so," says Ricky, strongly, encouragingly.

Did Kemp enjoy the practice? He did.

* * *

It's always been the same: the players who can tolerate unrelenting criticism are criticized more. Ray Tolbert had trouble hanging onto the ball, but if he fumbled, Jim Wisman would be attacked: "Why did you throw him a pass like that?" If Wisman didn't pass to Tolbert, he would still be attacked: "Didn't you see him open? Can't you see out of your left eye?"

"I don't care if you don't score a point, just play your role," Wisman would be told. "You played forty minutes and you didn't score a point!" he'd then be chastised. "I can put guys in who can kick it in a few times." Angry at Bobby Wilkerson, he would yell at John Laskowski.

The year after the 1976 championship season, the season of the jersey, Wisman's excellent performance in the Final Four victory over Michigan was forgotten.

"You know something?" Knight told Jimmy Wisman. "You didn't even play so well in the championship game."

For Wisman the moment produced an epiphany. What counted in basketball, as in life, was not what you once did, but what you are doing now. At the start of his own post-championship season, Dean Garrett grasps the same truth as he listens to his coach telling him he's worse than when he first came: "It's a motivational move for myself. What I'm thinking is, he knows you're out there, what he's trying to tell you is, just go harder. I want you to be better than you were before you came." Keith Smart sees that too: "He wants you thinking all the time, not only on the court, but outside in the rest of the world too, because there are a lot of people that can fool you and say things to you."

But no one rose to the challenge of Knight's motivational strategies more than Steve Green, now a dentist, one of Knight's first recruits.

"One year we got together in pre-season and decided we're not going to lose *any* games because we're not going to face him in a losing situation. We'd show him we were better than he said." It was a team that went into the NCAA tournament twenty-nine and zero.

At the end of that 1975 season after they had advanced to the regional against the University of Texas at El Paso, Knight stopped practice and demanded of his assistant, Bob Weltlich, "How bad are we going to get beat?"

"Hey, they're going to kill us."

The players then looked at each other and thought: don't you dare say that to us!

Motivation won out: Indiana triumphed in that game, losing later to Kentucky 92–90 in the regional final. The perfect season had been destroyed not, however, as it seemed, by one basket, but because of an injury to Scott May at Indiana's conference championship clinching game at Purdue with four games remaining in the regular season.

In the locker room, slightly raising his voice, Knight said, "Goddamn it, we should have won this game!" But then he said, "Why am I yelling at these kids?" Some had cried and Green had to console Tim Knight on the bench.

Knight was deeply pleased by that beloved 1975 team. He is a man light-years away in character from a Vince Lombardi, who after a victory could tell his team, "Don't think you're responsible for all this success . . . because I want you to understand that *I* did this. *I* made you guys what you are."[2] It is impossible to imagine Bob Knight speaking such words.

Because he did so many things well, as an Indiana player from 1979 to 1981, Isiah Thomas did not realize how much better he could be if he were more of a team player. Corrected, he would stare what came to be known as the "blank Isiah stare" and attempt to look right through Knight.

Was Knight too hard on Isiah? Piston coach Chuck Daly sometimes tells Thomas to control his game so he can play better with the other players. Isiah responds, as he confided to Bill Nack of *Sports Illustrated*: "I can't decide whether to play or to win." Winning means he must submerge his individualistic play, play Knight does not permit, not for the best player, and not for the weakest. In this sense Knight indeed runs an "equal opportunity" program. "I'm the only person in his life that's ever whacked him, ever," Knight says, "and I think he has a problem with that. No coach has ever gotten on his ass like I have."

Sometimes his teammates were perplexed by the degree to which Knight strove to shape Isiah's enormous talent to the team game, the winning game. But for Knight the team game alone justifies the expenditure of time these university stu-

2. Michael O'Brien, *Vince: A Personal Biography of Vince Lombardi*. New York: William Morrow and Company, Inc., 1987, p. 248.

dents spend on basketball. Only the team game encourages the development of character.

One day in the student locker room Knight made an accusation.

"I think Isiah is throwing games. He doesn't care if the team wins."

And then he quizzed the team: how many disagree?

Ted Kitchel raised his hand. "How can you say that?" he demanded. "I think Isiah is giving one hundred percent, giving as much as he can. I don't know how you can say that."

Missing the larger picture—that Isiah was not accepting the Indiana style of play—Kitchel had taken Knight literally. Knight, being Knight, would not explain, knowing that the best teaching involves the student's discovering the truth of what he's saying for himself.

"We're either going to play in the NCAA tournament with you or without you. It doesn't make any difference to me," Knight told Isiah that spring of 1981. "If we're going to play *with* you, you're going to play my way. Period."

"The only championship team he ever played on was at Indiana," Knight says. "He had to be babied, he had to be coaxed, hardest guy to coach I ever had, and the most talented. He was a hell of a player. He was a tough, competitive kid."

Obviously there was a side to Isiah's recalcitrance Knight admired. Later came that well-publicized Fort Wayne awards banquet where Isiah, responding to racism among the so-called benefactors, behaved childishly, lacing his acceptance speech with obscenities, regretting it all the while that he was doing it yet unable to stop himself. And then out of the view of the audience he made a peculiarly lewd gesture toward Knight.

"If anyone would stand up for him," Knight searingly told Ted Kitchel that day he quizzed the team, "I figured it would be you."

Kitchel might have been the greatest rebel in the Knight corps. In Kitchel's memory Knight never praised him for a great game. But one day, before the whole team, Knight announced, "If I were going to war, I'd want Kitchel on my side."

Once in a game against Northwestern, Kitchel pulled a muscle so badly he could hardly walk. Practice seemed out of the question. The coach, however, thought otherwise.

"When I played at Ohio State, John Havlicek once had two pulled groin muscles and he didn't miss a minute!"

As soon as Knight walked away, Kitchel turned to Phil Isenbarger and said, "If you were Fred Taylor, what would you do? Play Havlicek with two bad legs—or start your sixth man?" (The "sixth man" was, of course, Knight.)

At times, a player will stand up to Knight:

"Uwe, you picked up swearing really well," Knight told Blab one day. "Why don't you teach me some words in German?"

"No, Coach, then you'd know what I'm calling you in practice."

In an earlier era after a Knight dressing-down in the locker room, Tom Abernethy would turn to Quinn Buckner and, slowly, wink.

In a season opener, Buckner was indignant with Knight, who yelled at him because he missed a practice (he was on a football scholarship, playing two sports). After he had scored eighteen points, he looked at Knight so pointedly that the coach was driven to bark, "Don't look at me in that tone of voice!"

On still another occasion, particularly annoyed with Randy Wittman, whom he accused of not working hard enough to get open, Knight enlisted eleven-year-old Patrick Knight to guard him in practice. Then he demanded that the other players set screens on Patrick. This went on for three or four plays.

"Dad, I held him!" Patrick gleefully asserted. "He didn't score!"

Wittman, of course, wasn't about to give Knight the satisfaction.

On still another occasion Buckner made a pass that Knight didn't think he should have made and which cost them the game. Buckner maintained that it remained a good pass, only the guy missed it. He wanted to discuss it, but Knight simply refused. Disturbed, Buckner told his father.

"Maybe you want to leave IU?" his father said.

And Buckner saw at once there was jealousy between the two fathers.

"My father could see there was a male influence other than himself," Buckner says. Knight perceived it too. When after graduation Buckner's father began to help with his contract with the Milwaukee Bucks, Knight quietly backed away.

Kitchel was told he couldn't count to four (four passes), Kitchel was given a kick in the butt, not, as some reporters have written, right after an operation but four years later. In a game against Iowa, Kitchel shot on the first pass and was promptly taken out of the game and benched for eight minutes.

"How could you take that shot?" Knight demanded.

"I wanted to get us off to a good start," Kitchel said, undaunted.

When Kitchel was a senior and the team had a ten and zero record, Indiana lost a game to Ohio State by one point. Knight threw all the seniors out and told them that for the next week they could dress in the visitors' locker room. They couldn't prepare for the next game by watching films. Finally Kitchel said, "If we're a team, this isn't going to work." And he went off to the coaches' locker room to confront Knight.

It wasn't easy. Knight made fun of Kitchel before the assistants and seemed unwilling to relent.

"I don't want you back in," Knight told him, according to Kitchel.

"We're moving back in!" Kitchel said, holding his ground. And they did.

> *"You can bet the absolute goddamn farm that Kitchel never said that to me," Knight now says. "I don't even remember the incident. I remember throwing Dakich's team out of the locker room. But I can guarantee that Kitchel never told me anything. They've found they can become the center of a big party telling stories about me.")*

Mostly, however, the force of his will prevails, during their playing days and after. One day when he was giving a clinic in New Jersey, Knight called Jimmy Oxley, who had played for him at West Point, and asked him to meet him for dinner. Oxley was in medical school and very busy at the time, but he agreed.

At the clinic Knight asked Oxley to join him on the stage. He introduced his former player with many compliments, all the while discussing motivation. Oxley was in his late twenties, in street clothes, but as Knight beckoned him forward, demanding, "Walk faster, walk faster," Oxley found himself complying. "It made me so mad," he said later, "but I kept on going faster and faster. I just couldn't go slow. I almost ran across that stage when all I wanted was to go nice and slow." If this story sounds a bit like Thomas Mann's "Mario and the Magician," one might add that the commanding personality, that force of will, may be used, in the service of a variety of causes, some good and some evil.

After Knight's players leave, friendship begins. (Only a student's failure to graduate jeopardizes that relationship.) "The answer," Knight says in response to attacks on his methods, "is the product. The answer is all the kids that have graduated, the answer is their reaction to coming back to Indiana, the answer is their willingness to help us in any way they can." An annual summer golf tournament, which raises money for Indiana scholarships and for the library, draws nearly all of them back for a reunion. "If the product understands what was done to get it there and in every conceivable way," Knight says, "then that's the answer."

Playing basketball in Europe in 1977 and not doing particularly well, Joby Wright called Knight to say he wanted to finish school and perhaps coach.

"Come on back to school and we'll help you," Knight said. Joby arrived back in Bloomington only to receive a call to play in Finland. He slipped out of town without even telling Knight. Shortly after his arrival, however, Joby tore up his leg. He had to call Knight and ask for a second chance.

Joby, it was clear, needed a Knight lesson.

"If you want to play ball, play ball," Knight told him. "If you want to come back and rehabilitate your leg, come back. But there are no promises."

When Joby returned, he had to face the music.

"You're making an idiot of yourself," Knight said, "chasing a dream that's never going to materialize. If you haven't made it by now, you're never going to make it in basketball. Stop fooling yourself. If you're going to get yourself together, start by going back to school. I had it set up for you to go. You walked out on that. I'll help you get into school, but you've got to show me what you're all about."

The road back was slow. Joby first worked in Knight's basketball camp. Before he could be an assistant coach, for three years he had to mop the floors "if some kid puked," wash the backboards, do whatever Knight asked. "It taught me some things about myself," Joby says.

Each student is treated differently. When a former player accumulated gambling debts, Knight bailed him out—more than once. One day Jimmy Wisman, Wisman of that tearaway jersey, who had been working in advertising in Columbus, Indiana, appeared in Knight's office.

"I hear you're doing well," Knight began.

"I want to move to Chicago."

"You're not the most cosmopolitan son of a bitch."

"It's more than that..." Wisman began to explain, and even as he tried to tell Knight what it was he wanted, Knight was reaching for the telephone, calling the head of the School of Business.

"You remember Jimmy Wisman," Knight said to Dean Wentworth. "He would be successful at anything he does. I don't know anything about this business, but I'd like him to come over and talk to you." Out of this call came an interview with Leo Burnett in Chicago—and a job.

At their rites of passage, he materializes: funerals, weddings, illnesses, revealing concern that they might have anticipated while they were still at school. As a freshman, arriving for his first day of practice at the brand-new Assembly Hall, Steve Green was pulled aside by Knight and told that his Grandma Green had died in a car accident and his father wanted him home. Green hesitated. Couldn't it wait until after practice?

"Get dressed and get out of here!" Knight growled.

At times of personal crisis they may not notify him, but somehow he finds out. When Jim Crews' wife had a miscarriage, their unlikely early Sunday morning caller was Bob Knight. When Steve Green's baby was born with Down's Syndrome, the first person to call outside the family was Bob Knight.

"I'm doing fine," said Green staunchly.

"Hell no, you're not," Knight said, telling Green it was not necessary to maintain a brave front.

When Quinn Buckner's father died, he told Knight the role was exclusively his from now on.

And although he does not say so, Knight counts on their understanding, which explains why he could be incensed at an interview Kent Benson gave to the Akron *Beacon Journal*[3] in which Benson brags about having "survived that!" Knight recognizes that the remarks are positive in their intent, but misguided in their approach to helping him. Why didn't Benson admit that "for every time he hollered at me, there were twenty times when he patted me on the back"? In the article Benson remarks how Buckner and May, once yelled at, were lost for three weeks.

Knight shakes his head. "May and Buckner wouldn't break down in the face of the Gestapo," he remembers. "I've had Benson in tears out here over almost nothing."

"He swears at me more than at you two," Benson whined to Buckner and May one day. "I'm quitting!"

Buckner and May laughed. Member of the Fellowship of Christian Athletes or not, Benson did no small amount of swearing himself. After a visit to Father James Higgins, the unofficial team chaplain, Benson decided to stay.

And so they return, to be chided, encouraged, assisted in their careers, and, no less than anyone else, needled. "He's an important person in my life," Ted Kitchel says of Fred Taylor's sixth man. "I had to take being called the Dick Vitale of the Southside," Quinn Buckner says with ironic chagrin. No one seems to doubt it's worthwhile.

IV

"It's the inefficient people that bother me."

On the day after Valparaiso, I wait for him in his office. I'm eager to make an appointment for an interview, surely not too much to expect after close to a year of negotiations prior to my arrival. He saunters up the ramp and enters the office.

"How're you doing?" he asks, and abruptly turns away, making it clear that he has no business with me. He seems darkly intimidating, inaccessible to rational appeal. I dare not follow him into his private office.

"If you can," Bob Hammel advises, "treat it as if nothing has happened. Just continue." I decide that Hammel is cover-

---

3. "Count Cavs' Embry, Benson Among Knight Fans," Beacon *Journal*, Sunday, November 29, 1987.

ing up some truth too awful to utter, that he is being evasive.

But in the evening, after practice, as Knight sits chatting at the scorer's table with the head of the board of trustees, I make my way across the floor from where I've been interviewing Landon Turner. I ask when I might talk with him.

"Tomorrow," he says, loud, unfriendly, dismissive. I say good night. He does not respond.

The following day he takes no telephone calls. I think he must have changed his mind about cooperating for my article. I imagine that somehow on the plane ride to Valparaiso, or at the Big Wheel afterward, I said the wrong thing. I join the audience at the clinic, and chat with the fledgling coaches. I eat dinner with Bob Murrey, his friend who is running the clinic and to whom I reveal my disappointment. He's just busy, Murrey demurs, as if nothing out of the ordinary had occurred.

The clinic is about to open its concluding session on Sunday morning when Knight shouts my name across the floor. He takes me aside, keeping the four hundred participants waiting. He allows me to accuse him of bad faith, only to accept no blame.

"You have to come after me, I'm not coming after you!" he states categorically. "I'm doing five things. You're only doing one." Unbeknownst to me, I think, we've been competing. It's also apparent that he's half amused by it all. He promises to talk after the clinic is over.

And so we sit down in the coaches' locker room, although I'm annoyed that we'll only have a few minutes, that I must be constantly aware of my impending flight. I feel as if I have nothing to lose. I demand an explanation. How can he justify his not having returned my telephone calls? Surely I have him on that.

"You may have called," he says, "but you have not talked to me. Now if I say, I'm not going to talk to you, that's entirely different. You just can't ever use intermediaries."

My sense that this is sophistry is mediated by my relief that at least we are, in fact, talking.

Joby Wright puts his head in the door with news. Shawn Kemp has told him his mother had said that morning on the telephone that she doesn't want him to visit Nevada/Las Vegas. He's easily the best high school senior in Indiana and one of the top ten players in the country. Indiana wants him.

That his mother seems to view Indiana favorably is good news. As all college recruiters know, the support of a player's mother often makes the difference. It was, for example, the confidence of Mary Thomas in Bob Knight that ensured Isiah's choice of Indiana.

Knight turns to the subject of his own children. He really likes them both, he says, "Not every parent likes his kids. You love your kids, but you don't always like them." They're polite to people, which is important to him. It's clear he's proud of them both too—Patrick, who's shooting baskets outside at this very moment, and Tim who "works like hell" at his job here.

He feels a need to explain how inconceivable to him it is that a player and coach should be friends. This is something most teachers should know, but, he says, they don't. He acknowledges our mutual interest; we are both teachers at universities.

He waits. He offers me a grape. He is being friendly.

The issue for him is what makes teaching possible. Just as the notion of wanting a student to be his friend is alien to him, so is the fear among some teachers that an antagonistic, adversarial relationship might grow up between a coach and his players. "I'm not sure how many coaches I've ever known that were anybody's friend." You might, of course, say the same thing about teachers in general. He is as sophisticated in his approach to teaching as any professor anywhere.

As for the military metaphors that are perpetually attached to him, he says he rarely uses those quotations to support something he has done, although it's easy to attach military metaphors to a tough-minded coach. The military figure he admires most is Ulysses S. Grant, who, after his western campaigns, checked into a Washington hotel as "U.S. Grant and son."

Who is *he?*

He finds an answer in Themistocles, who, asked whether he would rather be Achilles or Homer, said, "Which would you rather be, a conquerer in the Olympic games or the crier that proclaimed who the conquerers were?" With his eternal adversaries, he is always ready to do battle: "I could be hired tomorrow as a sportswriter and I'd be pretty good. How many sportswriters could be hired tomorrow as coaches?"

He judges everyone by their fiber, no more on gender than

on race or nationality. "It's the inefficient people that bother me," he says, "male or female doesn't make any difference. I'm not intrigued by inefficient people, whether it be a house-wife or the Chairman of the Board of General Motors."

I return to the subject of his seeming intransigence, and now he has his full explanation of what happened.

"Let me tell you exactly what you're doing. You're doing the very same thing these people do, you're assuming, taking it for granted [that he's unreasonable]. You're saying that well, this must be true. You're doing everything you're trying to eliminate. That's exactly what you're doing. You let your-self fall into the same trap that you've been reading about!"

He pauses. There's no question but that I've been out-argued. I had come to challenge the stereotype only to behave as if it were the gospel truth.

He could leave it at that. But he does not, because, I sus-pect, at the core he's a generous man:

"You come out here for two days when we're practicing and you know now that all you have to do is say, 'Hey, god-damn it, I'm going to take you out to eat tonight. What time are we going?'"

CHAPTER SIX

Scrimmaging

"When we start playing, and we're starting into games, part of getting a kid not to make mistakes is getting him to a point where he doesn't want to make mistakes. Because he doesn't want to hear me when he makes a mistake, if that's what it takes. Then, eventually, he understands how much better he is when he doesn't make mistakes. Now his own willingness not to make mistakes supersedes his reluctance to hear me. Without developing that, I don't think you have a chance to be any better than anybody else."

On Thursday, November 5, Bob Knight calls.

"Where's my note thanking me for my hospitality?"

"I'm angry at you."

By now, of course, I'm not; it's rather that an adversarial stance seems appropriate.

"Just as long as you're five times as mad at yourself because you blew it."

I'm willing to grant I had been intimidated, so he seizes the opportunity to do what he does by reflex: develop your character.

"I hope I've gotten you out of that." He enjoys bringing up

people; it could be a player, or a TV interviewer, or me. We
set a date when I can listen to him give a talk in Indianapolis
"which might be interesting."

Noon on November 12: it's a luncheon benefit for Cathedral High School to raise fifteen thousand dollars for scholarships. He wears a blue nylon windbreaker over the red
sweater, and, today, sunglasses: no coat and no tie.

He dresses this way, he says, without a tie, to be accessible
to the people he speaks to; the red sweater bespeaks familiar-
ity. So, he confesses, he'll come up to the podium and begin
speaking before anyone can introduce him. Or he'll ask to be
introduced simply as "The coach of Indiana University."

He drives a Mercury, with his credit cards in the glove
compartment. He doesn't know exactly where he's going or
what time he has to be there. Mary Ann Davis, his indefatiga-
ble secretary, has taped the directions on his door. At the last
minute he grabs the paper and he's off.

On the hour-long drive to Indianapolis, his mind is on recruiting. Knight knows that other coaches recruit specifically
against him, insisting that Steve Alford was in "a concentration camp" for four years. "Our only difficulty," Purdue's
Gene Keady will say in the February 22 issue of *Sports Illustrated*, "is finding guys with courage enough to fight Knight
. . . it doesn't bother me. Or I'm too stupid." In the recruiting
wars among that fraternity it would appear there is little
honor, little sense of fair play.

Yet Knight continues not to coddle potential recruits, and
not to make promises he couldn't possibly keep. He will ask a
recruit, "Is there anything I can tell you?" He will not, "Call a
kid and say, 'How are you, baby? You'll play every day.'" If
he enters a player's home, and finds no books there, no newspapers or magazines, he doubts whether the player will
choose Indiana.

In fact, today's Louisville *Courier-Journal* has the story.
Both Shawn Kemp and Chris Mills who, as another of the
country's top high school players, has also visited Indiana,
have signed letters of intent with Kentucky. And some facts
are emerging. Mrs. Kemp, who said she did not have gas
money to visit Bloomington, the trip from Elkhart being "too
expensive" and her car too unreliable, turned up in Lexington,
Kentucky, more than three hours away. And if we look into

the future, there is Shawn Kemp driving a brand-new blue 1987 Z24 Chevrolet Cavalier automobile, and Chris Mills a 1984 Datsun 300 ZX.

Shawn Kemp's high school principal will confront him with a question: "Where'd you get that car?"

In Indianapolis at the door of the athletic club awaiting—or almost awaiting—his old coach is orthopedic surgeon Steve Ahlfeld. Only Ahlfeld doesn't have anyone at the door at the precise moment when the coach drives up. It doesn't matter that the coach is late. At once Ahlfeld is treated to a ribbing. Coach hopes his patients get out of surgery more efficiently than his car has been dealt with today. One of his first recruits, Ahlfeld, class of 1975, laughs. But he squirms a bit too.

Ahlfeld will not be the only recipient of needles today: the head table is filled with likely victims, from Dan O'Malia, president of O'Malia Food Stores and the chairman of the board of Cathedral High School, to the Reverend James P. Higgins, pastor of St. Martins in Martinsville and former director of St. Paul's Catholic Center in Bloomington, that unofficial team chaplain who set Kent Benson straight about Knight's swearing more at him than at Buckner and May. They are already through their chicken and canned string beans when Knight arrives.

The master of ceremonies is Bob Collins, columnist for the Indianapolis *Star,* who functions today as a friendly adversary. At once the two old combatants go one on one in merciless ribbing.

Collins is attacked for his pink jacket. "Father Jim Higgins," says Knight, "a longtime friend of mine, has just given me a note to read. 'Bob, please don't make any more references to Collins' gay leanings. We're trying to introduce a more tolerant view of this in the church.'"

Collins, who can both dish it out and take it, chooses, for now, to address himself to the priest, who sits happily smoking his cigar at the head table.

"Father Higgins, I'd like to say that, like you, I'm celibate. This came not through preference, but through aging."

"You have asked me so many questions over the years, and my answers have supplied so many columns for your rather feeble pen, that I would simply like to ask you this question:

Is your third wife merely a camouflage for all this?" Knight
rejoins.

Collins' comeback contains a sharp, an unmistakable needle, biting and pointed and effective:

"Coach, I'd like to say to you, 'Congratulations on your
recruiting season.'"

The audience—businessmen, former players, Indianapolis
professionals, nearly all men, largely Indiana fans—roars
with laughter. They too have heard the news about Kemp and
Mills. Knight laughs too. Collins has him—for the moment.

The ribbing goes on: Collins calls Knight "a dear sweet
man who teaches semantics," and begins a story about one
day encountering a player doing twenty-mile laps.

"I asked him why? He said, for 'absolutely nothing.'

"'Young man, that's not true. I happen to know for a fact
that the penalty for absolutely nothing is twelve laps!'"

In deference to O'Malia, the food merchant, there's a typical male joke about what to do with cucumbers. Then Knight
is awarded a plaque by Cathedral High School "for his unwavering leadership, dedication and love to the youth of our
country for these many years."

"Thanks for coming, Coach Knight," Dan O'Malia says
shyly.

But at moments of sentiment, within an all-male environment, it would be inconceivable for Knight to reveal his ten-
der side.

"I would rather the hell have had Barlow," he growls. Ken
Barlow, a former Cathedral student, and a fine basketball
player, a few years ago chose Notre Dame over Indiana. "You
can take that plaque and put it where your cucumbers are."
His timing is flawless. He pauses, and then he drives the point
home: "That's a hell of a thing," Knight says. "You send
[Phelps] Barlow and you bring me here to raise money for
you!"

Knight's affection for Father Higgins only ensures that the
"Padre" will be the butt of several jokes which include an
accusation that he used profanity from a seat just behind the
Indiana bench when Tom Abernethy tipped in a basket against
Notre Dame.

"I just don't condone that kind of language," says Knight.

After Knight relives some games for them, it's time for
questions. He becomes serious as he discusses the game

against LSU in the 1987 regionals: "That game expressed what I get out of coaching. You talk about patience and you talk about determination and effort and playing under control and reliance on one another, confidence in being able to get the job done under any circumstances. We were nine points down with 4:07 to play and we won. That's what I get out of coaching. Seeing all those things come together with those kids out there." The ribbing will resume in a moment—for now, unselfconsciously, he has stated his credo.

The supposed concentration camp victim, Steve Alford, consulted him about his present NBA chances only the other day. Knight went through the NBA roster team by team and found six players about Steve's size and athletic skills who have played pretty well. He was honest with his former star, for he is not one to flatter: They all handled the ball better than Alford did. But he shot it better than they all did! "What he had to do in my opinion was work on handling the ball better and getting it to people that were open. He's never again going to have the opportunity to score. His scoring is going to be secondary to everything else that he does."

Someone wants to know if Knight will be redshirting anyone this season, asking any players to postpone their eligibility. The speaker, however, has ignored the issue of tact and trust: the student might hear it first from a stranger or read it in a newspaper.

"Did it take you all morning to think of that question?"

Then Knight does reply. There will be a scrimmage tonight. "I want to see exactly where we are. Five or six players have already been redshirted. So we have only a couple of possibilities."

He behaves as if he's among friends, people with whom he can reminisce about his boyhood, when he listened to college basketball games on the radio, and knew the names of all the major league baseball players and all the football players. Thirty-one years ago someone had told him that there was a player better than Jerry Lucas and he couldn't believe it, because he had never heard of Oscar Robertson, although he was only one state away.

There has been another change, which he illustrates with an incident involving his son Patrick, who went to a basketball camp last summer with another coach's son. There the two boys posed for a picture with their feet on the bumper of a Mercedes Benz automobile:

"I heard about that and I went to the camp director and asked him if he wanted to run this camp next year. If you do, I better never see that picture anywhere." The corruption of kids has resulted in college becoming almost a stop to the pros. "Nobody even thought about this back when I was in school."

Now he introduces "one of the great people in the whole history of American college basketball."

"I think when he's right here among us we kind of tend to overlook this man. I don't think that if we were to rate a coach on the basis of what he has been able to do with talent, year after year, we could ever find a guy to place higher on the ladder than Tony Hinkle. Tony, stand up."

Hinkle, the retired basketball coach of Butler University, now a very old man, stands up at the head table, gratified.

"If they ever had a Hall of Fame for gentlemen in athletics," Knight continues, "the first two inductees in my mind would be Everett Dean and Tony Hinkle." It's Knight again showing respect for those in his profession who have preceded him; it's Knight participating in the living history of coaching.

And then, as if this were entirely too much emotion, he's off into a discussion of a Big Ten post-season tournament.

"You know, my feeling without knowing a hell of a lot about the subject would be the same as having women as priests."

The audience roars. Cathedral is a Catholic school, of course; no one enjoys the joke more than Father Higgins.

"How am I doing, Padre?" Knight wants to know.

Someone would like him to eat his words with respect to last season's predictions.

"Last year you said you didn't have a championship-quality team."

"Well, I was wrong."

"Are you going to repeat this year?"

"Nope!" But such a dumb question deserves a special needle:

"I was speaking down at the resort hall in French Lick and some guy in the corner stands up and says, 'Coach, we want two in a row!' And I look and I said, 'You wouldn't have been happy with what He did with a couple of fish and a few loaves of bread either'!"

Then he must rib the many Indiana University graduates in the room; there are simply too many to leave this group unmolested. He remembers a telegram from the Indianapolis Alumni Association that he supposedly received when he first came to Bloomington. "Coach Knight, congratulations on being named head coach at our alma mater. We're with you all the way—win or tie!"

It's time to go, and Collins gently rises. "I've got a feeling for Collins despite everything I say," Knight concludes. "I don't like Welch worth a damn (former chairman of the board of Cathedral and chairman of the board of the Landmark Bank) and if they ever get another Barlow here, you just keep your ass out of it."

He's happy to be able to have done something to help kids, "because that's what I think it's all about for all of us. Did you ever see a bad four-year-old kid? Think about this. Did you ever see a bad four-year-old kid? I don't care what color he is . . ."

But Collins has had enough; Collins isn't through.

"Your mother did," Collins says, and brings down the house.

Knight's final words are for education: "If we eliminated basketball at Indiana tomorrow, it would in no way affect the ability of the university to educate the kids in the state of Indiana," he says, "but if we took the chemistry department away, it would have a very adverse effect." Athletics is really only "the top of the tail of the dog."

He picks the winner of the door prize, an Indiana University jacket. (Collins calls it a Purdue jacket.) Knight, about to spend the next half hour signing autographs and posing for pictures, modestly hopes "that this season we'll give you a team you enjoy watching to play."

(At Cathedral's main fundraising event in February, called "the shamrauction," an uncensored videotape of his talk will be auctioned off and bring three hundred fifty dollars.)

Collins, returning to the *Star* office, is asked by one of his fellow writers, "Well, did you kiss His Majesty's ring?"

"No, but I'll tell you something," he retorts. "You'd kiss

his ass if he'd say three words to you, and you'd walk all the way to Bloomington to do it, and everybody in this office knows it."

And with that he turns on his heels and walks out.

"Did you enjoy it?" Knight asks me on the way back. He gives more than a hundred of these fundraising speeches a year. What *he* enjoyed was Collins' comeback. Have you ever seen a bad four-year-old child? "Your mother did."

The Seymour scrimmage is tonight. "Dress casual!" he orders.

II

"I had a terrific time this afternoon."

The intrasquad scrimmage will be held tonight in Seymour, sixty-five miles south of Bloomington, in the gym of the high school attended by John Cougar Mellencamp. It's that Southern Indiana Kurt Vonnegut calls "mean," where in the mid-1960s a sign still read "Black man, don't let the sun set on you here!" and the whole town boasted twenty-eight black households. "You'll find blacks in Clarksville or New Albany on the Ohio River, but not here," someone says.

Eighty-one hundred, a sell-out crowd, will watch Indiana play against itself, with nary a black face among them, not counting Professor William Wiggins, a member of the IU entourage. With the adjoining towns Seymour may be said to have a population of fifteen thousand.

Wiggins emerges from pre-game feasting into the lobby in front of the gigantic trophy case on the basketball side of Assembly Hall where he joins his colleagues. Professor Byrnes, the Sovietologist, is here along with Harry Pratter, the legal scholar, Drew Schwartz, the botanist, and Brion Mitchell of Comparative Literature.

Knight comes bustling down the ramp to decide who will go on the bus with the team and who will drive in the van with Ralph Floyd, the athletic director.

Driving the van, Floyd talks about how Knight "saved him, pulled him through" when his wife died three years ear-

lier. And now, he still looks after him, seeing that he isn't left
to eat alone every night.

*After the 1985 season, as exhausted as he was, Knight
took his team on a trip around the world. His final plans
turned out to include Everett Dean, Indiana's first All-
American who had coached Stanford to an NCAA championship in 1942 and also coached at IU, Henry Iba—both
of whom were in their eighties—and Ralph Floyd. Each
had lost his wife in the last year; each had been depressed.
By including them on the trip he brought them out of their
shells, back into the world, and as grueling as the travel
was (it included Japan), they all felt restored and ready to
go on with life.*

The team enters the gym by a side door, cheered by a
gaggle of waiting fans, but most of the applause goes to the
coach. When he comes out onto the court after his team, by
himself, his head down, his hands in his pockets, the applause
is thunderous.

"He's lost weight," murmurs a woman in the third row.

Dr. Steve Ahlfeld is here tonight, still worrying about his
temporary breach of efficiency in not having been outside the
Indianapolis Athletic Club this morning so that coach would
not have to park his car. Dr. Steve Green, the dentist, is here
too, as is Steve Downey, their former teammate and now an
assistant athletic director at IU.

Beside Knight on the bench sits Al Lobalbo, in 1965
Knight's assistant at West Point and before that the winningest
high school coach in New Jersey. Now in his sixties, Lobalbo
is visiting for a few days on temporary leave from his part-
time job as an assistant to Lou Carnesecca at St. John's.
Knight calls him "Grandpa."

The coaching tonight will be done by Tates Locke and Ron
Felling while Knight watches. Occasionally—since this is
only a scrimmage—he halts the action and walks out onto the
floor, puts his arm around a player and engages in talk, completely oblivious of the audience, of anyone's expectation that
this be a "game."

"Sometimes it was hard," Steve Ahlfeld says, "doing pre-
med and playing basketball."

"Post-exchange," Locke calls to his team. When Mark Robinson sits down, Julio Salazar, the head manager, advises him.

"Get the ball out and get it down the floor," Knight calls to the red team. "We're slower now than we are in practice." Then he moves over to talk to the whites.

"Good defense, Mark," calls Smart, sidelined by a groin injury, from the bench.

It's a teaching situation, with the score almost even throughout, 17–17 at 10:43, 39–34 with .59 to play in the first period. Knight even has one of the index cards he uses at practice. He tells Mark to give Lyndon some support. He calls Rick Calloway off the floor, puts an arm around his waist, and gives him a pat on the rear. He gathers the whole red group and talks to them, his arms raised.

No one is supposed to get tired. "If you think you are," he tells Todd Jadlow, "you'll be sitting next to me."

He begins to demand more intensity. "Judgment, judgment!" he calls to Steve Eyl, while Calloway yells to Pelkowski, "Get your feet set, Magnus." Will Calloway fill the role as the much-needed team leader? With the reds down 44–33 Knight comes over to tell Magnus, "You're only as tired as you think you are."

"Let's see what we can do," Knight tells the reds. "We're down eleven with three minutes to play." With 1.09 remaining, Knight takes the mike to thank the crowd for supporting the Indiana Basketball Hall of Fame, with which the Indiana Library fund will divide tonight's proceeds of around forty thousand dollars.

Does this scrimmage predict Indiana's season? Jeff Oliphant, who had been redshirted and then missed most of his first year with a broken foot, has scored three three-point shots and had nineteen points. Knight worries that he is not accustomed to playing as hard as he can. Calloway, Garrett and Mark Robinson played on the winning team in both halves.

But although Calloway scored twenty-nine points, he has not pleased Knight because he put the ball on the floor too much (the Isiah sin). Garrett only scored ten points; Mark Robinson had seventeen and Jay Edwards twenty-two. Joe

Hillman, back in Bloomington with a back problem, is still in everyone's mind as the team's floor leader.

Before they can board the bus, the team is besieged for autographs, not only by kids and nubile young girls, but by adults as well. Nor do they neglect Green, Ahlfeld and Downing, or Dan Dakich, all remembered as Indiana University basketball heroes.

As the bus wends its way back to Bloomington, there's a stop at a Holiday Inn for supper. Long tables have been set up in a private room, with a buffet of fried chicken, beef, corn, mashed potatoes, salad, cherry cobbler and bread pudding. Knight sits at the end of a table in the farthermost corner of the room; opposite him, in his customary seat, is Bob Hammel.

"I had a terrific time this afternoon," Knight tells Hammel, launching into the story of how he told O'Malia to stick the plaque in the place occupied by the cucumbers, how he had told them he would have preferred Barlow.

The target for ribbing at dinner turns out to be Steve Downing, at the far end of Knight's own table. He's too fat, his old coach decides, his cheeks are round and they stick out. Maybe he should grow his hair long so that his face would look "straight." And, more, Downing is ribbed about a free throw in a game against Notre Dame twelve years earlier.

"Is it like this traveling with Temple?" Knight asks me suddenly.

Then he turns to Professor Byrnes. What did the prof think?

"I never saw so many poorly chosen shots," says Byrnes.

"It's never as bad as you think or as good as you think," says Knight severely.

Byrnes, whose gentleness belies his distinction (shortly he will be off to Washington to take part in the entertaining of Gorbachev), remains silent. But later he will think: I give him the answer that I usually do and he jumps all over me. He asks the question so he can destroy you.

"The last thing I need is another piece of chicken," Knight says to no one in particular. Then, impatient, perhaps bored, he rouses himself. "Is everybody done?" he yells. "Let's go!"

Ahlfeld, Downing and Green come over to thank him for including them in the dinner. However intense the needling, grace and good manners remain the natural form of their discourse with him.

"You got to sit near the throne," Harry Pratter says to me affectionately, half-enviously, as we head for the parking lot.

Boredom is the villain, the enemy, which is why, the next day, sitting in his office, he will talk to me and at the same time leaf through old clippings, alternately favorable and unfavorable, dictate letters, talk to his secretary, today B.J. McElroy, make telephone calls and peruse sad stories of the death of kings. B.J. views Knight with an irony born of a worldliness which allows her to be amused by the anomalies of his personality. They are also friends.

He tells me he received a standing ovation at his annual talk to the student body. Thirty-five hundred turned up, five hundred more had been turned away, and so he told them, "You must be cheering because the university has done away with the school of journalism and we've made it a legitimate curriculum all the way around." As usual his remarks inspire a deluge of letters, from detractors and defenders both.

He believes he is emotionally close to those around him, to his coaches, to B.J., whom he insists upon calling Barbara, to all of them: "I want to get to know these people and I don't think I fail or am reluctant to get involved emotionally with people that I work around."

He asks B.J. to call David Ferrell at the library, one of the most important of his charities, and one for which he has personally raised hundreds of thousands of dollars since he began in 1976.

His friends are not hangers-on, or contributors, but people he plays golf with or goes fishing or hunting with—or whom "I just enjoy." Dinner parties with "mixed couples," by which he means men and women, are anathema and one doubts whether his marriage will alter this since what he objects to is the inane, the trivial, and the hypocritical and hence false attempts at intimacy. He did go to one "kind of a gourmet sort of a deal with little individual salt and pepper shakers and a spoon for everything. I went one more time and rented a tuxedo and wore it." Was he the only one in evening clothes? "Sure. I thought that went along with the whole scheme." His social life, he says, "is not built around bisexual groups."

"If I were to define my existence," he says, "it would be a fairly independent semi-solitary existence that I enjoy. Independent as much as a person in this job can be independent. I haven't ever held a party."

As for his favorite group: it's grandmothers. "They understand. They've been through it all. They know that not everybody can be perfect and not everybody can say what they think should be said. They look at everything with an air of indifference, an air of being set apart now." And, he says, grandmothers have been among his greatest defenders: One came up and said, 'I've got a grandchild in the third grade that knows more words than you do.'"

He laughs. "Maybe they all think they need to help me. They accept you for what you are and they understand why you are what you are. They're no longer competing with anybody for anything. See, most women are competing with other women for attention . . . and men compete too, and then you get to a point where you're really no longer a part of that competition for attention. I enjoy those people." (He has maintained a long friendship with the mother of those famous Indiana players before his time, Dick and Tom Van Arsdale.)

He seems a man with a lot of happiness in his life, enjoying the fullness of each day. "The last thing in the world that bothers me is somebody putting me down." He is thinking again of Collins, and that bad four-year-old his mother knew.

"I could have you in tears in about four minutes," he says to me suddenly.

How soon did he realize that?

"Very quickly."

Then he returns to his enjoyable life, "doing nothing, but the little bit I do. It certainly isn't an extravagant or opulent existence. It isn't full of cars and trips and glamorous people. I just enjoy from day to day. I just enjoy people, I enjoy going around and doing the things that I do."

He now asks B.J. to call Eddie Gottlieb. Gottlieb is attending a funeral, and Knight is concerned. He waits and returns to the subject of his sons, "the two people that absolutely mean the most to me in my life. I'm not sure how well I've done by them and that's a concern.

"Having Tim around is the most enjoyable single thing I've ever done."

"Tim has a more easygoing nature than you do," I say. He

disagrees. "But, see, I think I'm pretty easygoing. You could not get in to see any other coach like you've gotten in to see me. They wouldn't have time for you. I don't think I've even asked you who the hell you're writing this for."

Tim Knight passes by outside. His father tells him I said he has a nicer personality than his father. Evading a potential confrontation, Tim turns to business. He and his father now engage in a long discussion about the items sold at Seymour and what will be taken to Fort Wayne, site of the next scrimmage. Tim is imaginative, as he holds up a shirt with the season's IU schedule on the back, the biggest seller, like a concert shirt.

Knight returns to his attempt to define himself with the story of how a woman in real estate turned up at their summer golf tournament: "Here's this little old gal sitting there and she's thoroughly confused because this is just a players' thing and yet she had driven up from Louisville and had a room at the Ramada Inn."

Knight managed to include her in some of the festivities. Later he sent her tournament tickets. A former teacher, "she had problems with her self-image and she was really working hard to overcome this." He said to himself, "Here's a gal who is trying like hell to do something, make a life for herself. If she gets some enjoyment out of following our basketball team, I don't think there's anything really big about that. I don't ever take myself as seriously as a lot of people do," he says.

If he talks a lot about sports, a fact which strikes me as surprising because of his far-reaching intellect, it's because "I don't know a hell of a lot about anything else." And if he prefers Hammel to other sportswriters, it's because he never misquotes. He would never remind you of something you said unless he can show you where you said it. "Hammel is really the best sportswriter in the country, bar none," he says.

Being misunderstood, however, may be turned into fun. He recalls his response to the faculty council's 1987 statement on student athletes' rights, an implied attack on his treatment of his players. His retaliation began on his radio show when, asked as usual for the night's starting lineup, he said he didn't know because the faculty council hadn't sent it in yet:

"But they might be too busy since they are involved in a heated debate as to whether to plant petunias or daffodils in the flower bed behind the old library." Knight then decided for them: American Beauty roses, red and white, Indiana's colors. He instructed his television audience that those who think roses should be planted should send their view to the faculty council. The council received ten thousand letters along with rose bushes of every description. And at the next game—the whole audience wore roses so that there wasn't a rose remaining in a single flower shop in Bloomington.

While most "Bobby Knight stories" are exaggerations, designed to earn the teller a laugh, this event actually happened. Other such anecdotes are less accurate. Someone insisted he once emptied his bag of golf clubs in the direction of a rabbit who appeared at an inopportune moment. "I honestly can't remember swinging a club. By the time the story is told, it's emptying a bag of clubs. It's great to call people on things and just let them know. It's great to make them squirm a little bit. It doesn't hurt."

He asks B.J. to send a package to David Israel—an NCAA shirt, a sweater, extra large, and a blouse and sweater to his wife. "What better wedding gifts than Indiana clothes," Knight dictates. "However, I don't think of these as wedding gifts. I think of them as humble efforts on my part to help clothe the downtrodden minorities within the borders of this great country. Sincerely yours."

"What size is she?" B.J. asks.

The answer is in good humor and B.J. takes it that way: "How the hell do I know?"

A last letter goes to a coach: "Just a note to wish you the very best as this season is about to begin. I hope that the trip you made this summer with your team paid great dividends. I thoroughly enjoyed the book that you sent to me. Best wishes for a most enjoyable and successful year."

And then it's time for practice. Tonight for a period of time Jay Edwards only is permitted to shoot. Jay is being groomed as a strong offensive player.

Eight passes, Knight calls, no dribble. Jay must learn to get open off a screen. "Jay, you haven't set a screen yet," he is told a little later, "you haven't even looked for one. This isn't the kind of basketball you've played. But it's the kind you're going to have to learn to play fast. So the faster you learn it, the better."

In the middle of it all Knight asks Tim to call his brother and ask him to come over.

"I wasn't a very good player," Knight tells Dean Garrett. "But I never missed a lay-up under the basket."

No professors drift in on this Friday night. Nor is there any profanity. It's all teaching, instruction in the complicated Indiana screens.

"Work, Jay, work off those screens," Knight calls. The other freshman, Lyndon Jones, must also learn to get open for the shot. "Flare for it, flare!" Knight yells. Jones makes the shot.

It's obvious that everybody's habit is the reverse of what their coach desires; they dribble instead of pass; they shoot instead of screen. "You want to be ball handlers, you want to be shooters," he tells them, "but we have to have screeners."

When they get it right, they are immediately rewarded. "Atta boy, Brian," he calls. "Good set up and good cut. Brian, get open off the screen! Here he comes! Brian, you can always get open off the screen. Keep that in mind!" Now Brian Sloan must get Dean open.

After practice, Knight tapes a television commercial, invariably beginning with an out-take. Tonight's joke: "When one of our players gets hurt, we get rid of the S.O.B. and find someone else who can play!"

Well into the commercial, a technician asks him to speak more rapidly. He's indignant, or pretends to be.

"That's the way I talk," he says. "If you want to go faster, get goddamn Paul Newman!"

Suddenly he shouts my name, his voice ringing out to the far reaches of the floor. But I can't imagine that he is calling me in the tone he uses to get a player's—or a coach's—attention. The assistants, however, seem to have frozen in their places. They cast sidelong looks in my direction, as if I had committed some breach of ethics or, at least, decorum.

I walk, slowly, over to where he's sitting on the floor, his back against one of the basketball supports.

"Well, what do you think?" he asks softly.

I remark upon the complexity of the screens.

"If you spend a lifetime, you'll never understand the screens!"

There seems no logical reply to this, so I change the subject, thinking that I might get the last word nonetheless. The impulse to compete, in whatever arena you can, becomes irresistible at Assembly Hall.

"Was that four seconds or four minutes you said it would take to make me cry?"

He suppresses a smile.

"Maybe I exaggerated."

III

"I could never really understand why a meeting has any significance if articles are written about people that aren't there. That's always boggled my mind. And yet I was really pleased to be required to come here today."

On Saturday he goes hunting in Southern Indiana, bagging twelve birds. And on Sunday morning he attends the Big Ten Press Conference in Chicago, a meeting he boycotted for the past three years. Now there will be a one-game suspension for any coach who doesn't attend.

On this warm November day he drives up to the little Monroe County airfield in his black Bronco dressed in the blue nylon windbreaker with the red sweater underneath. He carries a briefcase full of clippings, quotations and mail, along with Tom Clancy's *Red Storm Rising*. Bob Hammel is already there, and Eric Ruden of Indiana's sports information department, as well as Jorja Hoehn, the women's basketball coach, who must attend her own press conference.

"Let's go, girls!" Knight calls.

Jorja doesn't seem to mind; he's been exceptionally supportive of her efforts with the women's team, attending their practices, allowing her coaches to attend his, and mentioning the women's team on his radio program. She is adapting his motion offense for the women's team.

Unlike the other Big Ten coaches, he has not dragged one of his players with him. It is enough that his time is being wasted.

"What's in it for me?" he asks Ruden.

"It cuts down on interviews," Ruden ventures.

"I never give interviews."

"Is it worth a day of your life?" he demands of Hammel.

"I might get a good line," Hammel says.

"For one good line?"

"Some days you don't even get one good line," Hammel laughs.

Yesterday, Big Ten Commissioner Wayne Duke had blustered, "If he's coming to knock the post-season tournament, let him not come." This is not a world in which the normal rules of civilized discourse, of democracy, apply. There will be a vote, but the "wrong" position merits chastisement, even abuse. Knight weaves his way through, comfortable by now in being a lone dissenting voice.

In the corridor of the O'Hare Marriott, a reporter comes up with his hand outstretched: "I know I should be an objective reporter, but I just want to congratulate you on a great season!"

"An objective reporter?" Knight jests lightly and gestures toward the man's nametag. "What newspaper?"

In the grand ballroom the coaches address the reporters, each doing his best to be charming. "Make sure nobody tells Bob Knight that we led the league in defense," says Illinois' Lou Henson. Bill Frieder, Clem Haskins, they're all in favor of the post-season tournament. "It'll give us half a million or more," says Henson.

When Knight comes up to speak, he has the devil in him. At once he attacks the purpose of the meeting—and the requirement that the coach attend "regardless of what it costs the school."

"Wayne, are you here?" he calls. Duke, of course, is very much there. Knight asks, again, what he has asked before: "Is there any meeting that the athletic directors are required to attend?" There isn't.

"Tell me if I'm incorrect," he persists. "Obviously Wayne's silence means that I am correct, but he doesn't agree with what I'm going to say." The money for these meetings, what it costs for the coaches to attend, Knight says, should go to women's athletics.

Abandoning his prey, he then turns to his audience—the press. Out of his bag come some clippings "which will reveal exactly what comes out of associations between coaches and the press and how much we're able to help you people and how much a lot of you know about what the hell is going on."

What he has brought are press predictions as to how the

1986–87 season was supposed to turn out: "Team most likely to come out of nowhere and win the NCAA: Western Kentucky. The Hilltoppers have a great front line." With great relish he announces what actually happened, lest they have forgotten: Western Kentucky got beat in the second game of the tournament by Syracuse, 104–86.

It gets worse: Virginia, picked to reach the Final Four, is beaten in the first game by Wyoming; who's hot? Georgetown, Missouri, Illinois and UCLA—only Georgetown making it beyond the second round. Who'll be in the Final Four? Iowa, Georgetown, Temple and Purdue. (None of these, of course, made it.)

In a loud clear voice, devoid of emotion, he concludes: "The number one seed least likely to reach the Final Four: Indiana. The Hoosiers are the most overrated of the top eight seeds with the possible exception of Syracuse!"

At this the reporters cannot help themselves; they erupt in laughter. He, however, neither reacts nor stops reading: "Indiana has a virtual bye into the regional semifinals, but the Hoosiers will never get past Missouri."

He waits. He pauses.

"Well, we couldn't because Missouri couldn't get past Xavier!"

He can't tell them much about this year's team because he doesn't know a lot about it. So "it's just nice to share more time with my fellow writers." He refers to the columns he wrote about the NCAA tournament with Billy Reed, who had been forced out when the Louisville *Courier-Journal* was sold by the Bingham family to the Gannett organization. Wanting to help Reed, Knight dictated the information, and Reed rewrote and edited the columns.

He used to feel sorry for reporters over the years, Knight tells them, but now he isn't going to do that, knowing "what your pay scale as daily writers has to be." (In fact, for their eight columns which appeared in forty newspapers Knight and Reed split a total of seventy-six hundred dollars.)

Who's going to play on his team? "I don't really know. Hell, you can get that out of Street and Smith. It'll only cost you about two dollars and fifty cents. It's a hell of a lot cheaper than a plane ticket all the way here. Anybody got a question?"

At first there aren't any. Then one brave soul, older than the others, who all seem in their twenties, does have one.

"Coach Knight, would you share with us your views on the proposed post-season Big Ten basketball tournament?"

"Don't you read Hammel's paper up here?" he asks.

"No!" says one of the Big Ten coaches who have wandered back in and now sit in a little clump at the right rear corner of the room.

No one has asked the players, Knight says. His students prefer to play each school twice, which would no longer be possible were there a post-season tournament: "Our players can see no reason why they should miss three or four extra days of class to play in a tournament that really decides nothing." The Big Ten already has four or five teams in the NCAAs.

"We talked about exploiting kids," he says. "The only argument I've heard so far from anybody is financial, and now we're really exploiting kids. We're telling these kids you have to play another week of basektball; you have to miss three or four more days of class so we can make more money." The source of this financial argument? Those who are in attendance at meetings "when they aren't on fishing trips or hunting trips or skiing trips."

There is a question about how he will replace Steve Alford. "I don't think you replace Alford with another player," he says, adding, "I don't think we should lose sight of how much Daryl Thomas contributed to what we did." Deliberately he singles out the player who disappointed him, who didn't graduate, yet who was a leader of that championship team—which he will always be. By hearing he is still appreciated, Daryl Thomas just might set his life in order. (And indeed by the end of the season Daryl Thomas will announce his return to IU.)

When Knight judges that he's talked to them enough, he suddenly demands, "OK?"

The taxi back to the airport is driven by a young man in tattered blue jeans. For a while he's silent, although he's well aware of who is sitting beside him in the front seat. At last he asks for an autograph—on his pants.

"There isn't enough thread for me to sign," says the coach, with seeming disdain.

But at the airport, as the driver is helping his passengers retrieve parcels from the trunk, the coach quietly, surreptitiously, leaves an autograph on the front seat of the taxi.

An article I had written about him for the sports section of the New York *Times* appeared today and I had raced to the Marriott newsstand to garner their last copy. On the plane back, I consider whether to show it to him. We're on the eight-seater, and his seat faces mine. Should there be anything he dislikes in the article, he might explode, or be cutting, sarcastic about my understanding of his methods. He might hit me with that favorite line of his distinguishing those who "see" from those who "perceive."

Then it seems absurd not to show it to him and so I make a motion with it in his direction. He, of course, is much too quick not to "perceive" exactly what it is I have in my hands.

"What makes you think I want to see that?" he challenges.

"It's your last chance, do you want to see it or not?" I say, pulling back my hand and the ungainly long pages.

"Let me see that," he growls.

He reads. I bury my head in *King Lear,* this week's assignment in my survey course in English literature. I'm watching him out of the corner of my eye. He finishes the article, puts it somewhere, and picks up his Tom Clancy novel, his face expressionless all the while. He neither says a word nor looks in my direction.

"You shouldn't have mentioned the Pan American games," he says when we are back in Bloomington, referring to my reference to the previous summer games in which Dean Garrett and Keith Smart participated. I realize that I have never once heard him criticize the coaching of anyone else. But if I had expected praise, I'm disappointed. That's all he says.

He heads for his Bronco. "You go with Hammel," he gestures as we make our way back to Assembly Hall.

He has arrived back in Bloomington in time for an hour of teaching, which will precede tonight's intersquad scrimmage. When he walks out onto the floor, the students are already there, holding their red notebooks. Today he is trying to teach them to see the whole court and everyone on it, to anticipate what the others are going to do before they do it. He is also trying to teach them how to concentrate, knowing that it isn't nearly enough to tell them to do it. "We can't get beat because I don't look at the outside and here comes Ricky and I don't see him," he says. It's still pre-season. In short, the lesson today is in seeing.

When they get down to mid-court, they must know who's there, what's outside, what's inside of you.

"As I'm coming back right there," he demonstrates, "I immediately look to see what's here."

He teaches defensive conversion by breaking the lesson into small parts so that each segment appears to be simple, possible, manageable: anyone can do it. As he breaks down the game, so he breaks down the floor, and as he completes each segment, he asks, "Now does anybody have a question on conversion?" No one has.

Part of the lesson is in communication: "Lyndon and I are coming along here. I'm not guarding Lyndon so I let Lyndon go and wait on who I'm guarding. It's Ron, but there's nobody to pick up Lyndon. So eventually Lyndon gets open for an easy shot."

"We don't play the man," he adds, "we're playing to stop the ball."

The other team sets up an offense, then the defenders must pressure that offense. We: Jump to the ball instead of waiting on what the passer is going to do *after* he gets rid of the ball. "I want everybody to write that down in capital letters," he orders. "JUMP TO THE BALL." Repetition reinforces his method; repetition has become so natural to him that it governs his conversation no less than his teaching: "Wherever the pass is made, anytime it's lateral or penetrating of any kind, jump to the ball, get to the basketball, the basketball is what we're trying to stop."

Once that principle is mastered, they work at keeping the ball moving toward the corners and taking away the reverse pass.

"Make him back up in reversing the ball; that's the hardest pass in basketball to complete, the back cut down the lane by perimeter play. Do you all understand what I'm talking about here?" He wants the opponent anxious about his offense because "the more anxious they are, the more mistakes they're going to make."

His voice rings out through Assembly Hall, clear as a bell, no microphone today. It's so clear, lucid, direct and overwhelming that it drowns out contrary thoughts; it drowns out doubts. It's the voice of authority telling them he knows this game better than anyone else has ever known it. As if basketball paralleled the labyrinthine plot of a Tom Clancy novel, he teaches them to maneuver, how to get the edge, how to outthink an adversary, how to find the loophole in an opponent's reasoning, how to beat him to the destination, all the while stretching the peculiar harmony of mind and body that is basketball.

In each coaching session these principles predominate: preparation, communication, self-discipline, competition, taking initiatives, hard work to anticipate any eventuality, taking responsibility. In his 1981 baccalaureate address he revealed he knew students sometimes come to college not knowing how to read and write. Unlike many educators, however, he admitted that there are some who *leave* "not particularly adept at writing and reading." Then he told the students that it was partly their own fault.

"We've got to be a team that doesn't make mistakes." Meanwhile "the more mistakes *they* make, the better we're going to be." He pauses for an instant. "If you've got any questions at all, I want them answered before we go through this. Because if there aren't any questions, we're all done with the defense and we can get into the offense."

There are no mysteries. They must: recover short to take away the drive, recover to put pressure on the shot, recover to make the interception if it's there. They've eliminated the lunge. But what is brother to the lunge? It's leaving your feet on the shot fake! They've already seen a Pistons-Hawks game and he's pointed out the times Isiah Thomas got caught in the shot fake: "Isiah worked for years here on the shot fake. We can't have that happen to us."

The implication is clear: if they work hard, if they follow what he tells them, they can supersede even Isiah, whom they know has more talent than all of them put together. More: if Isiah went through this, and it resulted in his outstanding career, hard work might bring them a similar success.

He teaches the possible. The shot fake is something they all can do. Not everybody will be a great natural shooter. But they all can learn the shot fake.

Already he suspects what the season will reveal. They are weak in making it tough for a post man to get position: "We don't have anybody fighting the post man. We don't have anybody taking away direction." He tells them what will happen and what they can do about it. "If the ball moves, step back and establish yourself behind him."

Dave has the ball and he makes a pass to Ricky. "But *this* is not jump to the ball. *This* is not what we want."

"Now Keith," he adds, "you're terribly guilty of this... the move that we want is directly toward the basketball with the back hand to the passing lane." It is this degree of detail that they must master: "The ball is above the foul line extended, I am one step on the man side of the bucket. The ball is below the foul line extended, I am one step on the ball side of the bucket."

There are many areas where they're weak. "Wherever we are," he tells them, "we're not doing a real good job of taking away cuts." In blockout situations, they're turning on the boards rather than on the man. The break should be on one side of the lane or the other, not in the middle of the floor.

Keith, Ricky and Jay must learn to work off somebody every time they come down the floor because they have the best ability to score. They cannot just get open. They cannot catch the ball: "That's not what your jobs are. You people are to get open to score and you don't score by being a ball handler."

The season is only two weeks away; he has decided that his offense must come from these three: from Keith, from Ricky and from Jay. He cannot know at this point in the season that Keith and Ricky both will disappoint him, that Jay will almost be lost to the team.

Everyone has a role: Jadlow, Garrett and Pelkowski get the ball to somebody who can handle it (after the rebound). Or you come right inside and you're set for the shot. No one is expected to do everything.

As the hour winds down, worry seems to set in. He's speaking and then, suddenly, his patience is gone. "Steve Eyl," he says, "for whatever the reason, you do this worse than anybody we have. You just catch the ball. You don't even look. You're just here and you throw it right back. You're not in any way looking to see what's going on. When the ball is brought toward you, you're going to screen. When the ball goes away from you, you're going to cut.

"We just don't do enough things right yet, boys," he concludes. "You beat people through execution; you don't beat them because you outjump them, outrun them or outshoot them. You outthink them and you outexecute them." It seems to be the most difficult lesson of all: "If you stay down and screen, you'll get shot opportunities. You'll get tremendous shots because you're a screener that you won't believe." He looks at them and he knows them. "You obviously don't believe it because you don't do it," he says.

"Be hard to guard. The more they have to guard you, the more we can get people twisted around." He looks at Ricky. "You're not getting squared up. You're not taking the shots that you have." He knows the game so well that it seems he is looking through a crystal ball. "And you're taking shots that you don't have."

When the ball comes across mid-court what he wants is movement, but passing, and not that Isiah sin, dribbling. "I want it passed right now so that the cut is made from up there and then he replaces himself or he inside cuts or whatever." What he hates is the "comfort zone." "Boys, he says, "you cannot be a good team playing comfortable. This team has no chance of being good playing comfortable. I don't want anybody handling the ball where he can't shoot it."

He teaches them all he knows; it's all he can do. And out of the simplicity, the clarity, he hopes will arise from within all of them—the will to execute.

"Well, what do you think?" he wants to know.

Then he turns to Patrick, who is practicing at one of the baskets. "You're shooting way up on top of the ball," he tells his son. "It just looks awful. You can't hit the front rim and score. That's three in a row on the front rim."

Patrick continues to shoot from the same place.

"Pat, get the ball right off the top of your head. Don't get the ball stretched way down your arm. The ball is too high. Don't even jump. Right there, that's good, that's the kind of release we're after. Shoot the damn thing long. Now concentrate. Hold your follow-through."

Tates Locke has an idea. He pushes over a chair. Patrick sits down and shoots baskets from the chair.

"Hold your follow-through. Now go out at the white line and keep it extended."

Knight goes out and demonstrates, holding Patrick's arms. "I can't tell you how much better that is," he tells his son. Patrick keeps on shooting one jumper after another.

Knight goes off to eat with Tim while Patrick keeps on practicing with Dan Dakich. "That's it," Danny encourages.

"When we go out to eat, he's my Dad," Patrick says, "but when I'm out on the floor, which is ninety percent of the time we're together, he's a coach."

Assembly Hall is now deserted. It's only Patrick Knight with Dan Dakich guarding him, shooting over and over again.

Then Patrick and Danny repair to the coaches' locker room, where they watch an old high school scrimmage of Patrick's team, Bloomington North. Patrick says he's not good enough to play for Indiana; it's this, it seems, and not any problem playing for his father, that will determine where he goes to college. (Tim has another view: "I think it's best for the son to play for somebody else.")

The tape is stopped every minute or two for study. Tim and Bob Knight return and Tim offers his brother something red in a plastic container, chili or spaghetti. Patrick declines. The remains of a homemade apple cake are oozing in the pan, beside the diet sodas. The tape is so faint you can barely make out Patrick, except for his black-and-white knee pad. "Is that you?" his father has to ask.

Patrick is sent home to change his clothes; he is not permitted to wear shorts, a T-shirt, cap and sneakers to the scrimmage tonight. Patrick departs. "Any people coming?" Knight asks. "Go look outside. Were there any cars out there?"

"It's not filled up, but it's getting crowded," Danny reports.

"Get up there and sell some tickets," Knight jokes.

He's still preoccupied with that Big Ten press conference. "Somebody will write how surly I was, and my arrogant ways," he predicts. "That's just me. I talked to them today just like you and I talk. There wasn't anything surly about what I did. But I just couldn't resist that"—by which he means throwing their inaccurate predictions in their faces.

Patrick concerns him too. "I'm not sure how good I've been," Knight says. He is sad now. "That's the hardest thing I've ever had to do. Not to be able to spend more time with him or see him in the morning or see him in the evening since I've been divorced. That really bothers me."

He offers me a frozen yogurt pie from the refrigerator. And he returns to the game, to motivating students. Anger is not a great motivational device, he has found, because the student can't get mad often enough. There's so much starting and stopping involved in playing the game that overcommitment is a greater error than undercommitment. That's where anger has limitations; it will cause a player to overcommit. Since his days coaching Army, he has believed that basketball is a game where the mental is to the physical as four is to one. "The great players are the guys that think constantly with good talent."

That the students didn't have many questions did not surprise him: "It's easy to get people to ask you questions," he says. "Don't explain things very well." At his summer camp he talks to the kids about not behaving, saying "'The first kid that tries me, I'm going to pack your ass on the next bus home. All right, are there any questions? Good. I'm glad you all understand me.' And I just say it that way so there isn't time for a kid to raise his hand."

The telephone rings. What about a starting lineup for tonight's scrimmage? "How many do we have available?" he asks. "OK, put Garrett, Calloway, Eyl, Smart, Oliphant and Jones in one color and the other seven in the other color to start with."

He remembers a game against Wisconsin at a time when Indiana was in first place in the Big Ten and Wisconsin in last. He asked his team to draw a starting lineup among both teams and "they picked two of ours and three of theirs and they were absolutely right. Indiana won the conference championship and Wisconsin finished last. The point is that what separates kids is not talent. And it's not skill. It's thinking."

He recalls the scene a few years ago when, annoyed at the cheerleaders for encouraging a chant as Steve Alford took his free throws, he kicked a megaphone which accidentally hit a girl, whose father was a good friend of his, in the calf of her leg. Shortly thereafter he received a letter laced with obscenities from the sister of another cheerleader who was working in Dallas.

"What would have happened had I found out the name of the president of this company and sent the letter to him, asking, is this the kind of writing you want your employees to do on your stationery?"

Two cheerleaders came in to see him; the one who was hit was not really upset.

"Before you even start," he told them, "let me tell you how unhappy I was. You cheerleaders are only out there for one reason—that's because I let you out there. You only go on trips because I let you go on trips. Did you two go to New York last year?"

"Yes."

"Which one of you sent me a thank-you note for being included in that trip? Expense-paid trip to New York for five days. That's a pretty good trip for an eighteen-year-old kid. I didn't get a thank-you note from you and I didn't get one from you. The shoes you have on I got for you. You get three pairs of Adidas shoes, don't you?

"I sent you those three pair of shoes. I haven't gotten one thank-you from one cheerleader as long as I've been here so don't come into me with this."

He returns to the theme of other coaches recruiting against him, even telling overt lies as a way of persuading students to play for them. They were recruiting a student named Glen Grunwald out of Chicago when an Illinois coach told Grunwald that at the half of a game, Knight threw a coat and a soda can at Quinn Buckner and hit him in the head. Buckner was a senior at the time, and he called the high school boy himself. Buckner's message was: "If you're too dumb not to see through that, then you're not smart enough to come to Indiana." (Grunwald went on to play for Indiana from 1977 through 1981.)

This is not to say that he never becomes angry at a player. Then it gratifies him when someone understands, as at a party a doctor's wife told the crowd, "Wait a minute. When was the last time one of you people either paddled, grabbed or slapped one of your kids? He's dealing with fourteen kids, everybody else's kids, and he's spending more time with those fourteen than any of us are spending with our own. And what the hell is so bad about him getting upset with one of them?"

He sits chatting, oblivious of the time, until the scrimmage is about to begin, and the band has begun to play.

A moment later, he is taking the microphone, and addressing the crowd: "We really appreciate your coming out tonight and I think I would be remiss if I didn't tell you that the three officials here tonight, all Indiana guys, Bob, Gary and Eric, have donated their services to tonight's game. But I told them as we've paid them a lot of money in the past for doing nothing . . ."

CHAPTER SEVEN

Interlude: Indiana Classic

"I don't have a doghouse. I have a birdhouse. If you fly, you get into the birdhouse and you get to play. You don't put guys on the bench. You put other guys in the game who deserve to play."

It's a Thursday at two in the afternoon in the coaches' locker room. Wearing a gray T-shirt, the nondescript blue pants and white athletic socks, Coach Bob Knight sits in his favorite chair watching a tape of practice. Simultaneously he talks on the telephone to someone he hopes will hire the son of one of his friends as an assistant football coach.

"He's really good and he's really bright," Knight says. "He's smart enough to do enough things so eventually you begin to lean on a guy like him. I've known him since he was in junior high school. He's self-motivated and he would be very, very good for you."

The conversation concludes with Knight not only polite, but even humble.

"I appreciate your taking the call."

Indian has already beaten Miami of Ohio, Notre Dame and Vanderbilt. It has also lost to Kentucky in overtime 82–76, at one point in that game failing to score on six consecutive possessions. Nor to be taken lightly is the fact that Keith Smart has six turnovers, including one in which he dribbled the ball off his leg in the last minute as Indiana had a chance to tie. Jay Edwards forced an overtime with a baseline shot at the buzzer. But then Kentucky's Rex Chapman, who had been shut down for most of the game, going five for seventeen, clinched the game with a three-point shot. For Indiana, Rick Calloway was the high scorer with twenty-six points.

Now Knight is scrutinizing his team on tape, while Ron Felling watches with him. Jay's got "an all arms shot," Knight decides. "He doesn't get his legs into it." While perusing the stat sheet from last night's practice, he talks about a potential recruit: "Do we have a record of his games to date, whether he scored or anything?"

"What's going on in the literary world?" he suddenly asks me without taking his eyes off the television set for an instant. I'm not sure to whom he's talking. "This is the worst thing that we can do, right here." Lyndon Jones "doesn't understand about dribbling in front of somebody." Something on the stat sheet does please him: Hillman was eight for nine from three-point range with one turnover and ten assists.

"What do your people think of this?" he wants to know, referring to the prospect of my doing this book about him, of this fascination with basketball.

"They say I'll get over it." I keep a straight face.

This evokes the barest trace of a Knight smile.

Ron Felling writes the names of the Indiana players who will start against James Madison tomorrow in the first game of the Indiana Classic tournament, and then the James Madison players against whom they will match up. Felling is asked to sum up James Madison's approach: "They'll bring in a big six-eleven white kid off the bench. They play a four-man motion around him. No screening. Just cuts and they play a little like the Kentucky back cut down into the post." The frame on the television screen is abruptly frozen as they decide:

> Jones - Gordon
> Smart - Ferdinand
> Magnus - Green
> Garrett - Brown
> Calloway - Winchester

With Daryl Thomas and Steve Alford gone, there is no indubitable starting five this year. Now, in December, Garrett, Smart and Calloway seem certain. Lyndon Jones is being developed.

Tomorrow's experiment, however, involves the starting of Magnus Pelkowski, the Colombian player, who is not only an excellent student majoring in international business, but an accomplished artist. Last spring, he drew a poster of Knight, Alford, Thomas and Todd Meier, sold one thousand copies for ten dollars apiece and spent the summer in Europe. ("Coach, thanks for everything," Magnus has inscribed on the print he reserved for Knight.) Son of the owners of a toy factory, he had as a boy designed remote-controlled airplanes: at twelve he built a 25 × 15 A-frame house, a retreat which housed two beds and to which he escaped on more than one occasion.

As a basketball player, however, despite his 6'10", 220-pound well-developed physique, he lacks the quickness, the overall skill of the first-rank college athlete.

But this weekend, because he scored fifteen points from the bench in the first half of the game against Vanderbilt on Tuesday, Magnus is being given a start.

Magnus is summoned to view the tape with Knight and Felling. He arrives in his bare feet, sits down on the couch, and waits.

For Knight must now telephone the father of the job-seeker to fill him in and to send a message to the son: he should tell his son, "I'll be glad to call any of these people for him. But he should not be concerned with whether he gets this or not. All right. OK." The conversation concludes with a joke about changing the prospective coach's resume since, "I'm not sure anybody has ever graduated from Purdue with distinction."

Pelkowski laughs and waits for Knight to get to him.

"If we start you in the corner," Knight explains, "that screws you up. You have a really good knack for seeing openings. You have to learn to move your body a little bit. I want you really working at moving, like you start down low and maybe you flash up high, then if the corner is open, you circle it or drift out to the corner.

"But when we start you in the corner, that screws you up. You're much better moving to open spots. I really want you working to go into open spots when we're playing against a two-three zone. When we're playing against a one-three-one, we're going to set you on the baseline, but not against a two-three. Just watch what you're doing here a little bit."

The tone is gentle, matter of fact, the mood, analytical. Coach and player study the tape. As he observes his mistakes, Magnus shakes his head in disbelief.

"You did a good job against Vanderbilt in going to the offensive board every time. See, this is excellent right here. You have a really good knack for seeing openings. Just make sure that you keep working and looking to go to openings. You turn and shoot the ball well in the openings. All right, now you've got to learn to move your body a little bit. . . ."

Magnus watches intently, seemingly confident that he will be able to accomplish what the coach requests.

"Right there you just go up left-handed and lay that in. See, this I don't want against a two-three zone because you just stand."

"You don't want . . . ?"

"No, I don't want that. Not against a two-three zone because you just stand and then you throw up jump shots with guys running at you . . . if you were on the low post and he were dribbling the ball back on the white line toward the lane, then you can just slide up on the open baseline . . ."

"How about coming across where Dean is? If I move right now and go where Dean is?"

"Well, but you'll come underneath and you're all right. But you see you have no follow-through here at all, Magnus. That's what I don't like about you shooting this shot . . . See your follow-through? It's just terrible. You're doing a good job screening. You need to come up in the middle a little bit more because you've got a good shot in the middle. Keep Dean down low and you come into the middle . . .

"Learn to pass the ball right off your ear. That's good, see, that's good right here. Edwards should hit you right here, this is a real good slide that you make right here. You slide right back out, excellent! And then you're ready to take the shot."

Magnus must watch his arm and how it doesn't snap back in his follow-through.

Pelkowski again shakes his head in disbelief as he watches himself.

"OK," he says.

Dan Dakich and Julio Salazar have both come in. Dakich is

asked to "get him out there holding his follow-through."

"Coach, he needs some high passes too," says Julio Salazar, an M.A. candidate in coaching, a Colombian who met Knight in Puerto Rico to ask permission to come to Bloomington to study Indiana basketball and stayed on to join the Knight staff. The coaching, no less than the playing, is a team effort, with everybody expected to do everything; again it's obvious that there is no distinction here between those who recruit and those who coach on the floor.

After Pelkowski departs, Knight turns his attention to Jay Edwards: "Edwards should be told he made thirteen out of forty-two, so he's shooting thirty percent." Knight makes a call about tickets for someone for Saturday, and another to Ralph Floyd to arrange dinner. Joby Wright enters.

"Joby, how are we doing today?"

"We're doing all right, coach."

"Did we recruit anybody today?"

At practice, Knight sits on the steps while his assistants coach. He calls Ricky Calloway over to talk. Quiet for a moment, he then yells out instructions: "Jeff, don't let him come over the top of you. You can't let him do it!"

But today most of his comments are for Magnus. "Magnus, just rotate away and Jeff come up." An instant later he's annoyed: "You shouldn't act as if it's a new idea, Magnus! Who's guarding Eyl?"

It's two months since the beginning of practice and the freshmen have obviously improved dramatically. "Joe, Joe!" Lyndon calls. You can see the point guard in Lyndon Jones emerging, like a newborn bird pushing out of its shell.

If there are students with whom he's displeased at this early moment in the season, it's Garrett and Smart. "Instead of screening and posting," he tells Garrett, scathingly, "here you are calling for the ball." Knight shakes his head. "Keith, you just got caught behind the screen and that's no improvement over your defense!" In disgust, he lets them rest: "Free throws!" (Smart himself attributes his faltering start to his experience playing in the Pan American games last summer: "It was a different type of basketball played there. You weren't pushed every day." Does he like it better at Indiana despite the unceasing, unrelenting correction of every mistake? "Without a doubt.")

Watching from the stands today is Dean Garrett's (and Mark Robinson's) junior college coach from San Francisco, Brad Duggan, who recalls the day Knight came to recruit his prize center:

> *"We spoke for four hours. Dean's mom was there, Dean's sister, Dean, me and one of my assistants. There were no highlight films, which coaches usually bring, a projector, a screen, films of the most beautiful campus, girls, the team with every shot going in, and endorsements such as, 'Magic Johnson says,' a prefabricated scenario to which you couldn't say no. . . .*
>
> *"He didn't do that. He just came in and the six of us talked about life, not about basketball. Where are you going to be in four years? he asked. You have to represent your family and yourself outside of basketball. What will you talk about to people outside of basketball?*
>
> *"Dean pulled me aside and said, 'Tell him I want to go.' I said, 'You tell him.' At the end Dean said, 'Coach, I really want to come.' Bob said, 'You don't have to tell me now, visit some other places. See if you like them, and if you like them better, fine. If you don't like Indiana, I'll recommend places for you to go to.' Any other coach would say, 'Great, sign here.'*
>
> *"When Dean said he was still sure, Bob said, 'Well, take a night, sleep on it, talk to your mom and Brad in the morning, if you still want . . .' and Dean said, 'I don't need that. I want to go.' About eighty schools were recruiting him; he was the number-one rated community college player in the country. Knight told him, you will never get any money, you will always go to class or you won't play, you will always act like a gentleman and I will scream and yell at you all the time. But I'll make you as good as you can be."*

From the other players, Mark Robinson heard that he might be redshirted. In dismay, he called Duggan, who suggested that he talk to Knight directly. "You don't have to if you don't want to," Knight told him, "but I think you'll be three times as good if you do."

Now Duggan must listen to some tough words sent Garrett's way: "Dean, you can't just go constantly to the ball."

Knight imitates Garrett, waving through the players, his arms up. "That's your game!"

"Good help, Magnus!" he calls. "Look for the open spot. All right. All right. Good cut."

"Dean, come out and screen Magnus," he orders. Garrett is blamed for thinking too much about his own scoring. "That's obviously all you have on your mind!" Knight covers his face in dismay. He controls his energy, as he does his voice, raising it during an unsatisfactory play, lowering it as he talks one on one with a player.

As for Magnus Pelkowski today, every move he makes is doubly scrutinized:

"Magnus, he shot over you as if you were six-one. I don't want that foreign mentality on this team. If you're tired, we can't use you." He goes off muttering. "That's why they can't play the game anywhere but here."

We're into the season and they should be doing better. "Do you guys think you're going to play again and again and again?" he yells. "How many opportunities do you think I've got for you, Hillman? Do you think I've acquired patience all of a sudden?"

In fact, he's exhibiting extraordinary patience, and if he's hard on Garrett, he's gentle with Calloway. "Really good cut, Ricky," Calloway is told. "That's the way to help out, Magnus. Ricky come over on this side with Magnus. Pop out, Magnus. Pick him up, Dean, and come back. Go ahead, Magnus."

Now Knight sits hunched over at the scorer's table. "White triangle, white triangle," he calls. When practice is over, he's surrounded by his assistants for more discussion: Dakich and Felling, Joby Wright, Julio and the trainer, Tim Garl.

The game against James Madison begins. Magnus gets the first basket and the first rebound; it appears as if the practice devoted to getting him ready to play has paid off. He gets the second rebound as well, and then manages to slap the ball away for Keith Smart to turn into an easy lay-up.

But soon Knight is driven to yell, "Magnus, get into it!" At 11.39 Todd Jadlow is sent in to replace him. It's Jadlow tonight who excels, making three field goals (of seven), five free throws, getting three key rebounds and being responsible for the plays that enable the team to go ahead.

Garrett's ineffectual play, however, enrages Knight, and Garrett is soon benched. Before long, Knight strolls down for a few words: "If you don't get off your ass, you're going to be sitting there a long time." Lyndon Jones and Rick Calloway, however, are given a lot of court affection tonight, pats and embraces.

You can see, as he coaches, his search for a team leader, the player who, as Ted Kitchel says he did, takes the coach's character out onto the floor. "Joe, he's going to go right," he tells Hillman about the team he's to cover. "Joe, call that switch, Joe!" he yells as the team comes down the floor. "Joe, tell him to get a good shot," he calls after Jay Edwards has attempted the impossible. But unlike predecessors like Buckner and Todd Meier, players who were also less gifted than many of their teammates, Hillman does not seem willing to accept the leadership role. Soon Jeff Oliphant is sent in for Hillman.

At halftime Professor Byrnes is presented with a check for $18,198.63, the share of the proceeds from the Seymour scrimmage that Knight has assigned to the library fund.

Starting the second half, Pelkowski is given still another chance. When he misses two free throws, Knight bangs down his program. Then he marches down the bench to tell Garrett again that he got nothing from him in this game. He calls Pelkowski over to the sidelines for a long talk and a pat of encouragement.

Pelkowski, of course, makes the next basket—it's the overwhelming reaction of nearly every Knight player who goes back onto the floor after having been coached on the sideline.

The mistakes accumulate, however. Jadlow misses an easy lay-up: "You didn't even look," Knight tells him. Eyl still isn't staying down in his stance. Jay has double-dribbled, excusable, perhaps, for a freshman. In the midst of it all, Knight turns to a young man sitting in the first row behind the Indiana bench and asks, "Where's Tim?" With ten seconds left, and the outcome long since determined, he's still shouting out directions.

Indiana wins easily, 84–52. The high scorer is Calloway, with 16. Garrett, playing twenty minutes, has 7 rebounds, and 7 blocked shots, but only 4 points. Pelkowski has played twenty-eight minutes. But although he has come up with 10 rebounds, he has scored only 6 points, going 3 for 10, a disappointing offensive performance.

On Saturday Knight finds time between practices to spend with friends who have come for the weekend. These include his own high school coach in baseball and football, Bill Shunkwiler, and Ed Gottlieb, his college friend.

Lunch is at the Jiffy Treat; he eats a Sloppy Joe. The talk is of basketball: how many good players there are from the state of Michigan. With Joby Wright's help, the list is exhausted. The men exchange the names of favorite restaurants in a variety of cities. "Aren't you eating?" he wants to know when I can't manage the Sloppy Joe. He notices everything. He has chosen this place, it would appear, because it is deserted; he is left unmolested to enjoy his friends. Another favorite, the Third Base Lounge, also attracts patrons who do not disturb him at his meal for autographs.

On Saturday night, Indiana plays the championship game of the tournament against Washington State, the team that had eliminated Indiana State and a disappointing Eddie Bird in whom the crowd took only a mild interest.

The students eat their pre-game meal in the stately Federal Room of the Union Building high and away from curious eyes. Over the leavings of the pancakes and honey and toast and scrambled eggs, the baked potatoes and overcooked hamburgers and spaghetti and vanilla ice cream, he addresses them:

"The stands are full, the lights are on, TV, the whole thing, so you've got all kinds of added distractions. But it's the ultimate chance for an athlete to go out and play well. That's what every single competition that you go into is about. If you don't play well in competition, then whatever you do in practice just disintegrates."

Last night, he tells them, they played well. But practice, with somebody standing there and telling them to screen or move or pass isn't the ultimate. "That's playing the game." And, he warns them, he expects some improvement tonight.

As they depart, he is very annoyed with Lyndon Jones, who has appeared for pre-game meal without a necktie. Nothing escapes him, although he seemed to be too absorbed in talking with Shunkwiler to notice.

"My tie was broken."

"What you had was a bad goddamn necktie? Is that right? Twenty-five years in this business and I've heard every excuse, but I've never heard that one. Even Garrett hasn't come up with a broken necktie!"

From the beginning it is clear that the game against Washington State will result in no easy victory.

Garrett starts—and plays badly. Early on he loses the ball, while Knight settles back into his seat. Then the coach begins to pace, and then he sends Pelkowski in to replace Garrett, who gets a lecture. "You stood here, he came out . . . you've got to be ready for the ball."

It's a close game and with .34 to go in the first half, the score is tied at twenty-six. A seven-footer named Todd Anderson has occupied the low post, and it is only Jadlow with three key rebounds, drawing fouls and making his free throws, who will finally turn the game Indiana's way.

The second half produces its own challenges. Calloway turns the ball over twice. "Garrett, stay on the ground," Knight yells. His man pump faked and Garrett—left his feet! Smart did not shoot, he "threw the ball!" At 7.26 to go in the game, it's tied again, 44–44. "Four passes," Knight yells at Calloway.

When a Washington State player named Anthony Kidd tackles Keith Smart to avert a lay-up, and the new intentional foul rule is invoked, Knight calls Kidd over to tell him he knows he didn't intend to hurt Smart.

This is the turning point of the game. Indiana goes ahead 48–46 with 5.46 to go. By 2.09 it's 57–47, and with .55 to go Knight can yell at Jadlow for his shirt being out of his pants.

Nor because the game is virtually over does Knight stop teaching. Smart is called over to be chastised: "We took a time-out to diagram and then we don't do it. Then we get into the game and we don't do it."

With .15 left, Steve Eyl receives some harsh words. "He was on me," Eyl tries to explain. Knight wanders down the bench for a few more angry words to Garrett.

The final score is 63–56. Knight hugs Kidd and shakes hands with a few of the other Washington State players. Then he walks off the floor and heads for the coaches' locker room, too disgusted with his team and all its errors, its "mental mistakes," to remain to witness the awards ceremony.

"You don't belong in here," Brad Bomba would have liked to tell him, as he did one year when Knight eschewed his usual rule of addressing the fans at the seasons' closing game. But Knight is deeply worried about this team. With Daryl Thomas and Steve Alford gone, natural leadership had not arisen from their ranks to replace the vacuum. It is mid-December, yet the teaching, the motivating needed to make them a creditable basketball team seems barely to have begun.

Dinner is at a local Italian restaurant called Leslie's Italian Villa, a generous buffet of homemade ziti and fettucini, lasagna and pizza. Here Knight entertains the three visiting coaches and their assistants—and his own friends, including the "Over the Hill Gang"—Knight's friends from Orrville who make this tournament an annual pilgrimage. He obviously enjoys these good simple people who knew his parents. Knight's father was the boss of the father of the Demlow brothers on the Wheeling-Lake Erie Railroad. Their sister baby-sat for Bob Knight. Harve Linder managed a softball team in Ohio long ago.

Those occasions when his Mom employed the paddle come up since one of her victims, Danny Markley, is here.

"She paddled me once too," Knight says, with obvious approval. "All those ladies [by which he means schoolmarms] did that then." Discipline and concentration—both seem to have been passed down to him from his parents.

Dr. Donald Boop, the dentist who treated Knight when he was thirteen years old and became his lifelong friend, is here too. Boop is planning to move to California soon.

"You'll never go," Knight says. Then the devil gets the better of him: "Convince Pauline [Boop's wife] to go, and you stay home!" But his words are laced with affection.

He sits between Ed Gottlieb and Shunkwiler, opposite Harold Martin, renamed "Adolph" after Adolph Rupp, a man who once got him into a Kentucky high school game, and stayed on in his life. And the talk is of business, of golf, and of girls who turned heads at Orrville High School some thirty years ago.

He remembers a teammate on his high school football team. When he was fourteen, and weighed 150 pounds, he would walk home every day with this older teammate, cutting across someone's yard.

"I didn't know you were that friendly with him," Shunk-wiler says, as if it had all happened yesterday. Long tables of men, former coaches, childhood friends, former classmates, colleagues in the coaching profession today—there isn't a woman in the room except the waitress, nor are women missed amid the reminiscing.

On such occasions it becomes apparent that a natural sense of continuity governs his life. Seamlessly he accommodates people out of his past. They are not to be cast out because he has moved on, or become successful. He lives strongly by values that have almost died out in our culture as he shares his success with the Orrville eight here tonight, with the college classmates, as with the parents of former players, former players, former assistants.

He assumes their trust; they're bulwarks against the corruption he otherwise finds endemic to the world in which he moves. With these people he can be direct (maybe too direct?), uncompromising, and frank. He can say anything and they will understand. He can relax.

Each departing coach thanks Knight for his hospitality. "Thank *you* very much," Knight replies.

On his Sunday morning television show (taped the previous night after the Washington State game, making him late for his own party at Leslie's), host Chuck Marlowe asks who will be the new team leaders. And indeed the subject of leadership gnaws at him as he ponders his team early in the season.

"Popular people don't make particularly good leaders," he says. "Decisive people with judgment, who aren't afraid to tell other people who don't have such good judgment that their judgment isn't very good, make good leaders." He has named no names.

Jadlow, however, was the key to the Washington State victory with his four free throws in a row, tipping the ball back out, an offensive rebound, a couple of defensive rebounds, and good position all the way defensively. The television show becomes one more opportunity to praise his players.

Having returned from a day of hunting, in rubber boots and greenish canvas pants, he sits at the scorer's table on

Sunday night surveying his team at practice.

"They're all good kids," he says. "But they're all followers. There's not a leader among them."

He asks me: "Do you know which one is best for enthusiasm?" I guess Ricky Calloway. In reply to the same question, Ron Felling also names Calloway.

"It's Todd Jadlow," Knight says. "Look at last night's box: he played nine minutes, had four free throws, which he made, and three rebounds.

"Jay Edwards is going to have problems," Knight predicts. "His personality is too blasé, academically as well as in basketball."

He wants to know from his assistants whom Eastern Kentucky, their next opponent, has played this year. Marshall beat them 62–61, Ron tells him.

He looks over at his players again.

"This won't be a very good team," he says.

In the coaches' locker room he continues: "Do you know the best guy we have at talking to other players. I mean, it isn't even close? By far the best is Jadlow. He encourages them, comes up and says something to them, makes some comments that are pertinent to what's happening.

"You know who knows more about how we play than anybody? Oliphant."

The starting lineup against Eastern Kentucky is discussed. Knight suggests Smart, Hillman, Eyl, Calloway and Jadlow. He believes that if Garrett had played the rest of the game against Washington State, Indiana would have lost. He does not plan to start Garrett.

Now he decides to give the team Christmas Eve off and let them come back to practice at seven in the evening on Christmas Day. "We could overload Alford mentally," he remembers. "But I don't think we can these guys." Fondly he recalls these players now gone: Daryl Thomas, Todd Meier, who knew "how to talk to people."

"Maybe none of them individually could have done it. Obviously Meier and Daryl couldn't and maybe Steve couldn't without their help." He pauses. "But, boy, we struggle right now."

* * *

Two days later against Eastern Kentucky Dean Garrett scores twenty-five points, grabs eighteen rebounds and blocks seven shots as Indiana wins 103–75. He even makes seven of eight free throws.

Garrett did not, however, start the game.

"I was gonna make me keep him in," Garrett said afterwards, accounting for his superb performance. But a difficult, an uneasy season appears increasingly likely.

And four days later there is an announcement. "IU freshman Jay Edwards is academically ineligible to play and probably will miss the entire Big Ten Conference season."

Part
Three

CHAPTER EIGHT

The Game's the Test, and There's No Multiple Choice

"I don't want him, I want you."

Christmas follows quickly upon an 81–69 loss to Louisville, as Christmas night looks ahead to the remainder of the season. After the Louisville game, the team dispersed, the players returning home. Their coach, however, went hunting for four days, thinking all the while about what to say to them when they returned. Against Louisville, Indiana committed nineteen turnovers. It wasn't Louisville's free throws or their press. It was Indiana's own play that beat them. His Christmas present to his mother on Christmas Eve, a week before her death, is the best gift of all—not a chair, not an appliance but—a visit to Orrville.

Practice resumes at six P.M. on Christmas night for this team that has lost two nonconference games, to Kentucky and to Louisville. Between now and the Hoosier Classic in Indianapolis on Monday night, they'll be spending every waking moment at Assembly Hall, he has told them. It's a crisis early in the season for a leaderless team.

Friday night inaugurates the first of five practices as Knight and his assistants try to teach these players how to be a team. He must "give them a game they can win with." What

157

he can teach them now will predict their season. They are not a good team, he insists. "I have parts of players." Now he must ready them for the Big Ten season, for which the Hoosier Classic is to be their dress rehearsal.

At five P.M he walks out onto the floor with Ron Felling and waves. Joe Hillman comes out first and jumps rope. Jeff Oliphant follows. Lyndon Jones and Dean Garrett do stretching exercises. Ron Felling goes over to greet the players and wish them a good Christmas. Knight talks for a moment to his son Tim before they all troop into the players' locker room for the first lecture of this long five days.

It is my fourth visit, the first at which I'm permitted to attend the lectures in the players' dressing room. There are no outsiders here, no banter, no smiles, not among assistants, managers or players. It is not because the discipline is Draconian, but because everyone is taking himself seriously. "Don't wear perfume in the locker room," Knight tells me, an order for the next time. There is nothing I can do about the *Ysatis* today. In his perfectly ordered closed world there are rules of appropriate conduct down to every detail. They include no talking at practice, no matter that the classroom seats 17,357 and you might not be heard.

Each student sits in front of his locker, his red looseleaf notebook open on his knees.

There is a notable absence. There is no one sitting in front of Jay Edwards' locker. Jay has received an incomplete in one course, and a failure in another, a 1.6 for the semester, when he needs a 1.8, just less than a C. Knight has not waited for the official date when he will become ineligible to play. As far as the coach is concerned, the day the grades were issued was the day Jay would be suspended from the team.

Nor, as we saw after the Indiana Classic, was Bob Knight surprised that Jay did poorly his first semester. After the victory against Notre Dame, during which Edwards managed twelve points in ten minutes of play, blocking a David Rivers shot and stealing the ball from Rivers, which resulted in a Garrett dunk, Knight called him into his office.

"You're going to have a lot of nice things said and written about you all over the country because of how you played last night," Knight said. "Three weeks from now those same people are going to write about how you flunked out of Indiana unless you get straightened out." Knight believes that Jay has not yet "looked down the line to see whether a college education is important or not. The other kid from Marion [Lyndon Jones] has."

Indeed, his words fall on deaf ears. Edwards does not believe that it will happen to him. The heady excitement of starting in big-time college basketball proves too much for many freshmen, of course. At Georgetown, John Thompson permits no freshman interviews or posing for pictures during the first semester. John Chaney at Temple attempted to deal with the problem of Mark Macon, a teammate of Edwards' during the Olympic Festival in the spring of 1987, by forbidding him to give any interviews. "I'm trying to keep my feet on the ground," Macon says when you meet him. And, near the end of the season, Macon thanks Chaney: "I appreciate what you did."

Edwards, however, falters. Given his autumn semester grades, he has lost his eligibility. But by an NCAA technicality, he becomes ineligible only on the first day of the spring semester, in the middle of January. He could still play.

For Knight, however, he is ineligible. He has chosen the student, the individual, over winning.

There is, however, an escape for Edwards. Indiana runs between-semester independent studies courses that anyone can take during the vacation period. Edwards signs up for "Self-Instruction In Art" for non-art majors, although he has never taken an art course in his life and has no interest in it. One project will involve a collage that will "express his personality," and on which he will paste a photograph of Mark Macon. There are eight projects in all, for which he must receive a B-plus grade for the group combined. Then he would be eligible to play in the spring.

Knight anticipates. He knows Jay's first thought will be to get Magnus Pelkowski, who is a professional-quality artist, to help him. "I put a stop to that!" Knight says.

Knight insists not only that the projects be done in the office of Buzz Kurpius, the academic adviser, but that Kurpius, or one of her assistants, deliver them to the art teacher. (On this point Kurpius demurs. She phones the art teacher ahead and lets Jay do the delivering himself, although Knight gives her "heck" for it.)

Meanwhile Knight worries. Edwards' mother is an older woman (he has a thirty-two-year-old-brother) and perhaps he's spoiled. She has sent him to Indiana because "I know you people would really get after him and make him work. That's the only place he'll be forced to do that."

Now, no matter that even if Edwards flunked out completely, he would still be eligible to play until January 14, Edwards is gone, Knight's best shooter off the team. Had Knight allowed Jay to play out the semester, making sure he did the art course, there would have been no questions from the press and Edwards would certainly have helped the team in the losses against Louisville and the ones in the Big Ten season to come. But the student himself is at stake. And so while Indiana practices and prepares for the tough season to come, Edwards pastes up his collages, paints his pictures.

"Do I trust you, Keith?" Knight had joked during the October coaches' clinic. Smart hadn't been able to control his ironic smile. The teacher who cares, intervenes. In his own course in Methods of Basketball Coaching, a student who cuts once automatically receives a C. As for himself, yes he took Woody Hayes' course in Football at Ohio State, his absences always noticeable because his upright friend John Havlicek *never* cut. Knight got a B; the football players, no matter what they did, all got As. They should automatically have gotten As, he thinks now, without the pretense of their attending the class.

"The first thing is this," he begins now on Christmas night. "To be a team hard to play against you have to put in an effort. We're a bad team. There's not a guy here who makes the play the way he's supposed to." As far as the games in Indianapolis are concerned, he tells them, we aren't even going to prepare.

This, of course, is relative. In comparison, perhaps, with other teams, they're preparing as if the course were a combination of chemistry, psychology and military strategy. Seeing, thinking, anticipating, reacting—there is too great a disparity between what they know and what they do. In this simultaneous exercise of mind and body, the intellect, the will and the body, each falls short. There is only one with whom Knight is at least partially pleased—Ricky Calloway.

The teaching involves this: Each must be convinced of what he's doing wrong. Simultaneously, each must emerge with a sense of his own ability, a positive sense that there is much he can do. At this crucial moment when they haven't coalesced as a team, he must both expose their weaknesses and convince them that he believes in their individual strengths. Otherwise they will not believe in them themselves. What makes this task possible is the force of Knight's will, his ability to make others act.

Now each sits, each waits. Kreigh Smith is told he "has no idea" where the three-point line is, however hard they've worked on this. The lessons are amplified by the prodigious memory; he remembers every play they've made in every game without so much as glancing at the running plays. Whatever they've done has been burned into his memory.

But that loss to Louisville is what infuriates him today.

"Keith," he says. "You scored twenty-four points. I'm going to tell you what you were worth." He draws a number five in red on the white blackboard. "You didn't get the ball to anybody. You didn't guard anybody."

It's not only a team without true forwards, but it's also one with weak guard play. "We don't have a single guard here that gets us the basketball because he sees what the hell is going on," Knight says in scathing tones. "I'm going to tell you something. I'm not sure he can play. I'm not sure that he'll ever be as good as anybody in this room. But if I listed the eleven of you with Patrick on a list of who sees what out there, you know where I'd put Patrick? You know where I'd put him, Ricky?" It's Calloway, his hoped-for leader, whom at every opportunity he singles out.

"Close to the top," Calloway says.

"Maybe at the top," says Knight, as if to taunt them with the assertion that the skinny high school kid, Patrick, is better than they are.

"Only Lyndon sees more than Patrick does out there, and you go too slow. You don't go hard enough and quick enough. Hey, I have not worked as hard with Patrick as I have worked with you guys. But the son of a bitch sees what's going on."

Already he moves from the individual to the group. Lest they believe that their inadequate play was the result of a lapse by any single one of them, he addresses them all. "I don't know what you guys thought beat us. It wasn't the press."

Then it's back to the particular: "Twice, Kreigh, you're coming up the floor with the ball and you throw the ball back to Hillman back here . . ."

Perhaps more than many of the others, Kreigh Smith has disappointed him. He seems to be attacking Kreigh now. "If you want to transfer over Christmas do so, because you won't play much here. You'd better learn to play basketball."

It's a device he will use whenever he must: urging a player to prove him wrong by demonstrating that he can in fact play well. As the closing days of this season will demonstrate, it does not always work. But it remains a test of character and an opportunity for a student to reach down for the extra ability he did not know he possessed. Like all of us, these student basketball players draw upon far less of their potential than they might. The demand that they plumb these depths is at the root of Knight's teaching.

"The closest we got to it [a leader] now is Ricky, and Ricky's not blocking out cost us the game at Kentucky," he tells them. The coach on the floor, the student leader, is essential to the college basketball game. Now in December Knight offers Ricky Calloway this role outright and before the entire team. Someone else might, perhaps, be delighted with Calloway for his concentration, his effort, and the seriousness with which he takes himself and the enterprise.

But Knight can't afford this. He sees the moment and he looks into the future. Calloway seems to be doing well according to the stat sheets. But his mistakes presage disaster, and the coach knows it. To ease the tension, he turns to someone else.

"Eyl, were you ever told to deviate from our rules?" He who has achieved as close to perfect an understanding of the game as anyone who has coached it remains dependent upon students acting upon his wisdom. When they make mistakes, it infuriates him because he has taught them how to play without making mistakes. If only they would allow themselves to be taught, they could achieve perfection, the golden bowl without the flaw.

Dean Garrett has particularly displeased his coach.

"Garrett, for some reason, I don't know, leaves Ellison" (Pervis Ellison, the Louisville star junior center). Garrett is summoned to the blackboard. "Draw for me where you should be." Garrett knows he hasn't done well. Garrett listens. "Now Dean," says Knight. "You don't have Daryl Thomas to lean on, to guide you . . . you've played three games out of eight, that's it. You've just been demolished."

There is nothing that happens in college basketball that he is not aware of, that he doesn't use to rouse them to perform. "Who in here can tell me the score of the Arizona-Washington State game?" He answers the question himself: it was 89–55 in favor of Arizona. The point is clear to them all. In the Hoosier Classic only two weeks ago Indiana had trouble beating Washington State. Now what does that say about their prospects?

"In the Louisville game, I absolutely lost interest." At the appropriate moment he will bring forth his ultimate threat, that he will no longer care. Do they appreciate the generosity of his vigilance? "The mature ones do," says former assistant Jim Crews. Students everywhere, in basketball as in life, resist change. They want the comfort of thinking as they already do. They're recalcitrant, stubborn and, left to their own devices, likely to sabotage themselves. The teacher who cares, however physically and spiritually exhausting it may become, never lets a student off the hook.

Knight directs his stare at Garrett and at Smart together, his junior college recruits, the "athletes" some sportswriters believe made the difference for Knight in the 1987 championship season. Replying to my suggestion that they would have come along more rapidly had they been four-year scholars in this program, Knight asserts, "No question."

"Here's where you are with your future," he tells them. "You two guys go ahead and say to this man in Orlando [Pat Williams, who has brought the post-season NBA showcase Aloha Tournament to Orlando this year], you're going to be gone out of class time for eight days. You think you're going to miss eight days and graduate? Do you think I'm going to let you?"

He has read an article from Orlando advertising this game and he doesn't like it. He addresses Garrett: "With the pro people you have dropped to rock bottom. I talked to five over the weekend. You're going to wind up a fourth- or fifth-round draft choice. You're either scared to play or you've been intimidated in three different games where you just quit. Your effort to rebound offensively in this game is the worst, bar none. You just back away. You never work to go to the offensive blackboard . . . I don't think you can think. I think you're the poorest thinker I've ever seen inside here."

Garrett listens, expressionless. But Knight is not through,

because Garrett must not be left believing he is incapable of being a good basketball player. "I don't think you're dumb," Knight says. "I think you're bright." Nor is it left at that. "We're going to be better next year, but where will you be?"

In fact, Knight is worried. For where indeed will Garrett be? Unless he improves at once, he will lose his opportunity for a pro career, for financial security.

"Ricky," Knight asks, "what did Daryl put into the game and what does Dean?"

"Daryl saw what was going on on the floor."

"Has he even come close?"

"Not very well."

Smart is drawn into the debate. Smart replies, "I don't think he's played well."

But Knight is not appeased. "Is the fact that you admit that an exoneration? I robbed the bank. I'm sorry?"

Now it's back to Smart. Knight saw Jack McMann over the weekend. He quotes others, quotes experts. "I can't believe Smart isn't playing any better for you," he was told. "You two can take that for what it's worth."

It's back to Eyl: "How many points have you scored in the two games we lost?"

"None," says Eyl.

"What are you going to do about it?"

For Knight, practice is the training ground; practice is treated as seriously as the games. "You don't play in a game anywhere like we do in practices," he tells them, and this is the key. Before each of the practices to come in the next three days he will show them ten minutes of the Louisville game. There isn't a move any one of his players makes that will not be scrutinized. Now, their heads down, Knight tells them, "You people are working to defeat the purpose of putting a team together."

The promising play of freshman Lyndon Jones, and his serious attitude, have not gone unnoticed. But what will help Lyndon Jones develop is not praise, reminders of his glory days as Indiana high school state champion three years in a row. Lyndon must perceive the disparity between what he is and what he can be; he must develop the ability to play against his own potential.

"Dakich," Knight says, turning to his youngest assistant, "you tell Jones how well he listens."

Dakich knows what to say. He too has played here.

"I don't think he listens worth a damn." Dakich addresses Lyndon Jones directly. "You don't ever do it."

"We're talking about trying to concentrate to do what we did last year," says Knight. "That's what this next five practices will be about. I want you to see how badly this game was played." On the large screen always ready in their locker room, the Indiana-Louisville tape begins.

Every few seconds, the frame is frozen to point out to a student what he could have done, as opposed to what he did do. "Joe," says Knight. "You can be up on top of the guy. There's no effort to get on top of him." Repetition is indispensable to any teacher, let alone one whose students must coordinate efforts of the mind, the will and the body:

"You people are just not thinking well enough, working hard enough to beat good teams. We haven't denied a pass. You're just out there, Joe. You're not doing anything. You are the most average player to be playing here. You have five assists in this game. Was there any other than a pass to someone out on the perimeter? We can't have guards playing like this. Look where you are, Steve." Again the film is stopped.

"Steve, what would be your reaction if you saw this happen with a fourth-year player at the start of a ballgame? What goes through your head? What's our defensive rule here?" He answers it himself. "Be one step on the ball side. Why aren't you there? I don't know."

The lights go off again, the film goes on. The criticism is leavened by a sense of what might have been, what they can do if only they would think. "Just with a little simple effort, we're going to get some shots," he tells them. "We were standing around. . . . Kreigh," he wants to know, "how much trouble was it for Steve to bring the ball up against the press?" The answer is apparent. Looking at the tape makes it clear. It shouldn't have been difficult at all.

Perhaps because people predicted that Joe Hillman might be that leader the team sorely lacks, Knight is upset with him. "Joe," he says, "you see less than anybody in here." That his team lacks a leader is never far from his mind.

Nor is he pleased by Keith Smart's jubilation on the floor when he makes a basket; unselfish team play is so much a part of Knight's ethic that it doesn't have to be mentioned. "I don't see you doing that when Ricky scores," Knight tells Smart. "I don't see you pat somebody on the back when he scores." Knight worries about Smart; he seems good only in open court play, and that won't be enough.

The film unfolds, the teaching intensifies. "Nobody contests anything," Knight says. "The ball is thrown around. It's a good thing Ellison walked because you aren't going to keep him from getting the ball. You had six turnovers within three feet of the basket." Nothing in Garrett's demeanor suggests that any of this is unfair.

It's constructive because with every criticism they are shown what they might have done, how they might have won the game. "Keith, you have to make a fake trap here.... Ricky, you don't go for the blockout. You just turn on the board."

Steve, however, whom Knight believes can do much better, is treated more harshly.

"What kind of athlete do you consider yourself to be?"

"Pretty good."

"Then why don't you keep anyone from getting the ball? You're not a good basketball player. You give the illusion of effort. There's no way you can count how many times Crook [Herbert Crook, Louisville's star senior] caught the ball against you. I counted four. What does that tell you? When have you ever made five jumpshots in a game?"

"Never."

"Then you better be doing something."

He teaches them the game. "You don't even think about the screener, Keith. They both jump to the cutter and you just throw the ball. If we take away open court play, you have no game."

He reverses himself.

"There's a bad call there, Ricky." Those who make much of Knight's supposed efforts to intimidate the officials ignore the many times on the floor he tells his players that a call against them was just, as here he informs Calloway of one that wasn't. To play the game at its height, which is the goal for them, they must approximate his understanding of it.

"See, this cost us a bucket later, Dean. I just told you about that in practice the other day." Here Knight isn't even as angry as most teachers would be when a lesson, only recently taught, turns out a few days later to have been forgotten.

"Joe, have you been taught to leave your hands at your

sides?" Knight asks. "Joe, what on a scale of one to ten is your defensive value out on the perimeter?"

"A one."

"Are you above average as a player?"

"Yes."

"Why not go out and play differently tomorrow than you did today?" That this is possible Knight demonstrates through the film of their defeat. "We're ahead thirteen-four, and we aren't even playing well."

"Why don't we draw a charging foul," he demands of Garrett and Eyl, "instead of both of you leaving your feet?" He treats watching the tape with them as another opportunity to coach this game. "Pass fake, pass fake," he orders.

"Dean, explain to me the sense of this. The ball is inside the basket, it's so far in the cylinder. Tell me what goes through a player's mind that goal-tends that ball."

"He doesn't know what he's doing."

"That ball's on the way down. More of that ball's below the rim than above."

"How many passes were made here?"

"One."

"Have I ever told you to go ahead and shoot whenever you think you're open?"

"Ricky," the exasperated coach asks, "how badly do you think these players care about playing?"

"Real bad. They care."

"Then how can you not do what we want done? We stay up hour after hour watching this stuff. We're trying to give you a game you can win with. Do you think it's a coincidence that you [Keith] take a shot on one pass and throw up an airball? I don't."

On this Christmas night, he's far from finished with them. The teaching becomes even more detailed, exact. "Now, Ricky, look where Garrett is, it must go to him. We don't see these things quickly enough. Joe, for what reason would you be running across the lane? Look where Ellison starts, Dean. Come up here, Ron. I'm Ellison, you're Garrett."

And he and Felling demonstrate. "Give Garrett a demonstration of the effort he extends to keep me from going into a low post position." Felling uses all the force of his body—no matter that he's a foot shorter than Knight—and keeps him from getting to the imaginary basket.

"You must not have enough determination, son," Knight tells Garrett. "You must not care about anybody in here. If you know we have no chance to win with you playing like this, why don't you do something about it?"

Garrett looks up at him. But it's still not over. "I have a friend of mine who really knows basketball and he told me it was impossible for him to believe you played as badly as you played. We're not going to rub something on your head [he rubs Garrett's head] and make you a better player. You play like you never listened to a minute of basketball teaching."

The point is that others have noticed, it's not just him, not just the coaches here. "I have no question about your being a good sincere kid, but that isn't going to get it done out here," Knight tells Dean Garrett. "You have to develop a game plan." It's Bill Russell who should be Garrett's model, Russell who "had a plan for every possession."

And there is more, words that will strike Garrett only later. "Do you know what pains me more than anything?" his coach asks him. "Not that Ellison got the ball, but that you're my center and you're my choice to play here. I don't want him, I want you!"

Allowing that to register, he goes on to the others. "Joe, do you think there's any chance we can get you out of slow motion? That slows down the pace of everybody."

"Keith, you're not guarding anyone. This isn't even a high pass. You jump up and catch this pass below your shoulders."

"How many passes have been made, Kreigh?"

"The first one," says Kreigh.

"That three-point line may be in Shanghai as far as you're concerned. You have no idea where it is. Tell me you're aware of the three-point line, are you or aren't you?"

But it's a lecture addressed to the team. No single individual is at fault. They look down, or at the film, and there isn't a trace of an argument. The evidence is right there before them. Failure awaits them should they not assume responsibility for themselves as individuals and as a team.

"You people may know there's a game going on, but you're not sure where it is or who's playing. You have no chance of winning in this league playing as you're playing." Each one of them must develop a basketball IQ, become a smarter player or they will have no chance. "We're the dumbest team that I've ever tried to coach right now. I can't coach players that play dumb. I have no patience with it."

There's also a threat. "If you don't make a hell of a commitment to doing what's right when it's right to do it, then this is going to be a goddamn long twenty games that we're playing, and I'll tell you another thing. I'll make it long for you and there isn't anybody in the world that can make it longer than I can. I don't intend to be playing dumb anymore like we are."

The session ends. Knight orders Ricky to sit there with them and find out who wants to play and who doesn't, who's going to come out of the locker room and play and who isn't. They have been "inside" for seventy minutes.

When they race out onto the practice floor into a particularly enthusiastic four-corner passing drill, calling out each other's names loudly, Knight orders Patrick Knight to join them. "We gotta have twelve guys. Let's go!"

II

"You have all worked hard. You have tried to do the things we want done. Let the other guy be dumb. Let the other guy lose."

Saturday morning in the students' locker room Julio passes out index cards. They are to write down the names of the two people, unrelated to them, whom they admire the most. First, two people whom you know. "I didn't say like the most, but admire and respect the most for what they are or for what they do." Then they must draw a line and write down the names of two they admire whom they don't know, a historical figure, living or dead, an athlete or a nonathlete. They write. Knight goes around the room, locker by locker, and asks why each has listed the four he has.

The answers are predictable: the winners are competitive, committed, successful, mentally tough. He neither asks whom they have chosen ("That's private," he'll say later) nor do they volunteer the names, except for Keith Smart who has selected John Hope Franklin and James Weldon Thompson. "They came out on top."

"Apparently you have an admiration for people who are

able to do the very things we want you people to do, and that's quite simply to get the most out of what you have."

The "we" is no accident; they are meant to see the assistant coaches as a team too. "Boys," Joby calls them. "Men," Ron says. Danny they enjoy; he played for Knight not long ago; he is closest to them in age, only three years older than the seniors.

It's the day after Christmas and Knight is making the speech of the season. He explores who he is and who they are, what he can do for them and what they must do for themselves. He asks if they believe the coaches are getting something extra for making them work this hard. "Not a dollar," he tells them. "We get paid the same whether we win, lose or draw. Do you realize that last year when we won the NCAA championship we as coaches did not get paid an extra dollar?" He believes they must be wondering about his motives, why he is driving them so hard. Is *he* getting something out of it? And he believes that if even one of them starts to think he's doing something *to* them rather than *for* them, he can no longer coach them.

"You want to know what the biggest difficulty in getting to the top of the ladder is? The biggest difficulty in getting to the top of the ladder is getting through the crowd at the bottom."

They are not being driven so hard "for some imagined benefit to the coaches. We're not pushing you for us. We're pushing you for you . . . there are a few of you in here who have to be pushed to excess, and that's not the way it should be."

Unselfconsciously, he tells his players that what he is doing for them is unique, and unlikely to be duplicated once they leave Indiana University. Once they're gone, "there isn't going to be somebody on your ass day after day; they'll just find somebody else." Always there's an example. It's Daryl Thomas, who failed to keep his commitments in the post-season and wound up a sixth- instead of a second-round draft choice, only to be playing in England for about ten percent of what he would make in the NBA.

"How many of you are reading a book right now?" he demands. He holds up the biography, *Vince,* which he is reading. "How many of you read books about people that succeed or fail? If you don't, how the hell do you know what's in success and what's in failure?" He takes from Lombardi an

"But I know they don't learn more in chemistry than they learn here. I know that."

"I'm not difficult to deal with like these people think I am."

Before the Russian game, with Bill Wall: *"I can't interfere...."*

At the Russian game: *"Just give them the ball back."*

Steve Green: "Keep your nose out of it."

Todd Jadlow: "I don't want that shot taken by you ever again unless you get your feet straight."

Steve Eyl: "Unless there's been divine intervention over the summer, shooting isn't it."

Dr. Steve Ahlfeld: *"The answer is their willingness to help us in any way they can."*

Ted Kitchel: *"If I were going to war, I'd want Kitchel on my side."*

Jim Crews: *"Joking, teaching, praising—with 10% devoted to yelling and criticizing."*

Tim Knight with Dan Dakich: *"I wanted him to know... that I thought enough of him."*

With Bob Collins: *"Did you ever know a bad four-year-old? Your mother did."*

With Tony Hinkle, left, and Everett Dean: *"If they ever had a Hall of Fame for gentlemen in Athletics, the first two inductees in my mind would be Everett Dean and Tony Hinkle."*

With assistant coach Ron Felling: *"I'm doing five things. You're only doing one."*

Knight with Patrick Knight: *"I forget you're my father."*

Patrick Knight: *"Move it, Patrick. Don't dance out there. Move through."*

Patrick Knight, Joby Wright: *"When we go out to eat, he's my dad."*

Ralph Floyd presents Professor Byrnes with a check for $18,198.63 for the Library Fund.

Knight: *"They're all good kids."*

Poster by Magnus Pelkowski: *"Coach, thanks for everything."*

Rick Calloway: "Ricky, how badly do you think these players care about playing?"

Steve Eyl: "Eyl, were you ever told to deviate from our rules?"

With Kreigh Smith: *"I think I made a mistake in not playing you against Kentucky."*

With Purdue coach Gene Keady.

Mrs. Lingofelter presenting Coach Knight with a red and white afghan.

Former player Tom Abernethy: *"If he needed anything on the spur of the moment, all of us would just jump at the chance to repay him."*

Ryan White, right: *"I heard Ryan was an IU fan...."*

With Don Fischer: *"The key word in this whole thing, Don, is bull...."*

With Julio Salazar: *"I needle Julio a little bit."*

With Joe Hillman: *"It's very demanding. But that's what you're here for."*

Meeting the press: *"Questions?"*

PHOTO COURTESY OF INDIANA
UNIVERSITY ATHLETIC DEPARTMENT

Dean Garrett: *"Dean, you're playing a lot better in practice the last two days. Why do you think that is?"*

With Todd Jadlow: *"I don't need anyone bigger than you or quicker than you or better than you."*

With Keith Smart: *"I want him to have a strong finish."*

With Jay Edwards: *"He knew I was a good kid."*

With Steve Eyl: *"I want Steve to get the ball."*

Fred Taylor: *"Hell, I've known him since I was seventeen years old."*

With Bob Hammel: *"Hammel walks around Assembly Hall like he owns the place."*

With Smart and Garrett, last game of the season: *"We do it after the game."*

With the author: *"This is this year's Feinstein."*

Against Michigan: Celebrating Jay's shot.

Jay hits the game-winner against Michigan: *"If it were baseball, he wouldn't swing at bad pitches in crucial situations."*

inspiration for his team, a "fourth dimension" determining success: "Selfless teamwork and collective pride which accumulate until they have made positive thinking and victory habitual." He searches for ways to motivate the leaderless team, the team without forwards, the team without a point guard, the team, unlike the legendary Knight teams which prided themselves on defense, which will have to succeed in high-scoring games. He does not give up on them.

Perhaps they are wondering why Coach Knight coaches. He tells them he "can't begin in the rest of my lifetime to spend the money I have." More, "there isn't any championship that a team I've coached hasn't won. There isn't any honor that a player I've coached hasn't had." He is not capable, he says, of influencing great multitudes of people. "But I think I can take a handful and influence them." And what does he want? "I don't just want you people to win in basketball," he says. "I want you to win in everything that you do."

He turns less soft. He looks at each of them hard, as if he were angry that they aren't doing as well as they might. "I only wonder why I coach when I have to get on *your* ass about catching the ball, or *yours* about applying pressure, or *yours* about thinking or *yours* about looking at what the hell's going on, or *yours* about playing intelligently." He hits every base.

The Louisville film comes on, exposing their errors once more: Joe has his hands on his knees, Smith's man "might as well be playing against a statue in the park as playing against you." He invokes Steve Alford with his "tremendous sense of wanting to win." On the wall facing them is a poem, "No one is beat 'til he quits,/No one is through 'til he stops/No matter how hard failure hits/No matter how often he drops . . ." And today on the bulletin board, photographs of the Pennsylvania players face them along with descriptions of their strengths, and clippings testifying to their abilities. The managers hung these posters the moment the Louisville game ended.

He leaves them alone in the locker room with Ricky again as his representative: "You people better talk again a little bit about what it's going to take to play. I don't know what you three, Eyl, and Garrett and Smart, want to be remembered for," he tells his seniors, "but we're a team of lazy players that does things conveniently and stays in a comfort zone and you can't beat anybody that way. If you have any questions about how to be good, ask me. If you don't know how to be good, then I'll tell you."

Out on the floor as they prepare for the Hoosier Classic, which Indiana University will host in Indianapolis in two days' time, it's practice as usual. At this tournament he will generally play the weakest team in the first game—unless a coach calls and asks that he not play Indiana that first night. Then he will play first, and, in all likelihood, be eliminated.

For lunch it's chicken wings at the Third Base Lounge, where all eyes are riveted on a movie-sized television screen and nobody bothers him. This lunch is on "the Eastern liberal establishment," he says.

"Move it, Patrick," he calls, once practice resumes in the late afternoon. "Don't dance out there. Move through." They must not attempt shots they are incapable of making. "You can make that shot, son, once out of a hundred times," Knight tells Keith. Magnus is also told, "How can you do something you've never done before? I never hit a golf shot left-handed so how can I do it?" It's the theme of the day, and the premise at the heart of his teaching: they will not be asked to do something they cannot. "What kind of shot is that for you, Steve?" he wants to know. "You have to know what you can do and what you can't do." That's their job—to know themselves well enough not to attempt the impossible, but to develop the abilities he knows they possess.

"Lyndon, everything was good, but you didn't see the cut. Tell him, Ricky." And so he continues to search for leadership, for a surrogate among them.

After a three-week absence with a back injury, Joe Hillman came back for one practice, only to have the team lose to Kentucky. It was at this point that Knight suggested he might become the team leader. With his intensity and determination, Hillman seems a quintessential Knight player, one limited only by his height: 6'2" rather than 6'8".

"I don't know if these guys will listen to what I have to say," Hillman replied, referring to a bad play he made in that Kentucky loss. Then he thought, you can't get on anybody if you're not doing a very good job yourself. He decided they should go out and develop some of their own leadership. But Knight thought otherwise, remembering Quinn Buckner, who had seized the reins of leadership, although he was far from being the best player.

"Get in there, Pat, are you going to play or not?" And then, "Dean, Patrick just blocked you off the board. Patrick can't block high school kids off, but he just blocked you off. Only Lyndon sees more than Patrick sees," Knight says, encouraging the freshman who had arrived so frightened. And then there is something more, a father's pride: "I have not worked as hard with Patrick as I have with you guys," he says. "But the son of a bitch sees what's going on."

Of course it doesn't end there. Pat's experience leads to a lesson for them: "Here's how Pat was playing the zone. Eyes riveted on the basketball with no idea of what's going on behind him."

The feel of these post-Christmas practices is: now or never. Dean Garrett seems incapable of improving. "When you get the ball at four feet, you've got to be able to score." And, later, "Where's the ball, Dean? You had no idea where the ball was. Why shoot a ball you fumble? If you can't catch a ball, you can't shoot it."

Always, they are told, the object is not a shot, but a *good* shot. It's nearly January, the start of their conference play, but the teaching remains rooted in fundamentals, as it will until the last day of the season. "Joe, you should catch, look at your feet and then shoot the ball. You should know where you are." It's that "sense of where you are," Bill Bradley's phrase, which makes a good basketball player.

If no mistake goes unnoticed, no good play escapes without praise. "Good leap, Ricky. That's good, Keith. Atta boy, Lyndon." That he feels affection for all of them is unmistakable. "Son," he tells Smart, "you don't begin to use your ability."

But there is also: "Patrick, when you drove right here, where did you have the shot?" and "Pat, you can't hold the ball over your head." Smart is asked, "What are you doing defensively?" Smart replies, "Nothing."

Finally, even Dean comes through: "That's good. That's the way to see. Come on, Dean. Every play like that!" Not that it ends there. "Lyndon, did you make that pass to Garrett?" he asks. "The next time he drops it, go over and slap his face. I want somebody out here that makes him pay the price."

A freshman chastise a senior? Nobody finds that unusual, not that shy, still slightly-in-awe Lyndon would do it. "Tell him, Ricky, tell him!" Knight urges. How well they bear up under his scrutiny is a tribute to everybody.

When Patrick Knight doesn't take a shower, his father notices this too. "How come you're not taking a shower?"

"I've got no clean clothes. I had to borrow underwear from you."

"Where are you going?"

"Home. Is that all right?"

As far as Patrick's career with Bloomington North High School is concerned, Knight has never interfered, not even to suggest that Patrick should first play on the *junior* varsity, which Knight believed would have been a good idea.

At five in the afternoon on Saturday they're back in their locker room. He tells them he has seen some "improvement in recognition." The tape comes on. "That big fat-ass beats us to the spot. That just can't happen. There's just no way that can happen." They are conserving their energy, something this team cannot afford to do: "Playing all-out means everything to this team, at both ends of the floor." He tries to reach Kreigh Smith: "Kreigh, you almost act like you don't want any part of the ball. You just throw it back as fast as you can get it back." Later in the season he will have little to say to this player: the focus now can mean only one thing. The coach is hoping Kreigh will be able to play.

It is not always easy, this scrutiny. "How many passes here, Steve?" "Two." "Would you consider this an on-balance shot? . . . Is this the best kind of pressure you can exert, Joe?" "No." "Then why are you giving it to us? That's my next question. If this isn't the best, then why is it what we're getting? Answer that for me!"

The issue again is leadership with nobody organizing any screening. They are not working to get open. He points out Keith's play: "You started in the middle of the lane, and that is it. That's all there is. You ought to just cry when you see yourself playing. You just represent yourself so badly. Watch yourself, Keith. You're back on the line again because of a bad pass and because nobody works to get open. Nobody screens. Ricky, you just stand out there and holler for the ball thirty feet away." As for Kreigh, "You don't even look to take the ball up the side. . . ."

"Play through being tired!" he calls out when it's obvious that they're exhausted. Later in the season practices will be only an hour and fifteen minutes. But not now. "You guys let the fact that you're a little bit tired dictate how you're playing. You're all feeling sorry for yourselves because you're a little bit tired. I can show you what being tired is like two hours from now. I have nothing planned for tonight." A few minutes later he announces, "I planned to stop twenty minutes ago. Every time there's something like that, it adds ten minutes!

"Concentrate on how you play, not on how long you play." They are to write this down in their notebooks, exhausted as they are now at ten of seven on Saturday evening.

"Be dressed and ready at ten in the morning," he tells them as they depart.

On Sunday morning he reviews the stat sheets that have been kept of these practices. Kreigh Smith has had the most baskets, twenty-six. But . . . he has been out-rebounded by Patrick Knight! In one practice there were forty-four rebounds and Kreigh only got one! He goes down the line: In one there were sixty-eight rebounds, and he got zero. Steve Eyl only got two!

Practice is the paradigm of Knight's teaching. They are all equally involved, no one waiting on the sidelines to take part. Each has an equal opportunity to show what he can do. More difficult than any game, the Knight practice is an exercise in pressure. And as in no other classroom, the teacher monitors every move, every thought of every single student.

Now the test papers are being returned to the class graded: Jadlow went eight for seventeen one night, yet made only two baskets the next time: "We play today and we don't play tomorrow.

"Ricky is the closest player we have to somebody who plays with consistency." So the coach decides . . . now.

"Keith, you get tired, and we're going to start playing you in spurts," Knight says. There may be a medical reason for this because, although he does not have the disease, Keith carries the trait for sickle-cell anemia. Off the bench, only Lyndon has played consistently. "Kreigh," Knight says pointedly, "that's why we can't think about playing you. You don't rebound. Let me ask you something. How can a guy be six foot seven and there be sixty-eight rebounds out here and you get zero? How many of you guys think Kreigh really wants to play?" Ricky, Steve, Joe and Magnus raise their hands.

"What would you do with this if you were a coach?" Of course the coach has his own answer. "The way you play," he tells Kreigh, "we're limited to playing you against the zone. You're not going to rebound, you're not going to scramble after the ball: the spot I have to have for you is one where we got some guy out here that never goes inside." Brian Sloan, on the other hand, has earned "a real chance to play and you're going to play." Hillman, who averaged forty-one points a game in high school, doesn't shoot enough.

"Do you think we inhibit your shooting?"

"No," Hillman whispers.

The point has been made: they all have a chance; there is no single starting five, no one whom he has decided simply will not play. "I want open shots taken by anybody that can make them. I want the ball passed four times, that's it. You don't have any requirement on your shooting other than that."

Why four passes? It's to test the defense, to reverse the ball twice, to get a chance to take the ball inside, to draw the foul, to get the three-point play. "It's an automatic sit-down for a guy that shoots the ball other than off the break in a wide open shot in less than four passes. I'm just tired of this," he tells them. "We just don't do things without a reason." They are also shown a tape of their own strong, aggressive, successful play. The moral is clear: They *can* do it, they can play well. He believes it because they have demonstrated it.

"How are you, Keith?" Ron Felling affectionately asks on Sunday morning.

Smart smiles. "I'm living."

Knight sees the season before him. He realizes that this team must gain an advantage in the first five minutes of a game (he puts the number 5 on the whiteboard). Then it must not allow a comeback for the opponent in the second five minutes. For the last ten minutes of the first half they need "steady play."

All but Kreigh are writing in their notebooks. And there's the goal Knight is famous for, the one that's no myth—"We have to be able to play mistake free." He points to the sign on their wall: "Victory Favors the Team Making the Fewest Mistakes."

This is not a team that will dominate its opponents.

As for Kreigh, "When I recruited you, I thought you'd be as good as Wittman. I can remember the first time I saw you play..." This he means too: "It just kills me when guys come in a game and give up points or throw the ball away or don't see.

"We have room for a lot of people to play, boys."

Garrett remains far from the birdhouse. Nor is Knight beyond using the players against each other to drive the message home:

"Ricky, if Dean happens to be here, and he comes over the top to this spot, and the ball's over in here somewhere, and he moves to the ball, and the ball goes back to the other side, tell me what he's going to do. I mean, what he's going to do ninety percent of the time."

"He'll go right back the same way."

"How many guys in here could have answered that for what Dean's going to do?"

All hands go up, save one.

"You couldn't have?"

Lyndon, still shy, nods. Yes, he could have.

"Then you better get your hand up!" But Knight is gentle with this shy freshman. "How are you today?" he asks, obviously only pretending to be gruff.

It's Sunday and they're about to leave for Indianapolis. No one has been immobilized by the scrutiny in the locker room and today players are called aside for private teaching. "Atta boy, Todd, good position," Knight calls. "That was perfect." "Good, good, good," he tells Magnus, "but stay on your feet." It's obvious that they have dramatically improved in these five practices since Christmas night. It's almost palpable. You can feel their spirits rise.

In the locker room for the last time, he tells them, "I think we've made some progress. You people each have to be better, but you don't have to be any better than you are. We're not asking you to be any stronger nor any quicker. We're just asking you to be as good as you are. That's all it takes."

It's a speech they hear again and again, but one they may not understand until long after they have left Indiana. "Play to win," he concludes as they practice for the last time before boarding the bus to Indianapolis.

Just before five, Everett Dean appears in Assembly Hall.

Nearly ninety now, he is unwilling to miss this annual excursion Knight prepares for him. Dean, whom Knight had praised at the Cathedral High School fund raiser, coached Stanford to an NCAA championship in 1942, and also coached Indiana. He is one of the old coaches Knight looks after, as, in their wisdom, they looked after him when he was a young man.

As soon as the players arrive at the Marriott in Indianapolis, Knight begins to speak not about Pennsylvania, an easy win, but about the Big Ten season to come. They should be encouraged by games like Eastern Kentucky, when they played well.

In twenty-two years, there's never been a bedcheck; there's zero chance of anyone being out. The players, "dressed," holding their notebooks, giggle.

III

"If you were to ask me to boil this whole thing down to the simplest form, it might be this: in order to be any good, you got to know what you're bad at, and so you play to your strengths and play away from your weaknesses. But somebody's got to tell you what the hell your weaknesses are and somebody's got to tell you the mistakes you're making. If they don't do that, you have no chance."

While Knight lies on the couch of his suite listening, Dan Dakich telephones a potential recruit.

"Tell him who you are so they have some point of reference," Knight coaches while Dakich talks to someone. "I'm Dan Dakich. I'm one of Coach Knight's assistants. I used to play at Indiana."

Unflappable, Dakich keeps up his conversation, unmindful of the prompter. "How old are you?" he asks the potential recruit's fifteen-year-old sister.

"All those are good questions except you never ask anybody how old they are," Knight points out after Dakich has hung up.

With his players resting in this interlude, the lull before the conference season, Knight ponders the enigma of his team. "You develop a game for a team to play and the game we developed for this team is a quick-paced game both on the full court and the half-court." But they're playing a slow-paced game. "The game that we developed is based upon recognition which leads into anticipation and being able to stop things defensively or do things offensively, and we're not playing with any reading or recognition at all.

"We're playing a smart game with no thought and that's impossible," he says, looking forward to the fate of this year's Indiana team. "They've not yet developed their judgment.

"The problem that you have with most players at this level is that they all think that they're really good players. Well, they aren't. There are only a few really good players. The rest of them have to understand that they're going to get by learning to do some things and learning not to do some things. Our guys haven't really done that yet. They don't have a really good player among them that just tells them all what to do and brings them all to his level. The best players are those that make everybody else a little better, either through their own play or through what they do and say."

If there is one player who accomplished that in this post-Christmas interlude, it's . . . Patrick Knight, close to his heart, but more, one who played with fire and intensity all week. "Patrick in this five-day session had more assists than anybody else on the team, which really pleases me." He may be a father, however, but he must also be fair. "He also had far more turnovers than anybody else." Then Knight adds, "But that's not being used to this kind of play. Patrick is the kind of player who can make other people better because he's creative and he sees." The coach demonstrates. "If I go here, I can throw there. Our guys don't see that." Patrick's strengths, Patrick's weaknesses: "He plays well around the ball. When he doesn't have the ball, either on offense or defense, he doesn't play well."

Knight focuses his rational intelligence on his own son no less than on the others.

And then the father re-emerges. "I'll tell you one thing. He was a hell of a lot better at these five practices than I thought he would be. He made some absolutely great passes. Not only did he have more assists, but he saw better. Hell, he had probably a dozen guys miss lay-ups on passes he made. He's got balls. He's not afraid to make a play."

Will he then recruit Patrick?

"If he can play, that's where he is going to play. I'm not putting all this effort into him and then getting somebody else to coach him."

Who can excel? "It's not an easy game for them. You have to be able to find something that makes it easy, like just simply playing hard because by playing hard you don't make as many errors. And you get into position so that all of a sudden there's a play you can make."

He remembers himself as a college senior being asked to speak at high school dinners. He started out by talking right over the top of everybody's head: "So consequently I'm never interrupted in my thinking. I've never locked gazes with anybody. I'm never distracted by what anybody does. Then gradually I would look. Even today when I speak I never look at somebody because you could be distracted for any one of a hundred reasons. And you lose your train of thought. Well, a lot of people are petrified when they get up to speak. How many people have you heard get up and say, 'I'm more surprised than you are that I'm going to talk,' or 'I had no idea I would be asked.' Well, why say that? These inane things don't mean anything. Just get up and say something and sit down!"

Do these reminiscences have a point; are they self-serving? In fact, they're about his basketball team. "That's what these guys have to latch onto as a basketball team," he says, "And I don't know where they're going to do it." He had hopes for Hillman, Hillman who had averaged forty-one points in high school. "But Hillman does not see the game well enough; he doesn't make enough things happen. He doesn't recognize enough; he's going to be cautious." Knight grants that Hillman's not going to throw the ball away. "I'll play him," Knight decides. "I'm not going to start him, but, I'll play him and we'll see if he makes five or six baskets in a night.

"The one thing that's disappointed me most about this team," he admits, "is that Smart hasn't been a good scorer. He's not a real tough-minded kid. He only does one thing to a superlative degree and that's play in an open court situation on offense when he has the ball."

Everything his team does interests him. "I would not have

had them wear a coat and tie tonight, except they all had them on when I went into that room, so I didn't say anything about it." He is pleased by this, pleased by good behavior in which they've taken the initiative. With no bed check, he is certain they're up there in their rooms watching the Movie Channel. It's not that they're entirely on the honor system. Once, he remembers, at Butterfield's, a Bloomington restaurant, a player ran up a seventy dollar bill despite his eighteen dollar limit. "I told them, here's what we're going to pay, and I almost told him, 'You can pay the rest of it.' The key word there, of course is "almost." "They've got the evening free, but they never go anywhere. There is no rule that they don't go out, but they never have."

In his hotel suite, resting between team meetings, his thoughts turn to the new Big Ten rule that decrees that a junior college player, who would not have passed the NCAA academic requirement under Proposition 48, would be required to sit out a year before playing. If adopted, it would mean, he predicts, that the Big Ten could never recruit a junior college player. He has had seven junior college players. Four would have been required to sit out the year, three—Jadlow, Smart and Courtney Witte would not.

As for the assistants that he hires, it's on the basis "of being able to teach, not recruit. There isn't a recruiter here, they're all teachers." Ron Felling, in particular, is an example of that. "He has a great way of telling people things," says Knight. "I really like the way Felling has great presence in explanation. He gets upset, but he doesn't get upset like I do."

This tournament, the Hoosier Classic, "isn't anything. What will tell us where we are is the month of January. If we could develop, we're in a great position. We couldn't be any better because they've already had to listen since they've lost. They haven't played well. The players who have to play well have not played well. If we had players who have to play well really playing well, and we're still getting beat, then we're in trouble." There is still hope for this season despite the losses to Kentucky and Louisville.

"We can't afford to lose one of these games. Then we have to get off to a reasonably good start in the Big Ten. Iowa could beat us, but we can't lose to Northwestern. We're in a good position to do some things, but we have to get better. My concern is, do we have enough kids for whom basketball

is an easy game to be able to do that? Or do we have too many
for whom the game is too hard?"

IV

*"I think we're at fault to this extent. I think we should
have played Smith a lot in the Kentucky game. We
overplayed Eyl. Smith really did a pretty decent job in
the Notre Dame game. I think he scored nine points in
the time that he was in there. He threw the ball away a
couple of times, but he was tired by then. Then we came
back and didn't play him in the Kentucky game. So as
fragile as his constitution is, that could have really
screwed him up."*

Venerable Everett Dean joins the team for breakfast on Monday morning, but Knight does not. At the Market Square
Arena, where they have come to practice, Knight sits reading
Vince while they dress and are taped. Knight's physical
strength extends to his eyesight; although he is never without
a book (it might be *The Reckoning,* by David Halberstam, or
Pentagon by Allen Drury), in his late forties, he wears no
reading glasses.

He sits in the empty gym and draws around himself a pro-
tective aura of unapproachability. It isn't hostile or directed
against anyone in particular. It's more an assertion, a visible
desire to be alone with himself. If someone assaults his privacy—this morning it's Don Fischer who does the Indiana
play-by-play on the radio, and Knight's pre-game show—he's
pleasant. A guest who does gain admittance to the closed
practice is Jim Strickland, an Indianapolis physician who,
certain that he is out of earshot, whispers how one year
Knight walked five miles in the snow to the University of
Minnesota hospital to visit an Indiana woman dying of leuke-
mia. Knight remained an hour in her room dressed in a mask
and gown.

Otherwise it's practice as usual: Lyndon Jones runs around
the perimeter of the court to test his injured ankle; everyone
else is immediately put under pressure. Todd pushes off, but
Magnus makes a good move. "I don't think we're asking too

much of anybody," he tells me. The implied question to them is always the same: "How much do you want to do the things you've worked at? Hillman, I'm going to isolate you and Smith because God put you on Earth to torture me." Smith's play has particularly attracted his attention. Smith is on his mind.

"Dean, you never moved . . . instead of getting over here and challenging him. Do you want to play?"

"Yes."

"You're not convincing me you want to play."

No one's place is assured. Knight turns to Ricky Calloway.

"Has Garrett convinced you he wants to play?"

"No."

Although Penn is probably the easiest team Indiana will play this season, he is infuriated at the lackadaisical practice. Suddenly he zeroes in on the culprit.

"L.J.," he calls to one of the managers, L.J. Wright, who is the best basketball player, "put on a white shirt!" And Kreigh Smith is banished to the showers. Revealing no emotion, sweaty with exertion, Kreigh departs.

The practice goes on, their effort up a notch. Keith is praised for a cut, Lyndon for anticipating, Brian for a good screen. But the hero of the practice is Ricky Calloway, Calloway whom Knight now sees as a creator. "Good, Ricky, very good," he calls. "Ricky, that was a really good step. You've got to create. You can't wait for something to happen. Atta boy. That's what basketball is all about. That's the way to play the game."

The others are told not to stand and wait to see what Ricky's going to do. And Ricky is given the highest Knight compliment: further instruction. "Ricky, when you hit him with the ball, come into the hole. Now you're posted. Don't let them match up to you. That was a great play, Ricky. I can't tell you how good a play that was." Now Ricky must "make the play. Think what you've got. Look at what you've got and have it register." A few moments later, Knight again praises Calloway: "Great pass, Ricky, that's the way to look." In his third season with Knight, having started on a championship team, Calloway is now treated as the team leader for whom Knight is desperately searching. Knight hopes Calloway will assume the role.

"What do you think, Jimbo?" Knight asks Strickland's wide-eyed thirteen-year-old son.

After practice a family comes up to Knight with their son, a boy aged eleven with his head shaved, obviously the result of chemotherapy. Knight takes a photo with the child. The father, a tall man with gray hair, tells Knight how someone, suggesting a resemblance with Knight, told him not to throw any chairs. Knight smiles weakly, and doesn't say a word.

The television interviewers have arrived, and their first question has to do with Jay Edwards. Is he ineligible? Will he come back? What happened? "Why should we talk about a guy who couldn't keep his grades up? We're talking about those who are playing," Knight replies firmly.

On the way back to the hotel in Strickland's car he sings: "Why, oh, why, did I leave Ohio?" The second button is broken on Strickland's brown tweed jacket. Knight reaches over from the back seat where he has chosen to sit with Jimbo and yanks it off.

"That was doing me for a long time," the doctor laughs.

"It's very hard to become something if you don't look as if you're already doing it," Knight answers emphatically.

Lunch is chicken and noodles, homemade biscuits and jelly, preceded by his inevitable bowl of chili, at Bob Evans, a restaurant he likes better than last night's mediocre Italian restaurant. His talk ranges from genuine pleasure at his national championships with three completely different teams—so unselfconscious that it is charming—to English history ("Anne Boleyn," he says, "not bad for a basketball coach") to the Russian game.

Autograph hunters descend, breaking into his conversation, as they invariably do when he eats at a restaurant. Today's shameless autograph seeker is a Baptist minister. We avert our eyes. No one says anything. The minister calls Knight "Bobby." Uncannily he knows the one right thing to say: he admires the team. The Baptist minister congratulates Knight for "building character."

Without missing a beat, as soon as the man is gone, Knight immediately resumes his conversation. He wants to discuss with Jimbo, a basketball player of course, which of three Indiana high schools would be the best for him. Knight becomes a parent: "At which would you be able to play the most?" Jimbo has demonstrated an interest in aviation, which provides the opening for a needle. Why isn't he coming to basketball camp? Does he want to be a pilot or a basketball player?

I can't argue him out of the check. Then he dons his pointy black-and-white checkered tweed hat which perches on the top of his head like a star on top of a Christmas tree and which functions well as a semi-disguise, and it's back to the hotel, to the team.

In his suite, the team awaits him. They are being lectured by Julio Salazar, who has done the scouting of Penn: "They run a regular UCLA cut. When they don't get it, they take the ball to one of the sides. . . ."

"Mark, are you here?" Knight teases the redshirted player who was given a few days extra off for Christmas because he is from California. "I thought you were transferring to the University of Trinidad. Look to your left, then look around the room, Mark, and then back to your left. Who do you think the guy in here most likely to fake an injury would be?"

They all laugh, slightly injured Lyndon Jones no less than the others. Knight goes on to tease Julio: "I understand exactly what Julio says. Todd, did you understand that? Julio, don't let these guys give you any shit now." Having excelled at scouting and research, watching endless tapes, weekends, evenings, boiling down an opponent to a series of cards, it is one of Julio's first walk-throughs and Knight is trying to put him at his ease. Julio, in turn, has an answer to each of Knight's questions. What is it percentage-wise, man to man versus zone? "It's ninety-five percent man to man, coach," Julio answers.

When the team is gone, Knight discusses Kreigh Smith with his assistants. (I ask him how Kreigh took being thrown out of practice. His reply is unrelenting: "The correct question from Kreigh's point of view is how *I'm* taking it.")

In fact, he is not happy with Smith's play because "everything he does is wrapped around his shooting, either positively or negatively. None of it has anything to do with the other ninety-five percent of basketball." Dan Dakich reports Kreigh told him, "I just have a real hard time. I'm supposed to be a shooter and I want to score because I think that's what I should be doing, that's what they want me to do." Kreigh cannot account for the errors in his play: "I don't know why I don't do that. I just don't know why."

Knight takes some of the blame. "I think we're at fault to this extent," he explains. Kreigh had scored nine points against Notre Dame, and had a right to expect to play against Kentucky. He should have played him instead of Eyl.

Dakich agrees. "Now his thinking is when he doesn't play in the Kentucky game, they're mad at me. What did I do wrong? Why are they mad at me? I don't know if he could have done any good for us," Dakich adds.

"Well, he certainly couldn't have been worse than Eyl," Knight says.

"He was sitting next to me in the Kentucky game, Coach," says Julio. "During the game he mentioned to me that he wanted to be ready because he'd played a big role in the game against Kentucky two years ago. He was really positive that he would be played again."

Dakich takes the opportunity to speak on Smith's behalf. "He played well this week. He shot the ball extremely well. In my opinion this is a game he'd play really well in."

Knight is skeptical. "This game? Well, that's the problem. He could score twenty points in this game and then where are you?" The point is clear. Playing against Penn is no test of anything.

But Dakich persists. "As far as getting him going a little bit, this whole tournament wouldn't be bad."

Patrick Knight telephones. He is exhausted after the five Indiana practices and won't be driving up for the first game of the Hoosier Classic. Today he just wants to sleep.

How did he do in his own practice today, his father wants to know.

"Awful," Patrick says.

Don Fischer arrives for his pre-game show to find a playful guest. Fischer, whose play-by-play is outstanding (he's an unsung Tim McCarver of basketball), enjoys the obstreperous Knight. As usual, he plays it straight. What about the field of the Hoosier Classic?

"I just don't know anything about it."

"How about Penn, the opponent tonight?"

"I really know very little about Penn. It's located in Philadelphia and it has a business school called the Wharton School of Finance which a lot of assholes have gone to and graduated from." Knight goes on to say something uncomplimentary about his own team. He is bored, trying to amuse himself and others. He would make life full, not boringly repetitive, as these pre-game shows invariably are, with the coach praising the best players of the opponent. He works at freeing life from becoming routine, as he demands that his players work at getting open on offense.

"What did you get for Christmas, coal and sticks?"

"Santa Claus forgot me."

Then he does get serious. Knight has invited two good California teams, California/Santa Barbara (which this season will go on to beat Nevada/Las Vegas twice) and Stanford to the Hoosier Classic. As for his own team, he turns the question back to Fischer. "What do you think?"

"I think the kids are working hard. I don't know if they've grasped what you're trying to get through to them, though."

And here comes the merciless Knight, the Knight who, if he so chooses, will not let anyone off the hook.

"What do you think it is that I'm trying to get through to them that they haven't grasped?"

Fischer ventures forward. He talks about their being alert, playing solidly. . . .

"Are you saying then that you don't think they're more alert, that you don't think they're playing solidly?"

"I still think there are a couple of people that have some work to do."

"Oh, I think there are more than a couple of people that have work to do," Knight slices in, "and I think that goes through all facets of Indiana basketball and that includes even the broadcast team."

Fischer reminds Knight that he's never had a team take this much time off since the last ballgame. They lost to Louisville on December 19, and didn't return to practice until the 25th. Knight wanted them "to get some rest and rethink where we were as players and what we had to do individually."

As all these pre-game coach shows do, this one ends with Fischer wanting to know tonight's starting lineup.

"If you pay careful attention to the introductions," Knight tells him, "you'll be able to pick it up."

* * *

With Fischer gone, and the game only a few hours away, he still wants to talk to me about his team, about Dean Garrett, who two years ago had "the worst run I had ever seen. He ran on his heels, didn't use his arms to run, just shuffled down the floor. He can't jump; he's not a very good athlete. He's just a guy who's been made to play because he happens to be six-ten. But what I know about Garrett is this: Garrett has to play on a team that's good."

His concern for Garrett extends beyond Indiana's own season: will Garrett be able to convince one of the pro people to draft him in the first round so he gets a good contract? "He isn't a forward and he isn't a center and he has a tough time moving from here to there with the ball and he doesn't see things very well."

As he speaks, one of the tapes of practice runs. He illustrates how Smart is looking the wrong way. "Now watch this whole thing unfold. See where Smart is. There's nobody close to him, nobody behind him, and the position he should be in is right where Smith is because that's the closest guy for him to guard. And Smith gets this uncontested shot."

He backs up the tape. "The guy for Smart to guard is right here. On that pass he should move across the line and look this way. All right, what is there for me? There's nobody for me to guard, so I look and I go right where Smith is.

"What can happen then is they can throw across court to Patrick, all right. But look at the bottom man here who has no one to guard either, so he comes out on Patrick's man. This is what you've got to teach in a zone defense. You've got to teach people where there aren't any players.

"Let me back this up for you and I'll show you. Now watch where Smith starts. He starts OK, they jump him. Now he can come back. But now Smart should be right on Smith. There's no one else. He can't expect a guy to cover the passer and the receiver both. You see what I mean? What Smart is doing is, he's expecting Hillman to guard the passer and the receiver and you can't do that. Now if the pass does come across to Patrick, then the bottom man comes out on Patrick, and Garrett comes over to play the bottom man, so Smart ends . . . this is what bothers me most about him. He just gives up plays like that because he really gets tired."

Knight does play zone defense, he admits, but only to affect the other team's play. What's more important is that his

team really works well against a zone. "Like Calloway has to
stay with the ball, there's nowhere else for him to go but
staying with the basketball. I don't know why he thinks about
going anywhere else . . ."

Teaching them is teaching them to see as he does, which is
both an impossible and the only possible goal. Now we watch
Calloway whose defender just stands. "There are more mistakes that can be made in basketball than in any other game,"
Knight says.

"Watch Patrick make a good move here. This is why I
think he has a chance to be good. Watch, watch him, he's up
on top of the screen. Watch how he starts in, then he slides
back and steps right into the shot. Perfect footwork, he
stepped right into it."

Did his father teach him when he was a child?

The reply is gruff. "Well, a little."

Even this conversation does not conclude without a glance
back at the sportswriters and the double standard they bring to
reporting about him. It seems not to occur to him that there
may be a casual connection between *ad hominem* reporting
about him and his attacks on them, range wars on the order of
the Hatfields and the McCoys:

"Constantly last year writers would write things about how
fat I was, or about how out of shape I was. Do I look like
I'm . . . ? I would say to Hammel, 'Have you ever seen a normal sportswriter? They're little short guys, or they're bald-
headed fat guys like you, or they're guys with some kind of a
physical handicap, they've got a bent arm, they limp, they
wear thick glasses.' It just amazes me that they could pick on
that. . . ."

V

"Do you have stock in Pennzoil?"

We are on the bus headed for the Market Square Arena and
the game with Penn, which he knows they must secretly believe will be easy: "Let's be as good on every possession that
we can be. Let's anticipate. Let's don't react. Let's get a possession over with and win that possession and win the next

possession. . . ." Tim Knight is on the bus and his father calls him up to sit beside him so he can discuss Patrick's success in practice. Has Tim talked to him? He has.

In the audience is Ryan White and his family, the sixteen-year-old hemophiliac with AIDS, an Indiana celebrity after his family has been hounded out of Kokomo by community pressure. Knight tracked him down and telephoned.

"I heard Ryan was an IU fan and would be interested in coming to a basketball game after January first," Knight told Mrs. White. Since Indianapolis is closer to their home, they chose this tournament. Now Ryan, a smiling boy in blue jeans and a blue-jean jacket, who looks more like thirteen than sixteen, sits chatting with his friends and Mom right behind the Indiana bench.

Nor can the game begin without a blind woman named Mrs. Lingofelter presenting the coach with a red-and-white Afghan that she has crocheted, complete with the IU logo at its center. Knight puts his arm around her, pats her on the neck. Tim Knight takes charge of the Afghan, which will wind up draped over a sofa in Knight's living room not far from the Olympic banner reading "To Our Coach, WE ARE ALL BEHIND YOU," signed in embroidery by all those who participated with him in the 1984 Olympics.

Against Penn, the starters in this year without a starting five are Calloway, Sloan, Garrett, Jones and Smart. The game is coached with all the intensity that the conference games will be. Knight draws on the clipboard. He screams for Smart to move, move your feet, watch your feet on the perimeter. He calls for Dean to flare. He praises Brian when he dives for the ball. Dean is called over to be told, "You were in the right position. That's all it took," and to receive a pat. Kreigh Smith enters the game and is given extra advice.

At 7.55, with Indiana leading 22–9, after a time-out Knight once again offers Rick Calloway the leadership of the team. "Get 'em together, Rick," he says as play is about to resume. Then he calls Smart over. But Smart is already shaking his head. He knows what he has done wrong.

"This is the best defense I've seen all year," Everett Dean tells me.

But Knight is not satisfied. "Come on, Ricky, handle the ball," he calls. "Step up to the middle. We've got to have good shots." Hillman is told he has just done "the worst thing

I've ever seen you do." And Kreigh, as he fouls, is told, "You've got to see it coming. That's a play you have to learn to make." In a minute and a half Steve Eyl scores six points after having scored hardly at all in the post-Christmas practices. It's the "I'll show him" response that Knight hopes will result from his announcement to a player that he's just about given up on him.

He's furious when Calloway loses the ball. "Ricky, he's just wearing you out," he calls. No matter that Penn has long since been blown away. The score is 61–37 with 12.23 to go. Calloway is taken out, to be followed down the bench by the coach. "There's just no sense to that," he says. The issue, now as always, is their doing well, their having assimilated his teaching, their commitment to effectiveness—none of which has anything to do with the particular opponent, whether it be Penn or Purdue. And so he can scream despite a thirty-point lead, "Get on the board, Lyndon, look at what you've got there!"

It is also true that the moods of the man, those clouds blowing across autumn skies, are at the wellspring of his coaching. Criticism turns to praise, the change as swift as a change in the weather and the players know it. The students know that the criticism can and will, like lightning, turn to praise with the next play. All they need do, which is what they want to do anyway, is perform at the level of their talents. "Atta boy, Joe, good pass," Knight calls to Hillman.

Ryan White dons a heavier quilted jacket as the game nears its end.

With 4.04 to go, and the score 76–47, in a huddle he tells them: "Let's have four minutes of really good basketball!" Back onto the floor go Oliphant, Jadlow, Pelkowski, Hillman and Smith. At 2.50 Kreigh gets his third personal and is mad at himself. "He'll go left every time. You've got to see what's going on," Knight says. Although Kreigh plays fifteen minutes, he scores only three points. Hillman, however, is four for five, with five for five free throws, scoring 14 points.

Walking off the court, Knight puts his arm around the shoulder of a Penn freshman named Dane Watts, who has been involved in some altercations with the officials. "Hey, you have a chance to be a pretty good player if you'll just shut up and play and quit bitching." "Thank you, Coach," says the rambunctious Watts, now gracious in defeat. Then Knight grabs Phil Pitts, the Penn senior: "You could play for me," he tells him.

In the locker room Ryan White appears to meet the players. He has his picture taken, and receives a hug from the coach. Does he have four tickets for the championship game? Ryan White stands there, his voice eerie and high-pitched, his complexion sallow. His courage refuses to allow him self-pity or to reject life. He's a person this coach would admire. Knight instructs Tim to get him some sweaters.

"Keith, wear a sport coat tomorrow," Knight calls as Smart heads for the bus.

At dinner he chooses lobster tails. Then it's more talk about them, how they live no less than how they play. Dorms shouldn't be coeducational: why make it easy? Churchgoing, midwestern values of clean living (no gambling, no smoking, no alcohol define his standard for them). Tonight he has a light drink, but this is rare for him. When his players complained of marijuana smoke coming into the rooms via a phone-box which linked rooms, delighted, he decided to allow them to live off campus.

He discusses the 49'ers football team with them; he shows respect to his son. Leaving Tim to deal with the check, he disappears before dessert only to have a sundae delivered to his room.

He joins his team for breakfast, ready to analyze last night's second game in which Stanford beat Santa Barbara. Julio has stayed up all night in his room studying the Stanford team, producing the cards, the preparation.

"What grade would you give Julio on his scouting report, Keith?" Knight wants to know.

"A-plus."

Magnus Pelkowski concurs.

"You're easy graders," Knight scoffs.

He looks at what they're eating. "It'll take more than coffee to keep you awake," he tells Todd Jadlow. Knight eats Rice Krispies and steals a last bit of bacon on his way out; he doesn't drink coffee, but milk, and teases Ron Felling for requesting coffee just to get a little closer to the waitress.

"A little bit of heaven," says Felling. It's his favorite line.

And then it's on to Stanford and Todd Lichti, to post exchange and Stanford's endless efforts to punch the ball inside.

The bus ferries the team to practice, but suddenly it stops, and a tall man in a blue jacket and a funny tweed pointed hat, clutching a sweater, gets off and walks toward a building, a solitary figure on the cold morning landscape. A sign reveals his destination: the Indiana University Medical Center.

The team proceeds without him to a very grand facility opposite an Olympic-sized swimming pool, the joint Indiana-Purdue sports facility in Indianapolis. Practice begins.

When Knight finally arrives, Bernie Souers of WTTV wants to discuss the tip-off program.

"Well, you don't mind if we do a little practicing first?"

The television, the VCR, the tapes have been brought to practice, which, this morning, is a lecture. The students sit on the floor, their notebooks open, as each Stanford player is examined. "He's right handed and likes to go to his right. . . . Butler is just like the kid from Washington State. . . .

"Most everyone will play zone against us," he tells them. "We have to take the ball one way and pass it back the other way. Don't take the ball with the pass the same way you're dribbling the basketball. Reverse pass and look to get the ball inside." Ron Felling lectures, with Knight chiming in: Taylor took four shots last night and they were all three-point shots. Lichti was nine for fifteen.

McSweeney, Wright, Butler, Taylor, Lichti—the names are repeated so often they become second nature, as do their achievements: Wright scored thirty against UCLA, twenty-four against USC. Stanford is treated as a formidable opponent. "I can't impress on you enough that these people are very, very good at what they do," Knight says.

"They work to get Lichti open like we work to get Ricky open." It's Lichti who will receive the lob pass, who will be screened for. "You got two things with Lichti in the corner. The ball comes to Lichti—which it shouldn't. We should be able to prevent that. The ball goes opposite and Lichti comes out of the corner. There he is on the drive. What's happened here is that they've been forced to switch it. . . . We want to make it tough for Lichti to go through here to the basketball. When the pass goes opposite, Ron picks and Lichti goes off of him. You can easily recognize that. The ball goes opposite and Lichti comes out of the corner. . . ."

The tape rolls. "You have to see that switch coming on or they'll just bury you there with Lichti. Lichti comes toward the ball again, and there he is. He finally gets it. . . ."

Knight anticipates the press: "I believe we can score against anybody that presses us," he tells them—as indeed the closing game of the season will reveal.

They return to the floor. He sits right under the basket, watching, the ultimate distraction. "That's good, Dean," he says. Or "Post, Steve, post." He uses his voice in all its range. "Downscreen, Ricky, downscreen and post. Good. Good. Screen, screen, that's good, Dean." Then, suddenly, he screams, "SCREEN, DEAN." Then, very softly, "Ricky, go outside and put the defense out." Then, louder, "HOLD IT, KEITH, HOLD IT. GOOD, DEAN, BE READY TO SHOOT, DEAN, DON'T HAVE TO TAKE THAT EXTRA STEP. . . ."

The value of his being a master is that he can predict what the other side will do. It is to a large extent this expertise, proven time and time again, which allows them the confidence, the poise to stop an opponent. They believe they have an edge because they will not be surprised as to who goes right and who goes left, who will pop out from where. No one can emerge from these sessions without the feeling "I can do it!", however formidable the reputation of the opponent.

All they have to do is what he tells them. "Under pressure they look to give Lichti the basketball." He has analyzed Stanford psychologically no less than physically. He knows what they will do in a crisis and what adjustments they will make when they can't follow their usual patterns. He warns how they will get open. "I want us to be able to make it tough for Lichti to get the ball out on the perimeter and keep the ball." They watch a tape of Stanford playing Iowa and then they get up and walk through.

"We've got eighteen of these coming up," he tells them. "We've got to be well prepared. We have to take it away. This is a challenging game. It's going to be a forty-minute basketball game. All right. Let's go."

Practice over, he motions to Kreigh Smith.

"What do you think it is?" Knight asks his student. "I just get disgusted. Just like yesterday morning" (the morning Kreigh was thrown out of practice). "You took a shot after one pass, or last night your foot was right there instead of right here."

But it's not all criticism. "I think you're a very good

player," Knight tells Smith. "You're also your own worst enemy. It's entirely up to you. This team needs you. I think you played very well against Notre Dame. I think I made a mistake in not playing you against Kentucky. You've got to keep your man off the boards. You've got to do all those things in order to be able to play. All right."

And Kreigh runs off—happy.

If you imagine that he's grown tired, you'd be wrong. He's not too tired to tease the television crew that has set up in the gym. "Bernie wanted me to start out tonight's pre-game show by talking about last night's game," he says, ostensibly on the air. "Look, I said, I'm going to talk about whatever I want to talk about. He also told me to talk about tonight's . . . , I don't know what's going to happen. How the hell do I know? The goddamn game hasn't been played yet. I have no idea what we're the hell going to do until the game starts. We do things that I don't see, that I don't know about . . ."

"Damn." "Hell." He ensures this will be an outtake. And, as he often does, he assumes both roles: host and guest: "We'll be back in just a moment after these words from our goddamn charming . . . sponsor."

"How would that be?" he asks Bernie, as if it were conceivable that they would broadcast the tape as is.

"People would really love it."

The real show includes compliments to the Stanford coach as well as to Everett Dean: "It may be the best start Stanford has had since Everett Dean was coaching there thirty-five to forty years ago." He warns the audience that zone will be played against Indiana. "I'm not sure that we have the kind of shooting that we usually have against the zone." With Steve Alford gone, and Jay Edwards ineligible, not by the NCAA regulations but by his own, Indiana lacks a three-point shooter with whom to beat the zone.

I try, I pester him three times, without success. He won't reveal whom he visited in the hospital this morning.

On the bus back to the hotel he has a question for trainer Tim Garl: Has he left the four tickets for Ryan White?

By one-thirty he's back in his suite, teasing Ricky Calloway about the fancy leather gloves he's now wearing indoors. Does he have stock in Pennzoil? "When was the last checkered flag?" And a moment later, "Do you use Pennzoil?"

Before the tapes are started, the lesson is repeated: "Two things can happen when Lichti goes to the corner. They throw the ball to him and it's a two-man game. They don't throw the ball to him and it's a reversal and a downscreen. He can go either way off of it. It could be a 'bak pik,' as Julio would say."

Knight puts his arm around Julio. "Your grammar is perfect, but we have trouble understanding you," he says. "You do awfully well with English, but we have to needle you a little bit. Here, Julio. That's part of being here." He hugs Julio. "Felling's grammar is such that your grammar overrides Felling's grammar so that the two of you are really a good team."

And now throughout the session they will hear about the "bak pik." "It's going to be a back pick . . . and there it is." Knight discovers that the remote control device is missing, and several people are blamed. "I want to tell you guys something," he says. "I needle Julio a little bit. The first time I met Julio he couldn't speak a word of English, not one word. He just worked like hell and I think you know how hard he works on your behalf. If anybody worked like he does, you'd be a goddamn all-American. Just keep that in mind."

The telephone rings and it's a Channel 13 commentator. "What the hell do you want?" Knight asks. "I want you to understand one thing. My whole team is sitting here. We're going through a scouting report. Do you know what Garrett just did? He just turned to Smart, and he said, 'Keith, that's that asshole from Channel 13 again.'" He hangs up. But he's not finished. "That's called public relations," he tells Julio. "As you get older and you're head coach at Indiana, I want you to handle public relations just like I do, OK?"

Is there anyone who can escape the needle? My camera rewinds automatically, and he pauses, about to turn on the television again. "Is our TV thing interfering with your camera?" he wants to know.

"Fake trapping, three-man stack against the zone, triangle, I want them in foul trouble in the first ten minutes of the game," he orders. Will they remember all this? (Dan Dakich confesses he remembered only his own part.) "Ricky, you be on the baseline," Knight says. "Read what that guy does like I'm you, and I'm the bottom guy on the baseline and the ball's brought off the point. Maybe he releases and that bottom man comes up. As soon as that happens, you replace the bottom man over here, coming right to get the basketball. Then if it's reversed, you can always come back the other way." All they need to do is read their maps and they will emerge victorious. Victory will be sweeter against a worthy opponent, and he has guarded against their contempt for this Western team, although they have been schooled in the belief that the Big Ten conference is the toughest.

"This becomes a hell of a test for us tonight," he tells them. "A really good test. Let's get to the point where good teams have real trouble playing against us. That's where we have to elevate ourselves. You guys better get together down there and talk things over a little bit." He likes the idea of their conferring without him, discovering leaders among themselves, maybe even conspiring against him, if only to prove him wrong about someone or something.

Now he does the show for Channel 13, although his best remarks are not those that will appear on the air. Again a reporter wants to discuss Jay Edwards and again he's told, "Keep one thing in mind when you're dealing with me. Talk about the goddamn kids that are playing and not the ones that aren't. If a kid's hurt, that's one thing. But if a kid screws things up, let's talk about kids that aren't screwing things up."

There's time for still another walk-through. Dan Dakich's pants are too long, in the coach's opinion, so he's told to put brushes on the ends of his pants and sweep the floor. "We'll play each of you a few minutes on Lichti just to keep somebody really fresh on him. I don't want you to go in there if you're not going to work to keep him from getting the basketball. That's the whole purpose in our playing him." He tells Keith he'll be relieved after playing Taylor; by now, Smart's lack of stamina has been taken into account. They take copious notes, freshman Lyndon Jones neatly, conscientiously, although no notebook is as elegant as Magnus Pelkowski's.

They must get used to the idea that "as we go down through the season we're going to have a different starting lineup almost every time we play because we just don't have enough people who have shown us we can play them in every kind of situation. And that's what we've got to have. One night we might need somebody to play defensively. Another night we might need somebody to shoot against the zone.

Another night it's our man-to-man offense. So don't worry about whether you started last night or don't start tonight. If you start thinking like that, then all you're going to do is get the thing screwed up." Joe Hillman will start on Lichti, then Steve Eyl. Keith will go in and "bust your ass" for four minutes. Even Lyndon may later go in on Lichti. In fact, although Calloway, Garrett, Smart, Hillman and Sloan will start, nine of them will play, Todd Jadlow for fourteen minutes.

By now there can't be anyone who hasn't conjured up the image of Lichti moving to his right, or who hasn't seen the ball being lobbed into the post. When the game begins, it will be almost a shock to see the real Lichti, flesh and blood, a handsome 6'4" 200 lb. guard. The instructions, even so close to game time, are minute, exact and spoken with the full confidence that they can and will be carried out: "Ricky, read what's happening. If you're over here, Rick, and you're being covered, let's say by McSweeney, and you see that when the ball's reversed, Wright has to go up and play the ball, then get over there as soon as you see both guards have rotated in your direction. Then go out. You're playing opposite the guards on the baseline." Above all they are warned about Stanford's post play. The post man might be standing there lethargically and then "all of a sudden the guy steps in, he's got the ball." He would hate it if they were fooled, a post player pretending to be asleep and then winding up with the ball.

They are warned. If they don't play as well as they can, they'll get beat. Always there are goals. It is December 29, their last game of the year. "Let's get this year ended with this tournament," he says. On the bus, he tells them, "Let's go out ready to play and let's come back with the championship."

Former players dot the crowd: Courtney Witte, Todd Meier, Steve Green and Steve Ahlfeld and Steve Downing, the old reliables, Phil Isenbarger, Ted Kitchel, Tom Abernethy sitting between his twin eight-year-old sons. Abernethy confides: "Anyone who played, who went through those four years here, any one of them would do anything he possibly could for him. If he needed anything on the spur of the moment, all of us would just jump at the chance to repay him." Not, of course, that Knight would ever ask.

Professor William Wiggins offers a holiday message to the crowd, thanking the fans on behalf of the parents of Steve

Eyl, Dean Garrett and Keith Smart, this year's seniors, "for helping their sons mature into fine young men." It's Knight's overriding theme: the development of his students into effective human beings who have transcended difficulty through hard work, who have come through.

Stanford, of course, plays zone against them. It's clear Indiana would do better with Jay Edwards. But teaching the young man a lesson about his studies came before winning basketball games. At 9.25 Lyndon is brought in against the mighty Lichti, while Knight chastises the team for dropping their lead from sixteen to ten. Immediately Calloway and Garrett score, a process repeated over and over. The harsher his criticism on the sidelines, in the huddle, the more likely you will see an immediate result: a rebound, a bucket, a steal. If they forget what they've been taught, he reminds them: "We told you fake left and drive left."

At the half the score is 41–31. Knight has a pile of IU T-shirts delivered to the White group. Ryan immediately puts one on, while his mother, a sweet woman whose courage seems to match that of her son, holds the rest on her lap.

Stanford closes to 59-53. Knight screams at them. Smart replaces Smith. Ricky is called over for instructions. Indiana keeps its lead, but only marginally. Eyl draws a fourth personal foul, then loses the ball, then is the victim of a steal.

"You threw the ball away twice," he screams at Steve Eyl. "You just can't throw the ball away like that. You can't play like that." And Knight shakes him by the shoulders. There's 1.16 to go and the score is 79–68, but that's never the point. And, like Jimmy Wisman, if Eyl will be mad at anybody, it will be at himself.

"Atta boy, Kreigh," Knight encourages as Smith makes a free throw. But when he misses another, the coach says, "For Christ's sake, how can you miss free throws?" And with less than forty seconds to go, he's still furious at their forgetting the preparation. "The ball goes in and we stand there waiting when we know what he's going to do. He's going to go to his right hand."

With .28 left Knight wants an intentional foul. "Read the rule when you get home!" he yells at the official. "He wasn't even trying to get the ball!"

The final score is 83–73. With 27 points Rick Calloway is

named the Most Valuable Player of the tournament. And the all-tournament team is: Pitts ("You could play for me"), Lichti (who has finished with only 15 points!), Garrett, Smart and Calloway.

"Todd [Lichti] had to work real hard for what he did get," Stanford coach Mike Montgomery tells the press. "They denied, they took him out, we just have to find ways to win without him." Knight has kind words to say about Stanford, toward which he's "a little prejudiced because I have a boy that went there [Tim]." And he praises Garrett for "the best defensive job I've ever seen him do. I think he was absolutely outstanding."

Kreigh Smith in his eight minutes scores three points, no rebounds, no assists. Taylor, for Stanford, hits four of five three-pointers, as predicted. And, in a statistic that no one mentions, Stanford commits nineteen turnovers to Indiana's nine.

It would appear that the players have indeed passed their test, the one, Knight says in the locker room after the victory over Stanford, on which "there is no multiple choice." Even without Jay Edwards, Indiana seems ready for the Big Ten conference season, which will begin on January 6 at Iowa City.

CHAPTER NINE

Learning as You're Playing

"I'll get five guys whoever they are, like I've always done, to pass, to listen to me, to work hard."

Those losses to Kentucky and Louisville, however, turn out to be harbingers of Indiana's season: a 1–4 opening to Big Ten play. They lose not only to Iowa, but also to Northwestern, that game Knight said they could not afford to lose, in a bitter 66–64 defeat. After missing six games, Jay Edwards returns on January 14 in a squeaker of a win against Wisconsin, which precedes a 75–74 loss to Michigan State, one of the sisters of the poor. A January 24 loss to Michigan, 72–60, comes as no surprise.

This Michigan game also generates a torrent of newsprint. After Steve Eyl throws away two passes with seven minutes remaining in the first half, Knight seems to push him down the length of the bench. A caller to Indianapolis radio station WIBC claims to have heard on ESPN that Knight is about to resign.

Jim Crews, now coaching at Evansville, is said to be ready to take his place. But Eyl apologizes to the coach for anything his parents might have said to reporters that had been misconstrued. On the radio Knight congratulates Don Fischer on resigning from *his* job to cover the bullfighting circuit in Montevideo: "The key word in this whole thing, Don, is 'bull.'"

As the Big Ten season roars into full swing, something else is happening on this team. It's Ricky Calloway's play, Calloway who had only two points well into the first half against Michigan. His failure to work with weights the previous summer, his resting on the laurels of the national championship, have resulted in his not being strong enough to contest for the basketball; at 6'6", he should weigh more than 186 pounds. The ball skitters out of his hands; he's playing forward and he can't hold onto a rebound.

In the first half against Michigan, Indiana commits nine turnovers. Meanwhile, Keith Smart is revealing the weaknesses of junior college players entering Knight's system. On defense, Smart is costing the team games. Early in the second half against Michigan, he picks up his fourth personal foul.

As Knight told them in Indianapolis, there is no starting five: Pelkowski had been started, unsuccessfully, against James Madison. Against Iowa, Calloway, Eyl, Garrett, Smart and Hillman start. Against Northwestern, Sloan replaces Eyl; Jones starts rather than Hillman. Against Michigan State, Calloway, Eyl, Garrett, Jones and Smart start the game.

The turning point of the Big Ten season comes on January 27, with the game against Ohio State. The team is now 9–6 for the season, 1–4 in Big Ten play. On the Wednesday of game day against Ohio State, during practice Ricky Calloway stands around chatting with Lyndon Jones, clearly not taking the drills seriously. For setting a bad example, he is thrown out of practice.

Later that day, the team is gathered in the ballroom of their hotel for the walk-through. Knight turns to Garrett.

"Dean," he says, "you're playing a lot better in practice the last two days. Why do you think that is?"

"These guys," says Garrett, pointing to Edwards and Jones, "are easier to play with than Ricky and Keith. *These* guys are looking to pass. *Those* guys are looking to score." Garrett is reminded of last year when "If things were going bad, I would say, 'Hey, Steve [Alford], you've got to help us out here.' That's how I think Jay and Lyndon might look at me right now. They're depending on me. That gives me more confidence. Helping others makes you a better player."

Smart, Garrett's best friend on the team, listens, remembering himself being asked one day, "How do you think Ricky played today?"

"Poorly," Smart admitted.

"Well, you tell him," Knight had said.

Knight, of course, is not shy about informing Calloway of his displeasure: After three Big Ten losses, he has sent Ricky to sit alone in the locker room and think, only after fifteen minutes to go back in and get him.

Listening to Garrett now, Knight is pleased at the honesty, if disheartened at the demise of "certain expectations" he himself had. He has examined the stat sheets comparing this year with last. After four big ten games last year, Garrett had twenty-eight points; this year he has sixty. But both Calloway and Smart are doing more poorly than they were last year. The "I'm gonna be a star" mentality has engulfed them. Shooting at sixty percent last year, they're down to forty. Against Michigan State and Michigan, Smart has scored a total of eight points. And meanwhile their ratio of assists to turnovers is appalling; Calloway is 35–35, while Knight hopes for a 3:1 ratio.

Is there really a choice? Smart and Calloway are both benched.

Smart is gracious. "Even when he got on me and made Dean and me run fifty or sixty sprints down the floor," Smart says, "I never did get upset. He didn't put me there [on the bench]; I put myself there." In Garden City, his junior college coach Jim Carey is less reasonable. He accuses Knight of not playing Smart because he doesn't like *him*. Knight telephones Carey's assistant with some sharp words: "Did you ever stop to think Smart wasn't playing because he didn't play well?"

Unlike Smart, an impressive person with a sense of perspective, Calloway sulks. He seems not to remember his own words spoken on October 15 at the special supper at which the team entertained Shawn Kemp: "You gotta listen to what he's saying, but don't take it and just fold up into a little shell. My family background was pretty good, so I already had that type of attitude going before I got here. Anything he says is just like a repetition of what my parents have told me over the years. He's telling us, never give up, always play hard. When you want something bad enough, go for it." And on that evening Calloway had remembered when Knight yelled at him "for something he says you did wrong, but you did it right, just to see how you're going to react. Are you going into a shell and not want to play or are you going to come back and not worry about what he said and just keep on playing?" He had seemed to understand as the season opened. But his failure to play well after being Most Valuable Player of both pre-conference tournaments seems to have unsettled him.

With Calloway's deterioration as a basketball player, the absence of team leadership is even more glaring. Knight had taken Joe Hillman aside and asked him to be their leader. But Hillman had been uncertain. And now there is no one.

Although he does not become a team leader, Garrett improves; he scores 22 points as Indiana defeats Ohio State, 75–71. The victory is not overwhelming, but it is significant, made more so in retrospect when four days later Indiana defeats Purdue. With his coach's confidence, Garrett improves. Now Knight reassures Jay Edwards that he does indeed want him on the team: ("Hey, there are a helluva lot of people who thought you couldn't play for me when you came, that you wouldn't work hard enough, that I wouldn't work with you," Knight tells Edwards. "Let's just you and I prove all of them were wrong.") Edwards at once becomes a player, on his way to becoming Big Ten freshman of the year.

Against Purdue, Edwards scores sixteen points in the first half, twenty-two in all. Jones and Edwards play forty minutes, side by side, effortlessly aware of each other, as they played to those three state championships for Marion.

Calloway remains benched; Smart plays less than two minutes. The winning basket against Purdue is scored by Garrett, who has thirty-one points in this game, the high point of his season. The player who sat there on Christmas night, his head down, as his coach told him he thought less well than anyone on the team, but that he was still the one the coach wanted ("I don't want him, I want you"), is coming into his own.

Ryan White again watches from the stands, as do the usual company of former players: Wayne Radford, Todd Meier, Stevie Ahlfeld, all of whom gather to be interviewed on television by Steve Green about old contests with Purdue.

"I screwed up," Jay Edwards tells Quinn Buckner, in town to do color commentary on the Purdue game.

* * *

Indiana goes on to struggle through its Big Ten season, winning against Minnesota, Illinois and Northwestern, then losing again to Michigan.

Pete Newell, a Knight mentor, is in Bloomington on February 4 for the game against Minnesota. He praises his student for creating a team where there wasn't one before. Garrett continues to excel.

But Smart does not bounce back; he scores only eleven points against Northwestern, his very average on the Steve Alford team when he was not expected to assume the burden of the scoring.

Knight continues to coach fundamentals to a team that cannot, as he puts it, "see." Against Northwestern on February 11 they commit twenty turnovers! With such play, Indiana cannot win and Jay Edwards' 29 points against Michigan on February 13 is meaningless in a 92–72 loss.

"How's the health of the team?" Don Fischer wants to know as Indiana is about to play Michigan State. It's mid-February and the flu has overtaken Garrett, Jones and Eyl.

"I'm more concerned about *your* health, Don," says Knight, never one to make excuses. But it has not been an easy winter. Hazel Knight has died on New Year's Eve, and the only solace her son has is that Christmas visit he decided to make. A rich man, he had allowed her the independence of spending her own money, figuring he'd take over when hers ran out. In her eighties, Hazel Knight still enjoyed life and was about to go out to dinner with friends when she was found dead. The friends from Orrville at once help to make the funeral arrangements; Bob Knight attends alone, gracious to those who have come to pay their respects. These include "Adolph," the Kentuckian he has adopted, Chuck Marlowe, with whom he does his television show, his secretary, B.J.

The loss to Michigan has eliminated Indiana from the Big Ten championship. Knight readjusts his goals. Now Indiana must "get in position to play in a post-season tournament." Calloway is given his first start in six games and goes eight for fourteen, leaving the game to a standing ovation. (Smart, however, comes in only off the bench.) Jay scores 24; in his last five games he is averaging 22.4 points, 20 for 32 from three-point range. He is the team's best shooter.

Both Calloway and Smart start against Purdue now on February 21, in a poorly officiated game. With Garrett in foul trouble early, Indiana falters. Calloway plays poorly again. Knight receives a technical, at first for stepping out of the coach's box, and then, when it's clear that he hasn't, for "unsportsmanlike conduct." Meanwhile, Gene Keady rants and rages at his end without penalty.

Purdue wins 95–85, but it's a closer game than that, close all the way. On the bench for much of the game, Garrett has only 10 points. Edwards has 20, but Calloway—only 8. It's a definite setback, one unmitigated by an 84–74 victory over Wisconsin on February 24.

II

"Did you see Smart put the ball behind his back down there? That's one of the most athletic plays I've ever seen on this floor."

After the victory over Ohio State, Knight announced a thirteen-game season in which Indiana could still do well. The losses against Kentucky and Louisville, the 1–4 start in Big Ten play, could recede as if they never happened; he had set them a new, a realizable goal. And, as always, he played whomever contributed to realizing that goal, and benched whomever did not.

If you expect anger and temper and impatience because this team has been disappointing, you won't find it. They prepare optimistically for their February 29 contest with Illinois, boasting a fine seven-two record in their new thirteen-game season; by this reckoning Indiana is only one game out of first place in the Big Ten. Only Purdue has a better record, he tells them, and Indiana beat Purdue, and then almost beat them again. "It's important that people think we're the second best team in the Big Ten," Knight tells his team.

On the practice floor he stresses fundamentals, adding an emphasis on their communicating with each other. Hillman is playing better, trying to lead. As his play has improved, he has become more relaxed with his teammates.

Knight is more irritated by Indiana's victory over Wisconsin than he is over the loss to Purdue. Smart, dazzling as he was, committed five turnovers. By not contesting a pass, he allowed Wisconsin a three-pointer, and then another three when he interrupted the shooter who had been stupidly moving in exactly the direction most likely to thwart him: toward the corner.

There is more praise than criticism in practice as the season winds down. Keith is told he's "as good as anyone in coming in hard and going up for the shot." He is chastised for a bad pass: "Is there a hole in the roof that would allow God to take that pass? Because I've never seen Hillman make it." This remark is much enjoyed by the contingent of professors. Knight tells Hillman, "Right where you caught it, there's the shot." The implication is that if Hillman would only see his opportunities, he could score.

The ball bounces out of bounds. "All right, all right, all right," Knight says. Joe is patted for taking the ball in well. "Keep it off the dribble," he tells them. "Every time we get into that goddamned dribbling, we get in trouble.

"You weren't even looking at the ball, Steve," he says.

He raises his hands in the air, exasperated. Then, walking away from them, to no one in particular, he says, "Patience, patience, patience." Seconds later, his hands in his pockets, the blue pants, the red warm-up jacket, everything the same, he turns and walks back to them.

Tates Locke tells me the new patience is a result of the happiness in his personal life. When I test out this theory on him, the coach raises an ironic eyebrow: "He hasn't seen me practice for twenty years!"

Preparation now begins in earnest for the February 29 game against Illinois, leap year evening. On Saturday at one in the afternoon they're in the locker room being instructed on how to handle the ball against the press, against Illinois' skill at making conversion baskets. As always, he knows exactly what will happen to them. "Don't get trapped down low where Kujawa can hang onto you and keep you moving up the lane," he tells Garrett. Only a few elements are stressed each day: today it's slipping the screen and preventing conversion baskets. "You're not a dribbler, Dean," he must say still this late in the season. "Stay with what you can do." Joe is told: "Think, think, think."

The team does not have a good practice. "You guys make a comfortable adjustment," he tells them once more. "Why not say, don't let him get the ball." Back-cut passes are going to be made against them. "Yet every time you prevent them from making the pass they want, that's just another nail in the coffin."

"You're relaxed down there," he tells Garrett. "They're eating you alive!" Joe Hillman is not in a contesting stance.

"Joe, where do we want you?"

"On the high side."

"You were all the way down here."

Yet the earnestness of Hillman, the effort, the dedication to excellence make him a paradigm of the Knight player. Hillman doesn't sulk, retreat, curve in on himself or allow his classwork to suffer. Garrett and Smart seated on one side of him in the locker room, Eyl and Calloway on the other, Hillman—the slow, short white kid—would be an asset at the heart of any team, and one to be measured without reference to games won or lost, or to stat sheets. If earlier in the season he had told Knight he wasn't sure he could be a team leader because "some of the guys wouldn't listen and hadn't listened to me at that point," nonetheless he has gone about "doing what I had to to be a leader."

Hillman admits: "It's awful hard to play here, I'll say that. It's very demanding." But then, he adds: *"That's what you're here for."* Knight indeed demands the analytic ability to master the system while simultaneously making the utmost physical demands on yourself. Not every player aspires to so high a standard of excellence. What some fail to perceive is that all college basketball players have a lot of natural ability; maybe most teams are equal. Something more must separate them. Knight appreciates natural athleticism, but he knows that it is not enough.

Suddenly he strides over to the scorer's table and says, with excitement in his voice, "Did you see Smart put the ball behind his back down there? That's one of the most athletic plays I've ever seen on this floor!"

Patrick enters Assembly Hall with two of his friends and sits down on the removable stairway. Tonight his school, Bloomington North, will lose its regular season finale to New Albany. Pat will go five for ten with nine rebounds, however. Who are you recruiting, he keeps asking his father. Any guards?

And then Knight's patience begins to wear thin. Magnus should have made a shot he failed to make: "All you had to do was catch the ball and lay it against the glass." "Strength,

strength," he tells Ricky. "You're a twenty-one-year-old guy with the strength of somebody fourteen." That summer without his building himself up has cost the team dearly.

Dean takes a shot he has no chance of making: "I'm not bringing you out there [up high] to be a shooter." Jadlow loses the ball—and Indiana suddenly seems to be a team of people all with suspect hands, hands that can't hold onto the ball and so can't rebound. "Hold it," Knight yells, loud now. "Eyl, if I hadn't watched you for four years . . . you haven't had a shot from fifteen feet all year. Then when you have a shot, you reach for the ball with one hand!"

"Get out of here!" he tells them. "Go take a shower!" He appeals to their sense of fairness, how much more he is putting into their common effort than they are. He went to a high school game to recruit last night. This morning he has been here since ten looking at tape.

"Get out of here!" he repeats, and he means it. "You started the Big Ten season one and four and if you want to finish one and four, go ahead. This isn't playing, this mish-mash."

He had warned them in October how difficult it would be to come back after the championship, but it appears they haven't believed him. It's as if that national championship has burrowed into their souls, the worm in the apple. They have been paralyzed by the disparity between what they think of themselves and how they're actually playing.

"Turn out the lights!" Knight orders the managers.

When they return at six, they hear a lecture by Tates Locke. He draws an analogy between their sloppy play and a pretty girl who doesn't take care of herself, so that after a while she ceases to be pretty.

"Ricky, how much time did you spend last summer squeezing rubber balls?" Knight wants to know at the next practice. "That's why you can't catch the ball." A segment of the practice is devoted to four people above the foul line getting the ball in to Dean, who is not to leave his position when the post man comes around him. "Ricky, don't make a move unless you come up with the ball," he adds.

And then suddenly Knight stands and claps his hands, applauds: "That's a great play, Keith!" he calls.

But when they practice working against the trap, Keith

loses the ball. "Set it again," he calls. This time Jadlow infuriates him, Jadlow backing away when he caught the ball, Jadlow who's been here for three years and isn't set to shoot.

Anticipating a comment he will make on television after
the season is over, Knight reveals his thinking to Jadlow:
"That's why I say to myself I have to find a better player.
That's why I have to get someone other than you. You could
have told me otherwise. You can't make excuses night after
night for three years and expect to play. I don't need anyone
bigger than you or quicker than you or better than you. I need
someone who'll do what I say." The words are meant to urge
Jadlow on, yet Knight, in fact, has done exactly what he says:
he has recruited Michael Boykin out of Atlanta, a big strong
player to work inside, a student who played only eight games
in the last two years because he had changed schools. But
Knight clearly hopes Boykin will play an important role in the
building of his new front line.

At 4:15, they're back: P A T I E N C E it says in Magnus
Pelkowski's notebook. Inside play will be Illinois' strength.
"None of them want to get it back out," Knight warns, as they
scrutinize the tape. "Dean, I swear to you," Knight tells his
center, "if you get up on his left shoulder, he's not going to
make a bucket."

Julio has a baby son! "Raise him right and give him soul
food," Keith advises. Then he turns to Dan Dakich: now it's
his turn to get married. Dakich laughs. Dakich demurs. At
this moment in the season only Joby and Julio are married.

At six-thirty on this Sunday night, after dinner, there is still
more tape, "directed and produced by Julio." "Duke got beat
today," Knight tells his team, "because they missed the blockout, a simple block-out." On the board he writes their record
and Illinois'. "There's a hell of a difference between nine-six
and eight-seven," he tells them. Out here in the heart of the
country, only your record in Big Ten play counts. Illinois has
very good athletic ability, but Indiana can neutralize that with
its basketball ability.

"This has to be us playing at our best tomorrow, boys," he
tells them. "Get a good night's rest." There's the sound of car
keys jingling as they get up.

About to go out to dinner with Lou Henson, Knight is
glued to the last scene of *The Vikings*. The heroic exploits of
men fascinate him. He has brought with him an interview with

Ted Williams, of note because it stresses how the man who had more natural talent than anyone else still stressed hard work and effort. "Do you think that you played up to your potential?" the interviewer asks Williams. "HELL, no," comes back the reply. As for people in other sports whom he admires—"Bobby Knight. I love his intensity. I love his discipline. I love his devotion."

On game day Knight sits on the sideline with two of his oldest friends, Dick Otte, of the Columbus *Dispatch,* who covered Knight as a college player, and Fred Taylor, his own college coach. Otte recalls how Knight, either a sophomore or junior, upset at the amount of playing time he was receiving from Taylor, asked Otte for money for the plane ride home to Orrville from Champaign, Illinois.

"Do you know how long it would take to go from Champaign, Illinois, to Orrville, Ohio, by plane?" Otte countered. The crisis blew over. Like so many players who don't believe they're receiving enough playing time, Knight was ready to bolt. Instead he was bolstered by his natural sense of the absurd, and his awareness that he wasn't as good a player as John Havlicek and the other Ohio State starters. Otte still wants to know if it was Knight who threw Otte's typewriter into the toilet nearly thirty years ago.

"I would have claimed credit by now if it had been me," Knight counters persuasively.

The friendship has continued over the years. When Otte's son developed a passion for West Point, he was entertained there by Knight. Today, his proud father announces, he's a major in the army.

Knight points to Taylor. "He's been all around the world and do you know where he says he had the best strawberry shortcake?" He's prescient, or he knows people, for Taylor has already told me about Knight's grandmother Sarah Henthorne's strawberry shortcake. Yet how could Knight know that?

Knight dispatches the two gentlemen off to a Bloomington steakhouse called Zagreb. "Order the tenderloin!" he demands and proceeds to offer extensive directions, left at the second traffic light, right at the old Southern Indiana courthouse, and it's a block down on the left. Otte and Taylor suppress smiles; they have been here before. Knight walks them upstairs to the door, repeating the instructions. And then, mocking himself with a straight face, he adds, "Unless it's one street further!"

Smiling fondly at the two older men as they leave, Knight says, "I wish we didn't have to win tonight."

In the coaches' locker room before the game, Fred Taylor tests out Knight's new set of golf clubs as if Knight didn't have a care in the world. The talk is of fishing: walleyed pike. "I bet they were three or four pounders." Trying to take his fish off the line, Otte's wife let them fall back in the water. The men laugh. It's not so much that women are not respected; women no less than men would do better not to venture where their competence does not warrant.

When Taylor retired as basketball coach at Ohio State, the ceremonies at his last game at Indiana were far more elaborate, grander than those in Columbus. Knight presented him with the traditional rocking chair. Now Knight recalls his days as a player. One day Taylor put up a sign, "Players Only," at practice to keep out a pesky booster, only for the booster to march right in. A brash Bobby Knight couldn't resist a needle: "Coach, either he can't read or you can't spell." (Was he always like that? I wonder. Well, so it seems.) And Taylor was so mad he didn't even say anything to Knight.

"What kind of steak did you have?" he wants to know. Fred had the tenderloin, Otte the strip. "Was it good?" The presence of these old friends soothes him. Their reunion is interrupted, however, by the entrance of Dick Vitale. "Dick, don't listen to anybody out here. Just talk," Knight advises.

"I want to come one time when you don't bust my chops."

"Then you'll know I don't like you anymore."

Tip-off isn't until 9:38, a fact which infuriates Knight. "If they truly cared about the kids they would play all their games on Friday night and Sunday afternoon."

And then he reveals he knows exactly what will happen in this game with Illinois.

"We can't play when every rebound is a struggle," Knight says quietly, seated in his favorite chair.

Just before tip-off, Quinn Buckner slides into a seat beside his old teammate Steve Ahlfeld.

Attending the game tonight too is Connie Chung, here to interview Knight for a documentary on stress. *Sixty Minutes* had called earlier in the season on behalf of Diane Sawyer, several times, but Knight did not return their calls. He suspected what their approach would be: the pro and the con. In fact, they had called Norm Sloan, the Florida coach, having read that he had attacked Knight. Sloan told them he didn't think they'd find a good coach in the country willing to say anything negative about Bobby. They had called Isiah Thomas too, telling him they understood he didn't have a very good relationship with Coach Knight.

"You want some guys to speak positively and some to speak negatively about Coach Knight and you want me to speak negatively, is that right? Well, I think you have me on the wrong side," Isiah said. and he let Knight know he said so.

That Chung had called herself ("although she doesn't know me from a jar of Vick's"), leaving both her home and office number, that she had answered the phone herself when he returned her call, ensured her the interview. "All these other people get some leg guy who calls. I don't do that. If I want you to do something, I call you," Knight declares.

The Illinois team is strong and big and athletic. They crash the boards; they come up with two or three offensive rebounds every time down. And they move out to a 8–0 lead.

They're a step ahead of Indiana on everything so that it's three and a half minutes into the game before Garrett scores the first Indiana points. When Eyl replaces Garrett, he immediately grabs a rebound, only to lose the ball. And meanwhile if Indiana scores at all, it's only as a result of Jay Edwards' three-pointers.

The game goes exactly as Knight predicted. Nick Anderson scores on conversion twice in a row, while Battle outmuscles Indiana on the boards. Fast and strong, Illinois excels in post play, taking Garrett completely out of the game. Jones replaces Smart, Jadlow replaces Eyl. All Knight can do, short of going out and playing himself, is shuffle his lineup. Nothing works.

Calloway has started this game, and early on Knight takes Keith and Jay aside to say, "Ricky gives us more movement in ten feet than you two have the whole goddamn game, now move!" (But Calloway will have only an average game, scoring thirteen points in thirty-eight minutes of play.)

"That's ridiculous," Knight tells referee Tim Higgins at one point. "He warns a guy not to push and then the call's the other way."

"You've made your point," Higgins says.

The coaching is calm, and measured, intense only where appropriate. "He didn't get up a couple of times where I would have gotten up," Buckner tells me.

Meanwhile, Indiana cannot hold onto the ball. Calloway loses it and Garrett is benched. In a run-down for a loose ball against two of Illinois' best athletes, hustling Joe Hillman, of course, doesn't have a chance. Illinois out-rebounds Indiana 48–26, and with that goes on to win 75–65.

Having won his five hundredth game in this unlikely venue, at the post-game press conference. Lou Henson is gracious: "I never dreamed we could get boards the way we did." Knight too speaks about the rebounding. "Questions?" he asks abruptly after a minute or two. He pauses. "OK," he says and walks out. There hasn't been a single question.

In the morning Connie Chung awaits him all set up on the court of Assembly Hall. "I wish I'd lost forty pounds," Knight says as he strides out to his seat. He is dressed in a nondescript brown sweater, the ubiquitous gray corduroy pants and moccasins, a man who would not stand out in a crowd.

But if personal vanity is alien to him, sharpness of mind is not, not even on this morning when his team is on its way to failing in its new goal of a four-game season. At once Knight attacks Chung's premise, quietly, softly and brilliantly.

The subject of the documentary is stress. But "stress" is not what he feels when he coaches. Stress belongs to people in life and death situations, such as a doctor performing a heart transplant. What *he* feels is pressure, some anxiety and frustration, which can be alleviated by preparation. It is hardly the flamboyant answer television would elicit to sell soapsuds or cars. "What are the stakes here?" he persists, returning to his challenge of Chung's definition of stress. "The NCAA tournament?"

"But what happens when you're yelling at the referee?"

Knight explains that, with seventeen thousand people yelling, you can't say softly, "John, John." It has to be "John goddamnit!" But if he allows himself to officiate, "the rest of the game slides away from me."

But does he feel better? she persists.

"I don't feel any better. I feel he now knows something he should be doing."

Quietly and methodically, he resists every attempt to sensationalize. Does he *ever* feel better? "I only feel better when the whole thing is over and I look back at how our preparation worked in the game." He mentions David Halberstam's book *The Best and the Brightest*, which describes how the Kennedy administration devoted three years to planning for its re-election. "If I coached like that, it would be chaotic."

But does he have headaches, migraines?

"I make the decisions. If they're wrong, I have to figure out how to make them right the next time."

The entire interview is a microcosm of the disparity between the man and how the world perceives him: angry, irrational, out of control, while he talks about how control, analysis and research have led to his success. These ideas, however, do not make for an exciting program. Talk about "preparation" is not what audiences expect of "Bobby Knight."

Chung persists.

"What's happening when you throw a chair, when you take the team off the floor..."

"I didn't," he says quietly. And he is willing even to talk about the chair. "I'm not saying that was a great and thoughtful action. I think it was frustration. Stress would be if I had thrown the chair at someone. I slid the chair away from everyone. It was something I had control over."

He admits to not holding things back. "In a position of leadership, you can't worry about hurting people's feelings."

"So, instead of eating nails for breakfast, you let it all hang out?"

"People who know me feel I have a lot more patience than people think."

"But you intimidate people." And she wants to know if *he* is ever intimidated: "The one thing that intimidates me is intelligence and knowledge...." This important truth about himself, however, is not pursued.

Chung presses forward: "What about your intimidating look?" And so she finally forces him away from any serious exploration of the issue:

"I can't help the way I look! I don't look like Robert Redford!"

In the course of the interview Knight has also used a cliché to describe how, perhaps, he would do better to behave when he becomes the victim of bad officiating: rape's inevitable, so why not relax and enjoy it?

At lunch, Sloppy Joes at the Jiffy Treat, Connie Chung forgotten, he has a test for Quinn Buckner: "Explain Keith Smart to me as a basketball player."

"I don't think I'll play Smart anymore," he decides. (Smart had eight points against Illinois, starting and playing thirty-three minutes.) "And I don't know about Garrett. You know who's the player who understands what we do best? Edwards!"

III

"Where's the newspaper? I've got to have something to read until these guys figure out an answer."

Tuesday, March 1.

Day by day with only three games remaining, he tries to salvage the season.

At Tuesday afternoon practice Knight is in his street clothes. With three games to go in their new four-game season, Indiana is 0–1.

On the board he writes: Garrett, Eyl, Hillman, Smart, and beneath that, 114 minutes, 57 percent, 21 points, 13 rebounds. The 57 percent represents the amount of playing time out of the possible 200 minutes available to all the players that these four used up.

"I just want you to look at that," he tells them. "That's your total for 114 minutes of play, the four of you. I want to know why." He pulls up a chair. He is prepared to wait until they can come up with an answer.

"There were a lot of kids in here that didn't get beat last night," he says quietly, "but you four just got pummeled."

That they have failed their exam is obvious. But this is not a teacher who will simply pass out the atrocious exam papers, having recorded the abysmal grades, and be done with it.

They must account to him and to themselves for their failure.

The four culprits look straight ahead. No one says anything.

"You got absolutely buried in the biggest game that we played all year or that we will play. I've never seen people less ready to play. I've never seen people do less in a game. I've really never seen people get beat worse." ("I thought we were ready to play," Joe Hillman told Quinn Buckner after the game.)

Three of the four, of course, are seniors. Joe Hillman is an academic senior with a year of basketball eligibility remaining. A finance major, he plans to study for a master's degree, an MBA, while he plays next season.

"I looked at the tape last night and I can't pick out one rational thing that you did in the game, Keith. It was as if we picked you up from a schoolyard somewhere, inserted you in the lineup and just told you to play."

Knight speaks softly, as if he were divulging the obvious. But he is not yet ready to let them off the hook. Three games remain. He is not yet ready to give up on them. He owes that to them, however human it might be to indulge in thoughts of the new recruits coming next season, or how dramatically redshirted Mark Robinson has improved.

"I want to know why. I'm prepared to sit here all afternoon. It doesn't make any difference to me. It was a game that means the whole season to us, and you four people let somebody come in here in a big game we're playing at home and just pound us. You hid the whole game, Dean. You never once flashed to get the ball, never moved once to get up into the lane."

He folds his arms. "Where's the newspaper? I've got to have something to read until these guys figure out an answer."

The only sound in the room is the ventilating system and the pages of the newspaper now slowly turning. No one stirs. On the wall the photographs of the Ohio State players, their next opponent, stare down at them.

He looks up. "Well, what are we going to do?"

Still no one speaks. As they can't realize what they did, so they lacked the superior basketball intelligence necessary to combat the unrelenting brawn of Illinois. The team is sent out onto the floor, minus the silent four, who must remain in the locker room to think. Practice begins. Teaching begins.

"Lyndon, what you've got to do is come in hard. Good plays don't just happen. You see them. You create them. You make them happen." Knight is quiet, patient. He tells Kreigh to stop and make himself available. Mark has faked himself into a bad shot. He criticizes Magnus for not practicing what he *doesn't* yet know how to do well.

Knight moves over to the free throw line and, as he talks to them, makes one free throw after another, a dazzling performance. "I can stand here all night making free throws but what good would it do me?" The lesson today is in what isn't enough. "Let's have a purpose to everything we do."

There are hints of preparation for the coming season. Mark Robinson is told to "dunk it as often as you can and let him foul you." Lyndon is told: "You've heard that possession is nine-tenths of the law. In basketball it's position. I don't have wings, but I have feet." Lyndon and Mark, part of the future: "You're dribbling while Mark is open," he tells Jones. "We missed one cutter after another last night."

But the defeat rankles. Keith Smart, who dribbled right into two defenders in the middle last night, made "the most ridiculous play I've ever seen in college basketball"; Smart came down the floor and picked up someone to defend who had already been picked up by someone else! "We need Calloway to score some points," he thinks. "I just don't know if he can. He's three years into playing; he should weigh 205 and be a lot stronger, but he isn't."

Wednesday, March 2.

Knight walks purposefully into their locker room. "I'm going to get some players. It's never going to happen again. Calloway, you lose the ball seven times when it's in your hands. Seven times it's jarred out of your hands. There isn't one of you who could jar the ball out of my hands and I'm forty-seven years old." He looks at Calloway, who alone had five turnovers against Illinois. "I don't know if anybody has come in and looked at the tape. I'm going to get me some players that are going to come in here and work at playing, that are going to lift weights to get better, that don't have to be pushed and shoved and kicked in the ass every time we turn around. If you people want to play like you just want to finish out the season, that's how we'll coach. Four corners!"

Out on the floor, he's exasperated. "I've coached five years before you were born," he tells Magnus and Brian, "and here's a guy that doesn't pay any attention to what you want [four passes]. What would you do?"

"Isn't coaching a lot of fun?" he asks me as he passes the scorer's table.

And then it's back to fundamentals. "Good cut, Ricky," he calls. "Now Ricky was wide open, but Brian didn't make the pass because he had the ball over his head instead of going around him for a bounce pass."

"How many buckets does Garrett have?" he calls to the managers keeping score. He's one for four with two rebounds. "I have managers who could have scored more," Knight snarls.

If we had won that game against Illinois, he agonizes, we would have had a pretty good season. He still believes Hillman would have made the ideal team leader, although he will acknowledge that players will respond only to superior ability among each other. Smart? He couldn't lead because "he couldn't control himself."

Today Knight has found a job for Winston Morgan, a former player back from two years of basketball in Argentina, with a chemical company in Indianapolis owned by a friend, Ames Shuel. He has not forgotten the night he had told Morgan he had no room for him on the team only for Morgan to transcend his own pain sufficiently to congratulate Jimmy Crews on landing the head coaching job at Evansville. Knight muses over what they learn here. Not one former student whom he has gotten a job has ever been fired. After being with him, they are not afraid of difficulty, of hard work, of competing.

"I don't think I can afford to bench Garrett," Knight murmurs. "I am going to bench Smart. Do you know who the best player is?"

Edwards?

"Yes, Edwards," he says impatiently, a man with no time for the obvious. "But Mark Robinson is really going to be a good player. He wants to learn."

And still the Illinois game rankles. At 54–57, if only Garrett had made that play. . . .

Then he's off to watch Patrick play basketball, an agonizing experience because he cares too much. "It's hard for me to watch him play. I get too upset."

Thursday, March 3.

Indiana and Ohio State are now tied for fifth place in the Big Ten, competing for the last open spot in the NCAA tournament, since six conference teams will surely not be chosen.

"Joe, we're never going to confuse you with Magic Johnson," he calls out.

After practice, Patrick is weighed and measured: 6'4¾" tall, 182 pounds.

And a new thought takes over that will not leave Knight until the season ends. He wants Keith Smart to have a strong finish. Could things have been different? Maybe, he even wonders, it shouldn't have been Smart who made the game-winning shot against Syracuse in the 1987 NCAA championship game, but Steve Alford. It put too much pressure on Smart. He tries to analyze the incredulous look that comes over Smart's face when the ball is stripped from him. Is he mad at himself, or is he surprised because he doesn't know the game well enough?

"Yes," he says sadly, "but I want him to have a strong finish."

Friday, March 4.

His eyes fixed on a tape of Ohio State, Knight is on the telephone in search of former player John Ritter's telephone number. "I've got some people lined up to help him." As soon as he's off, Tom Abernethy calls with an offer of another job for Winston Morgan. That they should be taking care of each other gratifies him. He produces a long list of telephone calls since February 24 from people in the media that he has not returned. They range from newspapers to television and radio stations everywhere. Tim Garl enters to suggest teams for the 1993 Hoosier Classic: Texas Christian, Western Kentucky and Princeton. "That would be great," he approves.

Fred Taylor arrives, inspiring more stories of Knight's high school days in Orrville with his baseball coach Bill Shunkwiler. It's as if only keeping the past alive makes the present tolerable.

Shunkwiler would allow you only four pitches, not four

swings, he remembers. And he'd stand back there and yell, "Get him out of there, that's it!"

"One day I was a junior and he had a kid pitching, a football player that I didn't like anyhow. I stand up there and I get four pitches and that is it. 'Get out of there, goddammit, you don't get any more pitches than anybody else.'

"So I slam the bat down and I walk away. It was cold and windy, the wind is blowing like hell, and I say, 'Well, if the son of a bitch could pitch . . .'

"And the wind just stops so you could hear me all over the park. Shunkwiler started throwing baseballs at me, he just started and I ran and he ran me right back to the high school. I can still see him standing throwing baseballs at me, running down the path. So I go up to the gym and I start shooting baskets. And he came in and played twenty-one with me and he never said one word."

His tone softens, turns gentle. "He was a really good coach. I was at Ohio State before I ever beat him at twenty-one. He's working for Gil Brandt of the Dallas Cowboys now." (Brandt is one of several men in sports other than basketball whom Knight admires.)

The telephone rings constantly. To one of his callers he confides, "At this point in time it matters not what you think, but just that we get the thing over with." That he must coach a team unreliable on defense is alien to him, painful, preposterous.

When the team enters, they are given photocopied clippings of their Illinois loss. "Why weren't *we* hungry?" he demands. "We're playing for the same thing they're playing for." He reads: Garrett "doesn't like the contact." His tone is scathing. Indiana "found itself overwhelmed in the category of intensity."

He faces them, furious: "We've played like good players and we've played like poor players. Which are we? What are we? Who are we? Where are we? It's running out. We have three games left to show who we are and what we are and this year's team will be in the book. And some of you will be more responsible for this year's team than you were for last year's team. [Calloway again, Calloway who was needed this year so much more than last.] Two different books and two different teams. But there's still time to write a good concluding chapter. That's up to you people!"

And so he coaches to the end a team without cohesion, without leaders, a team without a point guard, a team without forwards so that he's forced to play Hillman and Smart inside a lot of the time, a team without a ball handler who makes it his business not to turn over the ball, a team without players whose satisfaction may come from the unglamorous role of handing out assists.

In the stands at practice today is an invited crowd of donors to Knight's special library fund for which in the most recent drive he has raised nearly three hundred thousand dollars. They have come to present him with a little plaque. Trooping in from one of the balcony doors, on tiptoe, they have been warned to be silent. Professors, local businessmen and their wives, a diffident group compared to those down on the floor, they sit like stones in a little cluster, as if huddled together for comfort, waiting for the moment when he will join them for the little presentation.

But Knight ignores them, totally absorbed as he is in coaching his team to a finish they can remember with dignity. It is Fred Taylor he talks to, Taylor sitting at the scorer's table preparing for his television commentary.

"You said the only thing I could do is shoot," he says, putting his arm around Taylor's neck. "But I could get the ball to people."

He sits down and watches his team take free throws. "They just don't look."

"I think the potentially best player is number 10 [Mark Robinson]," he tells Taylor. "I'd like to play Magnus, but he gets us into so much trouble." He wants Calloway to be a third ball handler against the press. (Unbeknownst to him, Magnus has signed up with Pete Newell's summer camp for pros; he wants to give it one more chance; he wants to improve; he wants to play.)

Up to the scorer's table now marches . . . a cowboy, complete with white Stetson, a weatherbeaten, bowlegged man of about sixty.

"Do you think it's going to rain?" Knight asks his Montana hunting and fishing companion Jim Galt, who sits down to chat with Fred Taylor while Knight returns to the team. A moment later, Joby Wright comes over to ask Galt to please be quiet. Then the coach himself reappears.

"This is the first time Galt has ever seen a black guy, let alone talk to one!"

He turns to Fred Taylor:

"Well, coach, are they any better than Monday night?"

And there is still another visitor, a burly, quiet man named Gary Eiber, who played for Knight when he taught that season at Cuyahoga Falls High School. Eiber couldn't catch the ball. "You couldn't catch Marilyn Monroe in a telephone booth," his twenty-two-year-old coach told him. And Knight proceeded to blast one basketball after another at him, and he couldn't duck and had to catch them, and it hurt whether he caught them or not.

A few years later Knight recruited him at West Point, where he was in Mike Krzyzewski's class. One night Gary was hit in the eye during a game, but Knight told him, "It serves you right, you shouldn't be behind your man like that." And once when Eiber came up to Knight, who was talking to a major, Knight turned to him and said, "Didn't you forget something. This is Major——You're supposed to salute."

"Oh, don't bother," said the major.

But Eiber's arm was already going up and of course the major saluted back. Eiber resurrects: the twenty-two-year-old high school coach taking his team out for hamburgers after sending them door to door to collect money for the team, and correcting them in the proper form of introducing themselves to their elders.

IV

"If you're waiting on me to pull out a miracle, I'm all out."

Saturday, March 5.

Saturday morning, the day of the Ohio State game, and Knight is delighted with Patrick's play in his sectional against Martinsville. He scored sixteen points, rebounded well and handled the ball well.

"We can't have watchers," he tells the Indiana team, which assembles at 9:40. "We have to have five people rebounding. Getting beat on the boards cost us the game Monday night. The thing is going on like a battle and you're standing with

the best seat in the house and you're a spectator, not a partici-
pant." This time they better fight for loose balls.

His voice rises. "I don't want to lose a goddamn possession
out here today." Now he is at the top of his lungs. "If you
don't understand that, don't come to play! I don't want to get
our ass whipped one more time!" His voice grows still louder,
reaches its absolute top pitch: "I don't want to see one guy
stand while a post man moves under him instead of coming
right in on him. I don't want to see that once!"

How could they not want what he wants? "I want to win
this ball game!"

As they prepare always, so do they now: Burson, the short
white Ohio State shooter, prefers to go to his right. Francis
"will exhaust every move known to man to get the shot off."
Knight warns them, as always. "They're going to be competitive. They're going to be cocky coming in here to play. . . .
When we start well, good things happen. When we get behind
11–2, it's a long time trying to catch up." Endlessly he repeats the same things, in the hope of reaching them. "Boys,
individually you've got to give it everything you have, mentally and physically."

Again he appeals to their sense of fair play, to what they
owe him as well as the other coaches, to what they owe themselves. "If we can't get our best effort after what happened on
Monday, I don't know where to go, boys.

"If you're waiting on me to pull out a miracle, I'm all out.
What I'm waiting on is for you people to play like you're
capable of playing for forty minutes. I'm waiting on that."

At pre-game meal this ten-thirty A.M., a message awaits
each of them at his place. "Play like champions!" He usually
doesn't eat with the players, but this time he has joined them
for spaghetti with meat sauce and vanilla ice cream. His address is: "There isn't anything we have to do that we aren't
capable of doing. We've played a lot of basketball that's good
enough to beat anybody—individually and collectively. It's
just a matter of playing that kind of basketball. That's your
responsibility. You're good enough to beat anybody, but you
have to play that way and you have to think that way.

"You can win," he tells them. "You can do well." Achievement lies within their grasp.

After a brief nap in the coaches' locker room, he's in the
stands in his stocking feet discussing Big Ten officiating with

Ohio State coach Gary Williams. There ought to be a summer camp for referees, they agree. The referees ought to be accountable for their errors. He illustrates a play he noticed on the tape of Ohio State's game against Minnesota. A few people surreptitiously take his photograph. Otherwise he blends into the steadily filling stands, almost unnoticed.

Tates Locke has donned a pair of outlandish plaid trousers, almost as garish as Knight's old plaid jackets. Knight sits back in his armchair, raises an eyebrow: "He won with them once."

The starters are Calloway, Hillman, Garrett, Edwards and Jones. He does not start Smart. Indiana begins weakly: hands that don't hold onto the ball cost rebounds, with Garrett an offender. Hillman, alert, struggles with great intensity for every rebound. But Calloway has trouble with the Ohio State press and is called for a five-second violation. Meanwhile Ohio State has roared out, absorbing the lesson of the Illinois game. They play rough, testing Indiana, believing Indiana will not retaliate. Unfortunately, Ohio State begins to pick up fouls in the process.

At half time, with the score 39–35 in favor of Indiana, scholar athletes in each sport are honored. His A–average earns Magnus Pelkowski the award for basketball, while Joe Hillman wins for baseball. Each student has been asked to invite his favorite professor to a luncheon, and Magnus has chosen his professor of German literature in a 400 level course. But Hillman and Pelkowski must be praised in absentia. They are in the locker room being told by their coach that the next twenty minutes will determine the turning point of the season, that if they want to go on at all, they must win this game. A hopeful sign is that Indiana is leading Ohio State in rebounding 26–14.

Neither Garrett nor Smart start the second half. Jadlow does start, having earned the right by fierce play in the first half. Not being able to exert good pressure, they have few steals (Illinois had ten to their two), but they did shut down Burson in the first half: he had only six points.

Jadlow puts them up 57–52 and then Garrett misses a pass, and has the ball stripped from him. "Read the defense," Knight yells. "Triangle!" Jay is called over to the sidelines. "Get away from White, Jay, so he can't bump you on that screen."

It's only in the last two minutes that they solidify their lead. Having managed only three of twelve field goal attempts, Jay Edwards puts on a clinic in free throw shooting, going twelve for twelve, cool and calm, revealing the presence that will place him on the AP's all-freshman team along with Mark Macon, Kenny Miller, Livingston Chatman and Dennis Scott. As Indiana wins 85–77, Knight shakes hands with Ohio State player Jerry Francis, whom he thought had played well in the game.

Have the guards rebounded, as Knight had demanded they should? Hillman has had seven, but Smart and Edwards only three each, and Jones and Calloway, who played seventeen minutes, two. Calloway has scored only three points. Garrett has had seventeen points; Knight excuses his less-than-dazzling performance on the grounds of a lingering flu. Smart is "up and down," making, as usual, some good plays and some bad ones. He did draw one charging foul and one they called a block. "It's been a roller coaster for us," Knight says. Jadlow, who came in off the bench, gave the team a lift. And Hillman, less reluctant to shoot than usual, has gone four for seven.

The press leaves the students' locker room, having crowded around Jadlow and Edwards, ignoring the others, a cruel display repeated game after game, and up go the Minnesota clippings and photographs.

"You did a hell of a job here in the second half," Knight tells his team. "They're a pretty good basketball team, pretty good players who came to play. We wouldn't be easy to beat if we played like this all the time."

It's six P.M. There's still time to drive to the Seymour High School gym to watch the sectional finals where Bedford North Lawrence will play Seymour. Knight sits high above the crowd on a chair catercornered over the wildly cheering crowd of eighty-one hundred, a totally white crowd which cheers frantically at every possession.

He talks about two things: first, Damon Bailey, his discovery, a baby-faced fifteen-year-old, who wipes his hands on his sneakers like Larry Bird, scores magically both inside and out, fights for rebounds and blends in with his team. Bailey, still a sophomore, still only six foot three inches tall, may in two years drive down the road to play at Indiana. Tonight, Damon Bailey scores forty-seven points; on the road to the state finals, he will score in another game—fifty-three. But

Knight thinks also of Jay Edwards who, despite his cool demeanor, "has more heart than you think."

At ten P.M., it's chili and chicken with noodles at Bob Evans, and tea laced with lemonade. He grills Jim Galt, still wearing his cowboy hat, about next summer's Montana fishing prospects. In the car, he sings a song about Jesus wearing a Rolex while he saved souls, a satire on the television preachers, as he drives out of Southwest Indiana. This, he confirms, has been one of the last bastions of the Ku Klux Klan.

Sunday, March 6.

Parade magazine lists its All-America high school basketball team, and there on the fourth team is Damon Bailey. Knight returns from very early spring fishing. As he scrutinizes a golf tournament on television, I remark, if Damon and his team had enlisted all that intensity, intelligence and concentration, they could cure the ills of this planet, cancer, world peace, the homeless. It's one more facet of that down side of the Hoosier obsession with high school basketball.

"I think they'd settle for the regional championship," says the man with no illusions.

The team arrives. They've played five months and now only two games remain, one on the road against Minnesota and the last at home against Iowa: "It's going to all boil down to eighty minutes of basketball that we play this week. And every minute that everybody plays has got to be a good minute. Let's just make that our objective for the entire week. Let's make up your minds that you're not going to have a bad possession, that you're not going to have a thoughtless play, that we're going to have four hundred minutes of good individual basketball this week. That's really all I want to tell you." Then softly, he concludes: "OK. See you tomorrow."

V

"I've never felt worse for a kid than I feel for Smart."

A week remains, two more games, and he is still viewing the Wisconsin tape of February 24. Although Indiana won

84–74, at one point five straight Indiana turnovers and a few three-pointers for Wisconsin took the lead down to 73–70. Knight gets home from the movies only to watch the entire Wisconsin game one more time to see if there were things Smart did positively. Afterward, he thinks, I don't see how we won this game with Keith making all the mistakes he makes. Either he can't discipline himself, or he doesn't think quickly enough.

The next morning, Knight asks Dan Dakich to view the tape purely from the point of view of how Smart played.

"Don't watch anybody but him."

A few hours later Dakich reports back.

"He just gets lost. At the end he made four plays that very easily could have cost us the game."

In the coaches' locker room Knight illustrates the one play in that game that obsesses him: "We're trying to force the ball to the corner. Here's the man with the basketball and his first move is to the corner. Smart's guarding him and instead of keeping the ball going in the same direction, he tried to take away the direction we wanted him going in in the first place. He actually shuts that off. And now we've got three to block out four!"

Last year would have been the right moment for Smart to graduate, he thinks. "I just hate to see the kid wind up not having the kind of year that I envisioned he would have." Realistically, he concludes, "He'd be much better off playing in Oklahoma and I feel awful right now because he isn't suited to the way we're playing."

Keith Smart reflects upon that moment in the Wisconsin game when he moved ahead of that player heading for the corner:

> *"Sometimes I rely on anticipating where a player will go. He may seem to be setting up to go this way and pop back the other way. I'm thinking, 'Maybe I can make him think I'm going that way, and he'll go back the way I want him to go.' He reacts one way and I go the other way and the whole play is dead. But if he reacts the way I'm thinking, it's a great play!"*
>
> *Resilient, intelligent, realistic, Smart admits that he*

hasn't worked with Knight long enough. "If I could get two more years here, I would love it. You need one year to learn things and the next year you're more comfortable with the system. If I could have started the year again, I don't know if I could have been the leader the team needed, but I would have tried. I never thought of myself as a guy people looked up to. If I had one more year, I would be able to make up for all that."

Meanwhile, with only two games remaining in the regular season, Knight wants Smart to have a brave finish. Watching tapes in the coach's locker room, he examines his team as he does every day and concludes he has "a lot of hunters. But we don't have any warriors." He has also "a bunch of guys out there who are in their fourth year and can't play at this level and they've had opportunity after opportunity to have demonstrated it." Calloway, however, is improving. He's "finally putting forth an effort which he should have been doing since October 15. But he wouldn't listen, didn't listen, didn't comprehend. Now it's almost midnight."

Monday, March 7, final week of the season.

Today there's a team meeting rather than practice. At this point of the season the practices are short, no more than an hour and fifteen minutes. "To save our legs," Joe Hillman explains. They view Minnesota's offense on tape, commentary by Ron Felling, then go out on the floor in their street clothes for a walk-through led by Julio Salazar.

In his last words of the afternoon Knight says he has heard (from Tates Locke, although he does not tell them this) that some of them have been running around late. Now he does something rare for him: he imposes a nine o'clock curfew. "If I call or someone comes by after nine and you're not there, you won't play. I've heard of guys running out all kinds of hours. That isn't how we run basketball here." He's been told that whenever anything is going on on campus, Calloway is there.

The curfew is a measure of how desperately he wants the season to end well and how uncertain he is about this team. The motivation for the Knight player has always been expected to come from within. But this has not been a typical

Knight team. And even after their last game he will not stop searching for the reasons.

Tuesday, March 8.

"Let's set a tempo for our play for the week in what we do today," he tells them. "We've got our whole season riding on how we play this week."

Never does he forget how much he wants Smart to finish well. "Get Keith open and Magnus back pick for Keith," he calls. "Get set for the shot down there," he tells Keith. When Joe doesn't see Keith open, he's yelled at.

"Joby, was Keith open?"

"Wide open," Joby says.

Keith plays inside and outside both, as Knight looks for opportunities for this player to excel.

After practice, Smart reveals how surprised he was that Knight devoted so much of the practice to his offense, his surprise a measure of how the Knight players seem to understand him only in retrospect: "Today when he put me on the court and every play was Keith do this and Keith do that, I couldn't believe it! What I take away from here is knowing that if one day goes rough, another day will bring a smile. Coach would get on me, but a couple of days later, or the same day, or ten minutes later, he'd say, 'Great play, Keith!' I wouldn't trade places with anyone. I love it here."

Brian Sloan, with his double major in English and history, walks by, his Chaucer under his arm. He is a fine student despite his agonies with Spanish (he was put in Spanish honors by mistake). Like Magnus, he could graduate. Obviously not the best players, with no guarantees about playing time, nonetheless they choose to remain to complete their final year of eligibility because they too want to be here.

Tuesday, 6:00 P.M.

Patrick arrives for extra practice.

"Do you have a tape of the game against South?" his father wants to know. On Saturday, South defeated Patrick's school, North, for the sectional championship. The tension of watching Patrick play prevented his father from attending the game. South's leading scorer was Chris Lawson, whose thirty-two points, however, did not prevent North's almost winning at the buzzer.

Wednesday, March 9.

Former Knight assistant Royce Waltman, now a head coach himself, at DePauw, drops in. I am introduced.

"This is this year's Feinstein."

By now I should be accustomed to the needles, but I'm not. I wince, and can't manage a word for Waltman.

"We've got three days left," Knight tells his team, "Thursday, Friday and Saturday, and there isn't going to be an easy minute out of the eighty."

At Monroe County airport, they depart the bus onto the tarmac while he remains in the traditional head coach's right-hand front seat. He gives them each a pat on the back. Jay is complimented on his haircut, which looks more as if he's shaved his head. Jay can't resist a smile as soon as he thinks he's out of Knight's view.

On the plane Knight reads *Golf World* and passes around to players and coaches alike a big tin of homemade cookies and brownies. "These are really good," he says. Throughout the flight he's obsessed because he can't remember the title of a self-help book. Was it by the author of *The Peter Principle?* I ask.

"Don't talk! Think!" he orders me.

The plane is met out on the runway by "Jake," a favorite driver who's a Civil War buff and who presents Knight with a book about the Civil War each year as the team plays its road game with Minnesota. Today it's *Great Battles of the Civil War*. Jake announces that he has named his new cats Jeb (a gray) and Beaufort (a black).

On the way to dinner Knight jumps out of the car and rushes into a bookstore, emerging with the title which perplexed him. It's *Winning by Intimidation*.

Dinner is at Vescio's in Dinkytown near the university, an Italian restaurant of New York's Little Italy quality and then some. Knight and a long table of coaches, sportswriters, and two executives from Northwest Orient airlines are fed a banquet fit for Mafia dons. Sid Hartman, an old friend from the Minneapolis *Star and Tribune*, is there, along with John Gutekunst, the football coach of the University of Minnesota, and Jerry Burns, the Minnesota Vikings coach. Football coaches obviously are sitting targets for the Knight needle: who was at the bottom of Watergate? A football coach!

Could Lombardi coach today? Burns thinks he would have made the necessary adjustments. Knight is not so sure. The Northwest Orient president is a tourist here, wanting to know how being at Army influenced Knight's coaching. He solicits the obvious, only, obviously, to be disappointed. At Cuyahoga Falls high school Knight "blistered" the fifteen-year-olds at halftime. And they won. The next time he talked to them quietly and they went down 45–40. Knight *always* knew coaches had to be aggressive.

Corruption in coaching: the stories include one about a coach who fed his starters steak and the subs hamburger and pocketed the difference. Leadership? Black players respect ability. Talent? You need superior thinking more than athletic prowess. Coaching salaries? How much has your salary risen since 1970, Knight demands to know from the president of Northwest Orient airlines. His has increased twenty times. He was offered a job by Ohio State, but told them they would have to raise Woody Hayes' salary first. He refused to be paid more than the legendary football coach, who not only went home with a pittance, but never asked for a raise. There is neither self-consciousness about how Hayes' career ended nor so much as a reference to it. Glib comparisons to the contrary, however, it seems inconceivable that Knight could ever strike a student, as Hayes did.

Seated at the far end of the long table away from Knight, Tates Locke turns to Ron Felling: "Read my lips," he says. "I'm having a hard time." Then without a word Locke gets up and slips off into the night.

As for the food, it's out of Fellini: garlic bread spread with melted mozzarella, mounded hot and cold salads laced with hot sausage and red peppers, delicate many-flavored pizzas in long pans, and then the main courses, shrimp and broccoli over linguine, breaded chicken with peppers and spaghetti, flank steak roll-ups with cheese inside and a dab of fresh tomato sauce on top. Everyone eats a lot. The coaches drink beer, Knight, iced tea.

"What's that?" Knight calls down the table, spying the turtle pie, ice cream layered with caramel set in a chocolate nut crust.

In his suite the team awaits him.

"We're down to seventy-two hours," he tells them. "That's going to determine the whole outcome of the season for us. We have our fate in our own hands. We don't have to rely on anyone else to do anything. To borrow an old phrase, 'We are the masters of our fate.' People right in this room will determine what happens to Indiana."

What they talked about on October 15 is just as true today. "We've got to play hard and we've got to play smart." The opponent is never underestimated. Coffey is tough-minded; Burton, a fiery little shooter, is a hell of a player.

The Minnesota team has given everyone they've played real problems, Knight says. The Indiana players are not permitted to believe they are dealing with one of the sisters of the poor, although in fact Minnesota is hardly at the top of the Big Ten, coming into this game ten and sixteen overall, eight and seven at home and two and nine on the road.

After his players have gone to bed, Knight contemplates Indiana's tournament chances. He compares Ohio State's record with Indiana's, knowing that tonight Ohio State has defeated Purdue. He wonders where they are with Sagarin's computer ratings. Where would we be if we win these two games?

Ron Felling goes around to check on the players, but it isn't necessary; the Monday night curfew was unnecessary too.

At breakfast, Knight talks to them again about the opponent: Gaffney, Coffey, Hanson, Burton. He reads a clipping: "They hope to have effected a nothing-to-lose atmosphere." The players look up over their pancakes, eggs, sausages, potatoes, orange juice and milk, only to hear a lesson culled from last night's basketball. "Purdue goes into Ohio State, there is no way Ohio State can beat Purdue, none. What you had was a great inequity in attitude. Attitude can carry us a long way or it can keep us from going somewhere. This game tonight's going to be determined on that. OK. Ready to go?"

On the way to practice, the bus crosses a trickle of a river. He wants to bet me that it's the Mississippi. My sense of geography utterly deserts me. Could the Mississippi run this far north?

I bet him ten dollars, as much to test whether he would bluff as to stand behind something I know. Of course he wins. I pass him the ten dollars (he's sitting directly in front of me). But he adamantly refuses to take it and tosses it back to me.

"It would be like taking candy from a baby," he says.

Post-pre-game meal walk-through takes place in a mirror-lined mini-basketball court, part of the hotel's health club. They line up against the wall, Dean in his white jacket, Lyndon elegant in double-breasted gray, Magnus and Joe in college tweeds. Help and recover. Match-ups once more repeated. "Don't let Maxey or Shikenjanski get away from us," Knight adds presciently.

Williams Arena is the oldest in the Big Ten. Built in 1928, it still features the raised court, so that the players must go up a little flight of stairs to get from the bench to the floor. The benches are old wood, painted purple and yellow. Inside the scent of popcorn is so pervasive that, like Proust's madeleine, it calls up childhood memories, of the circus.

"Let's go red!" says Joe Hillman. "Right from the start. Right from the start." Off they race up onto the floor, the starters Garrett and Jadlow, rewarded for his effort against Ohio State, Jay, Keith and Lyndon. It's that team that must win on offense, the higher the score the better for Indiana. It will be another night for the freshman Jay Edwards, cool, oblivious to pressure and deadly accurate from three-point range. Jadlow begins with two quick rebounds while Smart, missing his shot, loses the ball.

As Jadlow grabs rebounds three and four, it's as if he were remembering his coach's words: "I would have been happy with you, I wasn't looking for anyone else." Jadlow makes two free throws.

Otherwise they are predictably themselves: Garrett has trouble catching the ball and trouble anticipating where a rebound will come down. Smart doesn't screen. Eyl is sent in with the command: "Let's get some strength." Soon he will be replaced by Jadlow. And all the while Knight keeps teaching: "Dean, work higher. Don't let him pin you against the baseline."

A 37–31 lead at the half ensures them nothing. What

Knight feared now comes to pass. Having scored eight points in the first half, Jim Shikenjanski does indeed "get away from them," keeping Minnesota in the game. They're learning as they play once more. Lyndon is no match for Gaffney, and Knight brings the whole team up higher so that they've got the baseline to work with. Calloway goes in, but is reluctant to shoot, even when the shot is clearly his to take.

Meanwhile, the sophomore Shikenjanski, fierce and scrappy, begins to pour in the baskets, as if he were taking the opportunity tonight to prove that slow white kids can be basketball players too. And, having scored only three points in the first half, Burton wakes up to score eleven in the second.

But by 7.37 Jay Edwards has accumulated thirty-two points, while Burton picks up his third and then his fourth fouls. Unable to contest for the ball, weak as Knight angrily said he unnecessarily was, Calloway picks up three fouls too.

In the huddle, they're told: "Your whole season boils down to four and one quarter minutes." Victory is still not certain as Shikenjanski keeps answering, no matter that his previous career high was twelve points. (He'll wind up with 26 points). At 3.09 Willie Burton picks up his fifth personal.

In the huddle again at 1.46 with the score 86–76 in Indiana's favor, it's "Don't leave your feet and get around Shikenjanski! I want everybody blocked out!"

"For the season!" says Dean Garrett as they go back out. "For the season, let's go!"

At 87–80 with 1.01 to go, Steve Eyl is shooting one plus one. "Be a senior, Steve!" Knight whispers. Eyl makes the front end. Knight winces as he misses the bonus.

Smart makes six of eight free throws in the final minute and a half of play, going twelve for fourteen for the game and having made his first nine to set a Big Ten record of thirty-seven straight free throws. He has had a splendid game, beginning the finish his coach so desperately wants for him. In thirty-four minutes, he has scored twenty-four points.

Jay has scored eight three-pointers to break a Big Ten record of seven held by Steve Alford. Indiana has turned the ball over only nine times. The final score: 91–85. And through it all he's aware that I'm sitting right behind the bench: "The next best place to being next to me on the Indiana bench," he'll say the next day.

On the plane back after the game he eats a banana and

reads *Pentagon* by Allen Drury. At one in the morning, the plane taxies down the mini-runway at Monroe County airport. A man is there not to speak to him, but simply to greet the team in silent approbation: it's a weatherbeaten man in late middle age named Charlie Deckard.

Once a service station man and a rather wild town character, and now a tree-trimmer, Deckard met Knight sixteen years ago. A friendship bloomed. Once a month Deckard wrote to Hazel Knight; he had visited her three weeks before her death. Of course he attended the funeral. A Pentecostal Christian, Deckard's religion forbids him from attending the games or even watching them on television: the attendant worldliness is alien to the spirit of his beliefs. But for every departure and every arrival as the team journeys back from the road, he is there, a long figure in the darkness.

Outside Assembly Hall, another solitary figure greets the Indiana team. It's redshirted Mark Robinson. How did he know he was expected to be here? "No one told me," he whispers, "but I knew what happened to Steve." Alford is already a legend among them, as Quinn Buckner became to the classes that followed his. Robinson recalls Alford appearing even when, having been suspended for a game by the NCAA, he would not be traveling with the team.

Their uniforms deposited in the locker room, the team assembles in the lounge to wait for him. By now it's nearly two. "You make damn sure you're in class in the morning," he tells them. "We have one more forty minutes. One more. One more."

And they disappear into the night.

Will he be sad on Saturday when, after the Iowa game, the seniors say their farewells?

The answer is gruff: "I'll be in the locker room drinking a Coke!" There's a clue in that: he *never* drinks Coke, believing it's worse than cigarettes!

VI

"I want to see these three guys go out of here winning tomorrow."

Friday, March 11.
   Good screens, good cuts, squaring up and taking the ball to

the bucket—the lessons sound as if they belong to October and not to March. "They don't have anybody that can guard Keith," he announces. "If you'll work to get Keith open, you can cause so many problems for these people."

Iowa is assessed: they are a very good team offensively. But open court play, driving to the basket, exactly what Indiana, what Smart does well, will be effective against Iowa.

"I don't want happpenstance," Knight tells them. "Think it out." The tapes help. "Most of what they got out of us was in conversion," he reminds them of that 84–70 loss on January 6 to Iowa which began their Big Ten season.

Danny narrates as the film rolls. "Why don't we do that?" he asks them. Then he has to laugh. "Because it's Daryl!" They've been watching a highlight from one of last season's games!

Listening in the students' locker room is Robert Quay Norris, Knight's high school principal, in Bloomington from Orrville for the weekend with his wife.

Watching from the scorer's table is former Celtic player and coach, Tommy Heinsohn, in town to do the game for CBS. "I've known him since 1962," Heinsohn says proudly. Knight joins him to help with his broadcast. "I rarely use superlatives," he says, referring to Jay Edwards. But, he adds, "No one here can be a partial student and a complete basketball player." He compares Jay to Mike Woodson. After Knight is gone, Heinsohn explains to a young assistant: "This is the way they're gonna beat the press."

Locker room instruction focuses indeed on the Iowa press. On the whiteboard Knight outlines the cuts he wants, and who is to be in every position. In these last two days he sums up their season. "Last year was not full of thirty-four easy games," he reminds them. "You're being driven and demands are being placed on you." He is fully conscious of Calloway's pain at having been benched, Calloway who did not come back to make the kind of spectacular plays Keith Smart did.

"Guys get benched. That's the way basketball has been here and will always be here. When you overcome what you've been benched for, then you play. This season had some rough spots because of that and now we're down to the last game."

His primary focus of course is not Calloway, who will play

only one minute against Iowa, but on those who are playing their last game at Assembly Hall.

"We've got three seniors. And I've been on Smart's ass and I've been on Garrett's ass and I've been on Eyl's ass. But I've been on the ass of everybody who's ever been a senior here before them, all the names on those lockers and they all went out of here pretty damn good people. I want to see these three guys go out of here winning tomorrow and a lot of it will depend on you three people yourselves."

Nor, despite going two and one in their four-game season and nine and three in their thirteen-game season, are they out of the woods as far as the NCAA tournament is concerned. A bid is still not certain. But the tournament is not their purpose; their goal is "for a team that didn't do some things and individuals that didn't do some things they should have been doing to come back." They have a chance to go ten and three in their thirteen-game season, "which is remarkable."

The game is at four in the afternoon "and we just don't have anything left after the game tomorrow."

A word remains for Eyl, Garrett and Smart. Without sentimentality, he tries to explain to them what their experience at Indiana has meant. "You three guys have done a lot for basketball here, but I think basketball has done, just as it has done for everybody that's ever been in here, far more for you three than you've done for it. I have and the coaches have a great appreciation for your having been a part of what we're doing here." He is telling them, he is not leaving it to chance for them to know: he appreciates them.

He wants only one more thing: that they take advantage of their opportunities to create "a hell of a memory for the three of you tomorrow."

After a six-thirty meeting they're sent home; "Whatever you've got planned for tonight, cancel. Let's get home and get to bed." They look exhausted; they yawn. They're young, but the late return from Minnesota last night has worn them out. Lyndon's head droops. Jeff Oliphant rubs his eyes. Jay leans against the side of his locker.

"Who's yawning?" I ask Magnus Pelkowski.

"Everybody," he laughs.

And still the coach is explaining: "Any time the ball is on top, his pass is across."

"Let's really be proud of what we do tomorrow!"

* * *

Saturday, March 12, final day of the regular season.

In the early A.M. he's there to watch Iowa on tape once more.

"Are you going to start Eyl?" Dan Dakich wants to know, as if there could be any doubt. That Dakich, who played for him for four years, and was a graduate assistant and now a coach, could ask such a question is a measure of how successfully Knight conceals his feelings, the enormous affection he feels for his players. Eyl has been an inconsistent player at best. That he would not start today as a graduating senior is inconceivable.

"Yes," is the complete reply to Dakich's question.

Robert Quay Norris wants to know if Knight will be coming to Orrville in the spring. There is Hazel Knight's house to see to. . . .

"Where'd you eat last night?" Knight wants to know. Certainly this is the most important basketball day of the season, but he doesn't relinquish the impulses of the host.

The team arrives to be reminded of the match-ups. "You can't make straight cuts against the press," he repeats. "You've got to make a V-cut on every single press cut."

Charlie Deckard wanders in and takes a seat in the stands to observe this last regular-season practice.

And now during this last practice Knight begins to run plays for Steve Eyl.

"I want Steve to get the ball."

It will also be Steve Eyl who will be bringing the ball in from out of bounds.

("That's because he's good at it," Phil Richards of the Indianapolis *Star* says when I mention this to him. The implication is that Knight would not do anything to enhance a senior's last game. But even Dakich wasn't sure.)

"When they've got this half court trap, Steve Eyl," Knight says, "you're on top. You cannot dribble into a trap. Reverse the ball. I don't care if you charge five times, I want you taking it to the bucket."

Expressionless, in keeping with the austerity of the moment, Eyl takes the point.

("We understand him," Eyl tells me. "We try to get his point, we don't sit in a room and cry about it. We just bounce back. That's one of the things he wants us to do; it's to be able to bounce back from adversity.")

Knight's message to them on this last day sums up everything he stands for, and his deep feelings. "If it were in my power to do so, I'd make this the best day any of us has ever had. I can't do that. That's up to you people." But it's not the impossible that's being asked of them either; they are not being asked to be Larry Birds, Earvin Johnsons. "Nobody has to play better than he can play. Nobody has to play smarter than he can play. And nobody has to play harder than he can play. But each guy has to play as smart, as well and as hard as each of you can play." And he sends them off to their pre-game meal.

At each place is a card:

> "We started the season as champions—
> *Let's End Like Champions.*"

The starters are the three seniors, Smart, Eyl and Garrett, and the two freshmen, Edwards and Jones.

"Let's go white!" says Hillman, the player to whom Knight is grateful because he doesn't mind not starting, knowing that he will play the same twenty-four minutes whether he starts or not. And so Knight can start the younger, more psychologically fragile Lyndon Jones.

Although it's spring break, the stands are full. Seventeen thousand three hundred fifty-one are here, including Professor Robert F. Byrnes and his wife Eleanor, who have postponed their Florida vacation.

Smart and Eyl go to work at once, but Eyl begins to make mistakes. He isn't looking for Lyndon, as he was supposed to do, and Iowa is playing hard. But then Smart begins to score, eight points in the first five and one half minutes, while Hillman cheers from the bench.

As early as 13.13 Indiana has begun to break away. When Eyl makes a basket, he receives a standing ovation, as does Garrett's dunk at 5.41.

Smart will score twenty-four points in the half. All seems to be going smoothly, except for one contretemps.

With a minute to go in the half, it isn't Eyl bringing the ball in against the press, but Todd Jadlow. If it's particularly difficult to bring the ball in against the Iowa press, it's in part because the Iowa players have obviously been coached to get as close to the baseline as possible to harass that inbounds pass. Not infrequently, their feet are on that baseline, taking advantage of the fact that officials rarely call this violation.

Putting his arm back behind his head, suddenly Jadlow bounces the ball off the forehead of Iowa player, Kent Hill. This play is not illegal in college basketball, although usually the ball is bounced off a leg. Jadlow's action is taken in the context of Iowa's persistent violation of the rule.

Hill's reaction, however, is one of instantaneous rage. He swings in anger, ready to deliver a blow that would send Jadlow into the seats. Fortunately, he doesn't connect. At once Hill is assessed a flagrant foul, an intentional technical, and is ejected from his last college game. The Iowa bench, led by a fiery assistant, is now assessed a technical of its own and the free throws are shot by the icy calm Edwards. Was it Jadlow once more remembering Knight's "I didn't want to look for anyone else"? The halftime score is 53–34.

But Knight wants to leave nothing to chance. He's on his guard against the enemy—complacency. In the locker room during the half he writes on the blackboard 0–0. Let them start again, win again, lest they, this team which depends on offense, blow their lead.

Iowa player Bill Jones passes the Indiana bench and Knight calls to him, "Jones, you could play for me," while Knight tells Steve Eyl, "Don't get in a position to let them make that lob pass."

"Dean, you've got to move," Garrett is ordered. And meanwhile the Keith Smart highlight film proceeds, basket after basket interrupted only by a Garrett dunk, an Eyl rebound, another Garrett stuff.

On the bench, Coach Knight is tense. "Let me handle the rest of this," he tells Ron Felling. He's alert to every mistake. "If you want to finish the game, get the ball inbounds!" he screams at Eyl. When Jadlow is scored against, he's frantic. He walks down the bench with a clipboard to explain to Garrett what he did wrong, while on the floor Indiana has passed the one hundred-point mark.

At 5.58 Eyl fouls out. He leaves to a standing ovation while Knight bites his lip. This was not what he had in mind.

At 108–86 with 2.31 to play, he's still demanding, "Why won't anybody commit to help?"

But when at .41 Garrett and Smart go out together, brothers as they've been, the junior college players who have had to work so hard to play here, Knight embraces them in a gigantic circular hug. Never one to do one thing at a time when he can do two, Knight simultaneously motions to manager Greg Burton to collect the basketball.

The final score is 116–89. Smart has scored 32 points and Garrett 26. To ensure that all would go well, Edwards, the future to their past, has contributed 24.

Everyone remains seated, everyone here knows what is coming. It's a tradition of Indiana basketball that the seniors say their farewells to the fans, introduced by the coach who has not (yet) retreated to the locker room for a Coke.

"It has not been easy in Steve's case to be told not to shoot the ball," Knight says. "There have been times when if he would have, he would have been a dead man!"

"With Keith, he and I differ on when to use his great talent and when not to use it." And now he grows serious, frank. Smart, he acknowledges, has had to use his talents within the framework of the way Knight wanted them to play. And as for Garrett, "There were caches out West who never believed he could play at Indiana and there he was, playing for the national championship."

On October 15, Smart had told me "he hasn't talked to me anything about making the shot, he hasn't said anything about that, not yet, so I look forward, when I finish here, ten years when I come back . . ."

It turns out, however, that Smart will not have to wait ten years.

"After Keith made the shot in New Orleans last year . . ." Knight goes on. And the crowd erupts once more.

"They have all carved a special place for themselves in Indiana basketball on and off the court."

The floor is theirs now and he walks off, indeed to retreat into his locker room, not, one suspects, because of the reason he gives, "I wouldn't listen to my own speeches, let alone theirs," but because he cannot abide being praised.

Flash-forward: he's about to leave for the Final Four, to cheer on Mike Krzyzewski and the Duke team. But he calls to

see how I am. "You must be a good teacher to have so bril-
liant a disciple," I tell him, and in a second he's off the
phone; he can't bear to hear it.

Steve takes the microphone first, immediately to invoke:
Kitchel and Wittman and his coaches, Wright, Felling and
Dakich, all of whom have remained on the floor to listen.
"Every move we make out here," he confides to the seventeen
thousand, "they told us what to do."

Dean Garrett takes the audience back two years to his and
Keith's wondering "how it would be, what we were going to
do, how long we would be here. . . ." to a roar of laughter.
Indeed there have been some, and there will be others, who
choose to eschew this struggle to excel.

Garrett's special appreciation goes to coach Joby Wright,
"the first one to come to me to tell me what I did wrong and
what I did right." It goes secondly to his "biggest buddy,
Keith Smart."

Eyl and Garrett are both gracious, but it's Smart, who
sheds a tear, who is the most charming. His mother, watching
him from the stands today, has told him he lost weight. He
thought to himself: "I guess coach Knight has taken the best
out of me." And then Smart adds, "By the same token he's
instilled in me some of the greatest qualities a young athlete
could ask for."

Smart invokes campus life too, students meeting him when
he was benched and telling him to hold his head up high. He
recalls the day he and Garrett were made to run fifty sprints
after practice and still his teammates waited in the locker
room until they were finished. That was his greatest moment.

As for Garrett, "we'll always be together, just like
brothers. Who knows," quips Smart, "we may get married!"

A model young man, Smart goes on to thank even more
people than Steve Eyl did. Smart's list includes last year's
assistants Kohn Smith and Royce Waltman as well as Ron
Felling, Dan Dakich and Julio Salazar, saving for last Joby
Wright who "represents what Indiana is all about." Nor does
he forget his trainer, Tim Garl, and doctor, Brad Bomba.

Mom is saved for last, a short, plump, beaming woman
who has brought along Keith's six-year-old brother. Keith remembers complaining about Knight to his mother only for his
mother to reply, "He **needs** to be on you." And she, who
Smart believes had to give up college when she became preg-

nant with him at nineteen, had told him, "I don't care what you do. I'm gonna be at your graduation in May."

"So, Mom," says Keith Smart, "I'll be there too." With that he brings down the house.

"We started the season as champions. Let's end like champions." And so they have.

Sunday, March 13.

They have been seeded fourth in the East to play Richmond at Hartford, Connecticut.

Having come to Indiana for the Iowa game, Michael Boykin and John White are taking their leave. "Get on those tests," Knight calls to Boykin, the student's ACT and SAT scores on his mind. Boykin leaves Assembly Hall, his future coach's arm around his shoulders.

Knight returns to peruse the NCAA pairings with Bob Hammel.

"I can't believe that Indiana is seeded," he smiles.

VII

"Boys, we've got to play a hell of a basketball game."

Four days of preparation against Richmond begin in Bloomington. On Tuesday, Rick Calloway is asked to leave the floor because he is not playing hard. After practice, Dan Dakich shows him a tape he has compiled of three or four possessions where Calloway has played badly. Calloway looks down. "That won't happen again," he says.

On Thursday, the team flies to Hartford directly to practice. For the coach there's a press conference where, inevitably, a reporter must ask him about LSU coach Dale Brown. Brown's team has also come to Hartford. But LSU is on the other half of the slate. The two can play only if both make the East Rutherford regionals.

Knight brushes the question aside, as if Brown, who in print has called him "despicable" and a "cheater," were no more than a pesky fly attempting to alight on the hide of a bemused elephant: "When you ask questions about him, you should direct them to a psychiatrist, not me."

A reporter in the audience sports a striking fedora that attracts Knight's attention, anything to escape the tedium: "Reminds me of one my Dad used to wear when I was a little kid. Brings back good memories." The next morning the Hartford *Courant* reporter will launch into panegyrics of how Knight is "nurtured by memories of his father," how he "worshipped his father."

Knight shakes his head: more absurdity. "All I meant," he says, incredulous at the reporting, "is that the hat was out of date."

"We'll let them relax," Knight tells Ron Felling while the team eats dinner, meaning only that there will be no tapes tonight.

He greets me as "the female John Chaney," asks when I arrived and sits down to bouillabaisse over linguine and orange juice mixed with Seven-Up. And then he is off for his ritual walk with Bob Hammel, indeed his closest friend, the person he turns to for solace amid the tensions of big-time college basketball.

"North Carolina A.&T. beat Syracuse on the boards," Hammel says with a chuckle.

"Really?" Knight answers. Hours out of Bloomington they are immersed in the texture of the happening. More properly, their concentration on the tournament began the moment the seedings were announced by CBS Sports. Having been one of the sixty-four teams is an achievement in itself; now the players and coaches must enter the crucible of real life raised one notch by the tournament, testing their concentration and their ability to play as a team.

At ten-thirty the team awaits him in a third-floor meeting room, part restaurant, part screening room, with a section of parquet floor where basketball plays may still be demonstrated. Here Knight reads from the scouting report, and conducts one more walk-through with tomorrow's starters, Keith and Jay, Lyndon and Dean and Steve. As in his Bloomington classroom, teaching is founded upon repetition: "The diagonal pass and the step-in post we have to take away . . . the reverse pass to the high post we have to take away . . . the post cross screen, the screener be ready to switch, we went through that. . . ." Keith is told he will be the help-side wing man; they must all work to keep Atkinson, the feisty Richmond point guard, under pressure. Knight is at the blackboard, one last review before tomorrow's test.

"What's he going to do, Steve?"

Eyl murmurs, but he's not made to hang in the wind. "He's going to step right out here and back pick," Knight predicts. "Now their guards will cut quickly inside too. They might have Kratzer and Stapleton in a stack. Stapleton pops out, Kratzer comes up and Rice will flash quickly to the low post on the other side. So just be constantly aware of their coming toward the basketball. Kratzer comes up, Atkinson with the ball, Stapleton has come out, Rice and Woolfolk, and Rice is right up there. So with you in here, Jay, you have to be really alert with the ball being over here, because, all the more important, Steve, that we really fight the ball right here. They are not a team that really looks to lob the ball. They're a team that wants to work through here from one side to the other. . . .

"They could play a box and one against you," he warns Jay, "and then we'll just start you on the high post and almost play a triangle inside.

"You can anticipate everything that's being done," he tells them. "You can read their defense and react against it." The lesson, of course, is also part psychology. "Here's a team that will approach this with, 'Hey, we're little Richmond and this is gigantic Indiana.' They have everything to win and nothing to lose. Let's don't give them a chance to think they have a winning approach."

As he broke their year down to a thirteen-game season, as he offered them the goal of making the sixty-four team field, now once more he adjusts their goals: "If we could win today and Sunday, there are only sixteen teams left. That's a good point of accomplishment." He sends them away to confer together, to "think about where we are, what we're doing."

One last trump card remains. "We're still the champions," he tells them, "and let's play like it. Let's make everybody that's in our path pay a helluva price. Let's just start that out on the first possession tomorrow."

Back in his room, he confers with Ron Felling one last time: "Is there anything else? I think we've impressed on Garrett all we can. . . ." Garrett has had bad practices all week. Garrett, essential to their offense, worries him.

* * *

In the morning, George Vecsey's characterization of Dale Brown in the New York *Times* delights him: "When he saw LSU and Indiana in the same subregional, Brown leaped off his sofa and brandished a fist, like Elmer Fudd about to catch that Wascally Wabbit." Knight chuckles. "That's pretty good," he says.

Friends from Orrville arrive, Dick Rhoads, who arranged Hazel Knight's funeral, Tony Yonto, who heads one of the foundries for which Orrville is famous. Only there is no room at the inn. Knight summons Tim Garl; within minutes the old friends have rooms and their wives can be rescued from the car out front. There is none of the tension of game day you might expect, or certainly none that takes precedence over seeing to the well-being of old friends. Knight reaches for the telephone to call Bloomington, to have a janitor open the basketball office so that someone can read him Mike Krzyzewski's home and office numbers. He watches the fate of his disciple's team, Duke, gaining ground in the other half of the Eastern subregional being played at Chapel Hill.

Suddenly there's a loud knock on his door. Without waiting for a response, in bursts a man in a rumpled tweed jacket, incredulous at the spectacle of Knight lying on his hastily made-up bed.

"I can't believe this! Get your...!" Knight is being given orders; Knight doesn't mind, not from this man.

Has his visitor arrived on a "chariot of fire"? "Where's your halo?" Knight asks softly.

"Tapes, tapes, tapes. Get them to play ball. Forget the goddamn tapes," the visitor retorts, no neophyte at administering the needle.

"Do you have enough tickets?" Knight asks with concern.

And he retreats with Red Auerbach to the living room of his suite for a private chat, basketball talk, those sentences that invariably begin, "We were playing..."

Don Fischer's pre-game show is preceded by the lecture that follows the team's eleven A.M. pre-game meal. Ron Felling is called upon to read an article from the morning's newspaper: "We're going to attack Garrett, get him off his feet and in foul trouble and that will be one less worry we'll have." This is to arouse them, fire Garrett with the spirit to prove them wrong. "We've got to pressure Atkinson and keep Kratzer from handling the basketball and we've got to make it tough for the ball to go inside to Woolfolk," Knight repeats.

Julio produces his painstakingly researched cards and a surprisingly long lecture ensues, as if the game were not just two hours away. Again they are told what they must take away: the diagonal pass, the step-in post, the reverse pass to the high post. "When the pass goes inside, we have to go inside with the pass. They're not going to throw it back out. We have to make it difficult for them to do anything with it inside."

As always, he combines infusing them with the confidence arising from their having played well, with an accurate appreciation of the other team's strengths. "You have to take this as a challenge to play smart and to play well," he tells them. "They have to guard you and that isn't like playing against Humpty Dumpty." He reminds them of their fine play in the first half of their splendid victory against Iowa when they did such a good job of taking away the diagonal pass and the step-in post. Now they must do it again.

Auerbach's needle notwithstanding, there are tapes, even now. At first the television set does not cooperate. "Here in the United States, Julio," Knight needles, "we don't have magic. We use electricity." Could he have read Gabriel García Márquez, is he aware of the magic realism that defines the culture of Julio's homeland?

No matter, off he goes into the details: "They want to go against you. Let's just turn that around and make it something they cannot handle. What they do offensively should really not cause us any problems. They move quickly, they get into things very quickly, *Rice is a very good shooter* . . . but one thing Rice does is come out of the stack on a reverse of the UCLA cut for the shot. Rice will line up on the bottom of that stack, and if they split it and Kratzer comes up opposite, and Stapleton goes out, Rice may quickly flash to the other side in the low post. . . ." How could the game not evoke déjà vu with this kind of preparation?

"But if we handle people, beginning with Atkinson on top," he goes on, "we have to be alert to switching the low cut, which is what we normally don't do. . . . One of the real things we have to be alert to, Steve, is not allowing Kratzer to handle the basketball. The less he handles the ball, the better we're going to be."

It's not only a question of what the others will do; there is much they can do, as he illustrates on the parquet floor. "We pass away from their movement. Woolfolk and Kratzer are really going to come at you hard. Look to lob the ball above Woolfolk and Kratzer. We can take the ball to the bucket and score with it. . . . I get it. I dribble hard away, and I pass back hard," he shows them. "Fill the baseline versus the isolated post. . . . We're going to start out playing with a three-man stack with Keith and Dean and Jay in a stack. Steve can then step right up and get the ball or start away and come back to the outside. Remember if that wing man stays down, and the point man takes Lyndon, then you just shoot into the gap right up there at the top of the key. That's the gap we want you in. . . ."

Whatever he can predict, plan, organize is done while he repeats over and over that "everything they run depends on these three things: Atkinson handling the ball, Kratzer handling the ball or their getting it into the post.

"Boys, we've got to play a hell of a basketball game," he concludes at last. "We aren't going to get by this game without playing well, and we won't get by the next game without playing well, and that's just the way it is, and that's the way it was last year." He reminds them. In the Auburn game during last year's tournament, they got behind by fourteen. Against Duke, they had trouble in the second half. Against LSU, they were down by eleven. Against Vegas, they gave away two good leads. Against Syracuse, they let them get eight points ahead.

"We know what has to be done 'cause we've done it," he tells them firmly "And that's how we have to play. Let's be playing Sunday."

He sits down at a table where vanilla ice cream sits melting, the spaghetti, rock-hard hamburgers, pancakes and scrambled eggs having been cleared off. It's as if he's thinking aloud, reinforcing his own sense of where he is, concentrating. Since 1975 he has failed to make the regionals only twice, "and it's hard to get out of the regional. When you get down to the regional, now you're down to the last sixteen teams in the country," he murmurs. "Then you're down to the last eight. That's a really good accomplishment. I think it's great for the kids. If we can win today and Sunday to be able to go home on Sunday thinking there are only sixteen teams left and we're one of the sixteen teams. I think that's a good

point of accomplishment for a season. And I don't honestly
know that we can."

In the elevator I tell him I'll be driving to the Meadowlands
next weekend. His reply is stern. "Let's win today!"

Out they come and again everything he has predicted
comes true. Richmond plays a box with one player chasing
Jay Edwards, so that in the first half he will score only seven
points. Richmond, coming out on fire, takes the lead, 3−0
and then 5−0, and 9−4.

You can see it in their play. From the beginning Richmond
believes that they can do it; they can win. Meanwhile what
Knight feared most comes rapidly to pass: Garrett has been
neutralized so that by the half he will have scored only one
point with two rebounds. Reflecting that he has been entirely
taken out of the game, Richmond leads 44−38. Meanwhile,
Jones and Edwards both seem nervous, freshmen at the tournament. Atkinson is as flashy a guard as Knight warned he
would be; Kratzer has five rebounds in the first half, and
Woolfolk is a presence. Rice, whom Knight warned was an
excellent shooter, has scored fifteen points. It's only Smart's
seventeen points that have kept Indiana in the game, and then
Smart doesn't screen, loses his man. He makes all the mistakes that led to his being benched in the middle of the season.

As the second half begins, Garrett both takes a bad shot
and bobbles the ball. He leaves his feet, as Richmond had
predicted they would make him do.

"Come on, men," Felling encourages. But Richmond
smells victory. Smart continues to keep Indiana in the game,
and Jay Edwards makes three three-pointers in a row. Yet Indiana still cannot take possession of this game. With fifty-four
seconds to go, the score is 70−69 in favor of Richmond.
Then, with twenty seconds to go, Smart has a chance to give
Indiana a 71−70 lead. He goes up for the shot, an acrobatic
move, but lightning does not strike again. "The shot" does not
repeat itself. Smart misses, and Atkinson, seizing the rebound, races off for a lay-up.

With scarcely two seconds to go, Hillman puts up a shot
that would tie the game, but, off-balance, he too misses. It's
over, 72−69, an upset. The press proclaims Richmond a "Cin-
derella"!

Rice has scored twenty-one points. Kratzer has had twelve rebounds, Steve Eyl having been unable to keep him from handling the ball. Pesky, ungainly Woolfolk has been dominating in the low post, scoring sixteen.

In the post-game press conference Knight is gracious. "Dick Tarrant was a good coach before I ever started coaching," he says. He praises the Richmond team for playing "patiently" and "smartly," exactly what he had hoped his own team would do. Why didn't he call time at the end? He never does under those circumstances: "That's what we practice for." Why didn't he play Calloway? "Because obviously I must have thought other people were better."

"Is everybody surprised that we lost?" he asks the reporters. "I thought there'd be a few people smart enough to know it was going to be a tough basketball game. I'm not surprised that we lost."

But the prize for the dumbest question must go to the elderly gentleman sitting stiffly in his seat who calls out, "How many times did you see Richmond play this year?"

"On tape . . . ," Knight answers mildly.

"Not personally?"

"How the hell would I get from Bloomington to Richmond during basketball season or for what reason? I think Tarrant's a helluva coach, but the son of a bitch isn't my brother!"

Moments later he is sitting in his dressing room. It looks like an actor's backstage dressing room with its mirror surrounded by lights. John Ryan enters with a word of solace. "You took us to the heights many times," he says. Knight is not consoled. The only person he wants to talk to is Bob Hammel; the only subject that interests him is the game. His eyes are small, set deep into his head, and his face is flushed, blotchy as he sits under the bright lights. He looks small, as if he's shrunk.

"I felt awful for Smart taking that shot," he says. "I told him he had kept us in the game until then."

"How many seconds were left when Hillman took the last shot?" Knight wants to know.

"Maybe two," Bob Hammel reports.

"Should I have taken a time-out? I don't know what else I could have done."

And he's back to them. "Eyl is . . ." "Garrett can't . . ." He speaks of the seniors in the present tense, as if he would still coach them, help them to overcome deficiencies, exactly as he had continued to coach Jimmy Wisman down the ramp after he had played his last college basketball game.

Then, obsessed as he is, he transcends his obsession. His natural sense of the absurd comes to the rescue.

"What's worse than a basketball post-mortem?" asks Coach Bob Knight.

Amid talk of weight-training, improving, within the hour they're off to Bloomington. As soon as he learns that the plane awaits, Knight orchestrates the seating arrangements on the small plane and the big. Then he slams his bag shut and races out the door, leaving Ron Felling and Dan Dakich to wait for the next interminable Ramada Inn elevator. It's the ninth floor, it takes forever, and then they realize . . . and bolt for the stairs lest he leave without them. In fact, the bus has begun to pull away as they rush out into the street. The driver hits the brakes, backs up . . .

"I'd like to see you on Monday or Tuesday," Knight tells Rick Calloway.

On Sunday morning, as usual, he is on television, if without Chuck Marlowe, who was not quick enough to arrange a taping before the team's departure. Knight calls this "my least enjoyable year of coaching." His reasoning: he has not been able to depend on his team's defensive skills, something on which he had prided himself throughout his career.

Being Knight, he is not interested now in assuaging his players' egos. He's Knight, and so he says exactly what he thinks. "We have players who are returning who will have to do an awful lot of work, players who really didn't work as I think they should this past year." It's Calloway of course he's thinking of, Calloway who was pushed out of the way time and again by a stronger defender, Calloway who had the ball knocked out of his hands. It was not Calloway's lack of ability his coach complained about, but his not doing his best with what he had. "You can lift weights and work your ass off, and he just hasn't done it," Knight had said time and again during the season.

Knight announces on television that he plans to offer an opportunity to two or three of his incoming players (Eric Anderson, of course, for sure, but also John White, Matt Nover and Michael Boykin). Some who "have played a lot for us in the last year *or two or three* ... have got to make some changes in their approach to how they're going to play." Richard Calloway in Cincinnati takes note.

On Monday morning Knight indeed meets with Rick Calloway. In December he had asked Calloway to lead, leaving him in the locker room in charge of the team. "Now Ricky, you talk it over with them...," he had said. And then when Calloway had been too weak to hold onto the ball, his failure to build up his skinny 186-pound body over the summer coming back to haunt him, Calloway had been benched.

"It's more fun playing with them," Dean Garrett had told Knight before the Ohio State game which marked the season's turning point. "Them" were Jones and Edwards; Calloway had failed not only to provide leadership, but to play the team game. After he had been benched, he had started and played an average of thirty-three minutes in wins against Michigan State and Wisconsin and in losses to Purdue and Illinois. But in the team's best games, the victories against Illinois and Ohio State on the road, and Purdue and Iowa at home, he had figured scarcely at all.

This Monday morning, forbidden now by NCAA rules to practice again, as it had after they had lost to Cleveland State in the first game of the 1986 tournament, Indiana has time on its hands.

Knight and Ricky Calloway meet.

"I think you ought to quit because I don't think you can make this a commitment. If you think you can, that's where we should start from," Knight tells him. So he had told Landon Turner in January of the 1981 championship season. "I've given up on you. Go to the NBA." At that point Turner had been transformed, sparking the team to play at its best, determined to prove Knight wrong.

But Calloway is not Landon Turner.

"What I came in here to tell you was that I was going to quit," Calloway says.

"That's entirely up to you. A lot of things happened to you here. There are possibilities, a dedicated weight program..."

But Calloway has listened, perhaps, to his father, distressed by his son's not playing. Calloway fears he will sit on the bench for another year; the same thing that happened to Keith will happen to him. He does not take the measure of how Smart came back with that superb game against Iowa, with late season triumphs.

Much more importantly, he seems not to believe that the transforming power of hard work would result in his being a starter next season. (And later his father will talk to the press about how many teams recruited him out of high school and about how his son still has the ability to help somebody win an NCAA championship. He does not acknowledge that Knight wanted nothing less than the full development of his son. . . .)

"I'm just not happy here," Rick Calloway says.

In the press Calloway replies to Knight's criticism that he hasn't built up his strength sufficiently to contend for the basketball: Knight, says Calloway, "harped on me about not lifting weights during the summer and I really didn't do what I was supposed to do." With this admission, he goes on to blame his teammates: "But I wasn't planning on coming back and having to play Daryl's spot. Jadlow and Eyl and Sloan, they knew the position was open. They should have worked on their games also, so they could play it. None of them came in ready to play there so I had to do it."

In fact, when Calloway was benched, it was 6′2″ Joe Hillman who moved into his position, and later Keith Smith would play forward. And of the nineteen games Calloway started over the year, fifteen were in a lineup with a bigger forward: Jadlow, Eyl, Sloan or Pelkowski. Further, as Knight had told his clinic audience in October, there are no number ones, two or threes or fours writ in stone on his team, only players.

After that Ohio State game when Calloway was benched for the first time, Ohio State coach Gary Williams said, *"That* was Indiana basketball!" Although Calloway claimed he was benched and then forgotten, in fact he returned to start and play more than thirty minutes in four straight games in February.

His teammates having been attacked by Calloway in the press, some of those not mentioned now step forward. Joe Hillman tells a story of how Calloway ordered a manager to get his shoes. "Get your own shoes," Hillman told him. Magnus Pelkowski remembers hearing Calloway say, "A player like me shouldn't have to work in practice like that."

Magnus, considering, realizes: "He was only happy when *he* played well."

It is still the week of the NCAA regionals. On Monday, Calloway tells Bob Knight that he will leave Indiana. On Thursday, Calloway receives a telephone call from Pontiac, Michigan. It's Larry Brown, coach of the University of Kansas.

In search of a new basketball coach, and having failed to lure Jim Valvano out West, UCLA announces a press conference for Saturday, April 9: Larry Brown has decided to rejoin the fold. The next day, however, Kansas announces that Brown has decided to remain in Lawrence.

And on this Friday morning another story has its origin in Lawrence. Rick Calloway is coming to Kansas, Richard Calloway Sr. is quoted as announcing. (At Kansas, of course, Rick Calloway will not find Larry Brown, who will have gone off to follow his fortune with the NBA and the San Antonio Spurs. He *will* find a school being investigated by the NCAA for recruiting violations. And indeed there were rumors of a car, of money having been offered to Rick Calloway.)

In a week, Chris Lawson, that skinny 6'11" redheaded junior from Bloomington who averaged 22.7 points and 10.2 rebounds for South (18–7) this year, will make his oral commitment to attend Indiana University.

Flash-forward to March 31: a diligent Emery Worldwide air freight inspector in Los Angeles rescues a poorly wrapped package that has fallen to the floor and broken open. Out of a video-tape box emerges an envelope containing twenty fifty-dollar bills. The origin of the package? Dwane Casey, Kentucky assistant coach. The recipient? Claud Mills, father of Chris, who, like Shawn Kemp, had preferred Kentucky to Indiana.

Mills is telephoned when the package breaks. "I've got a package for you with one thousand dollars in it. What do you want me to do with it?" the Emery worker asks. A conspiracy? "When you try to stuff a VHS tape into one of the eight-by-ten envelopes," comments Chuck Bullerman, head security agent for Emery in Los Angeles, "you're asking for trouble. They just break open."

"Did you send the money?" a reporter asks Casey.

"I would say 'no comment,'" Casey responds.[1]

Lacking subpoena power, and hence the power to obtain the truth beyond a shadow of a doubt, the NCAA nonetheless begins one more investigation of the Kentucky basketball program, the second in two and a half years. His son "could have gone anywhere in the country for fifty thousand or one hundred thousand dollars," Claud Mills says. "Chris Mills ain't no one-thousand-dollar player."[2]

At once the recruiting of Shawn Kemp is reviewed. Kemp's mother, Barbara Brown, had traveled by air to Lexington from Elkhart, Indiana, on October 31, although she had told Bob Knight she could not afford the gas money to come to Bloomington. Yet she paid cash, over four hundred dollars, for her airline ticket and over one hundred dollars in cash for a night at the Radisson Plaza Hotel. The NCAA learns that on October 28, three days before her visit to Lexington, Mrs. Brown received one of those Emery packages, one marked "urgent letter, next morning delivery."

The NCAA discovers that both Shawn Kemp and Chris Mills were suddenly driving automobiles within weeks of their signing letters of intent in November with Kentucky.

Claud Mills says he paid for his son's car out of a $24,000 Workman's Compensation settlement, although he has not worked consistently since 1984. Mrs. Brown, who works at Elkhart General Hospital, says the $11,000 car Shawn was driving was a birthday present from her. She put down $1,000 in cash and agreed to pay the balance in monthly payments of $225 over five years.

It is in such an environment that Bob Knight must recruit players for Indiana.

At Indiana, Chris Mills was specific in his conversations with the players who were his hosts.

"I have no money. I have to have a car. I have to live in my own place," he told Mark Robinson.

How much did he need, Robinson wanted to know.

"Thousands."

At Kentucky, they would accuse Knight of leaking the story about Kemp and Mills. In fact, the Lexington *Herald-Leader*, which won the Pulitzer prize for exposing recruiting

1. Philadelphia *Inquirer*, April 15, 1988.
2. *USA Today*, April 26, 1988.

violations at Kentucky in 1985, and had been the recipient of local harassment ever since, had known about Kemp and Mills since November. Only hard facts, which came with the Emery exposure, led to their resuming their investigation and publishing their findings.

On June 28th, NBA draft day, Knight's Christmas concern about the basketball futures of Dean Garrett and Keith Smart becomes a reality. Both players are selected only deep in the second round: Garrett at number 38 by Phoenix and Smart at 41 by Golden State.

But it's still only Tuesday, March 22, four days after Indiana has lost to Richmond in the first round of the NCAA tournament. The hard recruiting necessary to rebuild his team still incomplete (he will add one more player, an Illinois guard named Jamal Meeks), Bob Knight closes the door to his office. He has coached nearly seven hundred games. But now an idea new for him seems to dawn, a tribute, perhaps, to the degree of peace and personal happiness which has settled over his private life.

"Well, I've just made up my mind," Bob Knight declares. "If you're a coach, you're going to get your ass beat now and then."

CHAPTER TEN

Reprise: The Litany

"If rape is inevitable..."

The cruelest month? On April 25, Connie Chung's documentary, "Stressed To Kill," airs on NBC. Barely a moment into Bob Knight's segment, almost his first words are "If rape is inevitable, relax and enjoy it." It's as if the subject of the program were sexuality in the eighties, with a basketball coach a peculiarly unlikely commentator. Completely gone is the context in which the coach made the remark: Knight himself immobilized by unjust officiating, rendered as helpless as a rape victim, attempting to perceive what it might feel like to be completely and hopelessly vulnerable.

Recognizing that the figure of speech, no matter its origins in Voltaire's *Candide*, might be misunderstood, Knight goes on immediately to qualify: "That's just an old term that you're going to use. The plane's down, so you have no control over it. God, I'm not talking about the act of rape, don't misinterpret me there. But what I'm talking about is something's happened to you so you have to handle it. You have to be able to realize that there's nothing you can do about it."

The wire services alter the text, adding an emphatic "now!" after "so you have to handle it," whereas the "now" came later, after "nothing you can do about it, now..." as the transition to Knight's next thought.

But no matter, there it is—too charged in its overtones to be wise, because it might be misconstrued. And indeed how could it not be since no question precedes the remark; the viewer is left entirely in the dark as to what issue Knight is addressing. From the program you could not guess that Knight was responding to a question about officiating.

After the interview, which took place on the floor of Assembly Hall, Knight returned to the coaches' locker room and said to me, Bob Hammel and Quinn Buckner, "I just spent two and a half hours with these people on a morning after we got beat. It doesn't mean anything to me. I only made one request to them, that they not use that remark. Now let's see what they do." A few minutes later, at lunch, Knight asked me, "Did you think she was intelligent?" as if Chung's brightness would determine the outcome of his presentation on the air. But hadn't he told her he was intimidated by people of greater knowledge and learning?

Chung, of course, had every right to use his remark. Yet it took those of us who had been there aback when we saw the program. None of Knight's challenges to her terminology made it to the final cut, although over and over he had explored her premise that what a sports figure feels is "stress." Knight had devoted the lion's share of his two hours to defining what, exactly, is meant by "stress" and to whom it applies. He had offered analogies ranging from a surgeon to a state trooper. He had drawn on literary references, including a book by David Halberstam. Yet his segment amounted to little more than the one remark—and a clip of the chair making its inevitable slide across the highly polished basketball court of Indiana University three years earlier.

And then I forgot it. The remark had not seemed offensive to me as I heard it, although as a feminist my antennae had throughout the season been adjusted toward discovering in Knight any evidence of the sexism of which he has been accused. I listened and I heard the coach speaking about himself being raped, being the victim of injustice on the basketball court, mauled by inept officials. Ironically, he was speaking to one particular rape victim, himself! He was instructing himself to do what he rarely does: remain silent and so avoid that technical, "relax and enjoy it." A passive stance was one he neither could nor should adopt, any more than could a victim of criminal assault "enjoy" a violent attack.

In short, he was being ironic. In an absurd world, an unjust one, irony becomes the intelligent person's weapon. Should he indeed, Knight asks, any more than any other victim of abuse, relax and enjoy being attacked and humiliated? Knight is constantly and un-selfconsciously ironic, although most people fail to register this because he keeps that straight face. And irony, of course, makes no one comfortable.

Knight was attempting what few men will: putting himself in the role of the rape victim, and speculating, ironically, on his options. Far from being insensitive to another person's being raped, he was suggesting that in his own small way he understood the frustration of being rendered vulnerable and powerless. Far from suggesting that anyone could "relax and enjoy it," he was enlisting his entire career, his whole stance in all its aggressive activism, its rejection of passivity, to demonstrate that the only possible response to rape is to scream, both literally and figuratively, as loudly as you can. Indeed hasn't he done just that?

Should he have trusted Chung? Knight should have expected, given the litany held over his head by a hostile press, that the crudest and most literal construction would at once be placed on any figure of speech he chose. He had immediately asked for a tape of the entire interview. The producer agreed to send it. And then he never did.

It's that sound of Orrville again, with Knight the last provincial. He saw no insensitivity in the remark because he did not mean for there to be any. He had thought Chung was in good faith because she had telephoned him directly without employing an intermediary, because she had left her home number, because she had picked up the telephone at home herself. She had told him that she and her husband were fans of Indiana basketball. On this slender evidence, he had believed she would represent his views fairly.

Even before Chung's documentary aired, Malcolm Moran of the New York *Times* telephoned President Thomas Ehrlich for a comment. Without having seen the program, without talking to Knight, Ehrlich gave a statement to the *Times:* "Coach Knight was not speaking for the university. His reference to rape and his coarse language were in very poor taste. Period. That's all I really want to say." Then Ehrlich told the

Times to hold off printing his remark until the program aired.

That Ehrlich did not ask Knight for an explanation, or at least explore the context in which the remark had been made, was not surprising to those who knew that Ehrlich seemed to have arrived at Indiana the previous summer hostile to Knight. Richard Stoner, president of the Board of Trustees, and vice-president of Cummins Engine, had given him a copy of *A Season on the Brink;* that one-dimensional portrait was all Ehrlich knew about the man, the book about which Knight's player Todd Meier had told him, "Coach, it made you look as if you were crazy."

Contrary to popular opinion, there was no conflict around the Russian game. Knight had telephoned Ehrlich the day after and suggested a reprimand. Ehrlich had offered to send the text to Knight's office, and Knight had declined.

The overreaction to the Chung program was ludicrous when it was not vicious. If it resembled any of the other items on the litany of Knight's supposed sins, it was Puerto Rico. It was the misinterpretation we witnessed over Puerto Rico, but here doubly distorted by the wonders of modern technology where a remark taken out of context and then interpreted literally, when it was meant ironically, can seem to be the opposite of what it is. Yet if Knight could expect some public misunderstanding, and a great deal of press drumbeating, he had not anticipated that the president of the university would join the crowd in its antic furor.

Three days after the Chung program aired, Ehrlich sent to Knight's office a dozen anti-Knight letters, along with a copy of the letter he sent to each respondent. He thanks the writer and repeats that he found Knight's language coarse, adding that Knight did not speak for Indiana University. Ehrlich still had not spoken to Knight.

There was no covering letter.

In all her nearly twelve years at Indiana with Bob Knight, Mary Ann Davis, his secretary, said, she had never seen Knight so upset as when he saw that. He was offended and he was hurt. Insofar as any individual could speak *for* an institution, the principles of uprightness and integrity Knight instills in his players has granted him that right. His influence on them continues long after they have left him too; this spring, Bobby Wilkerson is graduating, one of four Knight players who played for four years who had not done so. Wilkerson is thirty-four. He played last for Knight in 1976. "Now maybe my name won't come up when somebody writes a book about Coach Knight," Wilkerson, in Bloomington for graduation during these tumultuous post-Chung days, says impishly. Daryl Thomas has enrolled in summer school, hoping also to graduate and thereby reduce the number of non-graduates who have played four years for Knight to two.

On the same day, Thursday, April 28, Knight attempted to explain the remark in an interview with Bob Hammel in the *Herald-Telephone:* "All I can say is that if this did, even through misinterpretation, focus attention on a very serious social problem, then I'm happy to have assisted." He suggested that anyone who thought fairly, who knew him, would know that his remarks could not in any way have been "tolerant of rape that is criminal assault." He spoke of the uses of the word rape, as indeed, metaphorically, we speak of the rape of cities, the rape of the minds of the innocent. But the matter did not die.

On April 30, the New York *Times* ran an editorial condemning Knight, quoting only the remark itself, "If rape is inevitable, relax and enjoy it," as if this were what Knight was advocating. It bore the style of Ira Berkow, who has attacked Knight so often and so intensely.

Cries of foul echoed as well from zealots in the office of Indiana's dean for women's affairs, seizing on the issue for their own ends. On Sunday, May 1, a rally attended by about two hundred people was held on the campus, its rhetoric devoted to turning Knight into an instrument for an effort to obtain funding for a Rape Crisis Center, which the university had denied the group only shortly before the Chung program aired. The goal of course is admirable. The ugly use of this particular man to pursue that goal seems unconscionable.

At that anti-Knight demonstration, the signs read, "Rape is Every Woman's Knightmare," and, "Rape is No Game." One woman demanded that mandatory rape awareness be taught Knight's players, as if they were more prone than other young men to be involved in rape, so ludicrous a turn had the rhetoric taken. The leader of the campus caucus of the National Organization for Women admitted, "I think Bobby Knight helped as a catalyst to bring out more reaction." The Indiana University women's movement had indeed learned a political lesson, if one they borrowed from less liberal origins: the utility of the scapegoat. Meanwhile the crowd, a mob as mindless as any mob, cheered while a rape victim said that if Knight had suffered her attack, he wouldn't be able to say "relax and enjoy it."

Nor were the zealots through. On Saturday, May 6, during commencement-day festivities, some feminists of the IU/Bloomington Women's Collective built a shanty near the center of the campus. On one wall were spray-painted the words, "IU supports rape," on another, "Rape Crisis Center." Six women and a large, black dog stood around the shanty as dusk fell. An organizer said she hoped they could capitalize on the momentum created by Knight to hasten progress toward opening a rape crisis center. A legitimate and important goal had been married to an outrageous attack on Bob Knight for insensitivity to violence and abuse. So these women expected their noble end to justify their spurious and deeply dishonest means.

The next day, Sunday, May 8, President Ehrlich telephoned Bob Byrnes of the history department and asked that he serve as an intermediary between himself and Knight. "I'm going to make mistakes," he told Byrnes. Amazingly, he had come to Indiana believing that he would find there the abuses endemic to college athletes, unaware that if there was one program in the country built upon honesty and integrity, a refusal to exploit students, it was Indiana's.

Byrnes found the conversation alarming. Ehrlich spoke of Knight as if he were a member of a different social class from himself, a blue-collar person whose behavior was bound to be different from his own. He made a remark about Knight's children and his personal life, which Byrnes found appalling.

Ehrlich, however, wished now to defuse the situation. And so Byrnes advised him to write a letter to Knight the following morning, saying, "I made a mistake. I hope you stay. I appreciate all you've done for the university." Ehrlich agreed on Byrnes' formulation, according to Byrnes, more than once in the course of their conversation.

Knight had told Bob Byrnes there were five schools for which he would consider leaving Indiana: New Mexico was one of them. Once New Mexico knew it had a coaching vacancy, they had discussed alternatives with Knight for two hours on the telephone. Four days later they had called again.

Was *he* available? The idea seemed appealing for personal reasons that would have prevailed had there been no Connie Chung documentary, no feminist hysteria, no failure in collegiality on the part of the president or, in fact, had he just won the NCAA championship. Knight decided to inquire further into the basketball program at New Mexico.

On Monday morning, May 9, Ehrlich's letter, hand-written, was hand-delivered to Knight's office. Neither "I made a mistake" nor "I hope you stay" had made it to the final draft. Only "I appreciate all you've done for the university" remained. Disgusted, Knight threw the letter in the wastebasket.

Later that afternoon, Knight retrieved the letter from the wastebasket to show it to Harry Pratter. He told Pratter he was concerned that New Mexico Athletic Director John Koenig had been looking for ways to explain the rape statement. Nonetheless the next day, May 10, he flew to Albuquerque on the private jet of Rick Galles, an Indy-car owner.

"Never tackle a folk legend," Bismarck is reputed to have said. On Wednesday, a full page advertisement, headed "We Feel it's Time to Say THANK YOU BOB KNIGHT," appeared in the *Herald-Telephone,* paid for with $1,026 by the "Friends of Bob Knight." A coupon encouraged readers to send Bob Knight an expression of their support. The text begins with a quotation by Abraham Lincoln, "To consent by silence makes cowards of men," and is an expression of Hoosier pride, Hoosier integrity. "These are not people who want to win at any cost," the Friends write. "Midwestern values run far deeper than that."

The Friends also take the opportunity to respond to those purveyors of the litany against Bob Knight: "It is not just troubling to read experts from afar, experts whose access to public opinion is as gigantic as the New York *Times* and *Sports Illustrated,* repeatedly sneer at the Bob Knight phenomenon in Indiana as love of victory run amok. The people of Indiana whom we feel we represent have personal ideals at least as high as those of anyone from journalism's aristocracy."

Indeed, the Chung special unleashed more chanting of the litany against Bob Knight with the usual mixture of truths, half-truths and misinformation.

On May 3, *USA Today* was ready with a list of "Bobby's

Nightmares." These included the 1976 grabbing of Jim Wisman by the jersey, a "pushing match" with the policeman in Puerto Rico, and a "shoving match" with the LSU fan "who tells reporters Knight stuffed him in a garbage can." There are eleven items to this litany, the penultimate of which is Knight's pulling his team off the court with fifteen minutes to play in the exhibition game against the Russians.

Sports Illustrated weighs in on May 9 with a column that includes two paragraphs about Knight's "insensitivity toward women, particularly those who invade his sacred basketball realm. He has ridiculed women reporters and has drawn obscene pictures when he knew they were watching."

I was, of course, one such invader; I witnessed no obscene pictures, experienced no such insensitivity. This litany includes Knight "assault[ing]" the policeman in Puerto Rico, "stuff[ing]" the fan into a trash barrel and of course pulling the team off the court. It implies, incorrectly, that Knight's problems with Ehrlich stem from the reprimand issued by the president after the Russian game, the reprimand Knight solicited.

Ira Berkow calls his May 14 New York *Times* column "The High Priest of Hoop Hysteria," a headline borrowed from the previous day's *USA Today*. The policeman is "punch[ed]." Knight takes his team off the floor. And Knight is "disturbed" that Ehrlich chided him after the Russian game. Knight is also attacked for "wearing red sweaters with the name of a manufacturer clearly emblazoned above the heart, like a man wearing a billboard in front of a sandwich shop." Berkow does not mention that fifty percent of that money goes to the Indiana Foundation for scholarships and grants for research. That Knight's students go to class and pursue degrees? "Knight is doing no less than a college educator is ideally supposed to do." That in Knight's program, as opposed to a large number of basketball programs, players are not bribed or corrupted? That's not mentioned.

Nor would any litany be complete without a contribution from Mike Lupica of the New York *Daily News*. "Bob Knight should talk to some rape victims before he opens his mouth on national TV and makes a fool of himself," Lupica writes on May 1, followed on May 15 by: "Bob Knight is trying to make it out like it was the president of Indiana University who made the dumb remark about rape. But I do think a change of scenery would be a good idea at this point in Knight's career."

To those journalists for whom the litany is bread and butter, no opportunity is foresworn, nor will evidence to the contrary ever matter.

On Wednesday, May 11, President Ehrlich releases a statement through his office: "I believe Bob Knight is an outstanding coach and I certainly hope Bob Knight will spend the rest of his career at Indiana." On this day Knight returns from Albuquerque with public praise for the people and for "an outstanding coaching situation."

Thursday, May 12, there is a "keep Knight" rally. Although the university is in summer recess, twenty-five hundred supporters gather outside Assembly Hall. In conjunction with the rally, the Governor of Indiana, Robert D. Orr, says, "I would hate to see Bob Knight go. He is someone who is so closely identified with the state of Indiana, someone who really exhibits what it means to be a winning Hoosier— bright, tough, loyal, a little stubborn, confident. He is not perfect, but I've yet to meet anyone in seventy years who is." So the governor suggests that Knight, in fact, does indeed speak for a larger constituency than himself.

It is a day Knight meets with his sons. You do what you have to do, they tell him, appreciating that this is a moment in their father's life when he is starting anew, and that it might be a good thing for him to begin his new life somewhere other than in Indiana. We'll get it straightened out at this end, they tell him. The appeal of starting over in his personal life in a new and hospitable environment is the strongest argument for his taking the job in New Mexico. He is pleased at this show of affection and understanding from Tim and Patrick.

And then he's off to Gary, to a little town called Merrillville, for the Hank Stram–Tony Zale Polish-Americans' scholarship banquet, where more than forty thousand dollars is raised.

A woman on the athletic committee for hiring at Albuquerque says in regard to Knight's hiring, "We're not happy about it." Meanwhile, Harry Pratter tells Knight what a personal loss it would be for him were Knight to depart. "I very much appreciate that," Knight says. "It may make me decide to stay."

* * *

Friday, the 13th. Knight flies to New Orleans for a basketball clinic. In Muncie, Thomas Ehrlich, sensitive to the hostility of those who want Knight to stay, says, "I think I'm doing everything that I can to urge that Coach Knight stay in Indiana. Of course I don't like it, the suggestion that I'm not doing all that I can to see to it that he stays at Indiana University." Knight's statement today is designed to lessen the anti-Ehrlich tide by speaking of his decision as a personal one, not "because of people now at Indiana."

On Saturday upon his return at nine-fifteen in the evening from New Orleans, Knight spends from ten to after one in the morning discussing what to do with Harry Pratter and Bob Byrnes and his wife Eleanor. He has decided not to go to New Mexico, not only because of the expenditure of energy it would require to build a program there, but also because the extra money for his salary would have come from people outside the university. "I don't want to get into that situation," Knight says. At Indiana he is not dependent on anyone for money, those boosters who might attempt to speak on behalf of the basketball program.

During this long evening Byrnes advises Knight to tell Ehrlich exactly how he has spent the last week. That Ehrlich seems to have little sense of the man has become painfully apparent as the days wear on.

At eight on Sunday morning Knight speaks to Richard Stoner. "I'm delighted you're not going to New Mexico," Stoner says. Stoner believes it is not a good idea for Pratter and Byrnes to accompany Knight to this evening's meeting with President Ehrlich. The professors had thought they might attend as character witnesses.

A full-page ad in this morning's *Herald-Telephone* from well-wishers in New Mexico welcomes Coach Knight to Albuquerque. Should he choose to accept the job, supporters would be awaiting him there.

Six months earlier Knight had promised a nun he would speak at a lunch for her Fort Wayne school for children with learning disabilities. Four hundred people have paid one hundred dollars to raise forty thousand dollars, and, heartened by this support, a foundation has agreed to add twenty thousand dollars more. No matter that his tenure at Indiana is about to be debated, on Sunday afternoon Bob Knight is in

Fort Wayne. Returning to Bloomington, he consults with Bob Hammel.

Before his ten P.M. meeting with Ehrlich, Knight announces that he is not going to New Mexico. Then Knight meets with Ehrlich, Stoner, Ralph Floyd and Indiana vice-president Ed Williams. If after the Russian game, when Ehrlich had suggest sending the text of the reprimand to his office, Knight had declined, this time their statements are discussed. But at no time does Knight raise any financial issue, as coaches with offers elsewhere attempt to renegotiate their contracts.

On Monday morning both men issue public statements. The president states that Knight had not been treated fairly by NBC because they had not honored his request that they delete the controversial statement. In effect, Ehrlich says that he would not have criticized Knight if he had known the facts. He assures Knight of his personal support and of the university's full support. Ehrlich does say, "This is where we believe Bob Knight belongs. This is his home. He is Indiana basketball to thousands of IU fans."

Knight attacks the notion that he had been "upset with a president who emphasizes academics. I think it's obvious I would be that kind of president's biggest supporter. Nothing could please me more." So he makes an effort to strengthen Ehrlich's position with his academic supporters.

In his public statement, Knight invokes the "energy requirement" necessary "to do the things that had to be done. Maybe other considerations would have gotten in the way also, but I just could not not get past that one thing." After examining the team roster in New Mexico, he had concluded that the recruiting alone would have been grueling since the school somehow drew few players from New Mexico itself.

"If Dave's got the job, I'm not going for it," Knight had said when he learned New Mexico might hire his former assistant and current Southern Methodist coach, Dave Bliss. New Mexico had obviously wanted Knight. But once he is out of the running, Dave Bliss is selected as the new coach of the Lobos.

At last, on Monday May 16, the issue has been resolved. How did Knight feel now that it was all over? "A little better," Bob Hammel thinks.

* * *

Looking back on these events, Knight reflects: "It's as though I orchestrated the whole deal to put this guy in a bind. I insisted the whole thing be done privately." He had told only Ralph Floyd, Indiana's athletic director, of his plan to visit New Mexico, as a courtesy, never believing Floyd would give this information to the press. Then Knight had taken that private plane, which was met at the Albuquerque airfield by a car in which Knight was driven to a private home.

"If I had known there'd be such a fuss," he says, "I would never have gone down there!"

As for Indiana's president, Thomas Ehrlich, a final word from Bob Knight, his father's son: "Always be suspicious of a guy that has to have a chauffeur!"

Tuesday, May 17.

"Joan of Arc!" he begins a telephone conversation.

"Say something positive!" I say.

"I'm not sure there is anything positive."

He's Coach Bob Knight, no matter that school is out. Academic difficulties have jeopardized the eligibility of two of his players, who have done poorly during the spring semester, and he's furious. There have been some behavior problems about which he has just learned. Nothing else seems to matter, he's that angry, his voice is shrill with anger.

"Go away for a few weeks," I suggest, something I might not do, but he would certainly not do. But the last three weeks had to be spiritually exhausting, debilitating to even the sturdiest of psyches.

"What good would that do?" he all but shouts. "The problems wouldn't go away!"

In fact, by the fourth of July, Jay Edwards will have lost his scholarship for "academic and disciplinary reasons." Despite taking first summer session courses, he has barely retained his eligibility. But worse are his not having shown up for his summer job, one arranged by the university, and his accumulating $700 worth of library and parking fines, including— parking in President Thomas Ehrlich's own space! Editor of the Bloomington Monthly *Michael Kelsey puts it well: "this is where Knight shines—in making a young man sold on himself see that the world is bigger than him." Indeed, Jay does see. He announces his decision not to transfer, but to*

remain at Indiana, paying his own way. Come fall of 1988
Jay would reveal problems with both cocaine and alcohol.

I'm listening to a very angry man; I hear a man so totally
dedicated to his players and to the integrity of basketball at
Indiana that he is all but incapable of asking, of taking anything for himself.

CHAPTER ELEVEN

Conclusion

"We do it after the game."

Had he ever gone to war, he would have been one of those officers set apart because they carry about themselves an unmistakable aura that seals them from mortality. Bullets whizzing by their heads, such men, at once recognizable, are protected by the invisible shield of their indomitable wills.

If you conclude from his violation of his own assertion ("Nobody else is going to write a book while I'm here unless it's me") a need to be understood, you'd be wrong. "A guy came here once for a few days and then psychoanalyzed me," he says with disdain. He doesn't wish to be explained, if only, perhaps, out of some apprehension that the magic might die.

He has been known to pick up the telephone to thank writers for having appreciated what he has created, a map for survival by which he believes he prepares young men against life's defeats. While they are players, they fear that they will not measure up. Some feel this more strongly than others, which is why Lyndon Jones had a better freshman year academically than Jay Edwards did.

Expressionless, they listen, unaware that never again in their lives will anyone care enough to scrutinize them for every mistake, look at them so closely. Sometimes, indeed, the tension becomes unbearable. But then, an Abernethy winks, a Kitchel jokes, "Look who their sixth man was!" Dean Garrett and Keith Smart, on separate occasions, wish they could stay just one more year.

It's all held together by a value system based on preparation, discipline and organization, not the fancier, more dramatic skills that few athletes—or anyone else—possess. The stiffer the challenge that will be met the better, shooting grouse rather than quail, attacking the roughest terrain. When you're sitting there day after day watching him, it becomes obvious. Only by discovering your capacity for excellence can you gain self-respect. "Make up your mind you're not going to have a bad possession," he orders, as if this were possible. Landon Turner smiles, as if to say, whoever heard of such a thing: "He wants perfection."

How to be, how to live, Stein's questions in Conrad's novel *Lord Jim*: Although verbal psychologizing is alien to him, he lives his life conscious of these questions. Easing the burdens of others, strangers no less than friends, is the duty of a strong man. This is to be done without fanfare, as if it would be tainted by exposure. On that Tuesday morning during the post-Christmas tournament when he disappeared into a hospital, he would not respond to questions as to whom he visited, where he went, a very far cry from the Dale Brown bragging this season about his visits to leper colonies, Brown who for some reason would ferret out any opportunity to attack him.

He is a man aware that there are other areas of life he might have studied. He reads in a world where often the printed word stops at the sports pages. Life is met with a sense of the absurd, a cold eye cast on life and death. But meanwhile, everyone is treated the same, men, women and children, black and white, players or friends or assistants—all potential subjects to be coached, or needled. The habit of leadership flings open a wide-ranging umbrella under which a host of friends might shelter. David Israel, the writer, laughs to find himself at Knight occasions surrounded by people who have absolutely nothing in common, other than that they are all Knight's friends.

Indeed, Knight is democratic to the core: first with his team, where anyone can earn his praise. All you have to do is follow his instructions, which never demand more than your ability can master. Fly into the birdhouse; the door stands open. Take his game, his character onto the floor and so predict what others will do before they are even aware they're about to do it. "Read the defense." "See."

He's generous to a fault, open to a fault, sometimes naively. Perhaps it's that missionary quality that led him to invite still another writer into his domain. Loyalty and generosity define his connection to those closest to him, and he seems startled when his good will is met by meanness. He retreats. He has resigned from the Olympic Committee, from the coaching organizations to which Mike Krzyzewski believes he could make an outstanding contribution. But however often he's misunderstood, he seems not to lose the open, warm side of himself that you do not see on television, the side that leaves him vulnerable. He's not a man who likes to be vulnerable, that's obvious, yet vulnerability is the price he pays for trusting. When it's abused, yes, he becomes very angry.

No one escapes the needle, not in his personal life, a woman or a boy, not his closest friends. "Hammel walks around Assembly Hall like he owns the place," he suddenly says. He venerates his own mentors, the older coaches who have defined the game he loves so well. Yet when Fred Taylor, his beloved college coach, walks into practice one afternoon in coat and tie, in Bloomington to do the color commentary for the Ohio State game, Knight's reaction is ironic: "I said to myself, who's that distinguished man coming in . . . and then I remember, hell, I've known him since I was seventeen years old."

"And don't you forget it!" says Taylor.

In answer to that sports editor who wanted to know, "What's he like?", the answer is not particularly glamorous. He's a person who has learned to savor the simple pleasures, except when, like any Indiana father, he must agonize over his son's performance in the high school sectionals. Otherwise there's hunting and fishing and golf, endlessly trying out a new set of golf clubs personally sent to him from god knows where, the gratification of being in the company of old friends, seeing his children respect other people.

If his players understood how deeply committed he was to their welfare while they were still playing, his teaching might not be so effective. Keith Smart says he missed the "player-coach relationship," not realizing that he had it, and unaware

of how often Knight agonized over his not having the fine
season he expected. Knight has discovered that, at times, to
draw on those abilities students have not grasped that they
possess, they must believe they are defying him. "The times I
hated him were when I was a player," Mike Krzyzewski remembers. "He forced me to do things that I really did not
want to do. They were good things, but sometimes I didn't
understand."

A malcontent? A person of limited understanding? That's
the Duke coach speaking, who as a West Point cadet suffered
the wrath of a coach who thought he was much too soft, but
who earned the respect of that coach by achieving the greatest
transformation Knight has ever seen in a player.

Knight's premise, learned somewhere on those playing
fields of Orrville, is that life is hard. You'll need fortitude to
live it. Survival is synonomous with successfully competing.
He's a former athlete, whose world is sports, a realist who
teaches adjustment to life as it is.

His players begin with the pride of his having chosen them.
So Jay Edwards after his academic troubles sent that message
through Joby Wright, whose humorous affectionate spirit en-
dears him to the players. Was Knight so disappointed that he
didn't want him to remain at Indiana? Jay pleases his coach
with this question, the initiative, the directness, the realism of
having to face what might be a very painful reply: that Knight
would rather that he not remain. The intensity of the competition, combined with the academic demands of the university,
attack all freshmen (why the question of freshmen eligibility
in varsity basketball persists). One has only to remember
Mark Macon's tears of anguish as Temple lost the regional
final in 1988 to Duke, or Jay's own sub-par performance in
Indiana's loss to Richmond.

"He said if he didn't want me here, then he never would
have recruited me in the first place. He knew I was a good
kid. But he wasn't going to sit there and let me not be what I
could be." Jay Edwards speaking those words proves the reverse: the freshman basketball player has, in fact, an advantage over other students. He has someone believing in him,
watching over him, teaching him how to develop from the
very beginning. If *he* believes you are valuable, you have no
choice but to believe it yourself. Hadn't he screamed at Dean

Garrett on that cold and rainy Christmas night: "I don't want him, I want you!"

Think of Bob Knight as a nineteenth-century man, formed before the Civil War, unshadowed by self-doubt, confident in the clarity of his principles, unselfconsciously relishing his triumphs, in the image of John Wayne who is his great favorite. He wants to win, but only "the right way," as obviously he could have won more games that season had he kept Jay Edwards on the team.

Toward his principles, he is unwavering. No matter how unfashionable they become, he insists upon hard work, going to class, no matter the liberal view that students learn more on their own. It was in large part radical chic that granted credence to those absurd charges in Puerto Rico.

Look again at that scene, that huddle in the final game of the Pan American competition. The seemingly insensitive coach clutches the jersey of his own player, Mike Woodson. He screams. He yells. He distracts his beleaguered team from the waves of hostility threatening to overwhelm them. Fear *me!* he demands, who will not allow you to be less than you can, and forget the screaming crowd.

Listening, an eighteen-year-old kid out of Chicago about to become an Indiana player, races back onto the floor, grabs an inbounds pass on the fly and bolts to the basket, in the process forcing on the Puerto Rican guard his fourth personal foul. Then, as not yet even a freshman, Isiah, having scored twenty-one points, tells the press, "Players with my size and my talent are a dime a dozen in America." Despite everything, the top-seeded American team returns home with the gold.

This is not meant to idealize him. There are the telephone conversations when he does not bother to say goodbye. There's the glinty hooded look; for no apparent reason on a Sunday afternoon he does not greet me. "There's a stare," explains Tim Knight. "He drops his head, shrugs his shoulders and it could blow over in two seconds or a couple of hours or a day or more." Knight intimidates, so that team doctor Brad Bomba regrets later not having forced him to leave the floor after that third technical foul in the game against the Russians, although he wanted to. Mike Krzyzewski and Tim Knight concur in their wish that his assistants might intervene at those moments when a cause is lost and still he won't concede because he is certain he is right.

There's the practical joker who turned the hose on Pauline Boop innocently tending her garden or pulled the rearview mirror off Ron Felling's car only hours before Indiana beat Iowa in the final game of the season. There's the needler who tells Dick Vitale to change the battery in his voice box. There's the unrelenting anger against ingratitude, the dean of the library's albeit ungracious complaint that Knight had transferred some of his fund-raising efforts to the refurbishment of the Indiana foundation airplane, which ferries the team to its road games, after he had raised literally hundreds of thousands of dollars for the library.

And yet at every turn he defies the stereotype. Supposedly given to Vesuvian excesses, he never once shows anger or irritation at a question. Supposedly a right-winger, he's much more a populist; supposedly a sexist, he treats men and women the same. Supposedly profane, he only occasionally is.

And always there's that pull of Orrville, the belief that life can be lived by clear and simple rules. His moral independence comes from there. Players who don't follow Knight's code of conduct off the floor, after being given a second chance, may find themselves off the team. A student takes marijuana, misses class—or doesn't pay his library fines or parking violations, and he's held accountable. That he may be the leading rebounder on the team, or a superb athlete like Jay Edwards, makes no difference at all. His sense of continuity between the past and the present, between the living and the dead flows from those midwestern roots too, his endless remembering of those who came before ("Now Tolbert would have dunked it!").

What stands out most is the love of kids, nurturing them and appreciating them, and it is this which has made Bob Knight's basketball program strong. It defines him and it doesn't matter who understands and who doesn't. These feelings are maternal no less than paternal in their tenderness, if one would dare distinguish between the two, and if he also likes John Wayne and digestion-destroying Sloppy Joes and shooting birds out of the sky, so be it. At Minneapolis, Indiana's final road game, play was postponed so that Minnesota's graduating seniors and their parents might be introduced to the crowd.

"You aren't going to do any of that bullshit here?" Tates Locke wanted to know the next morning.

"No," Knight said, "we do it after the game." And he walked away.

The habit of action has grown almost obsolete in our time. There are echoes in Bob Knight of the people who tamed the wilderness, of the man who shot Liberty Valance, portrayed on film by his hero. View him then as the victim of the corrupt newspaper editor in that John Ford classic, not Peabody (Edmund O'Brien), but his successor, the fool who speaks the line, "When the legend becomes fact, print the legend."

This book has been an attempt to discern some facts about Bob Knight, which demand equal time with the legend.

CHAPTER TWELVE

Indiana Basketball: Redux

"When I saw that team score 100 points against him, I was scared to death."
"This is the best season I've ever seen him coach."
Henry Iba

Never mind that *Sports Illustrated* picked Indiana 30th, Dick Vitale had them at 34th, and *Street and Smith* 7th in Big Ten play. The writers who cover the Big Ten picked Indiana to finish 6th or 7th. A superb group had been recruited for 1990; this year, as Billy Packer put it, "Knight is not a story."

Although everyone else had written off this Indiana season, the coach, of course, had not. After that first round loss to Richmond, the seniors had been given to know they must remain in Bloomington over the summer—playing basketball. But a disparate group of athletes awaited Bob Knight, fragments of a team. Todd Jadlow and Brian Sloan had never been starters. There were two unproven junior college players, Mark Robinson and John ("Chuckie") White. Lyndon Jones had gotten off to a slow start in his freshman year. And as for the new recruits, Michael Boykin failed to meet the NCAA's academic requirements and had gone off to junior college. Jamal Meeks was a late recruit, a second thought.

Only Eric Anderson seemed promising. And Joe Hillman, having graduated with a degree in finance and real estate, had gone off to pursue a career in baseball at the instructional camp of the Oakland Athletics.

By the measure of physical, basketball ability, strength and quickness, Indiana did not indeed seem to have the combination of players with whom anyone could win. "His team lacks true athletes," said Dick Vitale. "There is absolutely no lateral quickness. Any athletic team will have a tremendous advantage against Indiana. It's going to be a very up and down year for The General's team." About the purely physical skills—if by those we define the "true athlete"—Vitale was right.

Then, even before the season began, other problems arose, liabilities not peculiar to Indiana, problems of discipline endemic to the spoiled pampered athlete in a culture where the heroes of sport have replaced those of war. The Indiana players are all high school champions—or near champions—recipients of privilege and special treatment derived from their athleticism. They arrive as susceptible as any to behaving and believing as if everything would be made easy; and some try to find a way to get by by doing the minimum amount of schoolwork while partaking of the social high life of the athlete. Walk around campus in the company of a basketball player, one student told me, and *you* become special.

These attitudes are set long before the players encounter Bob Knight. Character will out, Bob Knight insists, refusing to view his students as victims of society. Why do some rise above adversity, while others, having grown up in perhaps less painful circumstances, do not? He was talking about Jay Edwards.

In this season where Indiana was expected to lose, dilemmas of character and morality emerged early. Jay had taken a freshman course called "Drug Use In American Society." One of the requirements involved talking with high school students about the dangers of drugs. No matter, Jay failed his drug test. Discipline, hard work, a sense of responsibility and humility were the goals Indiana set in awarding Jay a summer job in a brick factory where he was to work from six A.M. to noon. The car he had been driving ("SILK" read its license plate) was exchanged for a bicycle. Barely acquainted with habits of study, he hated schoolwork. His tutors smelled alcohol on his breath. I remembered how last spring I asked him what courses he had been taking. English and math, Jay said. In fact those courses were "Black Church in America" and Afro-American culture, in Jay's eyes less legitimate avenues of study. The disingenuousness suggested confusion, uneasiness with the role of being a student. The value of what you could learn in books—how that could help you in anything—was an alien concept.

Now in September Jay failed his drug test again. He was suffering from both cocaine and alcohol abuse. Bob Knight believed he should enter a thirty-day program, a choice which would cost him the academic semester. But on the advice of assistant athletic director Steve Downing and his family, Jay chose only ten days of rehabilitation. He could return to the team, albeit without his scholarship, which Knight had already taken away. Jay of course could have transferred to another school; that he chose to remain at Indiana, uncertain of whether Knight would allow him to play, seemed a positive sign, a suggestion that Jay might take responsibility for his life.

Knight too was uncertain—of whether Jay could change his values, of whether he would play him. As if that weren't enough to contend with, other students were embroiled in pre-season skirmishes. A young woman wrote a letter to Knight complaining that Jamal Meeks had "borrowed" money from her and she hadn't been paid back. Mark Robinson's automobile had to be confiscated, if temporarily. A player called Joby Wright at one in the morning desperate to straighten things out, aware that his coaches were as concerned with behavior off as behavior on the court. Even the local prosecutor had a word to say, only to conclude that while loose sexual morals may have been involved, rape was not.

None of the incidents amounted to anything, Knight knew. "But they should not have happened." Players new to Indiana, young athletes believing themselves to be surrounded by a special aura of invulnerability, were unaware of how visible they were, how vulnerable to malice, blackmail, or simple public scrutiny. It was not easy for some of the athletes to accept that playing in the spotlight of Indiana basketball would require of them something close to exemplary personal conduct.

Amid all these difficulties, the trials of what Bob Knight, when exasperated, will call the "business" of college basketball, came a bright moment. With a year of eligibility remaining to him, Joe Hillman decided to come back to Indiana. His mother demurred: "Why do you want to go back?" Joe answered, "Hey, why not? You never know what's going to happen." He imagined himself watching Indiana play on television and missing the crowds, the excitement, the "fun." A 41.3-point scorer in high school, at Indiana he had not excelled. It takes the necessary arrogance of the athlete for a young man to declare, "I didn't want to leave Indiana without having played well."

But there was a hurdle to surmount. Joe was certain that Knight would "be pissed" over his missing two weeks of practice; he knew the rules; he knew that no one was exempt. But instead Knight surprised him with only one question: "After that, do you want to come back?"

Correspondence courses were designed (Joe became a qualified referee of high school basketball). The pride, the determination, the work ethic of Joe Hillman were the first cornerstones on which Knight would build this unlikely team.

"How many times can I bend over backwards?" Knight demanded of Dick Rhoads as he debated still over whether to permit Jay to play. He talked with former players like Tom Abernethy who commented, "All he has is you." The reverse side of the privileges showered upon the young athlete was obvious to all: given his longtime habits, drugs and unsavory friends, choices he had made in high school, what would happen to Jay should he lose basketball, should Knight banish him from the team? And Knight was well aware of Jay's failure so far to discover the value of an education.

His schoolwork monitored, his behavior monitored, Jay would play basketball. There ensued, of course, criticism from the press, which reminded Knight of the players he had thrown off his team in 1979 for smoking marijuana during the Great Alaska Shootout. There was a harsh comment from someone close: "What's a drug addict like Jay Edwards doing playing for Indiana?" His own man, Knight would take responsibility for his own decision. Jay would play, if without the scholarship.

Had I any doubts that this would be a pale, transitional season, Bob Hammel confirmed the pessimism shared by everyone. In late September over breakfast at the Big Wheel, I speculated over whether I would have a chance to see Indiana in New York at the pre-season NIT championships.

Would Indiana be playing in my neighborhood?

"They won't make it to New York," Hammel predicted.
"They don't have the talent. This year they'll be lucky to win
fifteen games." It didn't occur to me to doubt Bob Hammel on
the subject of Indiana basketball.

And yet, beating Illinois State, and the seemingly superior
Stanford, Indiana did make it to New York. Then they lost
first to Syracuse and then to North Carolina, giving up more
than 100 points in each game. It was something that had happened to Bob Knight only once before at Indiana.

But even in those humiliating losses, behind the scenes
something was happening to this team. Predictably perhaps, at
the N.I.T. banquet the Indiana and North Carolina players
were well-dressed, in sharp contrast to Syracuse in gold
chains and jean jackets. But when some Indiana players de-
viated from the expected rules of conduct, Knight sent Joe
Hillman in to straighten them out. If last season the coach's
anger at Joe after his poor performance in the Kentucky game
(he was furious in the locker room) had led Joe to abstain
from leadership, this year he seemed ready to accept the role.

Indiana gives up another hundred points to Louisville. But
there are rumbles of growth, of students seizing on the meaning of Indiana basketball. At practice, wearing a white shirt,
Lyndon Jones suddenly says, "Why don't we play to make the
red team a better team?" Bob Knight hears these words, re-
wards that player for this pure expression of unselfishness, the
likes of which he had not heard last season. Lyndon has
earned himself a start.

With Lyndon Jones part of a three-guard offense, against
Notre Dame the team plays better, although again they lose.
It's a 3–4 start, "the worst ever for the Hoosiers in Coach Bob
Knight's eighteen-year tenure," gleefully reports *The Sporting
News*. Bob Knight, however, gratified by Lyndon's attitude,
not coincidentally matched by Lyndon's game, uses the word
"progress."

After Notre Dame, Joe Hillman too notices something different. Bob Knight is showing "patience." He has become
"optimistic." He has told his players, "We've got three guys
doing exactly what we need. Now all we've got to find are
two more." The three-guard offense is in place: Hillman,
Jones and Edwards. The chrysalis of a team is slowly emerging.

II

"We've got to have some people thinking about the word 'team,' about winning, about being good, instead of how do I get to play, how many points do I score?"

In "ex-Hoosier" novelist Kurt Vonnegut's *The Sirens of Titan*, the hero, Malachi Constant, takes a lifetime to realize that "a purpose of human life, no matter who is controlling it, is to love whoever is around to be loved." Out of the echo of Lyndon's unselfish suggestion, that the second team, the white team, think not about turning their shirts to red, but to developing the skills of the starters, Knight turns to teaching the Indiana players the lesson that will transform them into a winning team.

It's December, the weekend of the Indiana Classic, invariably an easy tournament for them. Yet this is a season when they can take *nothing* for granted. In the coaches' locker room Bob Knight at this crucial moment in the young season is not alone. Grandfatherly and calm, a shock of soft white hair falling into his eyes, Pete Newell sits on the couch watching the tapes of Louisville and Notre Dame. Newell wears soft leather loafers, a sapphire blue sweater. Knight is rumpled, as always. *Neither* of these men could be mistaken for Wall Street brokers. The unstated theme of their talk is this Indiana team and its discipline on and off the court.

He is puritanical, this provincial from Orrville. As an athlete himself thirty years ago, he did not live as his players do. Exasperated, he falls on blaming "birth control pills."

"Hey, I went to college," Knight suddenly demands of Newell, "I didn't have to get $100 from a girl to buy shirts. You just can't believe this!": Jamal and the shirts, a silly, unnecessary contretemps. Knight's premise remains that behavior off the court is inextricable from behavior on the court, no matter that his players do not always share this perspective. Nor, alas, do their previous coaches. Mark Robinson's junior college coach Brad Duggan says it was "unfair," too harsh of Knight to have taken the keys to the jeep after a few automobile episodes. "Good men are made here," Joby Wright has concluded. It isn't easy to effect that transformation, as this curious season will repeatedly reveal.

Pete Newell is quiet, but the influence he exerts is nonetheless powerful. He scrutinizes the tapes and he searches for the good. He sees something now in the Notre Dame game. "You do a lot of things like this that you didn't do before," he notes. "There was real quick adjustment. There was ball help. You didn't do that in the Louisville game."

Gratified, Knight remarks, "We fouled Ellison out of the game in twenty-five minutes of playing time." But he is not easily pacified. "I watch this and I just think there are some kids who are capable of playing under the pressure at this level and some that aren't," he tells his mentor.

And now the coach has an idea, which he will share with Newell.

"We've talked about read the defense, read the defense, read the defense. I'm going to devise a whole new. . . ."

Knight and Newell know each other so well that they speak in shorthand, often not bothering to finish their sentences. Knight rises from his chair and walks over to the whiteboard to illustrate his idea for Newell. He points to a place on the court. It seems arbitrary.

"Give a guy the ball right here," he says. Newell understands at once. The players are going to be reacquainted with the basketball floor, learning to react, and *to move,* as if they had never played before.

"The guy has the ball and Dakich takes the position. Dakich runs right here, and Dakich says 'move!' He passes the ball and then he has to react to where Dakich is. Like Dakich is low, so he immediately takes him lower and comes in here to get the shot. Or if Dakich would run to this position, he throws the ball and he steps up and then he back cuts. Or if Dakich comes out and really plays him tight, then he throws the ball and starts away and goes. Or if Dakich plays him loose, he steps up and gets it and shoots it. You have to recognize immediately what it is you should do."

What is he teaching? Defensive positioning, offensive movement, handling the basketball. Newell approves at once. It's another form of a drill he uses at his summer camp for "big men."

Knight grows more enthusiastic with this scenario. "You play tight or loose, here or here. As soon as a guy gets the ball, he has to read the defense. Just so he gets the ball in a ready position so if he's got the shot, he's got it up there.

"Well, then I'm going to have you turn your back. All right, now you've got your back turned to me. The ball is up here somewhere now. So you're over here like this. All right, now you tell me to move."

Newell obliges. "All right, move!"

"Then I'm going to do it with two on two. Then I'm going to go three on three. Because what happens with the way we're playing offense is, and the thing that happens that I think really hurts us is, we end up with our players watching the ball on offense and not really paying attention to the men. Then on defense, do you know what we do? We watch the men and not the ball. And, see, I think it should be the opposite. I think on offense you play the man. You don't give a shit where the ball is. You play the man and on defense you play the ball, knowing where the man is."

"I agree with you, Bobby," Newell says. "I would just go back and let those folks take them through the very, very basic things."

It's a clinic for this team Bob Knight is designing, opening the possibilities of offensive movement, tightening the defense, exposing a player's many options:

"He passes the ball over here. He goes down and he screens. All right. He makes a cut. The defensive man tries to fight over the screen so he makes a tight cut. OK. The defensive man tries to jump above him, so he back cuts. All right. The defensive man goes around the screen, so he pops back."

The motion offense, the Indiana screens, "the way we play": this is the ultimate in patience, the reiteration of the system from degree zero if that is what it takes.

"Pete," Knight says, all intensity, "if we have to take two hours to do this, then we have to do it, and that's what I'm going to bring them in here on Monday doing."

If Tates Locke had been nicknamed "Asbestos Gloves," one who fans the flames of intensity, Newell is the opposite, a calming influence with the interests of the team at heart and a knowledge of the game to inspire respect.

"But let me ask you this," he says quietly. "Why not in your practice plan for each day, take one of these . . . take the first one you were showing them and then take the second one and just devise these basic drills like that so that each day you're getting repetition. They'll understand more of *why* they're doing what they're doing."

Listening, you are struck by the simplicity of their approach; it sounds obvious, redundant, like beginning at the beginning. The key lies in Pete Newell's emphasis on the "why," on understanding, on the "mental" part of the game. "I've got some guys that I think have to be treated like 'you put the round peg in the round hole, and you put the square peg in the square hole,'" Knight laments.

Because the team is in trouble, because they are not winning, Knight calls every element of his coaching into question. There is not an aspect of the program that he is not scrutinizing at the beginning of what promises to be a disastrous season, even the way he and his assistants address the players in practice. He is worried that with his assistants yelling to the players, "help," "recover," "move," they won't develop the habit of thinking for themselves: "Well, if that's me, all I've got to do is listen to what you tell me to do and I can play in practice. I don't have to read anything. I don't have to recognize anything. I just say, 'Well, I'll listen for Pete and he'll tell me what to do.' And I don't think we've done a very good job teaching the fundamental things that we have to be doing. And I don't think they've done a very good job of learning them either."

Newell reminds him that he's "got JC (junior college) guys and they always have a sparse background as far as teaching is concerned." It's a theme that will surface again and again this season as Knight searches for people who can play "the way we play," students who are willing and able to listen and to learn.

Knight recounts a story Kohn Smith told him of a kid at Utah State "that he didn't recruit, but he inherited, a Proposition 48 kid that was a sophomore this year. He brought the kid in and the kid's whole approach was, Kohn is telling the guy, you don't play hard and you don't put out. And the kid's saying, well, that's not my game. My game is finesse and you don't understand my game. Well, Kohn said, no, I never will understand your game and you aren't going to play your game here. And I really think that kind of mentality is as prevalent in California as it is anywhere." It's Mark Robinson who is from California, and whose athletic skills he will desperately need.

Knight leaps to a question. "Who's the number one player ever to play in Southern California, ever to play the game of basketball?"

Too quickly I volunteer Bill Walton. This is greeted with rapid-fire scorn.

"No, Magic Johnson and all these kids have a relationship with Magic because Magic is cool. But Magic is a goddamn competitive son of a bitch and they don't understand that, see. Would you agree with that?"

Newell does.

"I'm going to quit," Knight announces. "You coach the team tonight. I'm going home!"

He walks out the door.

"Well, I'll play a zone," Newell plans. "That'll bring him back!"

He's back. He relaxes into his favorite chair and back on go the tapes. It's time to look at his players as individuals, foremost among whom is Jay Edwards, the most talented basketball player on the team. Jay's high school coach, Bill Green, is reported to have said, "You can't teach team defense. All you can do is take each kid aside and tell him his role." It is another graphic example of what Knight has to contend with this season, not only disciplinary peccadilloes and problems of athleticism, but—and this is the norm— players who come to Indiana with no appreciable training in defensive play.

As always his concentration is flawless. There isn't a movement a player makes that escapes him.

"See, Edwards helps there, but his recovery is slow. This has got to be dart and recover."

"Bobby, he's slow," Newell decides. "Basically his stance is wrong. He's slow because he's high. Watch how he comes up, now he comes down and he crosses his feet. If he slid to one side, he would have been able to slide to the other."

But for every criticism Newell makes, he finds something to praise. He locates what is being done right and then builds on that.

"See," he points out enthusiastically. "Now there's a positive play. Now watch Edwards on that. Edwards did good on that, all the way, now, go way way back. Now watch how he clears that side. He moves off all the way over to here. Now watch, see how here he comes. He clears out there, now he's coming on back in here for a rebound. He just doesn't have enough of a movement game off the ball."

Knight remains worried.

"He doesn't have any appreciation of the value of defensive play. He's going to win 100–98. I think that's his mentality. See, we need a guard that can take this guy right here and really pressure. And we just don't have that right now. Meeks is the closest we've got."

Not coincidentally, since, like the inseparability of mind and body, good defense in basketball releases and yields effective offense, Jay's shooting has been off. (He began the Notre Dame game 0–9, finally going 3–15). Ron Felling is asked to take Jay out on the floor for ten minutes to work on his shooting.

"Get his legs, his shoulders into the shot. Let's see if we can get some carryover into the game with that."

"Now he can shoot the ball," Newell says.

"I understand that," Knight replies quickly, "but. . . ."

The "but" speaks volumes. Jay's—or anyone's—shooting will not be enough. It never has been for Indiana, not only because dependence on spontaneous offense bespeaks an inferior understanding of the game, but equally because Knight's emphasis is on succeeding with what you can *learn* to do well. You can learn to play team defense. But there is something more you can learn and that will provide the key to this season. It was first spoken by Lyndon Jones and now it is introduced by Knight's mentor himself.

"They're mechanically doing things and they think that's enough," Newell remarks mildly. And then Pete Newell offers an insight that will elevate this Indiana team beyond everyone's expectations.

"There's a team aspect."

The point passes without comment. Knight rejoins, "But not for Edwards. Look at Edwards. He doesn't think it's important. He never has."

"Edwards hasn't been taught the team concept in high school," Newell adds, offering a precedent for Knight to make the allowances he knows he must make. "You have to understand that."

The stage has been set.

*   *   *

In the office it's banter as usual. Among Bob Knight's Christmas mail is a T-shirt from two friends who have visited here. "We survived Bob Knight." The shirt is deposited on B.J.'s desk, she of the ironic sensibility. But at lunch the theme of the team game, team defense, is resumed as Knight splits his Third Base chicken wings with Newell.

"Jay takes a help position, but he doesn't help. If they would just vocally help too."

The more he thinks about helping out, team defense, the team game, unselfish play, the more fierce Knight grows.

"We have too many kids thinking about their own individual game instead of our game," he bursts out. "All of a sudden we're going to be down 11–3." He has noticed that some of them when they're on the bench don't watch the game. After tonight, he sputters, he'll "cut the five of them and Edwards can go back to drug rehab!"

But it's clear. He is determined that they play as a team and he will settle for nothing less, whether or not they meet the expectations of their detractors and win fifteen games or less.

"If I had three Joe Hillman's," he murmurs, now softly, "six-two, six-five, and six-eight, I could win some games."

An hour later, in the players' locker room you are struck by one sight: Joe Hillman sitting between the two freshmen, Eric Anderson and Jamal Meeks. And it's at once clear on this cold afternoon in December that Knight is not going to have to build this team alone.

Knight enters talking, angrily.

"One of the reasons why this team doesn't play well is because, goddamnit, you people are out there playing and there is no feeling of somebody making a good play and saying something. It's the worst team going in different directions I've ever been around. I'm going to show you a classical example of it here in just a second."

Facing what seems to be the weakest team he has fielded at Indiana, about to go into the books with a humiliating record, he all but screams: "We've got to have some people thinking about the word 'team,' about winning, about being good instead of how do *I* get to play, how many points do *I* score?"

On the Notre Dame tape he has discovered two quintessential moments which sum up what's wrong and what's right with this team. Never last season was I privileged to hear this lesson: It is what made me interested in basketball from the start, the creativity of unselfishness which in the professional game has been epitomized by Larry Bird and Earvin Johnson.

"I want to show you something, Jadlow," Knight yells. "If I ever see this again, if I see this, your ass is gone. I want to show you something here that's as bad as I've ever seen on an Indiana basketball team, and it's a perfect goddamn illustration of why we have problems playing."

The tape isn't at the right place and has to be rewound. This increases his anger.

"All right. Now here we really need a basket and things are not going very well for us. We're down about fifteen; we need a bucket. Eric drives. He really scores on a tough play, and Jadlow, you don't even pat him on the back! You don't even tell him, 'nice play.'

"You're a goddamn senior and the kid's a freshman and you just walk past him because *you* haven't scored any goddamn points! Now you tell me where your head is! That's a great goddamn play right there that a goddamn eighteen-year-old kid makes that you haven't come close to making nor do you come close to making in the whole game. And you don't even goddamn pat him on the back. You don't even say 'nice play, Eric!'

"Now that is absolutely bullshit and it's not going to be on this team. I'm telling you, Jadlow. If I see it again, I don't want you around here."

Expressionless, very upset, Todd takes the point. He feels bad and he'll be depressed for a week. But it wakes him up and he decides to try "to encourage everyone I can because I know when you're down, you like other people to say something to you."

What's most important now to this team is, first, character, values, shared effort, and only secondarily the details of a game. Knight speaks as if the sense of pride in each other's achievements will turn this team into winners, as if athletics were a matter of morality.

The lights go down again, the lesson exacted at Notre Dame not yet complete:

"All right, Joe makes a move here, the guy gets around him, Frederick, recovers badly. Lyndon comes back, Eric helps. Joe gets a piece of the ball, knocks it out of bounds.

Eric is a goddamn freshman and he comes over and pats Joe on the back! That's what makes a basketball team a basketball team right there, Jadlow, and you don't know one thing about it! That's a freshman patting a senior on the back because he recognizes that he made a play, or at least made an effort. Now you people don't think that means much. You've never thought it meant much!

"You can't have a basketball team that ignores things that guys do on the floor. You can't have a basketball team that doesn't root for each other. You can't have a basketball team that doesn't recognize contributions that are made."

To solve the problem of their less than superior athletic ability, if for no other reason, they must choose to be a team. To think only of yourself is to destroy not only yourself, but the team. It's the Vonnegut lesson: they must "love whoever is around to be loved." And it may be on this day, out of this lesson, that they decide to like each other—and so become a team.

The anomalies will grow. Right now freshmen seem to be doing better with team defense than players who should be seasoned but somehow are not:

"How the hell can a freshman come in here and recognize what the hell is going on? I want to tell you something about Anderson and I don't know whether he'll agree with this or not, and I'm not trying to put him in a bind. I'm simply going to say this: do you think that in high school you were well prepared to play the way we play?"

Normally ebullient, by now Anderson has learned the appropriate demeanor. He offers a scant whisper:

"Not at all."

"And this son of a gun has tried to learn how the hell we play. He screens better. He plays better than any of you goddamn guys do. And he's a freshman!"

Sportswriters will in fact proclaim Eric Anderson "perfect" for Indiana basketball. Eric laughs at this: "I don't know whether it's the way I look [he's fair and blond, blue-eyed and clean cut], or the way I play."

"Now if I ask you to pick the guy that's around the ball, goes after the ball, knocks it loose, more than anybody in here, who would you pick?"

He tries to make them role models for each other, as if the

effort of one could stimulate the efforts of the many, as if by example they could accept the concept of team defense.

He's in a hurry so he answers his own question.

"I can't ask for any more than we get out of Joe. I can't ask for any more than we got out of you, Lyndon, against Notre Dame. But I sure as Christ can ask for something more than I get out of the rest of you."

At such moments of crisis, Jay's seeming nonchalance, his distance, the shell he has erected around himself (which will stand him in such good stead at crunch time), all this infuriates Knight.

"You've gotten by your whole life playing at half-speed," Knight accuses, "and the goddamn shame of it is you won state championships doing it. And now here you are caught in a situation where people are just coming at you so hard and you no longer can be cool about it."

Jay is his "project" this season, as they say in sports, Jay the student he will encourage, Jay whose shell of complacency he will attempt to shatter, not brusquely because he knows Jay will not respond to that. Rather, he'll talk to Jay on the sidelines as if they were collaborators, two coaches. Today Jay seems to be listening, but it's hard to tell.

"I pick Meeks to jar the ball loose and come up with it more than anybody on this team and he's a goddamn freshman."

Jamal listens; Jamal concentrates; Jamal is cheerful, enthusiastic, and seems so at peace that you might imagine he has led a life free of pain. Were you to ask him, he would describe it that way: "I was a spoiled little brat; I was the first grandchild and the first great-grandchild on both sides of the family so I pretty much got what I wanted." He does not mention the tragedy of his father's death when he was seven; he does not mention that his mother, divorced from his stepfather, has recently had another child.

Jamal chooses, chooses to remember himself as a fifth grader playing boys' club basketball. On the day of the big game he had not done his chores (throwing out the garbage, sweeping the pantry). And so his mother told him, "You're not going." Jamal pleaded, "This is a big game." But his mother did not relent. "I don't care," she said. "You didn't take care of your chores, you're not going."

Discipline neither surprises nor dismays him. What im-

pressed him at Indiana was Bob Knight calling the team inside during practice and saying, this will happen, do this and this will happen. "I couldn't see it happening on paper," Jamal says, "and then the guy was wide open exactly where he pointed, right there!" Lest we forget, the basketball genius of this coach ensures him a credibility he then seeks to apply beyond the arena of basketball.

When the off-court behavior of a teammate whom he had befriended troubles him, Jamal distances himself. Automatically he moves away from someone whose habits are not conducive to the discipline he has perceived Indiana basketball demands. "Give him lemons and he'll make lemonade," Professor William Wiggins says of Jamal Meeks." And, yes, he immediately repaid the woman who loaned him the money to buy the shirts.

"The best screener is Anderson, a freshman. The best help-out defensive player is Anderson, a freshman! Now these are things you people have to realize and do something about. Jones did something about his play in the Notre Dame game."

So intermixed are the themes of selflessness, team play and basketball that they become inextricable:

"I mean we got people in here who have given no thought whatsoever to what's going on out there. It's how I can score another bucket. 'They didn't throw me the ball.' I wouldn't throw you the ball either! If we don't get into position, if we don't read, if we don't think, we're going to get our ass beat four straight times." He tells them he saw no coaching in evidence in the Louisville game except from Meeks and Anderson, "and I'll goddamn guarantee you, we're coaching. We're working our asses off."

Giving up one hundred points three times, knowing every night his team will more likely than not face people better athletically and physically stronger, he has devised a game by which this team can win. It's that three-guard offense he had tried at Ohio State last season and at Notre Dame where Lyndon Jones had come into his own. He puts it as a challenge to Jay.

"We'll play a three-guard offense," he says just before they go "outside" for their walkthrough. "But it'll be Jones, Meeks and Hillman if you don't work!"

* * *

Edwards and Jones, numbers 3 and 4: At Indiana numbers are not retired; the players assume the numbers of their predecessors and attempt to do them justice, as Joe Hillman will explain on Seniors' Night. Offered Steve Alford's number 12, a scorer's number in keeping with his talents, Jay had chosen instead, not someone else's identity, but a tandem with Lyndon, 3 and 4.

Quietly, Jay tells me, "We read each other real well; he knows when I want the ball. When I get hot, he gets me the ball. It's fun playing with Lyndon." In fact, Lyndon reveals a constant sixth sense, an awareness of where Jay is on the floor, even when his own back is turned. They become doubles, alter egos, extensions of each other. But because he is a "player," Jay says it's good for Lyndon that Jamal is here to offer him competition, lest he relax and not produce as well as he might if he did not fear that he would not play.

The coach announces a team meeting, designating Joe as his representative. "Now there aren't going to be any coaches, Joe, over there at this meeting. You know, we busted our asses to get you ready to play, Joe. Not just this ballgame, but the Louisville game. Now if you can't get guys to do what you want done, Joe, then you tell me and they won't play. It's that simple. You're going to play, Joe, because I see what you do. I see what you put forth. I see what you try to get out of what you have. You're going to play. Now if anybody else wants to play, then you better play Joe's tune."

When Joe Hillman was a high school senior, a recruiting publication called "Hoop Scoop" said "Joe Hillman is the most spoiled, egotistical, arrogant player in the L.A. area." The Joe Hillman you see here today has channeled his natural arrogance toward the goal of creating a team.

He had tried to lead them last season; he had known what was expected of him, but he had not succeeded. Now Keith Smart and Dean Garrett, with their attitude of "don't talk to us, go talk to the younger players," are gone. "If you'd tell one of them something," a player remembers, "he'd look at you and say, 'Shut up, you don't know what you're talking about.'" And the universal judgment of the survivors of last year's team is that Ricky Calloway was a selfish player, out only for himself. As a more significant member of the champi-

onship team than Joe, he had undermined Joe's ability to lead. Yet Ricky was neither willing nor able to lead himself, despite Knight's many attempts to encourage him to do so. According to some members of the team, last season the black players went their way and the white theirs. Professor Wiggins attributes the fact that this year racial lines are not so tightly drawn to Jay and Lyndon and Jamal's having played in high school with white players while Ricky, Keith and Dean retained the ghetto mentality of the superstar.

Not that all his teammates enjoy Joe Hillman's leadership. "You tell them," Knight instructs. And sometimes abrasive, even crude, Joe tells them. He is often without humor, nuance, the wit that allowed Quinn Buckner to treat each of his teammates uniquely. "You knew when to let up," Quinn smiles that ironic smile of his, remembering.

"Don't yell at me!" a player will accuse Joe. He is not always liked, this leader who seems to have been imposed from above. But then liking has nothing to do with leadership. So the son in August Wilson's fine play Fences *learns when he advances the theory that his father has taken care of him because he "likes" him.*

Hearing this, the father is furious, indignant. "It's my job. It's my responsibility! You understand that! A man has got to take care of his family. You live in my house ... sleep with you behind on my bedclothes ... fill you belly up with my food ... 'cause you my son. You my flesh and blood. Not 'cause I like you!"

And so it is with team leadership: you fulfill your responsibility knowing some people won't like it—or you.

The benefit, as coaches well know, is unexpected. Leadership inspires others to lead where they hadn't before. Players talk to each other on the floor, so that a chain of leadership grows. It's the contagion of leadership inspired and sustained by Joe Hillman that will grace this team, one which will go on to defeat twice Michigan—the future national champions.

Even the normally distant Jay will begin to talk on the floor, if only to say, "let's get a D," a defensive possession, the next time down.

The quickest study will be Jamal, who has only to be told once what's expected. "One of these years I'll take the position Joe is taking," Jamal decides. "Some people might not respect what you're saying, say you're too young, you don't know anything, you're just fresh in the program, I've been here for three or four years, what can you tell me? That's the kind of attitude people get." Will that stop him? "If people can't respect someone who's trying to step forward and help, that's their problem. If they don't listen, you're going to start losing."

In Jamal, you find the natural dignity of a young man who refuses to be ashamed of what is not of his own making.

In Joe, you find the leader who is not a great player, but who transcends his limitations by acknowledging them.

It is still December, the moment of creation for this team. Knight has chastised Todd for not praising Eric, and extolled young Eric for praising Joe, even on a play not completed. They form a tandem today, Bob Knight and his mentor Pete Newell, as Knight introduces Newell who will address the students "about his thinking on the concept of the word 'team,' about how there isn't any 'i' in the word 'team.'"

"Mechanically you're playing defense," Newell begins in his soft monotone. "But mentally you're not with it. You're doing a lot of things you're supposed to do, but you don't seem to understand why you're doing it.

"As a coach, I always said if I had a choice between a player knowing how he did something or *why* he did it, I'd always take the player who knew why he did it even though the other player might be technically better. And that's what I think is basically wrong with the defense. You don't think about why you're doing something. If you don't know why, let the coaches know you don't know why. You've got to get your head in it. As the coach says, there's no 'i' in the word 'team.'

"Offense is 'i,' offense is 'me,' manifested in the names of the players as individuals. Defense is 'team,' manifested by the word 'Indiana.' Defense basically is one guy playing the ball and four guys helping him. The guy playing the ball has to know that the four guys are helping him. You just don't help him by standing there. You help by your voice, communication."

It's Pete Newell who sets the tone for this team, emphasizing unequivocally defense and how it can make them a fine basketball team, a winning team. But without certain qualities of character good defense becomes impossible.

"Defense is where your unselfishness starts. I've never seen a good offensive team that wasn't unselfish on defense."

Newell bestows praise. He noticed an improvement in their offense in the Notre Dame game: better screening, better spacing, hitting the open man, taking good shots. But such offense is not possible unless they help each other on defense.

"There's a great pride in defense," Newell concludes.

Afterwards the players are encouraged to come up and introduce themselves to Coach Newell. Little Jamal is on his feet first, stretching out his hand with a ready smile. Eric Anderson shyly steps forward next. The players seem less blasé, as if the day's lessons have been absorbed.

On Don Fischer's pre-game show, however, the coach assumes a persona of uncertainty. Asked, predictably, to comment on the three teams in the field, he responds with studied seriousness: "Virginia Commonwealth is in Virginia. Santa Clara is in California, Alcorn State is in Mississippi. Indiana is—I don't know where the hell we are."

It's as if I never left, at least this weekend it is. He offers a soft drink. "Do you want a cup?" I tell him it isn't necessary.

"Drink it out of a cup. It's more sanitary."

I accept the cup.

"Do you want ice in the cup?"

"You go from one extreme to the other," Newell tells him. "Joan, I'd kind of watch it. You may get that ice right in your face."

"What you expect is not going to happen," I venture.

"What you expect is the unexpected," says Pete Newell, "and that is what usually happens."

The game against Virginia Commonwealth is an hour off, but the tapes in the coaches' locker room are back on. "Edwards is not helping, has no idea where the ball is. I know," Knight says, "that when Edwards is on defense, he's given no thought to playing defense whatsoever. I mean, he's just there." On offense, he sees Edwards "just standing."

Indiana wins.

Early the next morning he's back in the locker room asking Dan Dakich for last night's stat sheet ("How many rebounds did Magnus get last night?"). Danny returns—with only the first half stats. He's sent back out and asked to call Magnus.

Magnus complains that he's "too tense." The psychology of success, of course, demands one reply. "If you're too tense to play, just tell me and I won't play you." But there's more logic to the argument: "Do you paint a picture with stiff hands? If you can do that relaxed, you can play this game just as well."

Among the coaches there is a joke about "problems with the final common pathway."

Everyone looks blank.

"Synapse," says Ron Felling.

"I'm surprised you came up with that, Felling."

"Coach, I just look dumb."

"Well, looks are deceiving."

"Is another team out there?" Knight asks, interrupting the laughter.

"Virginia Commonwealth was out there when I came in with Magnus," Danny says.

"Do you mean when you came in with the first half stat sheet?"

Virginia Commonwealth may not be an outstanding team, a ranked team, but for Indiana this is an important victory. Certainly Knight treats it that way. He praises his team abundantly for their help, for their pressure on the ball. "Our whole tempo, our awareness, our alertness, our intensity are all so much better," Knight tells his team. Only then does he zero in on their mistakes: "We let the rebound get away from us. And we don't move here, Jay. We've got to move to help." Eric has "waddled", Joe didn't see the ball coming, Jay has turned his back.

One year ago they played Washington State in the second game of this same tournament.

"What was the score, Joe, with four minutes to play in that game? Do you remember?"

"62–60?"

"No," Knight begins. Then he realizes that Joe is close to being right. "It was tied, and the final score was 63–56. We were just able to beat Washington State in the last four minutes of this ball game last year. And Washington State in terms of how they wanted to play is what, Joe?"

"The same."

"Identical to what I said about Santa Clara. Identical!"

His tone changes. "Eric, have you been trying to take out Hillman's girlfriend?" he suddenly wants to know.

"No."

"Did you make an insulting remark, have you insulted Hillman in any way in the last week? You don't know why Hillman wouldn't throw you the ball here?

"Joe, Joe, have you been trying to take out Anderson's girlfriend?"

"No."

"So that's why he throws you a bad pass here?"

And then he's back to praising them anew for the good game they had: "Good help! We're there to pick up! We're going back! We get back and we help. We had somebody, even Jadlow, for Chrissake. You must have smelled you might steal that and get a basket, Jadlow."

He is very hard on Todd Jadlow, as he will be throughout the season. Jadlow's erratic play angers him, perhaps because he knows Jadlow can play well. Why, then, doesn't he *always* play well? Of all his players, Jadlow might be the sweetest, the most vulnerable, and one who flourishes with praise. Today the coach is demanding an irony that may not be available to so young a person. But Bob Knight never hesitates to demand the effort suggested in Robert Browning's famous line: "Ah, but a man's reach should exceed his grasp/Or what's a heaven for?" Reach! Reach! he commands. "Smile, Jadlow," he says. Todd does not smile.

Knight speaks to Jay through the press. He tells reporters that Jay thinks, "I catch the ball, I come down, I lob it. He's got to get beyond that. I think his mentality is he's got to be a scorer or a shooter and we've got to change that. He's got to want to be the best basketball player he can be."

So he envisions a long range goal, three seasons of development for Jay Edwards, so that he might become the "compleat player."

Knight admits to remaining worried about this season. "We're just trying to win," he laments. "I don't particularly like playing that way. We're trying to win a game tonight rather than see a team develop. I always have an empty feeling when you have to play like that." The words do not seem ironic.

Yet he has devised a game with which this particular team can win. He spells it out for them once more as they prepare to attempt their second victory in a row: "You create problems for them by doing three things: you pressure the ball, you take away cuts and you help out . . . and we get it and we get out of there!"

Out of that one victory against Virginia Commonwealth he has carved a theme for the season.

"Hey, what's our advantage?" he demands of the team. "Tell me what you think is the biggest advantage we have offensively. What's the number one thing that we can do offensively?"

It's still early in the season. They don't know.

"Against Santa Clara?" Joe asks, buying time.

"Against anybody!"

Joe murmurs something, the wrong answer. The coach is gentle. "Well, that helps. . . ."

"Hey, this is not a big slow plodding team that we have to wait until everybody gets into position and everybody gets there and we set up. We punch the ball inside and we move! *Movement is the key to what we do offensively. Getting to the free throw line!* We get to the free throw line because we're trying to score! Where are you going to get fouled more than any other place? Trying to score!"

And there it is. They must drive to the basket, draw the foul and get to the free throw line, where a fundamental skill will make up for the absence of the jumping ability necessary for the tip-in, all those physical skills which grant offensive superiority. This is who they are. Self-knowledge will yield success.

If a team gets us "going one way while they come the other way, how do we combat that?"

"We switch," says Jeff Oliphant, so quietly you can scarcely hear him.

"You thought you were right or were afraid you were wrong? Why aren't you a little bit more emphatic? When Dakich played here, in four years he had an answer once. I bet you could have heard him!"

But his tone is almost joyous as he concludes, for he discovered on last night's tape a new enthusiasm for each other's efforts. His praise of them now is unqualified. It is a selfless team spirit that will be at the root of their success as a distinguished defensive basketball team this season.

"See, this is what makes all the difference in the world in basketball," he says with obvious pleasure. "Right here, boys!"

*   *   *

Patrick has improved as a player on his high school team, Bloomington North. Next year instead of going on to college he will attend a prep school to improve scholastically and in basketball. "I really have no choice in the matter," Patrick confides, "because he wants me to do it. " If Patrick chooses not to come to Indiana, his father has told him, "I'll understand." Meanwhile his father remains the coach, yelling at him, agonizing over his mistakes, while Patrick responds as a player: "It gets me pumped up. You want to prove him right."

Patrick laughs at his Freudian slip. He meant to say prove him "wrong."

Will Patrick then choose Indiana if he's good enough? One thing is certain: he doesn't want to play for "one of his buddies because he could always call him up checking up on me." Patrick imagines, not surprisingly, going "somewhere where I can be Pat Knight, the player," not Bob Knight's son.

An old West Point colleague of his father's, Rich Cardillo, asks Patrick where he'll do his prep.

"Military?"

"No," Patrick demurs.

"What's wrong with military?"

"I want to go somewhere I can concentrate on my grades."

On the sidelines Joe Hillman sits chatting with Knight and Newell as if he were an assistant coach. They're talking about baseball. It's another game Knight loves; that Joe should be successfully pursuing a baseball career pleases him. It's clear that Joe as a person pleases him. And at the end of the Indiana Classic tournament, having coached on the floor ("Goddamn it, Chuck!"), playing 38 minutes, Hillman is also the leading scorer against Santa Clara with 17 points. The sportswriters in attendance vote him the tournament's most valuable player.

"What did you think of our voting?" Hammel asks Knight after the game.

"If it had been any different, there wouldn't be any more voting," Knight growls, striding away.

The most charming of the visiting coaches at the dinner held at Leslie's following the tournament is Davey Whitney of Alcorn State. He recalls his 1979 team's perfect season broken only by Indiana at the post-season N.I.T. in Bloomington. "Who wants to know what happened yesterday?" he muses sadly. Then Whitney brightens as he remembers how Bob

Knight attended the Alcorn State basketball banquet that year, traveling to Mississippi at his own expense.

"Do you want a drink?" Knight was asked upon his arrival.

"People think I'm crazy now," Knight joked. "If I drank, I'd be stark raving mad."

On Sunday night in the quiet of Assembly Hall, Knight assesses his team. They have just won two games. "Let's see if we can get our season going in the right direction between now and the end of December," he urges.

One locker space is conspicuously vacant.

The students depart.

"Where was Jay?" Knight asks at once.

"He went home," says Tim Garl. He doesn't know why. There is silence as the coaches ponder this. Concern for Jay, interest in Jay is everyone's preoccupation this season.

"You don't know the biggest thing on my mind," Knight says when we're alone. "It's facing the first Christmas without my Mother."

Has Joe Hillman returned to give something back, in homage to Indiana basketball? Is Joe, by helping him create this team, honoring what Knight has achieved at Indiana? At this he scoffs. "He's a fifth year player. That's what he should be doing."

"But not all fifth year players do. . . ."

"Did you ever think that some people may just be smarter than others?" he rejoins.

But intelligence doesn't necessarily dictate virtue: one has only to peruse history, literature: Machiavelli, Napoleon, the Marquis de Sade.

"You're too romantic and idealistic," Knight asserts. "I've been in this business for twenty-seven years. It's not that romantic, believe me."

Requesting a blurb for the book he wrote for Dick Vitale, Curry Kirkpatrick remarked that if President Ehrlich had not made advance statements to the New York *Times* there wouldn't have been an issue over the rape remark last year. For Kirkpatrick the choice of words had been ill-advised, but everyone knew where Knight stood. "There wasn't anything there," Kirkpatrick had said, meaning no story. When *Sports Illustrated* had gone looking for a columnist to reiterate the litany last spring, Kirkpatrick has told Knight, he refused the assignment.

Was Knight unreasonable for refusing to allow the Basketball Hall of Fame to consider him again?

"My credentials are no better this year," he says. "Now they've set a standard. The next basketball coach they elect should have *four* NCAA championships and *two* Olympic gold medals. They won't be able to elect anybody!" Comparing his achievements with those of other coaches who have been selected, he has discovered some who never even made it to the regional championship.

"Even if it weren't me, I'd say it isn't right."

The voters, of course, are sportswriters. "I didn't get it because it was me," he concludes.

Thinking now of still new attacks on him, like Bob Cousy's in a book advertised on the strength of its containing new material about him, he throws up his hands.

"You couldn't stand to be me," Bob Knight says quietly.

The team has listened. They achieve five victories in a row, defeating Arkansas-Little Rock, Texas-El Paso and Kentucky. Their ball handling has improved so that Joe no longer has to function as a point guard but can concentrate more on his offense. Indiana has outscored its opponents on free throws in every game since they adopted the three-guard offense. St. Bonaventure and Utah State go down in the Hoosier Classic in late December.

Bob Knight's New Year's present is Lawrence Funderburke's commitment to Indiana. Funderburke's outspokenness led his high school coach to remove him from the team. "I think I need some discipline in my life and he definitely can give it to me," Funderburke says about Bob Knight, *this* boy no stranger to irony. When Dean Garrett is quoted in the press as suggesting that Funderburke would do well to think twice about Indiana, *his* former coach is not amused. Dismayed, Garrett apologizes, pleading that he was misquoted.

It is a winning Indiana team, a good basketball team, which roars into its Big Ten season. They defeat Ohio State. They defeat Purdue at Purdue, Gene Keady pronouncing Joe "the smartest player in the league." While Jay, all sangfroid, breaks Keith Smart's Big Ten record of consecutive free throws with 38, the hostile crowd chants "Just say no!"

The coach gains his 214th victory making him the all-time

winningest coach in the Big Ten. His response is self-deprecating humor, plus the kind of prediction which amazed young Jamal Meeks: "If I live long enough," he reflects, "what happens next is I outlive my enemies. Those sons of bitches will all be gone. I'll be an elder statesman, and everybody will like me."

Indeed as the season progresses, as Indiana wins and wins and wins, the press begins to treat Bob Knight as if he were an "elder statesman," the éminence gris of college basketball. Laments at the exploitation of student athletes notwithstanding, winning often awards favorable press. The New York *Times* is quiet on the subject of Bob Knight following the review of this book by a *Sports Illustrated* writer named Rick Telander.

To the *Times*, Telander had described himself, disingenuously, as the author of a book about urban basketball. Later the *Times* discovered that his column lambasting Knight after the Connie Chung interview (the assignment Curry Kirkpatrick had declined) had been criticized in the very book he was reviewing.

Honesty demanded he mention that he was criticized in the book, but no less that he was a senior writer for a publication called to task for some of its depictions of Bob Knight. Appalled, the *Times* printed a retraction on page three of the first section of the Sunday news. The "editors" regret having chosen Telander; they imply his behavior was less than ethical and that they had been deceived.

Should this book, while hardly suggesting that Bob Knight is a "saint" ("You pay a price for working with someone who's the best at what he does," Joby Wright points out), have been more "balanced"? In an important article in the New York Review of Books *about the Bush-Dukakis campaign entitled "The Intimidated Press," Anthony Lewis, the* New York Times *columnist, suggests that the press failed to fulfill its responsibility to evaluate each candidate because of some spurious concept of "balance." "The idea of balance," Lewis argues, "sounds appealing, but can be a menace to serious journalism. Fairness is one thing, but to pretend that all issues have two sides and that any print or television account must show both—is something else altogether."*

Lewis suggests that the framers of the First Amendment more likely had in mind the Madisonian thesis that truth will emerge from a clash of divergent opinions. Papers in those days "were far more biased, more partisan than ours"; truth would emerge not from a watered down "balance" in which no side is clearly taken, but from the free exchange of many strong points of view expressed in different places.

A single dissenting view, another way of perceiving Bob Knight, ignites some sportswriters. It's as if the only acceptable response to Knight has to be somewhat snide. Knight's response to Telander's review of this book?

"They don't like a woman having written it."

But with my dismay over the Telander review, Knight has no patience. "When was the last time you were on the best seller list?" he barks.

Since Notre Dame, Indiana's opponents have shot under .500. Indiana has now won nine games in a row. How are they doing it? "Ball handling is the answer," Knight says sharply, irritated at the seemingly endless repetition of the question.

When he secures his 500th coaching victory on January 14th against Northwestern, all he will discuss is how the inside offense did not produce. His personal statistics seem no more important to him than the individual exploits of one player.

The season proceeds without incident: Indiana quietly strengthens its defensive skills, the game plan working. But against Michigan State at home on January 21st, the crowd takes umbrage at the officiating while two technicals are awarded the coach, his first of the season. Objects rain down on the court; a coin hits a Michigan State player. At courtside Knight takes the microphone. "You don't throw anything in here," he says angrily, "regardless of the quality of the officiating." It's his four hundredth win at Indiana University.

Indiana proves equally successful against the strong and the weaker teams of the Big Ten. They go into the game against Michigan at Ann Arbor 5-0 in Big Ten play. Time after time they beat Michigan down the floor. In the first ten minutes Brian Sloan gets five rebounds. And when Jay beats Taylor down, but can't then get a handle on the ball, Bob Knight shouts words of encouragement:

"That's all right, Jay!"

When Sloan fouls out, having tirelessly devoted himself to setting screens, Jadlow takes over, the chain of unselfishness reasserting itself. After the game, Knight calls Sloan "totally unselfish, I mean absolutely, *totally* unselfish." It's again the lesson of that wintery day in December. Nor does Jay's progress go unnoticed. Against Michigan he's moving well without the ball, learning how to get open. It's Indiana's 13th victory in a row.

When the winning streak is broken at last with a loss to Illinois at Illinois on January 28th, Indiana's first since Notre Dame, Knight has enough faith in this team to argue that victory had been within their grasp. Had they not lost patience, they might have won. Had they not failed to block out, three to four more baskets would have been theirs. There was unnecessary improper positioning in the post. A workout at 2 A.M. marks their return from Champaign.

Has Bob Knight forgotten that Indiana lacks the physical skills of many of its rivals? It's irrelevant because he has found a way they can be an outstanding basketball team without those skills if only they execute in accordance with their strengths. Of course he never has a problem with demanding more than people believe they can achieve. "It's always better to overdemand," Bob Knight the teacher insists.

Two days later they face ninth-ranked (AP) Iowa. Playing, as always, in defiance of his limitations, Joe scores 15 points. But Todd Jadlow plays the way Knight knew he could, scoring 32 and going 18–19 at the free throw line (breaking a Ted Kitchel Indiana record). Todd pulls down 13 rebounds.

"Smile, Jadlow," Knight had said on that day in December. He must have envisioned *this* Jadlow. "This team is pretty unselfish. We pull for each other," Jadlow says after the Iowa game.

Somewhere along the way they have succeeded in liking each other (soon, as a group of friends they'll be watching the Mike Tyson fight). Somehow Bob Knight has made them a team.

"Benny" is here, rehabilitating from an injury after playing in Italy. Kent Benson had infuriated the coach last season with his talk of how Buckner and May were cowed by the fierce coach, but *he* was not. "We," "us," "we got a little shook," "our guys hung in there tough," he still sees himself as an Indiana player. Coach Knight, Benny says, "knows his players inside out . . . if they work hard and listen to what he says, then they win."

Indiana is 7–1 in league play. They have defeated both Iowa and Michigan, with Illinois their strongest rivals. But the astounding transformation of this team has not mellowed the coach, who launches after the Iowa game into his annual attack on the Big Ten conference for scheduling 9:30 P.M. games on school nights. He knows the argument: the weaker schools need the television "exposure." Knight has a ready answer: the weaker teams, Wisconsin, Northwestern and Minnesota, have not been offered these late Monday night games.

"I think it will be a magnanimous gesture on our part," Knight needles, "when we say the rest of you can have the exposure. Take our spots and expose yourselves in any way you want to." Then, to underline his point, he closes his locker room to the press. "If any of you reporters are unhappy about not being able to talk to our players like you want to, write a letter of complaint to ESPN or Wayne Duke."

Two days later Duke announces the Big Ten will renegotiate its television contract with ESPN to avoid late starting times for Monday night basketball games. (In fact, in 1990 Indiana will play three Big Ten games with 9:30 P.M. starts, but two will be when classes are out.)

How many Big Ten teams have their own planes to ferry students home at a reasonable hour for classes the next day? Only one, Indiana.

Wayne Duke is stepping down as Big Ten Commissioner. As he would with a recalcitrant player, now that their adversarial relationship is over, Bob Knight reassesses. Too much has been made of his criticisms of Wayne Duke, Knight says. In fact, his quarrels have been with the Big Ten and he agreed with Duke on many points: "Despite our disputes, he's a person I always liked and in the final analysis I felt had done an excellent job heading the Big Ten in spite of the oftentimes less than intellectual interference by some athletic directors and faculty representatives around the league. Wayne Duke is a person who through an eighteen-year relationship—sometimes adversarial—I came through liking." Wayne Duke, Bob Knight now concludes, did "a good job."

There are mellow moments. This season has been "fun" for Joe Hillman, Bob Knight tells me softly. But when on February 4th against Minnesota at home Indiana is down 28–22 at the half, having shot .350, made not a single offensive rebound, but eleven turnovers, Bob Knight is not amused. Complacency is the enemy of this team, which still outrebounds few, is less physically strong and is smaller than just about everyone. Playing according to the season's plan, playing mistake free (always the coach's quixotic, necessary expectation), they can defeat anyone. Playing at the level of their physical skills, they will defeat few.

At the half Knight arrives angry at the locker room where his team awaits him.

"Get out of here!" he demands.

No one moves. Where are they to go? He cannot mean it.

"I mean it, get out of here now. I'm going to start tossing you out."

They saunter back out onto the court, homeless. The crowd, unaware of their dilemma, begins to cheer wildly, ready to offer encouragement for the second half. Over the noise, the players cannot hear what Joe is saying to them. They try to reenter the locker room and again Knight throws them out; they have not earned their rest. Senior manager Stephen Trust suggests they meet out beyond the Big Red giftshop.

"This makes our season," Joe tells the team. "We've *got* to go out and play. Hey, we don't want to look back on this and think 'we should have, we could have, if it hadn't been for the Minnesota game that blew our chances....'"

To underscore his point, Joe goes out in the second half and scores 14 of his 20 points. It's the first time he has scored twenty in his five years at Indiana. Transcending his limitations while exposing them, he dives for loose balls, never waiting for a ball to roll out of bounds if there is the slightest chance of saving it. Indiana wins 66–62.

The workout in the middle of the night, throwing them out of the locker room—Knight searches for motivational strategies to keep this team from forgetting how strong an effort is required of them every night as they walk out against physically superior teams. As the second half of the Big Ten season begins, he talks about "the kind of recruiting we've had ... while we're waiting for that." To inspire *this* team, he invokes the excellent athletes already scheduled to come to Indiana in the fall: Pat Graham, Greg Graham, Chris Lawson and Calbert Cheaney, all to be selected by the AP for the Indiana All-State first team, as well as Funderburke and Chris Reyn olds of Illinois. Jay and Eric respond, each scoring 24 against Northwestern. Joe sits chatting on the bench with Julio as the game winds down, not having to work so hard tonight. Jamal Meeks pulls down eight boards, and laughingly ends the game with an unlikely three pointer just outside the buzzer so that it doesn't count.

Tonight Jim Wisman, Wisman of the yanked jersey, is on the radio pointing out that the Coach doesn't get enough credit for "being innovative." "You're still going to play it his way, but his way just changes now and then," Wisman laughs.

The December lesson of unselfish praise for each other's efforts continues to echo through this increasingly triumphant season. On February 12th against Purdue, there is Jamal running up to pat Joe for a good pass to Jay that leads to a bucket; twice in the second half Jamal does the same for senior Brian Sloan.

Meanwhile, Jay, much improved in his offensive movement, is emerging as a basketball talent. In the first half against Purdue he seems to play an ordinary game. In the second his face lights up with pleasure. It's as if he's transformed. There's a little smile, a special alertness as if he would win more appreciation were he to be the hero of the game's finish. With four seconds to go, Jay hits the game winning basket.

It's another cliff-hanger, 64–62.

As for the coach's role in this season of unlikely victories: "If he were commanding the army of Guatemala," Bob Hammel laughs, "he'd think he could beat Russia . . . because it's him."

III

"This is one of the great opportunities that you have in playing college basketball here, to play in games like this. If you're going to be the kind of team and the kind of players that you want people to remember, this is the kind of game that we, you, each guy has got to play well."

Dick Vitale, who seems to have camped out in Bloomington, pronounces "The General" "mellow." ("If he says 'The General' one more time. . . ." B.J. threatens.) In fact, the tension at Assembly Hall is overwhelming. The atmosphere is so dif ferent from last season I feel as if I've taken the wrong plane, arrived at the wrong arena. This is not the Indiana I knew. There is none of the easy camaraderie of last season. It seems difficult for Bob Knight to tolerate the presence of an outsider now.

"He was relaxed—until they tricked him into thinking they could win it all," Bob Hammel concludes, watching the Friday practice for Sunday's game against Michigan. "It's another of those games there should be no way they can win."

"If we win on Sunday, I'll take you out to a good dinner," Bob Knight says.

The scene, however, seems characteristic of the season. Out on the floor before practice Joe is working with redshirted Matt Nover, as in December I saw him helping Knight create the team he will no longer be here to lead. I ask Joe how this season differs from last, and Joe is vehement. "This year they listen to me," Joe asserts. I ask him to compare them with last year's squad. *"This"* team wants to win!" Joe says. "They listen!" And Joe Hillman's pride in "his" team allows him to make an even greater claim: "It's a better defensive team than the 1987 championship team! We do more switching."

Preparing for this crucial game against Michigan, Indiana may well be proud of its defense: the opposition is shooting 42 per cent against them. In physical size, however, Michigan is the largest in the Big Ten. In shooting, they're the best in college basketball.

On Friday, there is no lecture, only practice, preparation at its most scientific, with the demand that they play mistake-free. "Let's don't have a bucket scored against us because we didn't block out. They're going to nail you. Your hand on his arm doesn't do a thing but give them a crack at two easy points." Whatever the players may believe, the coach knows it will be close; a single lapse can cost them the game.

Eric has dislocated his thumb, an injury sufficient to have been treated by surgeon Jim Strickland in Indianapolis. Eric, however, is not coddled. "If you want to play one-handed, Eric, I want to know about it," Knight calls. "I'm not going to lose baskets because you play with only one hand."

These five sessions preparing for Michigan epitomize Knight's coaching this season, coaching to beat a superior opponent, coaching to know each individual on the opposing team so that you can take him out of the game, coaching to ensure the maximum discipline on the floor, coaching to win.

There is no underestimating Michigan: "They'll come down full tilt. They'll PLAY." Yet, as always, there is a way to beat them: "Stay spread, drive, get them the hell out of the game . . . we'll beat them . . . and here's how. We have to have patience and we have to make it very tough for them to play defense. They get lost. They don't know where the hell they're playing without the ball. They get to standing. . . ."

Jamal races down, makes a basket, and is at once rewarded. Turning his white shirt to red, his enthusiasm uncontained, he flashes a quick smile.

"Jay, move!" Knight calls. "You can't stand!" How many times has Jay heard that? Basketball teaching is above all about repetition.

Jay takes the last shot of the practice, and misses. "Jaybird," Knight says affectionately, has to shoot again.

You can't leave practice missing your last shot.

Jay laughs, tries again, and makes it.

On Saturday morning Knight sits alone in the coaches' locker room. "Proposition 42," he says, "is ridiculous." He contends that if scholarships are eliminated, it creates one more avenue for cheating. But like every professor he wishes students coming to college were better prepared.

Upstairs in his office he's searching for something. He sifts through the inevitable mountains of paper, mementos, tins of food, nuts, candy. At last he comes upon a sheaf of papers. They reveal the statistics of his graduation rate as compiled by a Harvard graduate student named Bob Sulek. "We've won three national championships with no problems of eligibility," Knight points out. "If we can do it, anyone can do it."

"Read this over and give it back to me."

The material is astounding: his graduation rate for players who have completed their eligibility is 90 percent, while the graduation rate for *all* Indiana University students remaining in school for four years is 38 percent! Of his 43 students who earned their degrees, nine have gone on to advanced degrees: there are two doctors, a dentist, four masters' degrees, two lawyers.

Through 1988, only five of his 43 graduates majored in physical education! Five of the 48 who completed 4 years of basketball eligibility majored in physical education. His students not only graduate, but they graduate having studied something. (Of those who have not graduated, four of the five are within a semester of doing so. Of his 43 graduates, 32 are white and 11 are black. And his black players have graduated at a near 70 percent rate, as compared to 31 percent for black students in general!)

I find Jay and mention that only five percent of Indiana players majored in physical education. Jay is impassive. I ask about his future. He muses that he would like to be a detective some day, a police officer. Long accustomed to reporters twice his age hanging on his words, Jay has learned that special brand of dishonesty athletes use in feeding the press. To his credit, he seems uncomfortable doing it.

The team arrives this Saturday morning at 9:45, always, of course, on time.

"I want to show you one play," Knight begins at once. "This is a basket Michigan gets against Purdue and this is a basket we just can't give up. Now watch the lunge right here. McCants makes this lunge. If McCants just holds his position, gets some help right back here . . . and that's the kind of play we cannot give up to these people. I don't mean just this lunge. I'm talking about bad plays. I'm talking about being out of position, missing blockouts. We do those things or make that kind of play and they'll beat us. We're not going to have enough margin to work on if we make bad plays. We just aren't going to have it!"

Michigan "offensively boils down to the break, the boards, Robinson driving with the ball, Higgins and Rice shooting the ball, and their post play. They're not really running anything to get anybody open. They screen for Rice. They try to get Rice open and that's it. They bring Rice up toward the ball, across the lane, which we should be able to stop, without exception, they bring Rice off a downscreen. . . ."

Their coach has just told them that Glen Rice, the leading contender at the moment for Big Ten Player of the Year, can be stopped "without exception." They believe him, as indeed Jamal discovered, because his knowledge of the game has long granted him a credibility few coaches have earned.

Michigan needs "to get baskets on breakaways, rebound breaks, offensive board play. We control that stuff, plus get to the free throw line offensively." Indiana's game plan will be enacted in the face of Michigan's offense, which is now anatomized: "Higgins and Rice don't really put the ball on the floor. Maybe one dribble and shoot. They both prefer going to the right. Robinson'll shoot it and Robinson will dribble a lot inside. He gets the ball, he dribbles baseline, he dribbles in the post. None of those big players, Hughes, Mills or Vaught, will put the ball on the floor outside. They're basically turn around jump shooters." It's the theory that knowledge is power put into practice at Indiana every day of basketball season.

Meanwhile he must encourage them to screen. "You people better go screen like Joe does!" He becomes indignant, as if remembering something: "Goddamn it, Joe goes to screen! And some of you guys meander into it. Go get somebody!" Offensively, of course, it's screening that epitomizes the un-selfish team game, and if any team has raised screening to an art, it's Indiana.

He leaves the tape viewing to his assistants only to reap-pear with a joke: "We interrupt this program to find my high school schedule book. . . ." Joe smiles. Jamal smiles big, tak-ing Joe's lead.

This is not about spontaneity, about running back and forth up and down the floor. This is about the discipline which leads to achievement, the concentration and strategy that will always defeat chaotic individualism. The Indiana players sit there and scrutinize a tape on which have been spliced to-gether every possession in which Michigan scored against them in their last game. For each score Dan Dakich explains how Michigan could have been stopped, how Indiana could have avoided losing those baskets. "We gotta have guys to shove guys back to places," Danny observes.

"I was ready to switch," Joe notes in one case.

"Don't do that this time," Danny advises. "Stay back. You don't need to cheat like that. Rice will back cut. Let's not fall asleep on Rice. Let's definitely not fall asleep on Rice."

They watch a play where Jay is seven feet out of position.

"If Jay's where he's supposed to be. . . ." Danny begins. "Your hand's on your shorts." But he's careful about being too harsh with Jay: "I know you just hit a couple of threes to keep us in the game."

And frequently this season you notice the implicit or ex-plicit comparison that Joe made:

"Last year Calloway got caught on screens."

Knight is back to tell them how disappointed he was last Sunday "that we just didn't dominate Purdue because I think we're that much better than they are right now." Then it's back to the vulnerabilities of Michigan. "Just watch Robinson when his man doesn't have the ball. Watch Rice when his man doesn't. Look at Robinson turn his back completely on the man! See, already, look what they've worn out of them! Scheffler just gets three points here by moving. He just moves right off a little screen. They don't switch it."

Movement on offense of course is what Indiana does best.

"Now look how far Rice has come to help. They've just left the guy completely open to get the ball back to Rice's man. Shot fake, you're past Rice.

"This is where they want to score. Robinson will keep it on the dribble just as long as he can. Right here. He's trying to get it all the way to the bucket to score and they don't cover very quickly here.

"Lyndon, Jay and Joe, Jamal, you guards are going to have to rebound for us.

"By just moving and having patience, we're going to get people open."

He's never too tired to remind them of "how we play." "We're not talking about setting up offensive plays or patterns. We're defending against talented players, not tricky patterns. We just have to beat individuals, OK?"

It is noon. Practice will resume at 3:30.

Jay sits down and reflects upon "making the decisions on the floor that need to be made" when Joe's not in the game. "I'm listening to what Joe does," Jay says. "I'm observing and learning and that will help me next year to be a leader which I wouldn't mind." He speaks as if he's looking forward to his junior year at Indiana. Now he pictures himself talking to the other players on the floor, saying, "We need a blockout, if the team is up two points and we need defense."

At Marion, where he went to high school, Jay says, he was "more flamboyant" than Lyndon and had a "bad attitude." Without a scholarship until this semester, when it was restored thanks to his above a C average, he could have left Indiana. Why did he remain?

"I put myself in this situation," Jay explains, "and I had to make it right. I put myself in this situation and I blew it and I had to get myself right. There were things I had to do. I did everything right."

Jay does not lie and say he enjoys school. Instead he says he enjoys "doing good." He has calculated that if he's going to get what he wants, he must live differently. It is difficult not to hear Steve Downing's voice in some of this, but it is still Jay who is speaking the words: "Coach gave me a chance and I'm thankful that he gave it to me. I'm going to prove to people that he made the right choice. Now a lot of them are eating their words and I'm going to keep that up. We have a goal, to win the Big Ten."

As for his game-winning shots, like the one last Sunday against Purdue, Jay smiles. No, he doesn't hold something back. The idea that saving himself for a game-winner, the better to be approved, seems alien. "Don't forget," *Jay says still smiling,* "during the game you have to follow the game plan. But then you have to come out of it and score."

At the second practice of this Saturday before the Sunday game against Michigan, Knight stresses communication. "We have too many coaches talking and not enough players." It's Brian Sloan he criticizes today. Then he threatens to "go and watch the golf tournament."

"You people have to talk to each other," he insists. "Todd, did you tell him there was a screen there?"

"Say 'I got the ball,'" Ron advises.

"I got the ball," Jamal calls out the next time down.

"Shot fake, shot fake, shot fake," Knight reminds them. "Play beyond their pace defensively and play beyond their pace offensively. We can't let Rice and or Higgins get that—or flash in the middle. The flash I can stop, the score I cannot."

Joe must call the pass.

"You're not going to hear me tomorrow."

Mark has been assigned the part of Glen Rice.

"Who didn't block him out?" Knight screams from the other end of the floor.

Eric raises his hand.

"Eric, you're more effective as a scorer and a screener than as a passer, keep that in mind!" (On Monday morning Knight will lament; the only really good passer he has is Jay.)

"I want to tell you something," Bob Knight says, "winning is hard. That's why so few teams win. You can get through college half-assed. You can get through life half-assed. But I guarantee you, you can't win!"

The unexpected star of this afternoon's practice is a senior coming off an injury, one who has seen little playing time.

"I have to say this, boys," Danny tells Joby and Tates, "Kreigh is doing it all. It's all Smith."

Back inside, they must watch a tape of Michigan's game at Bloomington last season.

"Now Garrett could post," Knight tells them. "Garrett could post, get the ball and turn quickly to shoot. I don't think that we can really do that. But we can put the ball on the floor, you inside guys. We can do different things and be every bit as effective and draw the fouls more often than Garrett could."

The failures of last season's team still gnaw at him. Michigan played a match-up zone "that we just stood around against. You'll see how Smart never makes a move into the zone."

"This is just what we don't want to do here," he tells them. "We never get any penetration. We stand. We hold. Look at Eyl's pass. Look at Keith on top, and we throw it away again." (One of the team has in fact remarked that last season Eyl somehow gave up on October 15th, and did not give his all.)

"If he goes opposite with the ball, look what he's got. Where Keith had the ball, if Joe just goes underneath him, he's going to be open on the other side. Just dribble it one way and reverse it back the other way. We dribble it off the side and then just go right back down the baseline, dribble away and throw back and we're going to be open all night against this zone." So the game plan against Michigan emerges.

They're about to go off for their steaks when he invokes that Big Ten championship, the unlikeliest of Big Ten championships of Bob Knight's tenure at Indiana, on which this team has indeed begun to close in. "We start to drive the nails in the coffin tomorrow. They're going to start to beat each other!"

The six P.M. walkthrough takes place in the press room while Michigan practices on the floor, Frieder having closed his session to the press. Jay must be ready to switch, switching the essence of this game plan: "The switch just takes the pass away. It doesn't make any difference who it is. They're going to downscreen for Rice. When they do that, we're going to have to switch it."

At the heart of this game plan seems so impossible a demand that it takes your breath away. Glen Rice has the second best field goal percentage in college basketball. No matter. "Always keep in mind," Bob Knight tells his team, "that the first thing you have to do is keep Rice and Higgins from shooting the ball!" The rest is detail. Jay must be "stronger than that. He just pushes you a little bit and he's there." Todd, Eric and Brian must screen. The ball must be driven from the perimeter, forcing the corner turn. Movement inside.

"Boys," Knight tells them, "if we change direction, we'll really hurt them inside with whoever we have. We can down-screen with one big guy on another. We have to keep a good spread to what we're doing and we've got to have a possession by possession mentality at both ends of the court that just prevents us from making mistakes."

The Big Ten championship is now at stake. "We're here to play for championships," he has earned the right to promise them. "This is what tomorrow's all about, and you can't play for championships unless you've got everybody's best effort, mentally and physically. We don't win championships without that. You can be half-assed at a lot of things but you can't be half-assed at winning championships."

They can go to an early movie if they wish. But they must be rested, remembering that tomorrow "is what we're playing for." They are part of a tradition: "You're in the same position that damn near every team we've had here has been in at one time or another." And they can do it: "We don't have to do anything different from what we've been doing all week long."

There are now seven games left to the season. To be Big Ten champions Indiana must be victorious in five of them.

After he's gone, they stay to sign a card to Ohio State star Jay Burson who has broken a cervical vertebra and whom Knight has telephoned, a fact that he does not mention, as he keeps secret the many letters he receives from those who are ill, or their representatives, pleading that his presence at a fund-raiser could save a life. If he agreed to them all, there wouldn't be time for coaching, he'll report sadly.

For Jay Burson, Jay adds a #3 beside his name; Jamal adds a 23. The most ornate, if illegible, signature belongs to Kreigh Smith, a measure perhaps of his disappointment at not having had much playing time.

On Sunday morning Knight is at the board, again emphasizing blockout position, then keeping track of Rice and Higgins on the perimeter. Passes into the post must be attacked: "We just can't let passes be made and let them wheel and deal inside. We want to play under their offense and by playing under their offense, let's not get caught on the lunge."

On game day the instruction is at its most specific: "Rice or Robinson will cut to the ball. Sometimes Rice will come up and look for the shot. More often than not they're going to come underneath. Let's don't get hung up in here and he beats us to the spot."

How to defeat the Michigan shooters is his subject:

"Every time we step in front of a cutter, that just makes them go one more pass to get something. The more we make them work at both ends of the floor, the better it is for us. Don't foul shooters. You're not going to block the shot. When any one of these guys gets it and takes a turnaround shot, get up into him, get your hand up in his face, obstruct his vision, make him move, but don't come up and swat at the basketball and get a piece of his arm."

Switching is at the heart of this game plan: "They'll set downscreens for Rice. We'll switch that, recognize Rice or Higgins coming off the screen. They screen Rice to the ball. Any time Rice is opposite the ball, they're going to try to screen him toward the ball, across the lane. Rice will just cut to the ball on his own but he's going to go to the ball in that post position. Be alert to our switches.

"When we've got a screen situation, and they're bringing somebody off it, we switch it to prevent the pass, not to change men. WE SWITCH IT TO PREVENT THE PASS."

Through these intricacies of defensive positioning, the intense demands for offensive movement, Knight teaches them how to compensate for their weaknesses in sheer physical basketball ability.

And, as always, desire to win will help them. Taking the basketball from Jeff Oliphant, he makes his point. "If that son of a bitch is loose," he says fiercely, "it better be ours!"

As for their offensive play, the game plan remains the same. On this Sunday morning of the pivotal game against Michigan, he is still teaching them how to draw the foul: The pass "comes down to Eric, and as he catches it, all he's got to do is drive baseline and it's a foul, right there!

"Go after the ball with both hands, take it right to the bucket, and you've got a foul!

"Now look at Rice playing you, Joe. You've got plenty of opportunity, Joe, when you get the basketball to be down in the shot position. I don't care where you get it, instead of in an upright position like this, be down. Don't be backing away from him, and go right into the shot fake. Where Rice is playing, if you're going to shoot, he's going to run into you. Now you give him a shot fake and he's going to come at you. Time after time as we watch Rice play, he gives you that kind of room and then he comes flying up at you. We get him up and we go past him!

It seems an impossible match-up, 6-2, 190 Joe Hillman against 6-7, 215 Glen Rice. Joe does not flinch from the assignment.

"This has to, boys, be the most active offensive play that we're going to have all year. The more active we are offensively, the harder it is for these people to play with us." They must, moreover, remain conscious of Rumeal Robinson who "as he goes away looks to make the steal, he kind of slips back. He's always looking to make the steal on top if we lay the ball out there for him.

"LYNDON JONES, LOOK TO SCORE, LOOK TO PENETRATE. LOOK TO TAKE THE BALL TO THE BASKET. YOU ARE A REAL KEY IN THIS GAME OFFENSIVELY.

"Jadlow and Anderson, White, Sloan, you people have to screen, but you have to screen quickly. You can't shuffle into the screen. You have to go at the screen hard. You can screen each other. They don't do a good job when two big guys are involved in a downscreen.

"Flare! In regular offense get everything going with the flare. They have a real tendency to get caught inside. We go outside, we screen opposite. Any time you're in the vicinity of the foul line, any one of you inside people, you set a flare screen.

"We can't have any sulkers," he moves toward his conclusion, "we can't have anybody with his hands down, we can't have anybody surprised. Each guy in here has got to play to his ability. We don't have to play better than we are, we don't have to have one person play better than he is. We got to have everybody in here play to his ability." It's a concept of which he is fond and it's at the heart of his coaching year after year, asking of players only of what they're capable.

It's still only 10:50 in the morning.

Trusting this team to ready itself, the coach does not attend the pre-game meals this season. Today it's Joby Wright who addresses them on how this is the "most important game of the season." At each place is a card: "*Make* Today *Our* Day."

In attendance are some of those new recruits: Chris Reynolds, whom Ron Felling calls "effervescent"; Chris Lawson, who scored 35 points last night against the top Indiana high school team, is with his assistant coach at Bloomington South, Chris Beyers. Lawrence Funderburke in red cap and red sweatshirt is here with binoculars, no matter that he'll be sitting at courtside. He announces his 3.6 grade point average. Pat Graham, who will be voted Indiana's Mr. Basketball, having averaged 32.3 points a game, chats with the notorious Damon Bailey, still only a junior, but a future teammate.

The crowd is packed like sardines in a sea of red as Indiana goes out to play the future national champions. Rice scores at once, and then . . . Lyndon Jones scores, as he was ordered to do ("Lyndon Jones has to score!"). With 12 points he'll be the leading scorer in the first half.

When Michigan comes down the floor, it's like thunder. Rumeal seems twice the size of Lyndon. Knight is forced to substitute. Felicitously, he calls on Jeff Oliphant who contributes five points in the first half.

Lawrence Funderburke stands up and cheers every basket, his brashness giving way to pure enthusiasm.

Gary Muncy calls the game closely, but Knight is less pleased with referee Valentine. "Don't ever make a call and look at me like that!" Knight shouts.

Jamal takes over as an exhausted Joe sits down. Eric plays hard, bandage or no bandage. And when Lyndon drives once more to the basket, Todd pats him, that lesson learned in December when this team became a team. When there's controversy, it's Joe who talks to the referee.

"I have a discipline in my life," Lawrence Funderburke insists during the half, in an implied response to his troubles with his high school coach. "If I come here, I'll be the best." (That "if" should have given pause, [Funderburke will delay his signing, waiting for one more word from Knight that he really wants him] but it did not.) Sizing up the current team's deficiencies, Funderburke adds, "I can jump!"

In the second half Eric Anderson fights hard for a loose ball ("If you can't play with two hands, don't play!").

"Watch the screens!" a Michigan player calls to a teammate; they too have been prepared.

Jadlow goes down, then up, as he was ordered not to do because there wouldn't be time. He makes the shot.

When Joe sits down, Jay is awarded a leadership role by his coach. "I want you to run triangle now with Sloan screening," Jay is told.

At the end we leave our game plan.

With nine seconds left, Indiana is down by two. Eric rebounds. He passes the ball to Lyndon, who has no idea of how much time is left. Knight is on his feet. He thinks: Lyndon has to make the shot!

The seconds are ticking off, down to zero.

But the instinct of all those years, those state championships at Marion High School, playing in tandem with Jay, yields its inevitable result. Lyndon knows where Jay is. Lyndon finds Jay and passes him the ball.

"Shoot, Jay!" Knight screams as the double zeros come down.

Jay lofts the ball into the air; it reaches its highest arc, the horn sounds, and then the ball goes in, and Indiana has defeated Michigan! This miraculous shot lifts the coach off his feet and somewhat into the air so that Mary Gottlieb's grandmother, age ninety-five, sends the message that "he needs a pogo stick."

Funderburke leaps wildly out of his seat while the Indiana players celebrate on the floor.

Indiana has won, 76-75. So superior was their ball handling that Indiana committed only 9 turnovers. Rice and Higgins weren't to score; they haven't. Rice has 7, Higgins 11. Played by Joe Hillman much of the time, Rice picked up 4 personals and could only play 24 minutes. As for Rumeal, while he managed only one steal, he did score 24 points, driving again and again to the basket. They couldn't stop him.

Most amazing is that Indiana outrebounded Michigan 32-30. Twelve rebounds were contributed by the Indiana guards, as they were ordered to do. And as so ordered, Indiana got to the free throw line 24 times to Michigan's 11.

Enjoying this particular press conference, Knight insists that the last thing he told the team was, "now when we come down the floor, let's get the ball to Jones, and he dribbles across mid-court and Edwards, you stay to Jones' left, and you shoot it just at the buzzer. I said let's have a controversial ending to this game."

Knight will not grant that the Big Ten championship is now within their easy reach: "Anything can happen to us. I don't ever think what the hell we're going to be."

In the locker room, he reminds the players that Indiana's now going on the road for three games, beginning with Michigan State, where they lost last year's game thanks to bad shots taken by Calloway and Smart. But for them tonight he is all praise: "Joe has been here for five years and Joe's never seen Michigan play any better than they did today. We let it slide, 69-66. You did a hell of a job coming back in."

As always, there's a needle for someone. "Lyndon was the brains at Marion," Knight cannot resist, "but it turns out Jay was the smart one." Jay allows himself a small smile.

Everyone is asked to leave now but the new recruits, who are warned with mock ferocity: what happened to Lyndon, forgetting the clock, better not happen to any of them. Funderburke sits chatting easily with his coach-to-be, who introduces him to Landon Turner. "He's a smart boy. That's why he's going to be good here," Knight says.

"What do you think of her book?" Funderburke whispers.

"Not bad . . . for a woman," the coach replies, louder.

At Lung Cheung's, the dinner promised if they won, there is talk of the game. Ayatollah Khomeini has just put out a contract on the life of writer Salman Rushdie, a story no one at the table mentions amid the talk of coaches, of what the president of the University of Oklahoma had to say about the football player scandals, and of today's game.

IV

"This is exactly how I thought we'd come out in December, 25-7. Only I thought we'd lose to Michigan up there and beat Illinois here."

"It's not that romantic, believe me," Bob Knight had said. Jay's game-winning shots at the buzzer can be explained by his being an "athlete": "If he were a golfer, he'd be a good putter. If it were baseball, he wouldn't swing at bad pitches in crucial situations."

Yet unselfishness and the choice to play as a team, the discipline necessitated by awareness of your limitations, these are the values Indiana brings to its quest for the Big Ten championship. As for his own role, he responds obliquely: "Some coaches sit and watch things happen."

After the Michigan victory, the AP ranks Indiana fourth in the nation.

An anomalous moment comes during the half at the Michigan State game when Indiana local television broadcasts a feature with President Ehrlich dressed in a red sweater. Ehrlich agrees with two professors on how intercollegiate athletes are a "rallying point" for the entire university. "Bob Knight's wonderful teams" give "pride" to "all of us," Ehrlich says. The scene appears as awkward as Ehrlich's leaks to the press did last spring.

Indiana defeats Michigan State 76-65.

Against Minnesota, Jay gets into foul trouble and misses 15 minutes of the first half. When Todd, carried away, celebrates on the court after a basket, he's yanked from the game at once; he'd had an excellent game, which doesn't save him from the coach's wrath. Win or lose, the Indiana code of sportsmanship prevails.

At Williams Arena in Minneapolis this season, Minnesota has managed to beat Iowa, Ohio State, Illinois and Michigan. Indiana wins 75-62.

At Ohio State, Indiana commits a scant six turnovers and wins 73-66. "They give each other heat in the locker room which shows they have confidence in each other," Quinn Buckner observes after the game. It's the kind of Indiana team of which Buckner can be proud.

Nobody says anything about their having clinched the Big Ten co-championship, although they have.

Ohio State was on Thursday, a game made easier for Indiana by the absence of Jay Burson. Now on Sunday, March 6th, back in Bloomington, Indiana must face Illinois playing for the Big Ten championship outright. It's a game Bob Knight desperately wants.

The preparation is meticulous, repetitive, minute and choreographed down to the last inch of the basketball floor. As they did against Michigan, they practice on Friday, three times on Saturday and again on Sunday. Knight tells them that Illinois is "the best team at both ends of the court that there is in the country right now"; it's obvious to everyone that Illinois is a likely Final Four team.

Yet, as always, there are "some things that we can take advantage of both on defense and on offense." The game plan against Illinois involves creating an open post; people will cut in the post. As always this season Indiana must get to the foul line by driving to the basket:

"There are three things we have to do. We have to take away cuts. We have to be in a position where we're not giving up post position. We can't be in a position where they step into the post. They'll get the ball and step in quickly. You have to be damn careful making this pass across the top of the key. WE MAKE THE PASS ON THE SIDE OF THE KEY, NOT ACROSS THE KEY. When we're on the help side part of our defense, everyone is responsible for taking away the step in post."

A group is created at each end of the floor. It consists of a post man and an offensive post, plus a guard. Each group has a coach throwing the ball inside.

"We look to go in; it comes back; we switch if it comes high. I want that tight cut made every time the ball is reversed.

"We come in here. We look to post. We don't have it. Reverse. Look to post it on the other side. Any time we take it across he steps out."

What will Illinois do? "They'll fake. They'll spin. We can't let anybody come underneath us. We have to be right here ready to pick him up."

Suddenly he calls, "There's Battle! There's Anderson! They're already here!" The Illinois quickness has not been overstated and Knight respects it.

"I want you looking to back cut into the post. I'm looking for you to reverse the ball. In our game over there we had several situations where we waited until the cutter was outside the lane before we hit him. Eliminate that! We got two guys holding hands here. We don't need that. Spacing!"

"Let's go guys," Joby calls. "No mistakes. No mistakes. Take that post! It's your post!"

Joe has just been named an academic All-American. If there is a connection between intelligence and leadership, it's exemplified here. But no matter that his final Indiana season is winding down—Joe still does not escape criticism:

"How could you miss that shot? I played nineteen years and I never missed that shot!"

Undaunted, Joe remains, his voice on the floor: "Whatever side you screen, we're going to go the other way," Joe calls out.

"Spin and back," Knight tells them. "If they don't let you, just go the other way." Like Michigan, Illinois will be far superior to them in physical strength. "If they don't let you" is understood by all.

"Jesus Christ, Joe! Don't be dribbling the ball! Look!

"Too late, too late, Brian. You're standing there. We have no post play. I want this goddamn lane open the whole game! Brian, when Joe comes off that high, then you have to spin. They're not going to beat you to the post. They're going to trail you.

"Was it a good pass?" the coach suddenly demands of Eric. He answers himself: "It was a damn good pass."

Knight has told reporters that he always had Eric in mind as a four-year starter. "I didn't believe it," Eric laughs. "I never believed it. He told me, but I didn't believe him. Because I don't know when to believe him. I still don't know when he's kidding or not."

"I start with a flare. Step up and I flare. I step right here. Keep going, Joe, or we flair to this side. We screen away."

"Everybody time it!
 The screener times it!
 The cutter times it!
 The passer times it!"

This is Indiana basketball. It's Balanchine and more, a ballet in which out of superior basketball intelligence you predict and contain the movements of five wild cards, those alien dancers with their own choreography in mind. Unselfishness is the glue, as Pete Newell had reminded them. By now everyone is helping; each player supports the others' efforts.

"Chuck, we have to reverse!" Joe calls, teaching what Bob Knight calls "the way we play."

"Go high!" Todd adds, also teaching.

Finally the entire group applauds John White for a good screen.

"Good job, John," Todd calls.

One of the most articulate players, Todd notes the difference between this team and last year's in terms of how the players "come in each day understanding how each of the others feels, what the others are thinking."

The gray T-shirts are soaked.

"Come on, Meeks, step back," Joe is still yelling. "We're all moving and you haven't brought the ball in. Bring it in NOW!"

Inside, moments later, Todd straps a bag of ice around his aching ankle with an ace bandage.

On Friday night, Patrick has a weak game, although his team advances in the tournament. On Saturday morning the coach suddenly wants to be alone with his players, without his assistants: "I don't want anybody in here but me!" Outside on the moveable stands ready for tomorrow's game, Felling, Dakich and Locke sit talking quietly. It's dead silent in Assembly Hall, so that all you can hear is the eerie hum of the ventilation system. Fourteen of the nineteen managers are scattered around awaiting further instruction.

The drill on Saturday afternoon is as intense as any you'll see here.

"I spent five days setting this up. Now do what I want! If Anderson goes to the baseline, he'll have to stand next to me."

On this day no one wants to stand next to him. Eric flushes, and goes on playing.

But then he is all praise. Lyndon has brought up an important point. "We want to play a little bit to the outside. If I'm the passer, I need to think if I make the pass, Liberty's going to get it."

To prevent Illinois from getting the ball inside, the guard away from the basketball has to help defend the post.

"Forget it if you're not going to go after the ball when it's loose," Knight says, kicking a basketball high into the stands for emphasis.

Now he is using his watch to show them how long a possession lasts: 15 seconds, 30 seconds. "We still got fifteen seconds to screw around with the possession. Back it out, take your time.

"Offensively we have to open the post and defensively we have to close the post. Move the offense high to have the baseline available to cut and fill the post."

The aim is to eliminate passes into the tight cut and post man, making Illinois play with less than their strength.

"Make them scratch and scrape for everything they get.

"One thing about basketball," he tells them as this exhausting day draws to its close, "you aren't going to throw a shut-out."

Finally he reads to them from a letter sent to him by a principal at an elementary school where Jay spoke to the students fulfilling an assignment which was part of the rehabilitation program designed for him at Indiana. The letter praises Jay. It urges Knight to tell the players how much they mean to kids, how visible they are, how deeply under scrutiny is their every act. Then Knight and Lou Henson along with an entourage go to watch Patrick play basketball. Patrick excels. "It's as big a thrill as I've ever had," Bob Knight says.

On Sunday morning the Illinois weaknesses and vulnerabilities are once more elucidated. On the board is written the halftime score of their loss to Illinois at Champaign: Indiana 35, Illinois 25.

"In this game," Knight tells his team, "defending individual characteristics is far more important than defending any movements or cuts that Illinois makes in its offense."

Individual characteristics: each Illinois player is anatomized. Battle will turn to his right shoulder: "he's going to post and he's going to step out and shoot the ball, post far more often than shoot the ball. He doesn't really put the ball on the floor. He doesn't try and drive you. He wants to turn so his left hand is away from the defensive man, turning to his right shoulder, no matter where he is. If he's on the baseline with the bucket over here, he doesn't want to turn in; he wants to turn away. He wants to get his right hand and shoulder between the defense and the ball."

Preparation means leaving as little as possible to chance. They write in the red notebooks. From Battle they go on to Hamilton who "becomes the opposite, getting to his right hand, so his right hand is away from the defensive man on either side of the floor. Protecting his right hand, when he's outside Hamilton will shoot the ball. Hamilton does not want to go through play without shooting the basketball. . . ." And so it goes down through the entire Illinois squad.

As usual, Joe draws the toughest defensive assignment. This afternoon it's Nick Anderson. "And that's why I jumped all over you yesterday," Knight says, half-apologizing, "because the first play out there with you on defense, you jumped and there he went baseline. We can't give Anderson the baseline. Anderson is very aggressive on the boards, Joe. If Anderson plays you, then we've got to exhaust every possibility of getting him into foul trouble. Now Anderson is very quick, and you're not going to get by him a hell of a lot of times. But make him play you every time. If you've got the slightest opportunity, force a pass. Get into him, make him bang you as you go past him going either way.

"Anderson is a hell of a basketball player," he adds. "Right now he might be the best basketball player inside in the Big Ten." If Indiana does not defense the Illinois front line, "we don't win the basketball game."

Part of the Indiana strategy, as always, involves drawing the foul. But there's another important reason why this is especially necessary today. "We've got to reduce the time we play against these people," Knight tell them. It's a David and Goliath situation, only worse, because Knight also knows that Illinois will "play smart at both ends."

On their board is also written: Anderson, Battle: 44 points. This is the number these players acheived in their victory against Indiana here last season. Finally Knight repeats the essence of their game plan: "Feeds from the side. Get the ball to the side, get the ball to the side."

So the five wild cards, those dancers from Champaign, can be tamed.

"Did you work out this morning?" Mike Gyovai, who played for him at West Point, asks irrelevantly.

"I lay on my couch and in three minutes I went around the track," Knight answers mildly.

"What do you think?" he asks his former student.

"They'll win if they have the desire."

"Even when they have the desire, they don't always win."

The card at pre-game meal reads: *"Forty Minutes of Indiana basketball."* He has never been more prescient.

*   *   *

Ranked third in the country this morning to Illinois' eighth, Indiana begins by playing hard. Jay immediately draws a foul on Liberty, obviously the weak link.

"Lyndon, keep Joe and Jay moving," the coach calls.

"Screen the ball, Jadlow!"

Joe drives, drawing the blocking foul on Anderson, exactly as planned. But Illinois does indeed play smart, and it does not happen again. As hard as Indiana plays, Illinois wears them down. "There he is, Joe!" the coach calls. And he screams again at Lyndon: "Move people! Move people!"

An Illinois player, passing, away from the ball, slaps Eric hard in the head. No foul is called. On a Jay miss, there is little Jamal for the tip-in.

"Which single Indiana player played in every game?" Hammel quizzes when the season is over.

It's Jamal Meeks.

Holding to the game plan, Indiana has Illinois shooting only 34 percent in the first half. "Jay, Jay," Lyndon calls softly out of his supernatural ability to locate Edwards.

And then with 8 minutes to go, Indiana falters, exhausted. Eric misses an easy lay-up. "Eric, Eric, make sure of it," the coach screams. "Eric! Eric!" Knight makes a cross-over motion.

"That's a charge! That's a charge!" Knight screams. "Eddie, that was a charge to begin with!"

"Coach," says referee Hightower, "I'm having a tough enough time as it is."

"Give him a technical," Battle baits the ref.

With 17 seconds to go, Indiana is down by 2. Indiana gains possession. And then Jay does it again, that impossible high-arching baseline shot, a replay of Purdue and Michigan. The crowd goes wild, seemingly assured of an overtime.

But even as Jay releases the ball, with the zeros of the game clock just about down, Illinois guard Stephen Bardo does what Bob Knight had predicted Illinois would do: he plays very smart indeed. Just as Jay lets go of the ball, Bardo makes the sign for a time-out. The shot falls. Jay is jubilant. Jay smiles a wide smile.

But the referees put 2 seconds back on the clock.

To Bardo's amazement, no one is at the baseline to disturb him. He fires—one long 50 foot inbounds pass, straight as an arrow into Nick Anderson's capable hands. Jumping high over the smaller Jay Edwards who is guarding him, Anderson fires what looks like a 35 foot shot. The basketball bursts through the net.

Illinois has won, 70-67.

Anderson and Battle? Today they scored not 44, but 42. "They shut us out completely inside," Lou Henson, ever gracious, says after the game. It obviously wasn't enough.

Outside an ice storm ravages Bloomington, setting a thick layer of ice down with hard snow over it, an ugly jagged surface of ice and snow. Inside Knight is beside himself. He castigates his team for not playing the 40 minute game they had to play to win. They depart, only to return at 7:30 to watch a tape of the game. They may not be Big Ten champions after all.

When Knight leaves Assembly Hall at ten, the windows of his car are thick and lacy with ice. "Get in!" he tells his guests while he struggles furiously with his windshield scraper. Leslie's is closed, but they open up for him, for veal chops and spaghetti and iced tea. It's clear that he's exhausted, and hardly up to a social evening. But his guests, former players, are important to him. He wants to know about their families, their work. The game is not once mentioned. Afterwards, Gary Eiber is advised not to begin the drive back to Ohio in the ice storm. "The people here aren't very good driving in the snow," Knight says in one of his wildest understatements. Even he drives cautiously tonight.

Throughout the week, unimpeded by man, ice carpets Bloomington. Ambulances race by, since the main arteries, let alone the secondary roads, are neither plowed, salted nor sanded. The wife of Knight's high school principal, Robert Quay Norris, falls and cracks her head on the ice outside her hotel parking lot. Jeff Oliphant falls outside his apartment, injures his knee and is forced to undergo surgery. Even the parking lot of Assembly Hall where athletes come and go is not plowed for days!

Practice resumes on Monday afternoon, however, despite the continuing snowstorm. Knight takes the Illinois loss hard. It presages the end of their miraculous run. And Indiana had been winning for most of the game. They were up by 12 and 10 for a good part of it!

"You did beat them," Hammel ventures, consoling, adding perspective.

"But we should have won!"

The culprits are Todd, and Lyndon and Jay who are accused of letting others do their dirty work, who do not block out. Only Joe, scoring 24 and picking up four fouls as he struggled against bigger, quicker players, gave his all. (No one mentions what the overtime would have accomplished given Joe's four personals had Nick Anderson not made that shot.) That their mental toughness was undermined by the other side's overwhelming physical superiority is also treated as irrelevant.

Two games remain: Wisconsin here on Thursday, and Iowa at Iowa City on Saturday, a game it is unlikely they can win. This is not an easy week.

"I want to see somebody proud of what they do!" he tells Jadlow on Monday. "Dunk the ball!" Jadlow does, twice. Joe is ordered to "straighten him out or he can't play."

Eric is summoned to the coaches' locker room. Knight sends out for a season stat sheet. Eric's game has fallen off.

Inside on the board it says: 40 minutes. 11:30 47–34, and 35 points, what Illinois will subsequently score. 72–52 is also on the board: this is Wisconsin's victory score over Illinois. If Wisconsin beat Illinois, and Illinois beat Indiana, how can Indiana beat Wisconsin, which they must do to be Big Ten champions?

Knight points to the "40 minutes."

"There are two guys in here who played as hard as they can play. Hillman and D'Aloisio (who was not in the game). The closest is Meeks. Lyndon and Jay did not block out. If you don't do as well as you can, I don't know how you can be successful doing anything. We rested eight and one-half minutes and that cost us the game."

He has figured out that in their two games Indiana has led Illinois 55 out of 80 minutes (they led Michigan 70 minutes). "If we can get to 40 minutes playing as hard as each of you can play, we can beat anybody! That's what this ballgame Thursday will be about. It'll be about making every play, every possession!"

And now he launches into his most imaginative motivational strategy of the season, an exercise which goes to the heart of his team's limitations and ends on a restatement of their strengths.

"Let me set up a decathlon, Joe," Knight says walking to the board, as if he were addressing not the entire team assembled in their locker spaces, but their leader, who represents them all. "Ten events." He writes: High Jump, Long Jump, 100, 220, 400.

He stops. "We'll throw something." He adds the shot, and then the hurdle.

"What are three more events? A 400 meter relay, an 800 meter relay, is that nine? Let's lift weights! All right. Let's go down through here. Ten events that to some degree are going to determine athletic skill. We are now in a game: our basketball team against the basketball team from Illinois in those ten events. Who's going to win the high jump?"

He doesn't wait for an answer. He moves on rapidly. This is no "mind game," however. It's a way of reminding his team of their limitations, the necessary step to playing to their strengths. They need only one more victory; it's late in the season; it would seem that these lessons have already been exacted. Yet he's willing to go over it again.

"Who's going to win the long jump? Who's going to win the hundred? I mean, what are we going to win in here? I don't care how you do it. I think if you take our best person in each one of these events, and they take their best person, we win none of them. I think if you take seven people and they take seven, we might never finish in the top seven in some of these events."

He pauses, ready to establish the point of the conceit. "Track is an athletic event. *Basketball we have a chance to win, even though we can't do some of these things as well as another team can do them.* But we only have a chance to win if we can play forty minutes, and that's not what we're getting. . . ."

There is more than one way to be a fine basketball team. There is a way to be a fine basketball team without superior athleticism. But that requires never forgetting that your limitations necessitate a different kind of effort.

There's a black bounded box at the center of their whiteboard. Inside it Knight now writes: steals, loose balls, rebounds, tip-ins.

"We've got to develop a mental understanding, boys, that we just have to play better than other people do. How many steals do we get per game? Loose balls? Rebounds? Tip-ins? How many? Not many. Not many compared to a really good athletic team."

They are not a "really good athletic team." But they are a good team: they have compensated for their weaknesses with their own set of strengths: "So far this year we shot 300 more free throws than our opponents have . . . that's one way where we make up for a little of this. We try not to throw the ball away. We have patience instead of tip-ins. . . ."

Appreciating their strengths, they can still be Big Ten champions, but it must be by an intelligent game, not by running up and down the floor, relying on athletic ability where they will be overmatched. They are not as physically strong as many of the teams they have defeated. Rarely do they outrebound the other side. Only seven of them significantly contribute. Three of them, he complains, Jones, Edwards and Anderson, too often retain a "high school mentality": "It just isn't high school; a missed blockout doesn't cut your lead from 24 to 22; it cuts your lead 5 to 1." High school all-stars, they are accustomed to winning by big margins, a luxury, surely they know by now, *this* team can ill afford.

There is much to be proud of. Knight tells them they have done "a great job in a game where we're down." Yet "when we get a lead, we're playing in high school again." He adds anger to his voice now: "I mean, when you've got the knife in somebody's heart, you have to stick it right out his back! You're not playing Our Lady of the Heart!"

It's midpoint of this excruciating week. Late in the afternoon after practice he asks Jones, Meeks and Anderson to remain for further work. Others are given a choice: they can leave or they can stay. It is in such situations that he evaluates his players. Mark Robinson is in the shower. Stephen Trust is asked to deliver a message: did Mark think there was nothing he needed to work on? Mark is not to be ordered to come back out.

"I should be able to play him, but I can't," Knight says. Others are missing as well. Jay is out with the flu. Chuckie White has "a headache."

"This is a better defensive team," Knight reflects, once again comparing this team with last season's. "Smart and Calloway couldn't play defense. That's 40 percent of your team. Then they weren't patient on offense."

Chris Lawson chats with his future coach about the game when Patrick's team beat his. "Who scored beside you?" Knight asks. "Did anybody shoot?" He knows how to talk to young Chris who is surprisingly matter of fact and seems not to be at all nervous.

"When you play for us," Knight tells him, "every game you'll play against somebody better than you. Too many kids retain a high school mentality. We played 32 minutes and then we got tired. You're done playing against guys you can screw up against."

He can't forget Illinois, nor will he all week. "Look at you, Jay, see, this is where I just want to cry. If you're right where we need to be, he's got to throw it back out. So instead they get a three pointer. See, that is it, fellas, that's the game. If you don't want to cry (his voice grows softer) when you see this. . . ."

Then, louder, he makes his case: "I don't care if you have heart failure on this play. I don't care if you give the last ounce of energy you got left in your body. This is the ballgame, see, nothing else means anything after that . . ." So he lets Jay know that basketball is not always about game-winning shots.

"Look at the way he's standing," Coach Henry Iba observes, having arrived for a visit at this crucial moment in the Indiana season. "He's churning inside." Coach Iba is tall, slightly stooped, gentle and courtly and kind; he is fighting a bad cold, not easy on this icy landscape for an elderly man; he has just about lost his voice, but not his enthusiasm, concentration and clarity.

"Let me see your hands," he asks 6-10 Chris Lawson. "How much do you weigh?" is his next question. Lawson, red-haired, freckled and boyish, is impeccably polite, the kind of Indiana player you saw in the movie *Hoosiers*.

"Inside," Joe is taking heat for not having known where the ball was on the last basket in the first half against Illinois. "If we're sitting on his left hand, he has nowhere to go. If we tell you someone's going to the left, he's going to the left!"

"I thought this year he'd change a little," whispers Coach Iba, alluding to the coach's new marriage. "Oh, I know him better than anybody!"

Now Jadlow is yelled at, Jadlow the scapegoat of the week. "You have a pair of hands! You're there to catch the ball! That's why they won't throw you the ball!"

Jamal too has lessons to learn: "You're not here to dribble the ball. You're here to get the ball where it has to go!"

"The worst play in basketball is a bad pass," says Coach Iba. Now he wants to know what position Joe plays in baseball. Joe passes by and whispers the answer: the outfield and first base.

"Jadlow, get right on line and make two free throws! Take your time!"

"He'll make it!" encourages Coach Iba. "He'll make this shot." As if hearing him, warming to Coach Iba's good will, Todd makes both.

"That boy with his thumb wrapped," Coach Iba now asks Ron Felling, "Does he have trouble with free throws? Get his shoulders straight, square up."

"How many games of basketball did you play last year?" Coach Iba turns to Chris.

"Fifty," says Chris Lawson with a little smile.

Coach Iba is creating an Indiana team. "What year is that player with the bandage?" he now whispers, eying Eric. "He's going to be a good player." Chris "will be a good player for him. He'll be good playing with the freshman (Eric)."

Meanwhile Eric is garnering some encouragement from another coach: "Good, really good. It only takes one second to see and then you can make the play. That cost us a possession against Illinois on Sunday. Because you went after the guy coming off the baseline."

Hammel walks in.

"He's a good writer," says Coach Iba.

Eric is shown a pass he can't make. "That's the difference between being a basketball player and you being a guy with blond hair. You aren't going to die. If you do, we'll get someone else. Get your mind made up. You're going to rip these guys apart. Do you know if you're Swedish or Norwegian?"

Eric goes off laughing. In fact, the college schedule is bound to exhaust freshmen. Eric is very tired.

Back in their locker room, they are finally on the subject of Wisconsin: "Wisconsin is looking to go inside against us. Hey, we had an opportunity to beat Illinois and win the Big Ten championship and we didn't do it. Sometimes you won't ever get that chance again. But we got the same chance on Thursday and it won't be any easier. Nobody can be too tired to win. Nobody can be too tired to win."

Lyndon is shy about women in the locker room, but not the younger Chris Lawson. "It doesn't bother me," he says.

There are gratifying aspects to this season which have nothing to do with basketball. Jamal has improved in his studies. Last semester he failed Uralics, a course about the history of Inner Asia. Now he has gotten 45 out of 45 on a geology test, a subject few can find fascinating, athlete or not. "I'm going to get an A in geology!" Jamal predicts. The gratification of doing well is stressed by Buzz Kurpius no less than by Bob Knight. She thinks about last season. "Ricky undermined academic discipline," Buzz has concluded.

"I've known Bob a long time," says Coach Iba, but Michigan "was the first time I saw him come out of his shell like that. I was so happy for him." But as this endless week progresses, tension accumulates like grime on your skin. "He's very tense," Coach Iba reports. "It's hard to lose when you have the other team beat."

"You're playing for the championship," Knight asserts. "I don't want a drop left!"

On Wednesday, Jay is named Big Ten Player of the Year.

"Hey, there isn't a thing I can do in terms of giving you this championship," Knight concludes. "If there was, I'd do it. There isn't anything I wouldn't do to see that you get it. But you've got to win it. You come in here tonight, you give anything less than your best, you miss the blockout, hey, you won't beat this team . . . but goddamn it, there shouldn't be a more determined team taking the floor anywhere in America than us tonight. The most successful people in life in any field of human endeavor are those people that can give their best effort in the most meaningful of situations. You give your best effort when it counts the most."

Sister Miriam Schultheis of Fort Wayne, for whose learning center Knight participated in a fundraiser on that day last season he told President Ehrlich he would remain at Indiana, is here. She wears a red sweater over her white habit. "Be damn sure you wear it," the coach had told her.

"Would St. Jude listen to a Methodist?"

"If he has faith," says Sister Miriam.

It's to the Patron Saint of Impossible Causes to whom Knight prays this season. "Pray for us tonight," Knight asks Sister.

Ron Felling addresses the team at the pre-game meal. "You

seniors, it's your last home game. It means so much to us. Opportunity knocks for Indiana tonight."

Privately, Ron and Joby agree. For Indiana to win tonight, as has been true all season, Jay must have a great game. "It's all on Jay."

In the locker room, proffering his gentle hand, Coach Iba has some special words of encouragement and praise for Todd Jadlow. "I want that center to have a great game," says Coach Iba as he takes his seat. "If he has a great game, they won't have any trouble. This is going to be a big night for Bob."

Kreigh Smith plays tonight, given a chance on his senior night, as Steve Eyl was last season. Jamal comes in and is effective. Eric dunks the ball, exactly as he had been taught to do in that late afternoon extra practice. Jay is covered with sweat and lies down on the floor during time-outs to soothe his sore back. But by the half he has 13 points to Eric's 14.

And Todd has another excellent game, as willed by Coach Iba. "Lyndon!" Todd calls as Lyndon momentarily loses his man. Todd scores, a leader out on the floor, alongside Joe.

Whenever Todd scores, Coach Iba calls out, "That's my man!" Jay too begins to lead, calling to Jamal to throw the ball to Todd. When Kreigh scores a field goal at last with less than a minute to play, from the bench Todd stands and cheers. Under Coach Iba's kindly eye, Todd has scored 18 points with 7 rebounds.

Indiana has had 39 free throw attempts, to Wisconsin's 15, and 5 turnovers to Wisconsin's 13. But, as usual, they're out-rebounded, 37–29. And so they have proven conclusively now that despite their opponent's physical superiority they have become the better basketball team. The ball handling, the offensive movement, the defensive positioning, the fruit of their mental game, their preparation, have brought them Indiana's most coveted prize: the Big Ten championship.

On this senior night, Bob Knight takes the microphone to attack "all the brilliant prognosticators around the country none of whom have ever played the game." (In fact, Ira Berkow has, others have.) When he says, "there has been nobody in nineteen years better at getting a team ready to play than Joe Hillman," Joe smiles and cries.

"The most valuable player in the league is the player that does the most to get his team to the championship," Knight tells the audience. "This team is the champion of the Big Ten and Joe Hillman has done more than anybody. We're not talking about the best player; we're talking about the most valuable, and if you run into Dick Vitale or anyone else that disputes the fact that Joe Hillman is the most valuable player in the Big Ten, then you tell them to stick it up their ass!"

A dean sitting near Harry Pratter expresses shock at this language broadcast out over the microphone to the 17,000 faithful.

Knight introduces his seniors, now, in "alphabetical order" with Joe last. Todd acknowledges players like "Kreigh and Mike who give the team so much that people don't notice." Like his coach, he thanks the sportswriters for giving them "an incentive to work hard." Joby and Ron are thanked, as is Coach Knight, who, as usual, has fled to the locker room. Brian thanks the Indiana managers and reminds the fans that "we never doubted ourselves. We always had a belief in Coach Knight and that if we just listened to what he said, and what he wanted done, we would get the job done."

Joe is poised and unemotional as he ribs Joby "because I wore his number. Hopefully I've done what he wanted me to do with his number." Hinting at how feelings change, he remembers how much he hated Dan Dakich when he was a freshman and Dakich "knocked me around to make me do what had to be done."

At the press conference, Knight lobbies again for Joe to be named most valuable player in the league: "It's hard enough to get some goddamn kids to go to class, let alone to take correspondence courses to stay eligible," he reminds the sportswriters, some of whom have a tendency to forget that they are writing about students. He compares Joe with Quinn Buckner, the highest compliment he can bestow. Tonight he also praises Todd for his excellent second half, and he confides that as he took Jamal out of the game, he realized "there is no way we win the Big Ten championship without Jamal Meeks."

Knight also spends considerable time at this press conference making the case for Indiana's receiving the top seed in the Midwest at the NCAA tournament. Didn't Illinois lose at Purdue, Wisconsin and Minnesota? Indiana won in all those places. And Indiana has won the conference championship by winning its last three games on the road.

He knows that with Kendall Gill back in the lineup Illinois will defeat Michigan on Saturday. He knows too that Indiana with Jay's back hurt, with Eric exhausted, with Todd hobbling, may well lose at Iowa. He has won the Big Ten and he argues his case: he should have the top seed:

"The Big Ten championship is what we play for. I don't know what the rest of them play for, but that's what we play for. And any time that we're able to do it, I think that's a great accomplishment for our team." (Later, he tells me that the other coaches in the conference "water down the Big Ten championship because none of them win it.")

"I would wonder," Knight muses, "when the last time a team unanimously picked to finish 6th or 7th won the championship. . . ."

He turns to Bob Hammel, seated in his customary front row seat to the right of the speaker's podium, as if Hammel the master statistician could come up with this answer on the spot.

"The son of a bitch probably picked us to finish 8th," Knight needles.

He admits to putting pre-season predictions up in the players' locker room. After the third time Indiana gave up 100 points to the other side, he took them down. He thought: "I wonder if they believe all this stuff."

In that locker room tonight Joe is pleased with his star pupil, Eric Anderson. "You were even talking out there," Joe tells Eric. "You said, 'come on, let's go.' I really liked that."

(Eric confesses that Joe will "hit me, nothing big, but he'll punch me on the leg. If I'm not playing well, he says, 'don't be a wuss.' He hits me all the time to shape up. Out of the view of everyone he gives me a punch. He hits me.")

To the reporters, Joe underlines the team ethic: "This team doesn't care who scores. That's one reason why we've done so well. We do the things that have to be done without anybody worrying about who does this and who does that."

Exemplifying the unselfishness that brought this team success, Joe next praises his disciple: "Eric played one of his best games of the year. I told him before the game, if he didn't I was going to kick his ass."

Jay is asked about his many honors: He's Big Ten Player of the Year, and he'll be a first team All-America (UPI) and a second team (AP). "I'll look at that when the season's over," Jay says cryptically.

At Iowa City two days later Knight tests how quixotic it may be to draw on players other than Lyndon, Jay and Joe, Todd, Eric, Brian and Jamal for the post-season tournament. He considers not even dressing four of them: Jay, who has had the flu, who lay on a table getting his back worked on after the Wisconsin game; Todd, who turned his ankle again (Larry Rink whispers that he's been playing on a stress fracture); Eric, who's exhausted; and Joe, who has to be exhausted.

The idea of four starters in street clothes obviously appeals to Knight's imagination. It's a way of asserting the value of the Big Ten championship and that today's games, Indiana at Iowa, but also Illinois at Michigan, have nothing to do with who will win the first seed in the Midwest, Indiana or Illinois. The stakes seem high: the first round for the top seed will be played at the Hoosier Dome in Indianapolis.

"What do you think?" Knight asks Hammel.

Hammel dissents. Having his four best players walk out in street clothes will excite too much "notoriety." It's too bold a move. Knight decides to have Eric and Joe dress for the game while Todd and Jay will not.

But this is about more than resting his starters. There is pride, the pride in four people who, battered and tired, clawed their way to a Big Ten championship. This hard endurance is something Bob Knight respects: he will not expose these students to losing their final game of the season, to ending their superb season on a loss. His pride in them forbids it. It's senior day here at Iowa for B. J. Armstrong, Roy Marble and Ed Horton. Mothers are laden with flowers. The crowd is ready for its final frenzy. Indiana may well lose, but Joe, Eric, Todd and Jay will not.

At pre-game meal before his arrival, players and coaches talk quietly. Ron Felling jokes about calling the pancakes "flapjacks." "Shut up, Joan!" Knight suddenly shouts before all from the other end of the room, apropos of nothing. Yet only yesterday when I did not attend practice, he had telephoned: "where were you?" And he found room on one of the planes for this trip to Iowa. He had told Connie Chung coaching basketball cannot be compared with brain surgery, suggesting a perspective placing sports in their appropriate place in our culture. He had benched Jay last season *before* he became academically ineligible, demonstrating that a student's appreciation of his education did indeed come first: a 1–4 start to the Big Ten season was the fruit of his benching Jay then. Winning is *not* everything for Bob Knight, as his detractors insist. And yet his commitment to what he does produces this stress, this intensity, this demeanor.

3-2-1: today Knight decides to change places with—Don Fischer. He'll be "Don." Fischer will be "Bob." Fischer has never had, and will never again have, so much to say.

"Bob," Knight begins, "how about a few comments on the performance of the team, first of all in the game against Wisconsin on Thursday night. . . ."

It will be a long time before "Bob" can get a word in.

"Don," Fischer finally replies, "I thought we played pretty well in some respects. . . ."

"Don" cuts Fischer off because he has more to say about how tight the team was, how they had just lost a very tough game to Illinois.

"Well, Don, I mean Bob," Knight says, "you had to be pleased, Bob, at the way your kids wound up playing that game with the championship on the line."

There is, however, method to this madness.

"Coach," Knight says, "far be it for me to offer any suggestions on how you should play this game. But if it were me, I would not play Edwards and Jadlow in the ballgame today simply because of the injuries they have sustained and the fact that Edwards during the first three days of this week was having a temperature hovering around 100 degrees. Don't let me influence your thinking in your lineup, Coach, but I would offer these suggestions to you."

As broadcaster Fischer, Knight suggests "this is a good game to develop your depth to play people who haven't played a great deal or people that are going to be called upon to play in a tournament situation.

"Let me ask you this, Bob. I have on occasion in the past been credited with the lineups you have used, and let me just throw out a lineup that I would use were I you in today's ballgame. . . ."

Knight slips again. He says "Don." Quickly he recovers. "We've talked about Edwards, we've talked about Jadlow, and we've talked about depth and being at an absolute peak for tournament play. How would you feel about a lineup starting today's ballgame, Bob, that would involve Meeks, Smith, Robinson, White and Sloan?"

And now Fischer rises to the occasion.

"Don," Fischer tells Knight, "you've done it again. I think you've come up with an excellent lineup to start today's ballgame and I think we just might try that this afternoon."

As "Don," or as plain Bob, it's Knight who claims the last word. But it's a word for his team, not for himself: "On behalf of all of us around the network, Bob," Bob Knight says, "to the Indiana players a tremendous congratulations for a job well done with the Big Ten championship."

"If you continue that, you'll be coaching the game," Hammel tells Fischer.

"No, no," says Fischer, "this is as far as we go, unless he wants to trade paychecks."

"I think people will like that," Knight says. Then he adds, "this game means nothing."

Kreigh will play because he played hard against Wisconsin, and "the other guys weren't too upset" with him. Then Knight repeats, "it's a meaningless game. I had them at their peak for Thursday night's game. This game means something to Iowa. It doesn't mean anything to us."

Before the game he eats an enormous sticky cinnamon roll, an object so gooey he has to attack it with a knife and fork. Maryland coach Bob Wade dehydrated during last night's win against North Carolina State and had to be hospitalized. "Maybe I'll dehydrate before the game," Knight murmurs. He remembers once when he couldn't coach and used that time to visit a recruit: "I brought Jadlow into my life."

By the time this game starts, Patrick's team, Bloomington North, has lost by four points and has been eliminated from the state tournament. But Patrick went 10–17, scoring 21 points.

Just before tip-off, Knight comes out and embraces B.J. Armstrong. He tells B.J. how much he has enjoyed watching him play. B.J. says "thank you."

Sitting right behind the Indiana bench is an Indiana student who at Knight's annual meeting with the Indiana student body stood up to ask a question only for Knight to tell him he had first to lose 30, no 50, pounds. Only then could he ask, this in front of thousands of his peers. But then Knight arranged for

Tim Garl to put the boy on a weight program. He has been given special access to practice. Now here he is at Iowa City, having traveled with the team, all smiles, an example of Bob Knight's special brand of tough love.

How the first team, sitting on the bench, responds to the second team, out playing Iowa, exemplifies today the unselfish team spirit that has fueled Indiana all this long season. Most vociferous in their praise for their less-talented teammates are Todd and Joe, Todd at once on his feet cheering Kreigh as he gets a shot off. Then, as Indiana spurts ahead, the normally cool, undemonstrative Jay is on his feet, yelling instructions, mixed with praise.

At the first official timeout, the starters on the bench rush out onto the floor to greet the second string.

"Go, Jamal," Todd yells to Meeks who started today in recognition of his contribution this season. "Mark, keep moving on defense!"

In a huddle, it's Joe, and not Knight, who addresses them: "Kreigh, you gotta move. You gotta screen and move." And so Joe teaches "the way we play."

"Mark, stay down. Don't go up with him!" Now it's Eric, Joe's disciple, who is yelling from the bench, exemplifying the chain of leadership inspired by Joe Hillman.

When Kreigh hits a three, Jay is off his feet. Joe too yells encouragement. Bob Knight, however, observing all this, is exasperated by Kreigh's mistakes: "Does he understand English?"

"I came to see the Big Ten champs," an Iowa fan complains during the half. "I didn't pay to see the third team."

"Did you find your family?" Jay asks Todd, a native of Kansas.

Fans come up to the bench before the second half begins in search of autographs. "Thank you, Sir!" a child says to Todd. Todd turns around and flashes an ironic smile, revealing the humility to recognize the absurdity of this. Jay is asked to sign a pastel drawing of himself, number 3. He signs, without even looking at the picture.

"Everybody calm down!" Jay says as they start the second half.

"Go sit next to Joe!" Knight orders Kreigh in whom he still has hopes of a good game (About such things he's never wrong—which may be why some players will say: he can *give you* a 20 point game if he wants to, he can *make you* an All-American.)

Jay takes to encouraging Jamal while Todd cheers Kreigh, as do Joe and Eric. They all enjoy Kreigh's game. Now he has his feet set. He's not backing up on the player guarding him. Kreigh scores 23 points, has 8 rebounds and does not turn the ball over once, in, however, a losing effort.

After the game, the press wants to know if winning this game was a secondary thing for Knight. "Winning the game has never been a secondary thing to me," Knight insists. Could it be interpreted as meaningless? they persist. "It sure as hell wasn't meaningless. I'm goddamn sweating . . . if the goddamn game was meaningless, I'd have been in Columbus, Indiana watching my kid play today."

In the players' locker room it is Kreigh's day, at last. But the taste is bittersweet, more bitter perhaps. Flushed, Kreigh seems more despairing than elated. It has come too late.

Knight's talk to his players back at Assembly Hall returns once again to that loss to Illinois, who battered Michigan this afternoon 89-73. "You think about the errors you made at the end of the Illinois game in the last ten minutes . . . we had them beat. We need to be a little stronger, not get tired and we could have beat Illinois by about fifteen here last Sunday. We let it get away from us. That tells me that we can play anybody."

How? "We can't make mistakes. We can't make turnovers. We can't miss open shots. We have to have secondary break where we're really going to the bucket and getting to the free throw line."

It's the game plan of the season reiterated. (The final stat? Indiana converts more free throws—718—than its opponents *attempt:* 637.)

"I don't want anybody taking calls from reporters," Knight demands. "I don't want anybody talking to anybody! Period. I don't want to see the first goddamn quote from anybody. I just want us concentrating on being the best goddamn basketball team in this tournament we can be." So he introduces the tone on this last day of the regular season necessary for tournament play.

As he wearily gets into his car, a mother pushes a child forward to get his autograph. Then she rushes up. "It's my fiftieth birthday," she croons. Knight quietly signs. "People amaze me," he says softly. He talks about this Big Ten championship compared with others he has won: of the nine, only twice did Indiana win more than fifteen games—what this unlikely, heroic team has achieved.

I begin to compare Joe to Quinn, Quinn who, covering the Iowa game, told me this very afternoon how he "treated each guy differently," Quinn as a leader who rose from the ranks rather than being imposed from above.

"You know nothing about leadership," Knight says.

As for Todd and Jay, the way they encouraged their teammates today? "That's what they're supposed to do."

There's still Chuck Marlowe's television show to tape, and that's his final stop before going home. He speaks to the Indiana faithful about how tired the team is, and how he'll need rotation from people on the bench. If he has any doubts about how well that bench can play "the way we play," he keeps them to himself.

The players watch the NCAA pairings together, Joe doing most of the exclaiming as they sprawl on tables and chairs. They leave the little television room off the court as soon as Indiana is listed as number two seed in the *West*. Not especially disturbed by that, they go out onto the floor to have their team picture taken.

But the coaches make them wait. And so they play a little schoolyard basketball, bouncing the ball between their legs up to the basket. Jay, sore back or not, does 360's off by himself. Eric makes 17 dunks in a row "straight up." The others urge Chuckie White to try. (Knight agrees, he's their best athlete, but one who has had difficulty with the Indiana system. He'd like him to transfer to a school where his skills would better suit the system, Knight says.)

"No steps, no steps!" the players call. Chuckie still refuses, but Magnus will try. At a far basket, Jay keeps shooting, basket after basket, alone.

Eric Ruden lines them up. He seems careful to mix black and white players. Joe teases Eric. Why doesn't he go into the coaches' locker room and tell them, "we're ready!"

When Patrick wanders out, Joe needles him: "You in this picture?"

When Knight comes out, after much delay, he says, "Let's go! We've got thirty seconds!"

Inside, with them, he is contained. He does not once allude to their having lost the top seed. Instead he brings them back to a year ago, to Indiana's defeat at the hands of Richmond. On Thursday in Tucson, Arizona, they will play George Mason, a team from the same conference. George Mason even has a player just like Richmond's Woolfolk, last year's nemesis.

The psychology is obvious. History must not repeat itself. Last year they could not handle the step-in post or the post part of the Richmond flex: "Garrett absolutely just got eaten alive. Garrett played as though these guys weren't supposed to play and if you'll recall, Garrett spent forty minutes whining and bitching in the game. He spent forty minutes whining and bitching and he didn't make shots and he didn't guard anybody."

Knight is too brilliant a psychologist, far too astute, to end on a negative note. He tells his players he likes where they are: "I like the situation that we have to play in. We're the kind of team that can really play the people well that we've got to play against here. There are a couple of teams in that bracket that rely on the press. We love to play against the press. . . ."

He talks about tickets. He's disappointed that their families will have so far to go. "Let's play our way closer," he tells them. "The regional is in Denver, isn't it?"

As for their practices this week, "you sure as hell won't be worked to death," Knight tells his team.

But spiritually no less than physically, this team is tired. Some of the players complain that Jay hasn't worked on anything since he's been here. Another had written the number 25 in his notebook and crossed out each day until 0 remained, yesterday. After that it wouldn't be so bad since once they lost, it would be over. Some feel the coach didn't yell at Jay because he'd "walk right out." One ventures that Chuckie deliberately played poorly against Iowa, knowing he would transfer.

On this Sunday too Ricky Calloway is in town. At Kansas, he confides, "Monday's drug tests are announced to the team on Friday!"

V

"You remember when you were a kid growing up and believed in Santa Claus? There's not that much difference between Claus and me today, you know. We're two overweight, lovable guys that kids really enjoy."

"Do they have a chance at the Final Four?" I ask Hammel, that Greek chorus of Indiana basketball.

"No," Hammel says confidently. "They haven't the talent. Someone will beat them."

Of course he's been wrong before.

Indiana handily defeats George Mason, a game Knight treats as a reprise of Iowa, a scrimmage with exercise for some and rest for others. Eric Anderson and Lyndon Jones play longest: 24 minutes each. Lyndon gets the most rebounds: 8. Whenever Jamal is in the game, the lead increases. Indiana commits 17 turnovers. It doesn't matter.

They beat University of Texas at El Paso, 92-69. Eric, who has been accused of being lazy and not ambitious enough (but it was his mediocre first semester grades, far beneath his ability, the coaches had in mind, not his basketball), stars with 24 points.

At Tucson, there is a press conference where Knight brings not, as is customary, his seniors, but Hillman and Edwards. It's Jay he compliments, no matter that he adds a needle about Jay's defense.

"We need him to get like Joe is, and he'll have to be that way next year," Knight speaks to his player through the public gathering. "What we need from him is him talking." So he offers Jay the team leadership: "Joe's done a great job this year, and that's exactly where we've got to have Edwards next year."

His players know it by now. But Bob Knight does not know that Jay has already decided to leave Indiana and turn pro.

Stoical as always, Jay remains impassive. Now that he's "hot," he has no intention of remaining at Indiana. He may never be this "hot" again. That Sunday night in December when he disappeared he traveled back home to Marion where his longtime girlfriend was having a baby, his baby. Now she must work in a department store to support them.

Jay is leaving. But still part boy, part man, he worries about whether the coach will let him come back to see Indiana games. A tread of paranoia colors his reasoning. Jay thinks: he'll announce that he is going pro first, and *then* talk to the coach. If he talks to the coach first, maybe the coach will say something to prevent him, lie about his drug tests, say he did something wrong. . . .

Is he frightened of playing against Michael Jordan? one of his contemporaries wants to know, not addressing the paranoia, the confusion of that statement.

Smaller than most pro-players, with thin, spindly legs, Jay confesses he is a little worried about that.

Indiana advances to the regional semifinal at Denver where they are matched with Seton Hall. In the media orgy of the NCAA tournament Knight speaks out about that lost top seed: "If the Big Ten champion doesn't get the first seed, the best league in the country according to every power rating I've seen, then why the hell play it? What we ought to do is schedule eighteen Hoosier Conference teams!" National reporters have their shot at him, questioning yet again his having allowed Jay to play. So in May Knight once more explains that after that Great Alaska shootout and the marijuana epidemic, the three players he got rid of had lied to him. Of those who remained, two "were not particularly important to Indiana basketball, and did not play much at all. We kept two kids who didn't even play. But they stayed to the end. So if I can try to help them, I don't have any problem helping Jay Edwards."

As the tournament progresses, Bob Knight is honored: Coach of the Year, by the U.S. Basketball Writers' Association, and then by the AP. Graciously, Knight praises his team: "I had a group that worked hard and pulled together and for one another. They did what they did as a team and this is a team award more than anything else."

Of course he cannot resist a needle, the irony of his being honored by his antagonists of the Fourth Estate: "If I had gotten an award from the NRA or the Fly Fishermen of America," he tells them, "I could say I have a lot of friends among them. But for me to get an award from the press, it really means a lot to me because I know it's not based on favoritism." In fact, some of the press has relented this season, and now even the New York *Times* prints a large photograph of a benign Knight smiling at player-of-the-year Sean Elliott. Is he being canonized, "the elder statesman" he predicted he would become?

There are social issues at this tournament. With his customary bite, Knight attacks those schools firing coaches who have done well. Always he's quotable: "What they ought to do is fire the Pope. There aren't enough priests. They can't keep nuns in their orders. . . ."

Toward Seton Hall he's playful. "Joe does a lot of our scouting," he says at a Denver practice, as he sits with Hillman. "I haven't seen them. I'll have to talk to Joe and get his opinion on their personnel."

"Somewhere down the line," Bob Hammel sounds his customary warning, "reality intervenes."

Indiana is outplayed by Seton Hall. When Joe isn't on the floor, they are scarcely a team. After a lackluster start, Jay picks up two fouls, and sits down; he plays only 4 of the first 20 minutes.

The altitude necessitates that rotation from the bench for which Knight had attempted to plan. The altitude does not bother Seton Hall, which never returned to New Jersey after their first round, and which has been here to acclimate. One wonders how many weeks of classes their players missed.

Robinson and White come in, but they make the same mistakes they had during the season. Kreigh plays 14 minutes without attempting a field goal. Joe, Jay and Lyndon then miss 22 of 31 shots. The superior athleticism of Seton Hall gains the day—aided by the spurious participation of Andrew Gaze, a virtual non-student and all-but-professional who had been paid for playing in his homeland "down under."

Bob Knight offers no excuses, least of all the altitude; his sportsmanship renders that impossible. "They're playing at the same height we are," he quips. "It isn't like our end is higher than theirs."

"I've played my last game for Indiana," Jay asserts, as he walks off the floor.

No tournament loss is easy, of course. In the locker room

after the game Joe is told he gave the worst leadership of any game the entire season.

Again that superb representative of college coaching, Mike Krzyzewski, gains the Final Four. At a Sunday CBS panel discussion, he sits beside Knight, touchingly still, although he is over forty years old, calling him "coach."

The day after Michigan wins the national championship, Jay announces he will participate in the NBA draft. "He got himself well—to go," Joby concludes. Jay does not speak to Bob Knight at all. He is too afraid. It's Steve Downing he tells. Jay's brother, a Muncie policeman who has long been in touch with agents, becomes Jay's spokesman. Now James Edwards tells the press, "he's not saying nothing. I'm his brother. I've got control over him."

The tone is unseemly, the accusations unfair as James Edwards attacks Indiana for not helping Jay and Bob Knight for praising Joe Hillman: "Indiana never has given Jay a fair shake—ever. He does good, you know he's the best player on that team. Period. And they say Joe Hillman is. It's pathetic."

As if to prove his brother wrong, Jay at once stops attending class, and this time there is nothing Buzz Kurpius can do, she who had been so proud of Jay's fall semester 2.26 average, she who keeps a picture of Jay's baby boy under the glass of her desk.

And then there is a chain of ugly incidents. At one of the post-season Big Ten all-star games, Jay arrives drunk. When someone fouls him, he kicks at the man and almost gets into a fight, something that never happened on the Indiana basketball floor. A visitor at Jay's apartment is overwhelmed by the scent of marijuana. Jay is there with an Illinois player, stoned.

Saying little to the public except that he wishes Jay well, and that "Edwards' priority I don't think is that of being a college student. Consequently Indiana is really not a place for that kind of a kid to be," Knight immediately moves Eric Anderson out of the apartment he has shared with Jay. He arranges for Eric to move in with Jamal.

Two weeks after withdrawing from Indiana, Jay tells the Indianapolis *Star* he left school because he feared he might be set up for a drug bust: "They were going to set me up and put drugs in my car or put drugs in my house and have the police come in and find them. I planned on finishing the semester. I had a decent grade-point average. But if I had to look in my car every time I got in or look around my house all the time, I wouldn't have much time to study."

"A point of fact," Bob Knight tells me, "is that Edwards was failing three courses at the time."

Certainly Jay's statement echoes his irrational fear at Denver that Bob Knight might not tell the truth about his drug tests so he better announce for the NBA before talking to his coach. From Marion, Jay urges "all young people to stay away from drugs and find positive ways of having fun and expressing themselves." The Indiana newspapers dutifully report all these statements, including Jay's regret that he did not meet with Bob Knight before announcing: "I guess I was just scared." This comment, at least, bears the ring of truth.

Neither John White nor Kreigh Smith nor Tates Locke, the new coach at Indiana State, attend the team banquet. Later Chuckie says, "I just couldn't make it. I had some very important things to do." When he makes his departure from Indiana official, Bob Knight tells me, the Indianapolis *Star* headlines the story. Three Purdue players leave and the story is buried.

Jay appears suddenly at the banquet, after the other players have assembled. He is the only one not to speak.

Nor is team leader Joe Hillman present—but for a good reason. Joe has rejoined the Oakland A's, class A. Together with some new teammates, he watched the NCAA championship game.

"How did *you* guys beat *them?*" the baseball players wanted to know.

"I guess we were a little smarter," Joe says, echoing another voice equating success and character with intelligence.

When the Big Ten announces its most valuable player awards, Joe Hillman's name is not among them. The coaches and the Chicago *Tribune* have selected Michigan's Glen Rice; the media has chosen Jay Edwards.

It's as if the conference is treating college basketball as a business, the notion that these are students and not professionals a travesty. Joe Hillman, the leader of the championship team, who represented values which cannot be measured on a stat sheet, goes unmentioned. Jay, who increasingly departs from the values which justify the amount of time these students spend on sports, is praised. For on Saturday night, April 22nd, Jay is at a party at Lyndon's apartment where he is involved in a nasty conversation with a woman in the kitchen. Perhaps the woman, who is his age, twenty, has been rebuffed, and is striking out. There are harsh words. "I wouldn't go anywhere with that slut," says Jay. He slaps the woman twice with his open hand. When she taunts him, "no one in the NBA will want you," he lunges and punches her in the forehead with his fist, according to witnesses. Jay is charged with two preliminary counts of battery, to which he pleads innocent. Perhaps as a consequence he is selected by the Clippers in the NBA draft only number 33, in the second round.

The sad story of Jay's self-destruction illuminates as much the schools, the family, the society as it does one confused young man. Bob Knight, however, is quick to disagree with the notion that, as he puts it, Jay is "a victim of society." Jay "lied and he lied and he lied," Knight says.

It is early one rainy morning in May and his voice rises. Talking about Jay makes him angry. "It wasn't anybody's fault but his," Knight insists. "Why have other kids come through the same situation and not been that way?"

As for the drugs and alcohol, why Jay needed these escapes when he had so much going for him, what vacuum they filled in his life, Knight sounds like Clint Eastwood talking about why the sniper kills in *Dirty Harry:* "In the final analysis he enjoys it."

And yet for years Jay had been the young athlete glorified for his prowess, while his off-court life became a perpetual pursuit of sensual gratification. What indeed can books say to a person taught early on to value money, success, physical prowess—and winning? Jay has been treated as if he were special, immune to the daily struggles of ordinary young people, and he is not the only one at fault for that.

The spectacle of Jay's self-immolation virtually the moment he discarded his Indiana uniform underlines the overwhelming difficulty of the coach's task. Personal discipline comes as an unpleasant shock to recruits for whom already life is a steady indulgence in drugs, alcohol, sex and the cheers of the crowd as they await what they fantasize will be the money to come. They mark time in college, suffering the coursework, going through the motions, as Buzz Kurpius puts it, "doing the minimum." And who can stop them, change their values?

For such young people the ideals of unselfishness, discipline and self-sacrifice are alien concepts. Unselfishness will lead to victory, Bob Knight told his team in December of this auspicious season. He was proven right. But Jay could not hear him. The moral failure of a value-free society faces college coaches like Bob Knight, and frustrates them. Because Bob Knight has struggled so hard to turn young men like poor Jay around, sometimes the frustration mounts, and once, yes, yes, he even unjustifiably threw a chair.

"It's not "romantic and idealistic," Bob Knight had said Clippers, perhaps anticipating Jay's slide downhill. And yet it's not cynicism that pervades here. The record of those who remained speaks to the value of submitting to the discipline you hate, to the relentless and painful honing of character. Taught in December how to like each other, this Indiana team reaped the reward of unselfishness, the most unlikely of Big Ten championships.

It was at times excruciating to watch Bob Knight coach Todd Jadlow on the practice floor: the cliché "tough love" does not begin to describe it. And on Seniors' Night Todd would not hug his coach "like Keith and Dean did," when he left the floor having played his last game in Bloomington.

Now, in May, Knight praises Todd for having been instrumental in Indiana's winning the Big Ten championship. Todd has traveled to New York on a trip organized by Knight trying to find him a job playing basketball in Europe.

Now, in May too Knight summarizes his season. He wants to "send a message to kids," he says. Indiana won as much through the efforts of Jadlow and "journeyman" players like Brian Sloan, and of an "enthusiastic freshman" like Jamal Meeks as through the abilities of Edwards and Hillman.

The essence of the games against Michigan and Illinois, Knight says, "is that basketball can be played in different ways. The great thing about basketball is that a team with average athletic ability—through defensive positioning, offensive movement and handling the basketball—can play against a team with better players athletically. Our players were able to take another side of basketball and make themselves a difficult team to play against. We had a team that wasn't that good athletically. But that doesn't mean it wasn't a good basketball team. This team was about finding a solution to the problem of athletic ability and going on to be successful. Basketball is not only about athletics and athletics isn't the only way to be successful."

Basketball is also about the moral development of young people—a process you could have witnessed this season especially in young players like Jamal Meeks and Eric Anderson.

I tell eighteen-year-old Eric that his coach has called me "romantic and idealistic," no compliment from him.

Eric's face explodes in a grin. Then he has to laugh, and dissent.

"But you're a writer," this boy insists, without a second's hesitation. "That's what you're supposed to be!"

"Good men are made here," Joby had said. You can see it happening.